Continuing the Quest for Morality Truly Christian, Truly African

Other Books of Interest from St. Augustine's Press

Maurice Ashley Agbaw-Ebai, *Light of Reason, Light of Faith: Joseph Ratzinger and the German Enlightenment*

Maurice Ashley Agbaw-Ebai, *The Essential Supernatural: A Dialogical Study in Kierkegaard and Blondel*

Maurice Ashley Agbaw-Ebai and Matthew Levering, Editors, *Africae Munus: Ten Years Later*

Maurice Ashley Agbaw-Ebai and Kizito Forbi S.J., Editors, *An African Perspective on the Thought of Benedict XVI*

Maurice Ashley Agbaw-Ebai and Kizito Forbi S.J., Editors, *Benedict XVI Rethinking Africa: Tasks for Today*

Georg Gänswein, *Who Believes Is Not Alone*

John Tanyi Nquah Lebui, *The Cross and the Flag: Papal Diplomacy and John Paul II's Struggle Against the Tyranny of the Possible*

Peter Kreeft, *Ha!: A Christian Philosopher of Humor*

Peter Kreeft, *If Einstein Had Been a Surfer*

Peter Kreeft, *A Socratic Introduction to Plato's Republic*

Kenneth Weisbrode, *Real Influencers: Fourteen Disappearing Acts that Left Fingerprints on History*

Peter Kreeft, *The Philosophy of Jesus*

Peter Kreeft, *Socratic Logic (3rd Edition)*

Marvin R. O'Connell, *Telling Stories that Matter: Memoirs and Essays*

Joseph Bottum, *Frankincense, Gold, and Myrrh:A Christmas Chrestomathy*

Scott Randall Paine, *Face to Face with Everything: How Philosophy Looks at the World and What It Sees*

Chilton Williamson, Jr., *The Last Westerner*

D. Q. McInerny, *A Quality of Loss*

Donald S. Prudlo and Paul J. Voss, *Merchant Saint: The Church, the Market, and the First Lay Canonization*

Continuing the Quest for Morality Truly Christian, Truly African: The Achievement of Paulinus Odozor, C.S.Sp.

EDITED BY

MAURICE ASHLEY AGBAW-EBAI

AND MATTHEW LEVERING

ST. AUGUSTINE'S PRESS
South Bend, Indiana

Manufactured in the United States of America.

1 2 3 4 5 6 30 29 28 27 26 25

Library of Congress Control Number: 2025939756

Paperback ISBN: 978-1-58731-161-1

∞ The paper used in this publication meets the minimum requirements of the American National Standard for Information Sciences – Permanence of Paper for Printed Materials, ANSI Z39.48-1984.

St. Augustine's Press
www.staugustine.net

Table of Contents

Preface

John Cardinal ONAIYEKAN
Archbishop Emeritus of Abuja
May 29th, 2025, Solemnity of the Ascension of the Lord

I am most honoured to be invited to contribute some brief reflection to this collection of essays in honour of my friend and brother, Rev. Fr. Professor Paulinus Odozor, CSSP. I have followed with keen interest and deep admiration the life journey of Odozor as a priest, religious, missionary and moral theologian. He deserves to be celebrated and acknowledged for his contribution to Catholic Moral Theology in the last three decades of general turbulence in Catholic Theology in particular and Christian Theology in general. He has to a large extent managed to successfully navigate that turbulence with deep faith and clear reason.

I commend and congratulate those who have put together this book in his honour: colleagues and friends, confreres and students, both past and present. I thank them for finding a little space for me in this their labour of love. My contribution will be a few brief and straightforward remarks, listed in no particular logical order.

Moral Theology, as Theology

I wish to start with the important observation that Odozor has clearly reminded us that Catholic Moral Theology is above all theology. It is a moral discussion that has God as point of reference. It is about the Christian God, understood and believed in as Trinitarian, Father, Son and Holy Spirit. This concept of God has its focus on the Person of the Lord Jesus Christ, who has revealed to us the Father and the Holy Spirit. This Jesus, who is God-Man, is also like us in everything but sin, and thus has become for us a clear model of Christian moral living. That is why Moral Theology cannot afford to fly off on its own, without reference to Holy Scripture and Dogmatic Theology.

Morality: Truly Christian, African and Human

"Fr Odozor's 2014 book *Morality Truly Christian, Truly African* ... has become a classic in the field of Catholic moral theology." This is the clear and unapologetic pronouncement of the editors of the book under reference. But before we raise issues about what is "truly African" about Christian morality, I am wondering if it would not be necessary, or at least useful, to talk about what is "human" in Christian morality. Our modern world is drawing our attention ever more to what makes us simply human beings, that which we have in common, before all our diversities of all kinds. The more we focus on this, the more we discover how much more important is our common humanity than the diversities that often grab our attention. A Christian moral theology, anchored on God, cannot fail to see the importance or even priority of the human dimension of our morality discourse. Is this not why the Ten Commandments are valid for all humanity, not only for the people of Israel? Is this not true also of what we call "Christian morality?" In the same way, when we talk of a Christian morality "truly African," can we be speaking about a set of Christian moral norms valid for only African Christians? Surely the message of Jesus is directed to all humanity. "Go preach the gospel to all nations": this is the mandate of Jesus Christ to his apostles. We do well to take note of our being Africans. But is it not much more important that we are human beings, like the rest of humanity, and that we are Christians like the rest of Christ's faithful? Nevertheless, this does not exempt us from bringing the fruits of our African experience to the table of humanity and of the Church. This will continue to be an ongoing task for us.

The New Law of Christ

When I was a theology seminarian at the Pontifical Universitas Urbaniana in Rome, 1965-1969, our Professor of Moral Theology, the famous Bernard Haring, CSSR, published his then ground breaking Moral Theology text book with the title, *The Law of Christ*. This title summarized his clear position that

Christian Moral Theology must be about explaining the law of Jesus Christ. What the gospels tell us is that the attitude of Jesus to the law was in two directions, confirmation and fulfillment. He said: "I have come not to abolish the law, but to fulfil it." He was talking about the law of Moses, which guided the entire life of the people of Israel, a law about which they were very proud. They were sure that no nation had laws as good as their own.

That Jesus did not abolish the law was clear from his constant reference to that law as valid guide for life. "If you want to inherit eternal life, keep the commandments," he told the young man who put the question to him. At the same time, he did what was before then unheard of among the people of Israel; he took the liberty to go beyond what the law prescribed, thereby fulfilling the law. "You have heard it said.... But I say...." It is only by the direct authority of God that anyone can talk like that, an authority that is enjoyed only by the Son of God. This was clear in his teaching on sexual morality and divorce.

The Lord Jesus handed over this supreme authority to the Church that he left behind to carry on his mission of teaching. It is on this that Christian moral theology bases its own authority to judge and correct any other human moral norms and practices. Thus, all cultures must bow before the Law of Christ, no matter how sublime and exalted. If the law of Moses, which was given by the God of Israel, had to make way for the law of Christ, how much more the laws and customs of our African ancestors? This was clear from the very beginning when the Church confronted the moral norms of the dominant Greco-Roman culture all around her. Therefore, if our moral theology is to be truly Christian and African, it cannot exempt itself from the law of fulfilment, correction and purification that the Lord Jesus demands.

Moral Theology for the People of God

"Moral Theology for the Common Man." This was my original title for this paragraph, and that is still what I mean. Our moral theology must aim at the proverbial "common man," which can theologically translate into the idea of "the people of God."

Scientific and profound language may be a requirement in certain academic settings. This is the kind of language we see in many of the contributions to this book. We may need to live up to some expectations of the academic world. Some branches of theology may be able to get away with such esoteric language. But if moral theology is to effectively address the real life issues of the Christian faithful, it cannot afford the luxury of an inaccessible profundity and high-level speculation directed to only academic colleagues. Jesus is our model in everything, and especially in this regard too. He addressed himself to crowds of ordinary people, teaching profound doctrines in simple language which everyone could understand.

It is noteworthy that our Christ's faithful are increasingly becoming educated and exposed to developments in our modern world. There is need to bring to their attention the many available resources to access the sources of our faith. This is all the more necessary in our social media and AI age when practically all forms of information are available online. Apart from Sacred Scripture, they need to be introduced to the major documents of the Church which give authoritative guidelines for authentic Christian living. Such documents include Council documents, especially of Vatican II, the Catechism of the Catholic Church, the Compendium of the Social Doctrine of the Church, the Code of Canon Law and the entire gamut of the Magisterium of the different levels of the teaching office of the Church. Even in Africa, we can no longer presume that the worshippers in our congregation lack access to the doctrines and moral norms of the Church.

Conclusion

But despite all recent developments among our congregations, the moral theologian still has his job well cut out for him or her: to guide the people of God in their search for the path to eternal life. I see three areas of special urgency for the attention of the African Catholic Moral Theologian. First is the area of sexual morality, marriage and family, an area where the impact of contemporary globalization is throwing confusion on the entire humanity. Second is about justice and peace, especially as regards the proper management of the resources of our nations. How do we deal with the growing gap between the very few rich and affluent and the sea of poor and miserable people all over Africa? Finally, there is the challenge of good governance and stable political structures in our countries. The quality of democracy in Africa in recent times has not been improving but rather deteriorating, so much so that military coups are becoming attractive and welcome to a people thrown into despair by a corrupt and irresponsible political class. We cannot continue to blame foreign interference for our woes. We must look inwards and hold our leaders accountable. This cannot make any positive impact without a spiritual and moral revolution. In this battle, the Church and her moral theologians must be in the front line.

Introduction

Maurice Agbaw-Ebai and Matthew Levering

Paulinus Ikechukwu Odozor is among the preeminent moral theologians of our time. He has reached the pinnacle of his profession, having served for more than two decades as a professor of theology at the University of Notre Dame. Among African theologians, he stands at the forefront of the generation that came of age in the early postconciliar period.

Fr. Odozor's 2014 book, *Morality Truly Christian, Truly African: Foundational, Methodological, and Theological Considerations,* has become a classic in the field of Catholic moral theology. The essays in the present volume take *Morality Truly Christian, Truly African* as their starting point, developing it, challenging it, or consciously approaching its topics from a different but complementary angle. The contributors to this volume are friends of Fr. Odozor, but, more than this, they are colleagues in constructive theological work in the service of Christ and the Church. Two of the contributors presently teach in Nigeria—Raymond Aina and Anthony Akinwale—while the others either teach at institutions in the United States or Canada, or else (Tegha Nji and Emmanuel Ojeifo) are currently doctoral students at the University of Notre Dame.

In an interview published on the occasion of the fortieth anniversary of his priestly ordination, Odozor remarks that when he arrived at the University of Toronto in the mid-1980s, he was confronted with a situation that he had not seen in Nigeria. The rumblings caused by the 1968 encyclical *Humanae Vitae* were shaping moral theology in Toronto, calling into question Catholic teachings that in Nigeria were received and taught without rejection.[1] In response, the young student Odozor opened up a dialogue with Notre Dame professor and Jesuit moral theologian Richard McCormick, eventually producing a Master's thesis and a doctoral dissertation on McCormick's influential thought. McCormick belonged to the school of Josef Fuchs, and he was often sharply critical of Pope John Paul II—including

John Paul II's 1993 encyclical *Veritatis Splendor*, promulgated two years before the University of Notre Dame Press published Odozor's revised dissertation as *Richard A. McCormick and the Renewal of Moral Theology*.

The young Odozor poured himself into discovering the Catholic moral tradition in all its richness and variety, as well as its conflicts. In 2001 he published with the University of Notre Dame Press a compendium of texts to be used in coursework, exemplifying the diversity of perspectives that he had discovered upon his arrival in Toronto—*Sexuality, Marriage and Family: Readings in the Catholic Tradition*. Then, in 2003, he published *Moral Theology in an Age of Renewal: A Study of the Catholic Tradition Since Vatican II*. This book remains a crucial primer for anyone interested in Catholic moral theology and the developments of the twentieth century. The book begins with the movements toward renewal in moral theology prior to the Second Vatican Council, and it then explores the Council and *Humanae Vitae*. Odozor examines such themes as the prominent postconciliar debates regarding the distinctiveness of Christian morality, the place and function of Scripture, the natural law, the role of the Magisterium, and virtue ethics. He focuses particularly upon the debate over whether there exist universal moral norms, admitting of no exceptions. As a last step, he evaluates (quite positively) Pope John Paul II's teachings.

This book was a fruit of Odozor's arrival at Notre Dame as a visiting scholar in 1999. After graduating from the University of Toronto in the early 1990s, Odozor had moved back to Nigeria where he taught at the Spiritan International School of Theology. In this context, he carried too heavy a teaching load to do much research and writing. When he arrived at Notre Dame, he had not only time but also dialogue partners from across the spectrum of Catholic perspectives, beginning with his University of Toronto friend and teacher Joseph Boyle (a disciple of Germain Grisez), and including at Notre Dame such scholars as John Cavadini, Michael Baxter, Jean Porter, Maura Ryan, Cathy Kaveny, David Clairmont, and Jennifer Herdt.

In *Moral Theology in an Age of Renewal*, Odozor recalls the 1899 warning offered by Thomas J. Bouquillon, the first professor of moral theology at Catholic University of America, who feared "that moral theology had become obsolete, a pathetic poor cousin of other theological specialties as a result of its inability to keep up with the times."[2] One of the main reasons behind Bouquillon's concern was the separation of moral theology from dogmatic theology. Despite efforts to overcome this separation after Vatican II, it still persists—but many scholars do cross disciplinary boundaries, and Odozor is one of them. As Odozor comments to his interviewer James Nkemngong, "The constant question I keep asking myself is the difference that the belief in Jesus makes to these [moral] matters; what does being a Christian mean with regards to the way should [...] construe life and to live life."[3]

In this context, Odozor emphasizes the Pauline teaching that through faith in Jesus Christ and baptism into him, we are a new creation. He also gives particular weight to the sacraments and hearing the Word of God. These are often the subject matters of dogmatic theology, which indicates Odozor's theological breadth. Already during his seminary years in Nigeria, influenced by one of his young professors, Odozor read a significant amount of the writings of Edward Schillebeeckx, Juan Luis Segundo, and Karl Rahner. In his published interview, he praises the influence of Elochukwu Uzukwu, and he recalls reading Schillbeeckx's book, *Jesus,* as soon as it appeared in English. As a young scholar, he was as interested in systematic theology as in moral theology, especially the doctrine of God and Christology.

The fruits of this ability to move between moral and dogmatic theology are fully found in *Morality Truly Christian, Truly African*. In this work, we find serious reflection on the nature of God, Christian theology, interreligious dialogue, ecclesiology, and so on. He critiques the Protestant moral theologian James Gustafson for insufficient attention to dogmatic theology. In this regard, Odozor raises two points, one about the doctrine of God, the other about Christology. He states, "The first [...] is that Gustafson's position limiting what can be asserted of God to what is justifiable by science is a rejection of the reality of the importance of faith and reason as ways of 'knowing.' [...] The second point is that because of his attitude toward the reality of Jesus, his ethics [...] is anything but Christian."[4]

In *Moral Theology in an Age of Renewal*, Odozor positions his work within the context of postconciliar moral theology. On the one hand, he observes that despite their conflicts, postconciliar moral theologians shared a basic agreement about the Church's purpose and goal, and thus about the nature of the good and the ultimate end. In this vein he contends that postconciliar moral theology, for all its discontinuity with preconciliar moral theology, nevertheless retained many connections with the latter, "as a legitimate and much more complex offshoot of a more monolithic forebear."[5]

On the other hand, Odozor recognizes that there exist real disagreements among postconciliar moral theologians. He had to determine what perspective he himself would take as a constructive thinker. In the postconciliar debates, theologians such as Josef Fuchs, Bernard Häring, Richard McCormick, Charles Curran, Bruno Schüller, Joseph Selling, Alfons Auer, Louis Janssens, and Lisa Sowle Cahill butted heads with Joseph Ratzinger, Phillipe Delhaye, Servais Pinckaers, Pope John Paul II, Germain Grisez, and others on such topics as "autonomous ethics," proportionalism, the existence of absolute moral norms, the distinction between "moral rightness" and "moral goodness," the status of human nature and of human teleology, the contrast between "classicism" and "historical consciousness," the principle of double effect, the truth or falsity of *Humanae Vitae*, the nature of legitimate dissent from Magisterial teaching, and so on. Odozor deems that the first thing that should be said about these hotly contested debates is that both sides were arguing from within the Catholic moral tradition, so that the debates evince shared Catholic beliefs. But Odozor also leans toward one side. His appreciation for *Humanae Vitae* and *Veritatis Splendor* is evident throughout *Moral Theology in an Age of Renewal*—an appreciation not shared (to say the least) by many of the moral theologians whom he surveys. For example, he states, "The very discussion on contraception is important in the Catholic tradition not just because it is a matter of human sexuality, but more fundamentally because it is a God-question. What is involved are particular understandings of God and of God's purposes in the world."[6]

Odozor's *Moral Theology in an Age of Renewal* sets the stage for Odozor's arrival as a major twenty-first century Catholic moral theologian. Notably, however, the form in which his mature scholarship—preeminently his *Morality Truly Christian, Truly African*—took shape was to some extent an accident. Coming to the University of Notre Dame impacted his research trajectory. He states in his published interview, "When I was hired in the department, the dean asked me to help bring Africa to Notre Dame and Notre Dame to Africa."[7] Behind this initiative of the dean's, Odozor identifies the inspiration of John Cavadini, who as department chair first arranged for Odozor to be a visiting professor at Notre Dame and then hired him into the department. Cavadini enabled Odozor to organize a two-part conference, the first held at Notre Dame and the second in Nigeria, in 2003–2004 on the topic of "Solidarity with Africa." The first part of the conference included hosting at Notre Dame the Nigerian president, Olusegun Obasanjo; and fifty-two persons traveled from Notre Dame to Nigeria for the second part of the conference. Furthermore, Cavadini helped to spearhead the recruitment of African graduate students to study theology at Notre Dame. Cavadini also joined Odozor on trips to several African countries.

Odozor's research agenda was shaped by the Notre Dame department. He found that other professors in the department were doing bioethics, Thomistic ethics, and social ethics—all areas in which he had competence—but no one else was an "Africanist."[8] He therefore decided "to concentrate on matters about Africa at various levels," and especially to concentrate upon "matters relating to fundamental morals and foundational issues as they relate to Africa."[9] Of course, the postconciliar debates among European and American Catholic moralists remained important for him. African Catholic theologians are trained in Europe and America, and so these debates inevitably impact African moral theology. Yet, Odozor's primary focus became reading, learning from, and engaging with African theologians in order to develop and serve African Catholic theology. In the process, he has emerged as one of the greatest African theologians. Thus he has become a theologian whose work is of profound importance also for non-Africans.

As he recalls, when he came to Notre Dame, "it became necessary for me to give visibility to African voices and issues."[10] The absence of these voices at Notre Dame and in the United States had to be remedied. African theologians distinctively draw upon a cultural matrix that includes African Traditional Religions, in addition to the history of African colonial and postcolonial developments and crises. At the same time, as will already be clear, African theology is not separated from the wider Catholic world. Not only is there a shared Catholic tradition (from the Church Fathers onward), but there is also the aforementioned fact that African theologians generally do their doctoral research either in Europe or North America. In *Morality Truly Christian, Truly African*, an example of this link to the European Catholic world appears in Odozor's lengthy engagement with Bénézet Bujo, who taught at the University of Fribourg (Switzerland) for many years and who belonged to the generation of African theologians just prior to Odozor's. As Odozor shows, a number of trajectories in Bujo's work reflect "certain tendencies and trends in recent Western Catholic moral theology which Bujo absorbed in his studies in Europe during the 1980s."[11] Bujo's work has rich roots in African thought and problems, but it could not have taken the shape it did without the heavy influence of such thinkers as Alfons Auer and Josef Fuchs.

It can happen that theological work by African scholars engaging with other African scholars is presumed by non-specialist readers to be *solely for* the African context. Odozor has the African context in view, but he makes constructive theological claims that require the attention of the whole Church. His work is firmly rooted in the sources of moral theology, Scripture and Tradition. He grounds himself in Christian beliefs about God, creation, and redemption. He underscores "the universality of the God of Jesus Christ and of his love; faith in the reliability of God's creation and in the intention of God; hope borne out of faith in the life, death, and resurrection of Jesus."[12] His perspective contrasts with other paths in contemporary theology that place their hope not in Jesus' life, death, and Resurrection as the redemptive and eschatological inbreaking of God, but rather merely in the liberative praxis modeled by Jesus. In addition, Odozor attends to the moral significance of God's wisdom as manifested in the created order.

Odozor's insistence upon these foundations puts him at odds with influential strands of Catholic theology even among some African theologians. It would be a mistake to assume that African theologians are in lockstep about the major moral issues of our times, or even about the centrality of the God of Jesus Christ. Readers of the work of African theologians will know that this is not the case. As one also finds among Western theologians, some African theologians privilege "praxis" to such a degree that the experiential or practical dimension of theology is set against dogma. In this situation, as Odozor recognizes, there is a theological failure to perceive the deeper intelligibility of the Church's (and Scripture's) teachings vis-à-vis contemporary understandings of the requirements of equality, dignity, and tolerance. By contrast, Odozor's commitment to Scripture and Tradition enables him, from a richly Catholic perspective, prophetically to challenge cultural abuses such as patriarchy and statism, which are rooted in a lust for domination.[13]

Odozor is not only an academic, but a fervent believer in Jesus Christ. This love for the realities of salvation affects his scholarly writings. He remarks in *Morality Truly Christian, Truly African*, "Christian ethics is a response ethics. It is a response to God's loving initiative in Jesus."[14] Such an ethics has discipleship at its center. Discipleship means listening to, imitating, and obeying Jesus. In Jesus' life and teaching, says Odozor, Jesus "took God seriously; he took the human person seriously, especially as poor, vulnerable, sinner, outcast; he took women seriously as daughters and creatures of God; and he took reconciliation seriously."[15] These elements are fundamental to living the Christian moral life in Africa today, because they are fundamental for Jesus himself—they are "truly Christian." They are also fundamental to Odozor in his own life; the "response ethics" that he envisions begins with him. Robert Sarah remarks about the danger of a Christian life without interior conversion: "[M]an incessantly struts like a peacock but takes no care of his own soul."[16] In his published interview, Odozor makes a similar point: "If in the end it cannot be said of you by God that you loved, then your life was not worth it. If in the end, you're not remembered by those close to you as one who cared for or about people, then, whatever else you've done is not significant."[17]

In *Morality Truly Christian, Truly African*, Odozor is deeply aware of the problem that Cyril Orji has analyzed in *Unmasking the African Ghost. Theology, Politics, and the Nightmare of Failed States*—a problem that has also been addressed by Odozor's Notre Dame colleague Emmanuel Katangole in writings such as *The Sacrifice of Africa: A Political Theology for Africa* and *Born from Lament: The Theology and Politics of Hope in Africa*.[18] Orji does not mince words in his diagnosis of the brutal "ghost state" or "vampire state" in Africa. As Orji makes clear, the situation is not easily solved even by the best of ideas. He observes, for instance, "The problem of too much government and too little government plays out in a number of ways. Military dictatorship almost always results in too much government, while political squabbling among the ruling class and the plundering of resources that goes with it often result in too little government. Nigeria is a classic example of the latter."[19] For Orji, the path forward involves a modified and de-romanticized version of *ubuntu*, including spelling out *ubuntu* in actual legal precepts as well as ensuring that *ubuntu* does not reinforce patriarchy or violence against persons with same-sex attraction. Orji suggests pairing the strengths of *ubuntu* with political democracy, along with the "legal rights" and "legal economy" of capitalism, re-envisioned for "community-based societies."[20]

Although Odozor generally does not do social ethics directly, he regularly adverts to the crises ongoing in Africa. In his essay "The Church as Family of God," for example, Odozor recognizes the seriousness of the poverty, caste systems, ethnic favoritism, violence, and corruption that Africa faces. He concludes that "the metaphor of church as family of God in Africa must not be taken as an expression or as an assertion of a theological truth already achieved or evident in the life of the church on the African continent. It is still rather for the most part a statement of theological hope."[21] As is his wont, Odozor broadens the lens and asserts that the problems faced by Africa include—most fundamentally for Christians—the problem of God. As he puts it, "The God of Jesus is yet unknown. Therefore, every renewal of church life and mission must begin by revisiting this God. To the extent that we can get closer to the image of and an understanding of the one Jesus called his Father, we will be able to live right and do right in this world."[22] Often in African theology, as in Western Christian theology, it is assumed that the main desideratum is fixing the world by ensuring that human dignity is finally upheld. Odozor's radical realism ensures that he does not fall into this assumption.

For Odozor, the central thing is faith in Jesus Christ, who transforms in a powerful way all earlier ideas about the living God (or gods). Thus Odozor emphasizes the distinctiveness and transforming power of the God of Jesus Christ—the Trinity who loves us so much as to become one of us for our salvation. It is this Triune God of love and humility who secures the anthropological truths that all human beings are created and loved by God. It is this Triune God who suffuses all created things (including our ensouled bodiliness) with his wise purposes and who invites us to a sanctified life of self-sacrificial love. Ultimately, "Christian life must be understood as friendship with God, and this understanding changes everything."[23] The Christian life boils down to loving the divine Friend who has given everything to us out of love, and who calls us to love as he loves us.[24]

Much more can be said and will be said in the chapters that follow, where, as noted above, Odozor's contributions are taken up, challenged, and extended by some of his many friends in Christ. In his own chapter, which concludes the book, Odozor sums up what *Morality Truly Christian, Truly African* aimed to achieve. His chapter is itself a further beginning to the conversation.

May this volume serve the building up of the kingdom that only God can build in Christ and by the Holy Spirit; and may this volume be a fitting tribute to our friend Paulinus Odozor and a work that gives glory to God. Let us end this Introduction by recalling the "last things"—eschatology. In his published interview, Odozor briefly reflects on his own eventual death and on "preparing for a future with God" in the midst of our earthly activity.[25] He anticipates that heaven will be a state of glorious blessedness, filled with the presence of God in the midst of the vast assembly of friends. He expects that our bodies will be radically transformed, so that heaven cannot be univocally described as a "place." The consummated kingdom of God is the ultimate end toward which all Christian life tends. It is only here that we will find the transformed fullness sought by esteemed author of *Morality Truly Christian, Truly African*.

May our friend Paulinus, teacher and mentor in Christ, be blessed and continue to bless us by his care and writings. And when all labors are done, may we together rejoice in the new creation, suffused by the Trinitarian love poured out by Christ Jesus and his Holy Spirit. Then the psalmist's command will be realized in full: "Kings of the earth and all peoples, princes and all rulers of the earth! Young men and maidens together, old men and children! Let them praise the name of the Lord, for his name alone is exalted; his glory is above earth and heaven" (Ps 148:11–13).

Chapter 1

Ratzinger's Theological Anthropology in Conversation with Aspects of Paulinus Odozor's Understanding of the Human Person in Christ

Maurice Agbaw-Ebai

Introduction

It is a truly gratifying experience to take part in this volume dedicated to the scientific study and systematic engagement of the great work, *Morality Truly Christian, Truly African*, by one of Africa's finest minds, the esteemed Rev. Fr. Prof. Paulinus Ikechukwu Odozor, C.S.Sp., of the University of Notre Dame. In many ways, Fr. Odozor has helped to provide a theological framework for Africa's young and upcoming theologians, demonstrating to us that we must not[1] set aside our Africanness in order to be authentic Christians, even all the while, allowing the message of Christ to challenge us towards a more humane direction. But even more, Fr. Odozor is teaching us, I believe, that to be intellectually gifted should not result in setting up a parallel magisterium of experts against our mother, the Church. Here, I am reminded of the title of the enduring work by Henri de Lubac, that is, *The Motherhood of the Church*. I believe the gift that Fr. Odozor is to the Church in Africa and beyond, could be read through a hermeneutical framework of three dynamisms, which, in my opinion, provides the theological and philosophical framework for engaging *Morality Truly Christian, Truly African*: the dynamism of being an authentic African; the dynamism of being an authentic follower of Jesus Christ; and finally, the dynamism of a scholar who believes in order to understand, and who understands in order to believe—*crede ut intelligas* and *intellige ut credas*—as Augustine of Hippo fitting captured it centuries ago.[2] Fr. Odozor's ongoing work gives us a living, concrete example of what Augustine wrote after his conversion in *Contra Academicos*—namely, that faith and reason are the two forces that lead us to knowledge.[3] At a time when African theological scholarship is gaining wider esteem, Fr. Odozor has provided an inspiring example to a new generation of African scholars, that we can be all three without feeling out of place—namely, African, Christian, and a genuine intellectual, comfortable in both the Kingdom of God and the Kingdom of Thought, to use a Hegelian terminology.

Given this framework, it becomes obvious that only someone of Fr. Odozor's intellectual, spiritual, and human caliber could give us the framework for an interactive theological investigation of the anthropology that emerges from the rich corpus of Joseph Ratzinger/Benedict XVI. This is the particular aim of this essay: to attempt a study of Ratzinger's theological anthropology in view of certain aspects of the understanding of the human person in Christ in Fr. Odozor's *Morality Truly Christian, Truly African*. The Dogmatic Constitution on Divine Revelation, *Dei Verbum*, taught that "the Sacred Scriptures contain the word of God and since they are inspired, really are the word of God; and so, the study of the sacred page is, as it were, the soul of sacred theology" (DV 24). It is to the Scriptures, then, that we must turn to for the guiding light regarding the question of anthropology today. In this light, the noted rhetorical question of the Psalmist could serve as the path for engaging the theological inner rapprochement that is discernable in the rich corpus of Paulinus Ikechukwu Odozor, C.S.Sp. and Joseph Aloysius Ratzinger/Benedict XVI: "What is man that you should keep him in mind, mortal man that you care for him?" (Ps 8:4). This question posed by the psalmist has taken on greater significance and urgency today.

Das Problem: The Crisis of Anthropology Today

The question of what the human being is in terms of his origin, meaning, and purpose, is as perennial as it is topical. And this question appears to encapsulate the major challenge facing the theology and the Church today. It has been noted that the Church has witnessed three monumental challenges in her long history. The first eight hundred years saw the Church grappling with the question, what is God? The Christological councils of the first eight hundred years dealt with that question, and the existence of the Coptic and other Monophysite churches till date, tells us that we did not do a successful job in resolving the question as a community of the Body of Christ. The next major phase of the Church's life appears to have concerned itself with the question, what is the Church? If the question about what God is was borne from heresies, the question of what the Church is appears to have been borne from what was construed to be a reformist desire. The Protestant Reformation resulted in the Council of Trent, that affirmed the supernatural dimension of the Church in terms of the origins of the Church especially in the light of her sacramental and biblical economy. Further on, Vatican I would clarify the place of the Bishop of Rome as the visible principle of unity in the heart of the Church, and the unfinished business of Vatican I, namely, the place of the bishops as successors of the apostles and not mere emissaries or the Pope, who, together with the Roman Pontiff, constitute the apostolic college as willed by Christ, would flesh out what would be construed as a theology of communion as the pathway for the Church, in which Pope and Bishops constitute a college charged with the *munus docendi* flowing from the sacrament of episcopal ordination. This ecclesiology of communion was not limited to the episcopate alone. In fact, as we read in *Lumen Gentium*, *Dei Verbum*, and *Gaudium et Spes*, the whole body of believers, thanks to the sacrament of baptism, form a community that is born from faith, sustained by mutual love, and looking forward in hope to the life with Christ in the Kingdom of God, whose seeds are already planted here, thanks to the entry of God into history in Christ.

Now, it would appear the Church today is facing its third major challenge, namely, what is the human being? It goes without saying that anthropology, the meaning of what we are as human beings, is the new battle field that Christian theology must confront today, as I have already stated. But theology today cannot respond to this question in a vacuum. As the Danish philosopher Søren Kierkegaard perceptively remarked, life must be lived forward but understood backwards. Hence, theological anthropology today must remind itself of the steps and achievements made towards the question of the meaning of the human being especially in the Western philosophical tradition, given the obvious influence it has had on the development of Christian thought. For Plato, especially in the *Phaedrus* and the *Republic*, the human being is a duality, and to understand the who of the person is predicated on the what, in this case, a soul imprisoned in the body. In Aristotle, there a shift towards a more positive estimate of the materiality of bodiliness, matter, with the soul is the first principle of animation, its form, as we read in *De Anima*. This body-soul framework does not suck up much of the oxygen when we enter medieval Western thought, perhaps with the notable exception of Aquinas. Earlier on, Augustine's *Confessions* and *De Libero Arbitrio* wrestle with the human being as a lover, *amor meus pondus meum*, who has to choose between self-love and love for God. The human being is broken, fallen, and only in the discovery of God does the human being arrive at the great discovery of the self. Only in God does the human being find the rest that the human heart has been seeking all along. But even more, in his beautiful *Sero te amavi* of Book X of the *Confessions*, Augustine makes a great realization that I believe both Ratzinger and Odozor subscribe to, namely, that God was within Augustine, all the while that Augustine was outside! But God's love was so profound and so patient that God called and shouted, breaking through Augustine's deafness.

This vision of the human being that comes to the fullest realization of the self in the encounter with God likewise animates Aquinas, Pascal, Husserl, Blondel, Wojtyla, and others, with obvious different accentuations. Of course, that being said, we must also acknowledge the Cartesian *res cogitans* subjectivity, the Marxist economic person, and the Freudian reduction of the person to sexual drives. In Cartesianism, Marxism, and Freudianism, one can discern the seeds of the contemporary attractions of relativism; socio-economic utopia in the form of an economic revolution; and finally, the sexual revolution.

These immanentist visions of the person have come to a head today in forms that were barely discernable just a few decades ago. We see this reflected in the controversies surrounding gender and sexual expression, in which once-widely-held beliefs about maleness and femaleness as anthropological givens, and about the complementarity of the sexes regarding the question of sexual expression, are largely being rejected especially in contemporary Western culture. Added to the question of gender and sexual expression is the fundamental question regarding the inviolable dignity of human life, hitherto considered as a gift, but increasingly being degraded to such a degree that the right of the mother is considered to trump the right of the child to life. And besides this, is the very reality of scientific/genetic manipulation in which that which is possible by science is immediately translated to that which is doable. And alongside these cultural and scientific challenges and rejection of classical anthropology is likewise present, in very real forms, the rejection of the humanity and personhood of the other, seen in conflicts that never seem to diminish across Africa, the Middle East, and other parts of the world. I would contend that these realities, and more, constitute a panoramic existential context in which we can allow the theological-anthropological interaction between Ratzinger and Odozor to inspire us to reflect on how to best serve the needs of the hour, as theologians in the Church of today.

In my estimation, the anthropological conversation between Ratzinger and Odozor has a conceptual dimension, on the one hand, and a practical dimension, on the other hand, in an interwoven manner. For both thinkers, the foundations are Christological, biblical, and philosophical. These foundations provide for a Christian anthropology that is communal and transcendental. Ultimately, for Odozor as for Ratzinger, the origin, meaning, and purpose of the question that is every human being entail, to use the beautiful phrase of Professor Emery de Gaál, a *Christocentric shift.*

1. Jesus Christ, the Basis for the Understanding of the Human Person

To start with the conceptual framework, one must acknowledge that for both Ratzinger and Odozor, there basis for theological anthropology is the person of Jesus Christ, the Second Person of the Blessed Trinity. This is how Odozor concludes chapter seven of *Morality Truly Christian, Truly African*. Odozor says, "African theology must refocus its attention on Christ as the basis for the anthropological renewal we seek on the continent."[4] Odozor reflects a profound ecclesial consciousness with his choice of Christ as the starting point for his anthropology. He places himself squarely in the living tradition that find its most articulate expression in the legendary articulation of Christian anthropology of the Second Vatican Council's Pastoral Constitution of the Church in the Modern World, *Gaudium et Spes*—a phrasing that is strikingly Ratzingerian (as well as de Lubacian) in tone and texture: "It is only in the mystery of Word made flesh that the mystery of humanity truly becomes clear. [...] Christ the new Adam, in the very revelation of the mystery of the father and of his love, fully reveals humanity to itself and brings to light its very high calling."[5] As Odozor explains, "Christianity's loftiest ideas concerning the human person are contained in the incarnation and the redemption of the human person in Jesus Christ. The incarnation is God's profound statement about the goodness of being human [...]. God is with us; God is for us. In the incarnation Jesus took all human flesh in his own flesh."[6] I believe this Christological foundation to anthropology to be a fundamental common ground between Odozor and Ratzinger.

As I argued in *Light of Reason, Light of Faith*, Ratzinger's anthropology is solidly and unequivocally predicated on a Christological foundation. To cite Ratzinger:

> In Christ alone appears the complete answer to the question about what the human being is. In him alone appears the deepest meaning of what is for the present a rough draft. He is the definitive human being, and creation is, as it were, a preliminary sketch that points to him. Thus, we can say that human persons are the beings who can be Jesus Christ's brothers and sisters. Human beings are creatures that can be one with Christ and thereby be one with God himself.[7]

Along these lines, the human being is one whose essence is to be in transition, transitioning to Christ. In this sense, Easter enters the core of what it means to be a person: Human beings must die with Christ like a grain of wheat in order to truly rise, to stand erect, to be themselves (cf. Jn 12:24). In this sense, anthropology is essentially Christology, for Christ, as the new man, constitutes the defining hermeneutical framework shedding light on human grandeur and our ultimate destiny. Chalcedon (451) was right in its declaration of Jesus as true God and true man, for Jesus is both God being human, and God teaching humans the meaning and value of true humanity that is predicated on self-love and not in the self-assertion that characterizes the Nietzschean *Übermensch*. In all, this Christological foundational framework serves as a common element in the anthropologies of Ratzinger and Odozor. This Christological hermeneutic (Christ as the New/Second Adam: 1 Cor 15:44–48; Col 1:15), is so crucial that both Ratzinger and Odozor see as the medium for interpreting the data of the second aspect of the conceptual framework of their theological anthropologies, that is, the normative vision of the human being as testified to in the creation account of the Book of Genesis.

2. The Biblical Basis for the Theological Anthropology of Ratzinger and Odozor

Another common area between Ratzinger and Odozor is the role that the Scriptures serve in establishing and understanding who and what the human being is. Both theologians show a deferential regard for the text of Genesis 1–3, creation and the fall, in their theological anthropology, which Odozor characterizes under the subtitle *Elements of a Christian Theological Anthropology*.[8] As Odozor declares, this biblical vision of man and woman as a community willed by God into existence out of pure love and called to love, is the basic form of human communion and the foundation for what constitutes the human family today.[9] To spell out some salient aspects of the Ratzingerian reading of Genesis, one might state the following:

> A truth that is humbling: The human being is from the earth (Gen 2:7): The human being is not God; Genesis refutes the thought of natural necessity and its radical evolutionism that often accomplishes it. Like all living things, the human being is destined for death;
>
> A truth that is consoling: The human being is not a demon or an evil spirit, though it might occasionally appear to be one—*homo homini lupus*—"the human being has not been formed from negative forces but has been fashioned from God's good earth" (*In the Beginning*, 43).
>
> A truth about sameness and equality: this transcends all

racial pathologies: "Despite every distinction that culture and history have brought about, it is still true that we are, in the last resort, the same. [...] Emperor and beggar, master and slave, are all ultimately one and the same person, taken from the earth and destined to return to the earth" (*In the Beginning*, 43). The unity of the whole human race becomes immediately apparent—from one earth. "There is only one humanity in the many human beings. The Bible says a decisive 'no' to all racism and to every human division" (*In the Beginning*, 43).

A truth about God's image and likeness (Gen 1:26–27): While taken from the earth, God has breathed his breath into the nostrils of the body that was formed from the earth: "In the human being heaven and earth touch one another. In the human being God enters into his creation; the human being is directly related to God. The human being is called by him" (*In the Beginning*, 44–45).

Image and likeness form the basis of relationality. Ratzinger declares, "Human life stands under God's special protection because each human being, however wretched or exalted he or she maybe, however sick or suffering, however good-for-nothing or important, whether born or unborn, whether incurably ill or radiant with health, each one bears God's breath in himself or herself, each one is God's image. This is the deepest reason for the inviolability of human dignity, and upon it is founded ultimately every civilization" (*In the Beginning*, 45). The essence of an image consists in the fact that it points to something beyond itself. Image represents something else. In this light, humans as image implies humans can never be closed in on themselves, for image implies relationality, pointing the person beyond the self. We are most ourselves when we enter into relationship with God and address the Creator. Being created in the image of God implies we are beings of word and love, beings capable of thinking and praying, for without these, humans cannot enter into a relationship with God which eventually points them back to one another. As I have noted elsewhere, "Imago Dei is about self-communication and self-transcendence; the former regards other persons, the latter, the opening up to a God that is discovered to be love."[10] To Ratzinger, therefore, the whole of biblical anthropology from creation to redemption, is premised on God's love for the human being that finds its apogee in the God-Man, Jesus Christ, whose person provides the interpretive key for all of Scripture.

Odozor reads the biblical data along similar lines to Ratzinger with regard to human nature. What is further developed is the reality of the fall with its personal and structural sin.[11] Given the reality of the socio-economic and political situation of much of contemporary Africa, Odozor's considerable treatment of social sin and the structures of sin is quite understandable. He proposes tenets of Catholic Social Teaching such as solidarity, reconciliation, truth, and a transcendental sense of freedom, as possible paths that could aid Africa's liberation of itself and its peoples from the dehumanizing situation of an anthropological crisis that is manifesting itself in both material and even spiritual lack. Where do we locate this anthropological crisis that Odozor sees as reflected in the socio-economic and political hardship for many an African? Odozor points to the human conscience, the most secret core of the human person, as explained by *Gaudium et Spes* (GS, 16). This is where the law is made known that calls us to the love of God and of neighbor. For Odozor, there is a relationship between individual freedom, conscience, and the community.[12] As an objective and not a subjective norm of morality, conscience can aid the human being in discerning both the wrong acts that are dehumanizing and hence must be avoided, and the good acts that are life-affirming and hence must be done. God's grace is never wanting to help the person live out the good that conscience has discerned.

3. The Philosophical Basis for the Theological Anthropology of Ratzinger and Odozor

The last aspect of the conceptual framework of the theological anthropology of Ratzinger and Odozor has to do with the philosophical sources engaged by both authors. At the risk of over simplification, Odozor appears to be decidedly Thomistic. His basic definition of a person as a *compositum*, not just a soul, nor just a body, but both body and soul, follows Aquinas' Treatise on Man in *Summa theologiae* Ia, qq. 75–89. Of pointed significance is Odozor's reading of Aquinas' philosophical anthropology through the lenses of the imperative and the indicative, in that what one ought to do, is grounded on what one is. The person is therefore a subject and a moral actor. Odozor likewise engages Boethius's *Consolation* and its classic definition of the human being as an individual substance of a rational nature.[13] Though he does not deny the significant space that the Boethian definition of a person has occupied in Western thought and in Christian theology, Odozor seeks to break what appears to be an individualistic understanding of person that could be read from the Boethian definition, and perhaps from much of Western culture at large. From an African perspective, Odozor complements the Western idea of the person by insisting that African anthropology be grounded in African cosmology, which includes God, spirits, and human beings.[14] Though highly prized, Odozor is candid about the challenge that a communitarian understanding of the person continues to pose to African anthropology. Remedying it would not only include a rediscovery of relatedness as an essential quality of life, but even more, the question of the necessity of the respect of comprehensive rights.

Ultimately, the resolution of this anthropological crisis attested to by Benedict XVI in *Africae Munus* will be no small feat, Odozor recognizes. But there is no room for despair. In the Christian faith, Africa can find resources to save itself from the current anthropological crisis. This is the forceful argument that Odozor makes in the subsection titled *An African Christian Anthropology*. His proposals to remedy Africa's anthropological crisis include, amongst others, the following. First, he suggests an extension of the sense of family, giving respect and worthy attention to those beyond the nuclear family, to the point where all African Christians can affirm the statement made by the fathers of the First African Synod that the same blood, the blood of Christ runs through our veins as Africans. Second, he refocuses the fundamental vision of what it means to be a human being in the light of a transcendental prism. Third, he reemphasizes the sacredness of the gift of life from God, from conception to its natural end. Last but not least, he places Christ at the center of what it means to be a human being.[15] If Africa is to recover from what Benedict XVI and Odozor diagnose as Africa's anthropological crisis, which the Cameroonian Jesuit, Engelbert Mveng depicted as an anthropological deficiency, I believe that these proposals of Odozor will constitute a remedial first step. In this, Odozor and Benedict are in tandem.

If Odozor largely follows Aquinas, Richard of St. Victor, Boethius, Scotus, John Paul II in terms of his philosophical framework, Ratzinger appears to largely follow Augustine and Buber. We find the following in his recollections:

> We then found the philosophy of personalism reiterated with renewed conviction in the great Jewish thinker Martin Buber. This encounter with Personalism was for me a spiritual experience that left an essential mark, especially since I spontaneously associated such personalism with the thought of Saint Augustine, who in his Confessions had struck me with the power of all his human passion and depth (Ratzinger, *Milestones*, 44).

> I revered Martin Buber very much. For one thing he was the great representative of Personalism, the I-Thou principle that permeates his entire philosophy (Benedict XVI, *Last Testament*, 99).
>
> From the beginning, St. Augustine interested me very much—precisely insofar as he was, so to speak, a counterweight to Thomas Aquinas (Ratzinger, *Salt of the Earth*, 60).
>
> The personal struggle which Augustine expresses really spoke to me. Thomas' writings were textbooks, by and large, and impersonal somehow. That said, there is of course a personal struggle standing behind them, which you only discover later. Augustine battles with himself, and indeed continues to do so after his conversion. And that is what makes the subject compelling and beautiful (Benedict XVI, *Last Testament*, 79).

From Augustine, Ratzinger uncovers the human being in the full drama of freedom apparently God's most gratuitous but delicate gift. Augustine's conversion experience epitomizes the human quest for meaning, with each stage defined by an apparent irresistible promise of happiness that mirrors, in strikingly similar terms, the philosophic journey between Boethius and Lady Philosophy in the *Consolations*. The options for wealth, power, pleasure, fame, and honor are not satisfying. We long for more. Augustine teaches Ratzinger that every human being faces what the French philosopher Maurice Blondel calls the wedge between the willing will and the willed will, between desire and the fulfilment of our desire, with a retrospective realization of the inability of anything creatural to meet our greatest longing. If Aquinas saw superstition as an excess regarding the virtue of religion, Blondel saw superstition as placing the infinite into the finite, a false sense of self-sufficiency that results in an abortion of action, an existential dilettantism that refuses to accept the exterior help that must save action. Here, one is reminded of Pascal's realization in the Pensées: wretchedness away from God; happiness with God. This is great discovery that Augustine makes, resulting in the greatest formulation in theological anthropology, and the most quoted verse outside the Scriptures: God has made us for himself, and our hearts are restless until the rest in God.

In all, Odozor's Thomistic path and Ratzinger's Augustinian point to an identical realization: the human being, as attractive as self-sufficiency appears, as a being that reaches his or her fullest potential not by excluding the supernatural, what Odozor refers to as the transcendental sense, but rather, in embracing the reality that we are transcendent being called to a higher form of existence. I am reminded here of Kierkegaard's stages, in which the meaning of human life starts from the aesthetic, then moves to the ethical, and then, with the necessity of a teleological suspension of the ethical, the religious stage appears on the horizon as the most logical path, even if faith is presented as a leap into the unknown.

The challenge that faith continues to face today, due to Kant's reduction of believing to a postulate of practical reason, is the relegation of believing to the domain of the phenomenologically irrational. It would appear that once Kant shut the door on reason in order to make room for faith, the world of rationality, what Hegel calls the Kingdom of Thought developed a life of its own that was destined never to enter into dialogue with the world of faith, with the Kingdom of God. I believe that the philosophical framework adopted by both Ratzinger and Odozor shows that if the human being does not allow faith and reason to rise to the contemplation of truth, to use an image of John Paul II in *Fides et Ratio*, the result, as Ratzinger repeatedly averred, would be pathologies of reason, on the one hand, and pathologies of faith, on the other, with an existentially schizophrenic human being in the middle.

4. The Dialectics of Person in the *I-Thou-We* Hermeneutic

To Odozor, the African sense of community provides the definitive context for understanding who the human being is, almost to the point that relatedness and solidarity shape how a person is defined. This makes for a reading of African personalism in language reminiscent more of Buber than of Boethius. The I is precisely I because there is a Thou, that is, there a community. This I and Thou dialectic is what brings forth a we-structure with respect to what is constitutive of the African. In effect, the boundary lines between the subjective I of the individual and the objective Thou of the community are very thin and easily transgressed if need be. There is, therefore, a network of interconnectedness at the horizontal level, which is humanistically enriching and supportive.

While this I-Thou Buberian concept captures the interpersonal relationship from the perspective of African personalism as espoused by Odozor, Ratzinger appears willing to stretch Buber further. When Buber posits the I as the starting point of human subjectivity, Ratzinger holds such a starting point to be a misconstruction of God's nature, a theological reductionism in which God appears absent as primary cause, only appearing in the Thou in a somewhat secondary relationship. To put it plainly, and with Book X of Augustine's *Confessions* in mind albeit not referenced, Ratzinger wonders if it is possible to posit a subjective I without a corresponding Thou of God? Can there be the being of an I without God as the ground of all being? If Buber's I-Thou dialect is allowed to stand in its sharpness, holds Ratzinger, then God eventually appears distant, and his infinity compromised.[16] As Ratzinger argues, human identity is not found within oneself, but outside oneself, outside not in a sense of the spatio-temporal, but in the sense of finding it in God. Hence, there is an I only when there is a prior Thou, and not just a consequent relational Thou. In this sense, if one's identity is only in Christ, who offers the world identity and meaning as Emery de Gaál points out in the Epilogue of his *The Theology of Pope Benedict XVI: The Christocentric Shift*, then it follows, as has been noted, that the I-Thou dialectic breaks down, for the I is not encapsulated.[17]

This is the meaning of being new in Christ, of a new humanism, that Benedict XVI pointed out in the homily before the conclave of 2005.

And as Ratzinger would point out in various writings, it is precisely when God in Jesus Christ is the ground of my being, that I find the meaning of personhood in a community that is both vertical and horizontal, God and the neighbor. Odozor and Ratzinger agree and acknowledge that even the etymological and historical evolution of the term "person" is traceable to the Trinitarian reality, as first articulated by Tertullian in the West with his Trinitarian formula, *una substantia, tres personae*. While we are able to go into details here regarding the place of Trinitarian language and the Ratzinger-Odozor anthropological structure, it suffices to say that their insistence on a communal understanding of who we are as persons, in a context that has increasingly privileged the Cartesian subjectivity, has a great theological warrant behind it, in the image of the Trinity, Christianity's first basic dogma.

Conclusion: *Ecce Homo*: The Human Being in Ratzinger and Odozor: Overcoming the Anthropological Crisis of Hope

Kant was motivated to write his three *Critiques* by the questions: *What can I know? What must I do? What can I hope for?* Kant was a moral thinker like Fr Odozor. Kant was also a German like Ratzinger. I find it fitting to employ his paradigm in order to bring these thoughts on the theology anthropology of Pope Benedict XVI and Prof Odozor to a close.

First, by way of summary, what can we know from the Ratzinger-Odozor theological anthropology? In brief, we can know that the human being is not just a one-way-street, nor an intellectual construct. Because personhood is rooted in the Trinity, God as Person, we can know ourselves as persons by living in unity and communion with others, especially in the mystical body of Christ, as sons and daughters of God.

Second, given the state of anthropological crisis that both Ratzinger and Odozor acknowledge (different contexts notwithstanding), with Kant again, what must we do? Again, in brief, because every human being is made in the image and likeness of God and redeemed by Christ, we can proceed to build a new civilization of love, a new humanism, on the basis of the inviolability of each person's dignity, made in the image and likeness of God (Gen 1:26). A person is not just a number. As Benedict XVI beautifully expressed it in his homily inaugurating his pontificate, we are not some accidental product of evolution. Each one of us is known. Each one of us is willed by God. How urgent is this message today, with the increasing wars all over the place! One of the beauties about Professor Odozor's theology is his optimism. I also noticed this in his preaching, some of which I have watched on YouTube in preparation for this conference. Even when he laments the state of things in Nigeria as he did during the homily he delivered for the 40th anniversary of John Cardinal Onaiyekan of Abuja, Nigeria, Fr Odozor does not despair. He ends on the note that Christianity can make a difference. To hope against hope, Benedict XVI declared in Yaoundé, Cameroon, is the beautiful description of a Christian.

And this brings me to the third and final Kantian question, what can we hope for? With Benedict XVI and Fr Odozor, we can hope and work to bring about a world in which the human being is not a means to an end, as Kant points out in his *Groundwork of the Metaphysics of Morals*, but also an end itself. We can hope, not in the sense of a Marxist utopia, but as Benedict XVI points out in his encyclical *Spe Salvi*, that in prayer, action, and suffering, we can proceed in a way that, as persons-in-communion with others, and not only ourselves, we will experience the star of hope, for no one is an island, no one lives alone, and no one is saved alone, and we can hope that this communal sense of personhood would contribute to build a better world anchored in the person of Jesus Christ, the God-Man as Chalcedon proclaimed. And we thank God for the sure and certain guides that we have along this Christian path, and we wish Fr. Odozor many more years. May Fr. Odozor continue to be an inspiration to us regarding what it means to be a theologian of the finest caliber, but even more, a friend of Jesus Christ the incarnate *Logos* of God, who fully reveals us to ourselves as persons and points us to our highest calling.

Chapter 2

Paulinus Ikechukwu Odozor's Unfinished Quest for a Truly African and Christian Moral Theology of Marriage

Raymond Olusesan Aina, M.S.P.

Professor Paulinus Ikechukwu Odozor's scholarly career resembles a magnificent mosaic, meticulously woven with threads of vibrant African culture and profound Christian doctrine. His contributions to the field of fundamental moral theology are vast and commendable. Odozor's insightful engagement with the work of his mentor, Richard McCormick, and his critical reviews of post-conciliar Roman Catholic moral theology stand as testaments to his intellectual depth. Notably, his most comprehensive offering to African Christian ethics paints a rich fusion of cultural values and theological insights, offering valuable perspectives on the continent's unique moral landscape. Yet, despite Odozor's sustained and significant contributions, a crucial element remains incomplete: the construction of a truly African and Christian moral theology of marriage. This endeavour, akin to the unwoven sections of a masterpiece, awaits further development. It is here that Odozor's younger colleagues and fellow scholars are called upon to carry the torch. Our task is immense, demanding the careful weaving together of diverse threads from African cultural practices and Christian theological principles. This combination envisioned as both beautiful and transformative, will require challenging established norms, exploring uncharted territories, and embracing the boldness to imagine new perspectives on marriage. The journey will not be easy. It demands a critical examination of the status quo, a willingness to explore novel possibilities, and the courage to envision a future where marriage is understood and practised in ways that resonate deeply with the African context. Yet, the stakes are high. Only through the completion of this synthesis, with its harmonious blend of African cultural wisdom and Christian theological insights, can we hope to build a more just and equitable society for all Africans.

In his book *Morality Truly Christian, Truly African*,[1] Professor Odozor presents a revolutionary new framework for moral reasoning in African Christian theological ethics. His approach seeks to weave together the richness of African cultural worldviews with the deep insights of Christian moral theology. Odozor argues that this convergence is essential to ensure that moral concepts within the Roman Catholic tradition are not simply imposed constructs, but are instead firmly rooted in the lived experiences of African individuals and communities. He provides compelling case studies that illustrate the efforts of the African Church to integrate moral discourse into a religiously diverse continent and to connect the healing gospel message to African realities. Through his groundbreaking work, Professor Odozor seeks to empower African individuals and communities to take ownership of their moral discourse and to create a truly African Christian theology that is both authentic and relevant to their everyday lives. Two key questions, which will be explored further in my discussion on Professor Odozor's impact on my classes, serve as the driving force behind my engagement with him in this dialogue. The next section will explore the questions and their relevance to my pedagogical approach.

Afro-Christian Sexual Ethics and Conjugal Morality: A Classroom Perspective with Paulinus Odozor

In the hallowed halls of our seminaries, vast libraries stand as testaments to the intellectual discourse on sexuality, marriage, and family life. Yet, amidst the familiar cadence of Western voices, whispers of African wisdom echo, yearning for recognition. Driven by this potent undercurrent, I embarked on a journey within my Moral Theology course at a Nigerian seminary, weaving these whispers into a synthesis of African Christian sexual ethics and conjugal morality. This course became a pilgrimage into the vibrant cultural heritage of Africa, where Christianity has found fertile ground and blossomed in unique and captivating ways. Armed with the groundbreaking work of Professor Odozor, my students and I have over the years explored the intricate and multifaceted world where African

Christians grapple with the complexities of living a faithful life in the 21st century. Through this shared exploration, we unearthed a wealth of insights, illuminating the nuanced perspectives that shape African Christian approaches to marriage and sexuality. Driven by a desire to ignite a fusion of idealism and dissent, I conceived "Afro-Christian Sexual Ethics and Conjugal Morality," a novel course merging two previously overlapping subjects. This third-year theological studies course aims to equip the next generation of African theologians and missionaries with a robust foundation in ethical reasoning, particularly within intercultural contexts.

The curriculum explores deeply contemporary issues related to sexuality and conjugal morality, exploring them through the lens of the African Church. Students engage with ongoing discourses on inculturation's implications for Roman Catholic sexual ethics, grappling with the delicate tension between particularity and universality, tradition, and (re)contextualization. Immersed in the richness of African Fundamental Moral Theology, they delve into its methodology and its postulations on sexual ethics, the marriage process, and conjugal morality. This bedrock of knowledge equips students to confidently navigate complex sexual ethical dilemmas. They actively participate in current moral debates, considering the lived experiences of individuals and communities within the African, and particularly Nigerian, contexts. The course reader, a vibrant mosaic of African voices, serves as a springboard for their understanding of African ethical reasoning. Empowered by this multifaceted perspective, graduates of the course emerge prepared to minister and live as African Christians. They possess the confidence to navigate the intricate ethical landscape of the 21st century, weaving together faith and cultural wisdom in their personal lives and professional pursuits.

Professor Bénézet Bujo's pioneering work in African Christian ethics[2] laid the groundwork for the moral values explored in this course, harmonizing Christian teachings with traditional African wisdom. However, Professor Paulinus Odozor's critical interrogation of Bujo's assertions on "palaver" and natural law invites us to reimagine this synthesis, incorporating new threads of reflection and possibility. In his groundbreaking article, "An African Moral Theology of Inculturation: Methodological Considerations,"[3] Odozor challenges us to reconsider the place of palaver, a traditional African communal dialogue process, and natural law in an inculturated moral theology. He argues that palaver is not simply a tool for conflict resolution, but rather a holistic approach to moral reasoning that is deeply rooted in African culture. Similarly, Odozor contends that natural law should not be understood as a universal and abstract set of principles, but rather as a dynamic and contextualized process of discernment that is informed by the lived experiences of African Christians. In the classroom, we relive the lively conversation and debate between Professors Bujo and Odozor, two towering figures in African Christian ethics. Both scholars agree that African Christian ethics must be grounded in methodological principles that account for the continent's cultural diversity. However, Bujo's view of African tradition is static, while Odozor argues that Bujo idealizes African culture, overlooking potential negative aspects such as the insular and ethnocentric tendencies of African hospitality and the potential for misuse of the African palaver. Odozor emphasizes the need for fixed boundaries, such as human rights, in ethical discourse. The dialogue between Bujo and Odozor is essential to the development of African Fundamental Moral Theology, which challenges Western moral claims. Their juxtaposing contributions help us to explore the rich mosaic of ethical thought unique to the African continent. As we moved to the core of the course, with Bujo's *Plea for Change* as our major text and inspiration,[4] two questions about Professor Odozor always arose:

> Is it not a curious twist of fate that Professor Odozor, a leading African moral theologian, finds more inspiration in the work of his American Jesuit mentor, Richard McCormick, than in the work of any African pioneer of theology?
>
> As Bujo's journey from critique to creation unfolds, what tapestry of African marriage rites and theology has Odozor woven?

Professor Odozor's critical response to Bujo's practical proposals for transforming African marriage customs and theological interpretations of marriage offers a valuable lens through which to assess the applicability and impact of their discourse. These questions inform the direction, scope, and depth of my contribution to this conversation by shaping my exploration of the intersections and implications of their viewpoints.

A Contextual Hermeneutical Framework in Progress

While Professor Odozor's exploration of sexual ethics and conjugal morality has yielded a valuable hermeneutical framework, it remains incomplete. Significant gaps exist, and I am driven by the desire to push these boundaries forward. This pursuit is not merely academic, but rather an attempt to engage Odozor in a dialogue that might inspire him to address these unresolved matters. Professor Odozor's stature within African Moral Theology is undeniable. His potential contributions to our understanding of sexual ethics and conjugal morality within an African context are vast. By provoking his curiosity and encouraging him to delve deeper, I aim to prompt further development of his insights and elicit additional commitments to advancing this field of study. This proactive engagement would capitalize on his wisdom and experience, harnessing his expertise to enrich the ongoing discourse and scholarship on sexual ethics and conjugal morality in Africa.

One of Professor Paulinus Odozor's earliest contributions to the construction of Afro-Christian moral theology of marriage is his article "Thoughts on African Christian Theology of Marriage and Sexuality."[5] Professor Odozor's work on African Christian theology of marriage and sexuality strikes a delicate balance between respecting African cultural and social dynamics and upholding Christian principles. He emphasizes the importance of a holistic approach to understanding marriage and sexuality, one that encompasses the emotional and spiritual dimensions beyond the physical. He also stresses the need for a nuanced and contextualized interpretation of traditional African practices related to marriage and sexuality. Odozor's contribution is particularly significant within the context of the African bishops' interventions at the First Special Assembly of the Synod of Bishops on Africa (African Synod I). These interventions highlighted the need for an African Christian theology that is both authentic to the continent's rich cultural heritage and faithful to the core teachings of the Catholic Church:

> At the recent African Synod there were calls for an African theology of Christian marriage. This paper is an initial response to this call. . . . I will go on to offer some thoughts on

> certain elements which ought to be considered important in any construction of a theology of marriage which is truly African and fully Christian.[6]

The most pressing task in developing an African Christian theology of marriage for Catholics is to forge a unified form of marriage that integrates the three existing layers: traditional, civil, and ecclesial.[7] Odozor asserts that African Catholics should boldly forge their theological frameworks, unconstrained by the fetters of Rome. He envisions a clear path forward, one that has been overlooked for too long.[8] Odozor takes up the gauntlet thrown down by the African bishops at the First African Synod, focusing on the foundational principles and caveats that must underpin any Afro-Christian theology of sexuality and conjugal morality. While he lauds the more relational, communitarian, and deeply religious processive African marriage rites and values, he also acknowledges that certain aspects of African culture are irreconcilable with Christian teaching. Specifically, he notes the following:

- The place of children in marriage and family life, which is often overlooked or undervalued in African eschatology.
- The patriarchal construct of marriage and family life, which often subordinates women and children.
- The polygamous system in Africa is not compatible with the Christian ideal of monogamy.

Odozor contends that these aspects of African culture must be challenged and transfigured to create a truly Christian theology of sexuality and conjugal morality. He envisions a new synthesis, one that draws on the best of both African and Christian traditions, one that is both relevant and liberating.[9] Professor Odozor's critique of proposals for transforming African marriage customs and theological interpretations laid a valuable foundation for further exploration. However, a crucial question remains: *in the years since, has Odozor himself made significant contributions to the construction of this envisaged Afro-Christian theology of marriage and conjugal morality?* Examining the trajectory of his work allows us to assess the development and impact of his ideas in this crucial field.

1. Feminist Critiques of Afro-Christian Sexual Ethics: Odozor and Cahill in Conversation

Our scholarly inquiry led my students and me to a fascinating exploration of the writings of prominent African moral theologians, specifically focusing on the challenges facing marriage within the continent. Among these works, Odozor's monograph stood out for its insightful analysis and compelling arguments. While it does not present a definitive solution to the intricate issue of dual marriage rites in African Catholicism, it offers a robust and persuasive defence of the traditional African marriage process, highlighting its validity and inherent reasonableness. Odozor meticulously lays the foundation for his defence by invoking a pivotal quote from the 1981 SECAM Working Paper on Christian Family and Marriage in Africa.: "Marriage is considered a vital ministry of the life and future of the lineage all over Africa. It is a covenant not only between two persons but also between the couple and their respective lineages."[10] This excerpt powerfully underscores the critical role marriage plays in African society, setting the stage for Odozor's subsequent arguments and analysis. While his work is not a panacea for the issue we seek to address, it is nonetheless a valuable contribution to the ongoing debate on African marriage traditions. His elegant apologia, a spirited rebuttal to the assertions of Professor Lisa Cahill of Boston College, highlights the ethical dimensions of this complex and nuanced topic. Cahill argues that African marriage traditions may undermine or even infringe upon the fundamental principles of women's freedom and dignity. Odozor, however, vehemently contests this assertion, positing that Cahill fundamentally misunderstands the true essence of African traditions in this context. With eloquence and erudition, he constructs a compelling defence of his position, meticulously dismantling Cahill's arguments and offering a fresh perspective on this important issue.

Cahill argues that the communal nature of African marriage can sometimes limit individual freedom, especially for women. She maintains that everyone has the right to choose their spouse freely, but that this right can be infringed upon when the community's views and expectations are given too much weight. Cahill also argues that community involvement in marriage decisions can entrench traditional gender roles and reinforce patriarchal norms, which can further erode women's autonomy and agency.[11] Odozor counters Cahill's assertion that community involvement in African marriages inherently restricts individual autonomy, especially for women. He contends that this inference unduly simplifies the complex interactions and dynamics within African societies and their marriage traditions. By challenging this notion, Odozor underscores the imperative for a more nuanced understanding of the relationship between communal participation and individual agency.[12] Odozor further asserts that African couples enjoy a unique structural support system that sets them apart from their Western counterparts. He emphasizes that in African societies, marriages are often embedded within a holistic communal framework, providing couples with a web of familial, social, and cultural support. This support system, he maintains, fosters a greater sense of cohesion and collective responsibility within African marriages. He posits that this contrasts starkly with the Western model, where individual autonomy can sometimes lead to isolation and limited social backing.[13] Odozor's counterpoints engage in a discourse that highlights the multifaceted nature of African marriages and challenges Cahill's sweeping generalization. He underscores the importance of considering the unique dynamics and support systems that shape marriage processes in African societies, ultimately advocating for a more balanced and nuanced understanding of the relationship between communal participation and individual agency within these contexts.

While acknowledging the genuine concerns about community involvement in marriage decisions, Odozor asserts that these concerns are not unique to Africa. He emphasizes that communities can exert subtle pressure on individuals who are contemplating marriage, regardless of culture. Odozor points out that the potential for external influence and pressure in the process of choosing a spouse is a global phenomenon, suggesting that the challenge of maintaining personal autonomy in matters of marriage is not unique to African communities. Odozor raises a significant concern for African Christian moral theology, advising caution and advocating for vigilance against both "communitarian imposition" and "excessive individualism."[14] This highlights the need to strike a balance between communal values and personal freedom. Odozor's objective is to galvanize African Christian moral theologians and practitioners to critically evaluate the potential risks and benefits of community involvement in navigating the complex landscape of contemporary marriage dynamics. By presenting these diverse perspectives, Odozor contributes to a nuanced understanding of the challenges associated with community influence on marriage decisions. His acknowledgement of the global prevalence of these challenges, coupled with his call for vigilance against undue external pressures and unrestrained individualism, serves as a clarion call for thoughtful reflection and discourse within the realm of African Christian moral theology.[15]

In my research for this study, I discovered Odozor's seminal 1994 article, published in the aftermath of the First African Synod. As already stated, this article presciently anticipated the ongoing debate between Odozor and Cahill on the role of communal involvement in African marriages. Odozor's 2014 book can be viewed as a continuation of the discourse first sparked by his 1994 article, which suggests that the fundamental tenets of the debate can be traced back to that earlier engagement, in which Odozor forcefully challenged Cahill's assertions.[16] One may contemplate the potential evolution of Cahill's stance since her 1994 article, raising the question of whether she has modified or revised her views over time. The persistence of assertions and counter-assertions in Morality Truly African, Truly Christian suggests that the issues addressed in the earlier discourse remain salient, necessitating continued exploration of the diverse perspectives articulated by Odozor and Cahill. The ongoing dialogue between Odozor and Cahill exemplifies the inherent fluidity of ethical deliberations. Their exchange of contrasting ideas and the potential for shifting viewpoints highlights the intricate and multifaceted process of interpreting cultural norms within a modern ethical framework. The exchange between Odozor and Cahill highlights the complexity of this issue, which transcends the mere role of community involvement in African marriages. It also implicates the broader question of the relationship between culture and ethics. How can we balance the need to respect cultural traditions with the need to uphold universal human rights? The debate further engages the role of women in society. Cahill asserts that community involvement can oppress women by denying them the right to choose their partners. Conversely, Odozor contends that community involvement can empower women by providing them with a support system and a voice in decision-making.

The Odozor-Cahill debate continues to rage, with no easy answers and valid arguments on both sides. Nonetheless, this dialogue is essential, raising critical questions about the intersection of culture, Christian ethics, and gender. Their ongoing exchange serves as a reminder that ethical discussions are dynamic and evolve with societal change. Thus, open, and honest conversations are imperative, even when we disagree. By engaging in dialogue, we can learn from each other and gain a deeper understanding of the complex ethical challenges of our time. Professor Odozor's pursuit of authentic African and Christian moral theology necessitates a nuanced approach to feminist perspectives, such as those of Lisa Cahill and Afro-Christian feminist theologians. Dismissing these perspectives as superficial or approaching them with excessive caution would hinder the development of a truly comprehensive framework. Instead, engaging with feminist theory offers a critical lens through which to examine power dynamics, dominance, and disparities within African Christian marriages, providing invaluable insights for navigating their complexities.[17] Christian feminist theology further enriches this exploration by interpreting religious concepts from a gender equality perspective, seeking to understand Christianity through the lens of lived experiences.[18] This vibrant and diverse field of thought, encompassing scholars from various backgrounds,[19] offers a wealth of rich and nuanced insights that can be fruitfully integrated into Odozor's project.

Unravelling the extent and impact of Christian feminism and gender studies on Afro-Christian theology, especially in the context of marriage and conjugal ethics, warrants further inquiry and scrutiny. Professor Odozor must grapple with the concepts articulated by Christian feminist and Afro-Christian feminist theologians and scholars to construct a truly African and Christian moral theology that is both just and inclusive, particularly when addressing sensitive aspects of traditional African marriage practices and conjugal ethics that may not be congruent with authentic Christian principles and practices.[20] At this juncture, let me highlight the works of two African theologians, Mercy Amba Oduyoye's *Becoming Whole* (2004) and Musimbi R. Kanyoro's *The Power We Have* (2002), which engendered discourses on the intersection of gender, African culture, and Christian tradition. Oduyoye affirms the rich legacy of African women's resistance to oppression, offering profound insights into the essence of wholeness and healing. Their narratives have the potential to shatter stereotypes that justify the subjugation of women, paving the way for a more equitable and inclusive world. Similarly, Kanyoro asserts that African women play an active role in both religious and social spheres, wielding significant influence in promoting a more just and equitable world. It is imperative to acknowledge their perspectives and value their insights. As a result, there is a clarion call to reorient both the church and society to reflect the full humanity and equality of women. Considering these and similar disputations, it is essential to ascertain Professor Odozor's stance on these matters.

- How does Odozor perceive the potential of Christian feminist and Afro-Christian feminist perspectives to contribute to the development of a holistic African and Christian moral theology?
- Specifically, how can these perspectives be used to interrogate contested elements within traditional African marital customs and ethical norms?
- What are the challenges and opportunities inherent in this process?

Investigating these questions would contribute to a more nuanced understanding of Professor Odozor's approach to and perspectives on this topic. This challenge is particularly relevant given that his curriculum vitae on the Notre Dame website does not list any publications on feminism or feminist theology as of 2020, except an invited presentation on Catholic theological perspectives on female sexuality and violence against women following a performance of The Vagina Monologues at the University of Notre Dame on February 14, 2006.[21]

A meticulous scrutiny of Professor Paulinus Ikechukwu Odozor's works reveals that his Afro-Christian moral theology, particularly in the context of marriage and family life, does not adequately integrate or engage with the perspectives of Afro-Christian feminist and womanist scholars. While Odozor has engaged with some scholars in this field, such as Lisa Cahill, his work has not fully explored the breadth and depth of Afro-centric feminist and womanist discourse. For instance, in *Morality Truly Christian, Truly African*:

- The index does not contain any entry on "female," "feminism," or "womanism."
- It contains a reference to "gender theory" (p. 290), but no other references to feminist or womanist perspectives on morality.
- It contains references to a few female theologians and scholars, includ-

ing Mercy Amba Oduyoye (pp. 80–83) and Carolyn Osiek (p. 234), as well as to the place of 'women' in *Africae Munus* (pp. 289–90).

- It contains references to women in African Christianity (pp. 26–27), African tradition (pp. 75–85), the Igbo people (pp. 84–85, 311n51), the praxis of the kingdom (pp. 199–200), African Synod II (pp. 288–91), trafficking (p. 289), and widows (pp. 78–79, 311n51).

Women and African Moral Theology: Odozor's Perspective *in Morality Truly Christian, Truly African*	
African Christianity	Women's involvement in Church life and ministry predates the Western church's agitation for the same.[22]
African tradition	Odozor emphasizes the importance of eschewing romanticism about African tradition and challenging harmful practices such as violence against women and disinheritance of the girl-child, even though these practices exist in some African cultures.[23]
Oduyoye, Mercy Amba	Odozor recognizes Oduyoye as a renowned African feminist theologian and world-class theologian.[24] However, he critically engages with and contests Oduyoye's assertions that African culture is always full of abundant life.[25]
the Igbo people	Igbo culture, both past and present, demonstrates that it is not irredeemably patriarchal, as some people stereotype African culture and life.[26]
the praxis of the kingdom	The Kingdom of God, as envisioned by Jesus, is a place where all people are treated with equal respect and dignity, regardless of their gender, social status, or family background.[27]
Osiek, Carolyn	Odozor, in his discussion of the most appropriate anthropology for an Afro-Christian moral theology, cites prominent female scripture scholars who argue that the family in antiquity was closer to the

	traditional African conception of family than to the Western conception. This is because both the nuclear and extended members of the family unit were included in the family, reflecting the inherent relational anthropology of both groups.[28] Odozor's focus is not on Osiek's feminist theology and advocacy for women's roles in the church.
African Synod II; *Africae Munus*	Odozor's chapter on Afro-Christian moral theology explores the emerging culture wars between the West and Sub-Saharan Africa over gender ideology, which he sees as threatening African theology of sexuality.[29] He expresses some unease about feminist advocacy, viewing it as too radical, and approaches feminist hermeneutics with caution.
Trafficking in persons	Odozor emphasizes the Church's prophetic and liberative role in addressing the trafficking of women and other forms of women's debasement, and in promoting greater inclusion of women in ecclesial governance and decision-making.[30]

Table 1: Source—Author

Examining the table reveals key insights into Professor Odozor's views on women, feminist hermeneutics, and their place within the framework of African Christian moral theology. His approach resembles a captivating dance of gender, culture, and faith, where he acts as a gifted weaver, skilfully interlacing threads of African tradition, Christian teachings, and feminist thought to create a mosaic that is both aesthetically pleasing and intellectually stimulating. At the core of Odozor's hermeneutics lies a fervent commitment to promoting gender equality and challenging the negative aspects of certain African traditions. He acknowledges the long-standing vital role women have played within the Church, emphasizing its responsibility to address existing gender inequalities and actively promote women's inclusion in leadership positions. However,

Odozor's dance takes a unique turn, deviating from the approach of some feminist theologians. He expresses wariness towards certain feminist interpretations of biblical texts, potentially perceiving them as overly radical or Western-centric in their application to the African context.

However, despite these reservations, Odozor recognizes the crucial role of feminist thought in challenging harmful traditional practices and affirming the value of women's voices. This recognition underscores his commitment to navigating the complex interplay between cultural norms, religious teachings, and the pursuit of gender equality within the African Christian context. His insights provide a delicate balancing act between tradition and liberation. He acknowledges the value of African cultural traditions while also challenging practices that perpetuate gender inequality. For instance, he argues that the African traditional conception of family emphasizes community, interdependence, and mutual respect. This conception of family can be a powerful source of support and liberation for women, especially in the face of patriarchal oppression. Nevertheless, Odozor also acknowledges that African traditional marital customs and ethical norms can be controversial. He recognizes that certain practices, while deeply embedded in the cultural fabric, may be incompatible with principles of gender equality and individual autonomy. This tension between tradition and progress lies at the heart of Odozor's ongoing exploration. He has not yet provided a comprehensive analysis of the challenges and opportunities involved in incorporating Christian and Afro-Christian feminist perspectives into Afro-Christian moral theology. Engaging with these perspectives would enrich Odozor's work by fostering a more nuanced and inclusive understanding of African Christian ethics and challenging patriarchal biases.

2. The Reception of Amoris Laetitia in the Church in Africa[31]

Pope Francis' post-synodal exhortation, *Amoris Laetitia*, is a significant document that addresses the challenges facing families today and their enduring role, despite these challenges. However, many people in Africa mistakenly believe that the 2014 and 2015 synods focused solely on broken marriages, civil divorce, remarriage, access to the sacraments, and same-sex unions. Unfortunately, many people in Africa or of African descent have allowed the media and Western narratives to shape their understanding of doctrinal and pastoral developments in the Church today, overlooking broader issues relevant to the African Church. I argue that Professor Odozor's interventions on *Amoris Laetitia* could have been broader than what many people in the media currently remember him for. In this section, I will begin by summarizing some of the urgent areas of pastoral and theological reception of Amoris Laetitia in Africa. I will then compare these with Professor Odozor's interventions on *Amoris Laetitia* for the Church in Africa.

Amoris Laetitia raises complex questions in the African context, particularly regarding the interplay between morality, law, and pastoral practice. Specifically, Chapters 4 and 5, which focus on fruitful love in marriage, and Chapter 7, which addresses child education, raise questions about their implications for canon law. This includes their potential impact on the understanding of "*matrimonium ratum et consummatum*." The document's eighth chapter presents challenges related to "*salus animarum*" and the dynamic between love, law, and mercy. The application of internal forum solutions in African contexts, the tension between *Amoris Laetitia* 300–311 and Canons 912 and 915, and the interaction of *Amoris Laetitia* with the norms for obtaining nullity declarations outlined in *Mitis Iudex Dominus Iesus* are all important areas for further exploration. However, despite these indications of interest, the *Amoris Laetitia* remains largely unfamiliar and unexplored among Africa's faithful.[32]

Professor Odozor's 1994 article rightly points out that the discussion of African traditional marriage rites raises unresolved pastoral issues. This topic has been repeatedly discussed at Nigeria's National Pastoral Congresses in 2002, 2012, and 2022. However, Chapter 8 of *Amoris Laetitia* does not address the conflict between the Church and African marriage rites, particularly about non-communicants in conjugal relationships. While there has been much focus on divorced and civilly remarried couples, there are also many active couples in Africa who are non-communicants because they are married customarily but not "*in facie ecclesiae*." A significant expression of Africans' theological and pastoral reception of *Amoris Laetitia* would be to develop a unified and inculturated marriage rite to address these issues.[33] Despite advocacy for such a rite since the 1980s, few regions in Africa have done so. Some non-communicants in Africa may be allowed to receive communion even if they are living in certain irregular conjugal relationships. For example, the Congregation for the Propagation of the Faith has responded to an inquiry from the National Episcopal Conference of Cameroon stating that a person who has been married civilly under the law of monogamy but whose partner refuses to solemnize the union according to Church law may still receive communion.[34] This requires pastors in Africa to exercise discernment and consider alternatives to separation from the community or exclusion from the sacraments.[35]

Amoris Laetitia also addresses the pastoral care of people with same-sex attraction. While acknowledging that same-sex attraction is not ideal, the document emphasizes the need to treat people with decency and respect and rejects unjust discrimination. It calls for a balance between avoiding negative judgment of people with same-sex attraction and their actions and providing compassionate care and support for them and their families. However, in Africa, there is a need to balance this moral objectivity with moral decency towards people with same-sex attraction, and to provide pastoral support and understanding for their families.[36]

3. Odozor's Moral Theological Reading of Amoris Laetitia

In one of his earliest scholarly interventions on *Amoris Laetitia*, Professor Odozor argues that Pope Francis' post-synodal exhortation on the family has revived the debate over the existence of absolute moral norms in Catholic morality. He notes that some people believe the document leaves this aspect of Catholic moral thought open to unacceptable interpretations, while others believe it provides a much-needed reassessment of the role of individual consciences and intentions in determining moral rightness or wrongness. He concludes his discussion of *Humanae Vitae* and its apparent conflict with *Amoris Laetitia* by stating that the debate is likely to continue for some time, as it goes to the heart of what it means to be a Catholic in the 21st century.[37] I find it difficult to determine Professor Odozor's precise position on *Amoris Laetitia* regarding the issue of eternally and universally binding moral norms. However, he prefers the more categorical tone of *Humanae Vitae* to the more nuanced liberationist approach of Pope Francis's *Amoris Laetitia*. This liberationist approach gives rise to what Stan Ilo refers to as Pope Francis's hermeneutics of multiplicity and inclusion.[38] Professor Odozor appears to favour a more static and universal interpretation of natural law over hermeneutics of multiplicity and inclusion. His use of the natural law methodological approach, which emphasizes the objective and universal nature of moral norms, suggests that he may be more inclined towards a traditional understanding of natural law. This approach has been criticized by some for being out of touch with the realities of our time, where moral norms are often contested and debated.[39] This will influence how Professor Odozor engages with *Amoris Laetitia*, as we shall soon see. I believe this is problematic, given his prior casuistic approach to certain sexual issues, such as the use of condoms among HIV/AIDS discordant couples.[40] This approach appears to be closer to *Amoris Laetitia*'s moral reasoning in chapter eight.

Odozor has expressed concern about the HIV/AIDS epidemic in Africa and the ethical dilemma posed by discordant couples. While he adheres to the official Church teaching that prohibits the use of condoms, he advocates for a nuanced consideration of this issue, drawing on the Thomistic casuistic tradition, which allows for flexibility and nuance in applying moral principles to specific cases. He argues that moral principles should be interpreted considering the conditions of each case.[41] John Odeyemi summarizes Odozor's argument that casuistry can reconcile moral idealism and practical rigour in addressing HIV/AIDS and condom use. Casuistry is a flexible method of moral reasoning that considers the circumstances of each case. Odozor believes casuistry helps address HIV/AIDS because it allows for a nuanced understanding of the risks and benefits of condom use. One may ask, what does this mean?[42] Odozor has noted that the Catholic Church is facing a difficult moral challenge in the form of HIV/AIDS. The Church teaches that all life is sacred and that marriage is a holy union, but HIV/AIDS is a deadly disease. This forces the Church community to rethink its moral principles and beliefs to address this new and daunting challenge. The goal is not to abandon the Church's teachings, but to find new and creative ways to apply them to the specific context of HIV/AIDS. The Catholic tradition of moral casuistry can be a valuable resource for the Church community in its search for solutions to the challenges posed by HIV/AIDS.[43]

Does *Amoris Laetitia* not teach exactly this? The Catholic Church has always upheld the sanctity of life, the sacredness of marriage, and the importance of following God's law. However, we are now facing certain life situations that are creating a growing chasm between the Church and some of its members who are in irregular unions. The Church is faced with a choice: either find a new way to apply its principles to this growing trend, or risk losing touch with a significant portion of its flock. *Amoris Laetitia* chooses the former path. Drawing on its rich tradition of moral casuistry, *Amoris Laetitia*, like Odozor in his earlier article, seeks to balance the competing values of protecting the sanctity of marriage and being merciful to the innocent victims of failed marriages or other forms of irregular unions. However, in a 2017 interview, Professor Odozor expressed surprise at the West's obsessive focus on the issue of whether divorced and civilly remarried Catholics should receive Communion. He argued that the debate has been settled in Africa, with the answer being no, and that the Western focus on this issue detracts from the richness of *Amoris Laetitia*.[44] I am surprised by the apparent departure from the nuance and sensitivity to conjugal contextuality Odozor demonstrated in earlier discussions of discordant couples.

4. Odozor's Unfinished Business: Completing the Model for Marriage

Professor Odozor's unfinished quest to construct a truly African and Christian moral theology of marriage culminates in the creation of a structured teaching module on Afro-Christian sexual ethics and conjugal morality. As previously mentioned, Odozor is particularly driven by the development of a comprehensive model for marriage that remains faithful to Christian teaching while resonating with African cultures. This is a pressing issue, particularly in Nigeria, where the lay faithful have consistently emphasized the need for a unified and culturally relevant rite of Christian marriage during the National Pastoral Congresses held in 2002, 2012, and 2022. This reflects a deep desire to reconcile traditional values and practices with Christian tenets, a crucial endeavour that continues to demand attention.

Developing a Teaching Module: Addressing the Needs of the Future

This endeavour directly responds to the needs of the younger generation, who will be responsible for developing teaching materials for seminaries and universities. By crafting this module, Odozor equips future generations with the tools to educate others on this critical topic, ensuring the continued exploration and understanding of Afro-Christian sexual ethics and conjugal morality. This teaching module from our elders like Professor Odozor is necessary for us, their younger colleagues, who have had to construct something for teaching in seminaries and universities to assess their module with the wisdom of the elders. This module is absent in almost all tertiary institutions in Africa. The discourse on African marriage models and their integration with theology encompasses a multifaceted analysis of cultural, ethical, and theological intersections. Central to this conversation are the perspectives of diverse scholars, particularly Bénézet Bujo, whose calls for transformative changes in the structure of marriage hold pivotal importance.[45]

Bujo's proposals for change highlight the crucial communal and anamnetic nature of marriage. Rooted in the communal fabric of African societies, marriage is perceived not only as a union of individuals but also as a connection between communities. This perspective also encompasses the anamnetic function of marriage, where it serves as a means of remembering and honouring ancestors, traditions, and lineage. Bujo examines notions like polygamy, sorority, and levirate within the context of African marital practices. These practices, while diverse in their manifestations, highlight the intricate interplay between cultural norms, familial ties, and societal expectations. The overarching theme of Bujo's proposals is the question of overcoming Africa's marriage challenges. His vision for an African Marriage Project, characterized by a comprehensive five-stage process, presents a roadmap for transcending current obstacles and revitalizing the institution of marriage in Africa. This project seeks to harmonize traditional practices with contemporary perspectives, fostering a more integrated and meaningful marital experience

I challenge Professor Odozor to go beyond simply reevaluating existing paradigms, as he did in his 1994 article. I urge him to explore uncharted territories to address the complexities of African marriage in an evolving context. Questioning Africa's sexual traditions and their reception across different regions and disciplines highlights the diversity of perspectives and historical dynamics. By uncovering sensitive points across Africa's history and present, this exploration delves into the past and current tensions that influence sexual ethics within the continent. We want to know what he has to say about how some sexual ethical "*aporiai*" shed light on nuanced concepts, such as the positive Afro-Christian theology of sex, in which sex is considered not just a physical act but a spiritual communion. Nevertheless, sex is sometimes associated with the dark side of domestic violence in African homes. This deeply ingrained issue poses significant pastoral and ethical challenges, necessitating a holistic approach to address and redress it. In this context, the teachings of *Amoris Laetitia* find relevance in the African milieu. The document's insights on marriage and family life need to be evaluated and taught in our seminaries and theological institutes within the prism of the African Marriage Project, raising questions about their applicability and potential to shape the course of African marital traditions.

Professor Odozor, how should moral theologians such as myself go about teaching these topics in our classrooms? How can we teach the current realities of African marriage and family life in a way that is both faithful to the African tradition and the Christian faith? We challenge you to offer us your thoughts and proposals on how to impart an authentic understanding of African marriage and family life that aligns with both the African tradition and the Christian faith through a thoughtful and comprehensive approach. To effectively achieve this goal, the development of a dedicated one-semester teaching module is essential. This teaching module would necessitate the collaborative efforts of a diverse team of African scholars and theologians. Their collective expertise would ensure a holistic perspective, encompassing the intricate dynamics of African traditions, the Christian ethos, and the contemporary challenges faced by marriages and families on the continent. Central to this module's success is its grounding in the wisdom of the African tradition. The module should draw upon the richness of indigenous knowledge systems, cultural practices, and historical context, respecting the intricate intermingling of African societies. Simultaneously, it should also be designed to address the complexities and transformations that modernity has brought to the African landscape. The module's curriculum should emphasize the integration of these dual perspectives. It could encompass themes such as the communal nature of African families, the historical significance of marriage, the evolution of gender roles, and the ethical dimensions of family life. By addressing these topics through the lens of both tradition and faith, students would gain a nuanced understanding of the intricate interplay between cultural heritage and spiritual values. How long shall we wait for Professor Odozor's valued contributions and collaboration in this regard?

The dearth of comprehensive teaching content on African marriage and family life in many tertiary institutions across Africa underscores the urgency of this initiative. By offering a dedicated module that bridges the gap between African tradition and Christian teachings, educational institutions can equip future generations with a more informed and nuanced perspective on ethical considerations within the African Christian context. Ultimately, the development and integration of such a teaching module hold the potential to reshape perceptions, enhance critical thinking, and foster a deeper appreciation for the intricate dynamics of African marriage and family life. By nurturing an environment where tradition and faith coalesce, this educational initiative can play a pivotal role in shaping the moral consciousness of African societies, guiding them toward a harmonious synthesis of their cultural heritage and spiritual convictions. This is because African marriage and family life is a complex and multifaceted issue, shaped by a variety of factors, including African traditions, Christian principles, and the broader societal context. To provide students with a comprehensive understanding of this issue, teaching materials need to be able to address all these factors.

Professor Odozor is a renowned scholar of African traditions and Christian principles, as well as a recognized expert in African Christian ethics. This unique combination of expertise makes him uniquely qualified to contribute to the development of teaching materials on African marriage and family life. If Professor Odozor were to develop or collaborate on such materials, they would likely have a transformative impact on future generations of theologians, scholars, and individuals. These materials would provide students with a holistic and culturally sensitive understanding of marriage and conjugal morality, equipping them to navigate the complex challenges of contemporary African societies while remaining rooted in the values of their faith. In essence, the anticipation of Professor Odozor's involvement or collaboration underscores the urgency of infusing African theological education with materials that align with the multifaceted realities of African cultures, Christian teachings, and the ethical imperatives of our time. Such an initiative would hold the promise of empowering African theologians and leaders to guide their communities towards marriages that are life-affirming, just, and enriched by the principles of the Christian faith.

Concluding Remarks

Professor Odozor's work goes beyond scholarship: he masterfully weaves African culture and Christian doctrine into a vibrant new fusion of African moral theology. This synthesis resonates deeply with African communities because it considers the full spectrum of human experience—physical, emotional, and spiritual. This holistic approach sets him apart, offering a richer understanding than purely doctrinal or cultural perspectives. Furthermore, Odozor fosters dialogue between African and Western theologians, inviting them to collaborate on a theology that's both relevant to Africa and liberates from restrictive interpretations. This has immense potential to enrich Christian thought globally. Ultimately, Odozor's work is a gift to the African church, laying the foundation for a transformative theology of marriage and sexuality. This theology empowers individuals, strengthens families, and contributes to building more just and equitable societies.

While the celebration of Professor Odozor's work acknowledges the richness of his insights and their potential contribution to building an authentic African Christian theology of marriage and conjugal morality, it also, like a weaver scrutinizing a tapestry, identifies areas where greater clarity and concrete solutions might be needed. This does not diminish the significance of Professor Odozor's endeavour; rather, it underscores the ongoing nature of constructing such a theology, a journey we must all undertake together. Therefore, we invite Professor Odozor to offer further clarity and intentionality in his approach to building a truly African and Christian moral theology of marriage. His guidance is invaluable in shaping the understanding of future generations of theologians, pastors, and pastoral agents across the continent. However, we also challenge ourselves to engage the potential of Christian feminist and Afro-Christian feminist perspectives in this development. How can we move beyond Professor Odozor's perceived wariness towards these approaches, fostering instead a more inclusive and nuanced dialogue?

Finally, we call upon esteemed scholars like Professor Odozor to develop teaching modules on Afro-Christian sexual ethics and conjugal morality. These modules, grounded in African tradition and Christian faith, must also embrace new perspectives and solutions to equip the next generation with the tools for navigating this complex terrain. As the younger generation of theologians, we envision a synthesis woven with diverse threads, representing the dynamic African Christian theology of marriage and conjugal morality we strive to create. Professor Odozor has laid the foundation with his pioneering work, but the weaving continues. We must incorporate new perspectives, solutions, and boldness to challenge the status quo and explore possibilities. We request Professor Odozor's continued guidance and support on this journey. Together, we can create a unification that is truly African and Christian, guiding our communities towards a more just and equitable future. However, our project is incomplete without the threads of Christian and Afro-Christian feminism. These offer invaluable insights into marriage and family, urging us towards a more just and equitable society. We commit to weaving an Afro-Christian moral theology of sexuality and marriage that is inclusive, egalitarian, and liberating, incorporating the voices of the marginalized and oppressed, woven with hope, love, and justice.

Professor Odozor's scholarship and unwavering dedication to constructing a truly African Christian theology demands profound gratitude. His work has ignited within me a fervent desire to cultivate a platform for amplifying and celebrating African voices. Together, we embark on the weaving of a novelty of African-Christian sexual ethics and conjugal morality, one that is both authentic and profoundly resonates with the lived realities of contemporary African Christians. This cohesive fabric, woven collaboratively, will illuminate the path for generations to come, serving as a beacon of strength and inspiration. Through this joint effort, we aspire to create a rich and meaningful mosaic that embodies our collective endeavours to build a brighter future for all Africans. This shared testament, imbued with enduring beauty and significance, will stand as a lasting reminder of our commitment to this shared vision.

Chapter 3

Politics, the Common Good and Holiness

Anthony Akinwale, OP

To the extent that painters mediate a vision of reality, philosophers are painters, and philosophers of politics are painters of cities.[1] To the extent that theologians see philosophers as allies in their encounter with reality, theologians too are painters.[2] And to the extent that theologians are interested in the reality of the city, political theologians are painters of what a city ought to look like before God.

Theologians speak of God. Not only of God, but also of other things in so far as they have God as their beginning or end.[3] Theologians assume the task of painting the city in relation to God who created human beings, inhabitants of the city, to be rational, relational and religious. Their rationality is manifest or ought to be manifest in their relationality, and restlessness in their rationality and relationality points to their religiosity. It is in their nature to be political, that is, inhabit cities, loci of intelligently ordered common life in search of the common good. It is in their nature to be political because they are rational. Their rationality and relationality manifest an openness to God, their religiosity, in so far as the truth and the good they desire is beyond the reach of their nature. The restlessness characteristic of their rationality and relationality cannot come to an end without God.

At the beginning of the *Summa theologiae*, Thomas Aquinas was speaking of the sapiential vocation of the theologian when he described theology as wisdom. At the beginning of his other *Summa*, the *Summa Contra Gentiles*, using Aristotle as ally, as he often does, Aquinas painted the portrait of those who are called wise.[4] "They are called 'wise'," he said, "who put things in their right order and control them well."

The moral theologian, considering the sapiential vocation of theology, seeks to put order in human action. Considering the fact that the human being is an animal who lives in the rightly-ordered common life that the *polis* ought to be, ordering the action of the human being living in the city is necessarily included in the job description of the moral theologian. In concrete terms, the moral theologian today must be interested in moral theology not just from the point of view of the human person, often presumed to be living alone, but from the perspective of the human being who, because of relationality, lives in the city.

With these remarks in mind, I intend in this essay to examine the inextricable relationship between politics, the common good, and, by extension, the call to holiness of life made by Jesus to his disciples in the Sermon on the Mount.[5]

Here I recall the sequence to the words of Aquinas I have just quoted. "Now," he said, "in all things that are to be controlled and put in order to an end, the measure of control and order must be taken from the end in view; and the proper end of everything is something good." The goal of politics is to rightly order the affairs of a nation so as to attain the good.

It is my contention in this essay that the moral theologian, with philosophers as allies, must assume the task of articulating the relationship between politics, morality and the call to holiness of life. Since this essay is written to honor Paulinus Odozor, a Nigerian moral theologian, it represents a reflection on the Nigerian political landscape.

Politics and the common good

Preceding remarks announce that my subject of inquiry centers principally on three themes: the first is politics, the second is the common good, and the third is holiness. Establishing their inter-relationship is the task of painting what a city and its inhabitants ought to look like. But success of the task of painting a city is largely contingent on our ability and willingness to walk through the museum of paintings that political philosophy is.

In the museum of political paintings to which I have just referred, one sees a Thomas Aquinas who, following the example of Augustine, the most quoted thinker in his writings; following the example of Plato by following Augustine; and following the example of Aristotle, the second most quoted source in his writing, left an intellectual tradition in which there is no politics without the common good, and there is no common good without politics. Whereas politics, according to Niccolò Machiavelli, is separated from morality, and whereas the monstrous Machiavellian misconception of politics has gained currency over centuries and in many places, the tragedy of the otherwise noble act of politics can be found in a repeated failure to grasp what the two are, and in a corresponding failure to appreciate the inextricable relationship between politics and the common good.

Machiavelli would have us believe that politics is about the acquisition of power for the sake of the egotistic intent of the politician. The title of his famous work *The Prince* says it all. In his conception, politics is not about the common good. It is about the political fortunes of the prince, that is, the politician. That overrides the interest of the citizen and the common good. The intellectual orientation, posturing and prescription of *The Prince* sharply contrasts with two other titles, two landmarks in political philosophy—the *Republic* of Plato and the *Politics* of Aristotle. Whereas Plato and Aristotle devoted their intellectual energies to the common good—the good of the *res publica* in the former, and the good of the *polis* in the latter, Machiavelli decidedly deployed his intellectual arsenal to the acquisition and retention of power without regard for the pursuit of the common good. What matters for him is not the interest of the polis but of the politician.

Broadly speaking, therefore, it may be asserted that there are two types of politics: politics of the common good, and politics of selfish interest. The former is proposed in the writings of two Greek philosophers—Plato and Aristotle, to which Christian thinkers like St Augustine of Hippo and St Thomas Aquinas subscribe.[6] For these Greek and Christian thinkers, politics and morality must never be separated for politics is itself an ethical project. Politics is not to be separated from the human search for the common good, that is, the search for the best way to live together.

But there is also the latter, that is politics of selfish interest, of the politician described by Machiavelli. It is not politics of the common good but politics of the narrow self-centered definition of the good. It is politics without morality. Many are politicians who practice this type of politics. What matters for such politicians is what is good for them even when it is to the detriment of their fellow citizens. They are ready to sacrifice anything, including human life and the common good, for the sake of their selfish interest. But there are other voices one must not ignore. Two—Jean-Jacques Rousseau and Thomas Hobbes—are cited here.

In Rousseau's romanticized state of nature, the French political theorist idealized in the human person two instincts—self-preservation and compassion.[7] What we see in politics, however, is self-preservation without compassion. In the absence of compassion, what obtains is rugged individualism, an antithesis of the common good, in which the human person desires and works for his own good by working against the good of other human beings. It is what Hobbes, in another account of the state of nature, describes as the conflict of desires and aversions in the war of man against man, in a state of nature where life is lonely, short, and brutish.[8] But Hobbes's prescription of a commonwealth to which he said we must submit ourselves, or to which he presumes we have agreed to submit our will, a commonwealth that adjudicates when one person's desire collides with another person's aversion leaves us in the hands of a ubiquitous state presumed to be omniscient and placed above the law. A state that is more powerful than the citizen.

A state that arrogates ubiquity, omniscience and omnipotence to itself cannot be checked. And even when citizens "freely" submit themselves to such a state, their effort amounts to self-inflicted tyranny. Nigeria and much of Africa have, for years, operated on this wavelength of the ubiquitous and omnipotent state. The state, its institutions and functionaries, ought to be subservient and accountable to the citizen. But the reverse has been the case. A typical African state arrogates virtually limitless powers to itself, and, with these powers, takes over the land and its resources from its people. In the history of virtually every African country, the presumedly omnipotent state, by way of a tragic further extension, is personalized in the head of state—sometimes in the First Lady—who, instead of presiding, sits over the resources and shares them with those he wants.

The state must be at the service of the common good, and it must secure the common good by respecting the rights of the citizen. Such is the expectation. But in the wide gulf between expectation and experience in these matters, the typical African state and its functionaries operate like a security man hired to protect you and your property, who instead takes over the property, and decides that his security post will be your kitchen. Such a state, personified in the political leader, will impoverish and starve the citizen, the real owner of the land and its resources, and then present itself as benefactor of the citizen. Nigeria is no exception. Our country is fast becoming a place of apotheosis of state functionaries, a place where the citizen worships the politician, where the typical political office holder poses as Santa Claus, but who, in fact, is a robber offering proceeds of his robbery to victims of his robbery, where the deified victimizer dresses himself in the stolen robes of the victim.

On Saturday, January 23, 2016, on a popular programme on an Ibadan radio station, Splash FM 105.5, anchored by Edmund Obilo, he posed the question: which two of these are the greatest problems of Nigeria: corruption, ethnicity, religion, mediocrity, or external influence?

Of course, from the response that came from actively participating listeners, top on the list was corruption. The most fashionably pious presumption in contemporary Nigerian political discourse is that that the country can fight and eliminate corruption. That would have been the case if other countries in the world had eliminated corruption. But, even in countries that lay claims to longstanding democratic credentials, corruption remains uneliminated because many political actors have divorced politics from the common good.

I humbly submit that human beings cannot eliminate corruption. However, what we can do is to work very hard to prevent it or drastically minimize it and or efficiently manage it and curtail its debilitating effects on the common good. Corruption, as an ailment found in every society, is the world's oldest pandemic.

The term "sin" is largely absent from the writings of philosophers. It is an almost exclusively theological category. But we need this category to explain what is before us. Yet, there is widespread reluctance to use the word today in a world that is increasingly intolerant of passing judgement of value, increasingly exclusive of anything considered to be antithetical to inclusivity. In theological terms, corruption is sinfulness, and sinfulness is an ailment. Human nature is wounded by sin and prone to sin. We are, in a sense, challenged here to widen our understanding of corruption, to see it for what it truly is, so that we do not end up dealing with symptoms while neglecting the ailment. Corruption is by far bigger than graft. It is disdain for virtue, desire for lawlessness, and non-appreciation of grace. Virtue makes its possessor good; law, just law that is, with its precepts and prohibitions, compels the human person to be good; while grace assists the human person to be good; and the three combine to form a vaccine against the pandemic that sin is.

Aquinas defines law as an ordinance of reason, not of the whims and caprices of the ruler, promulgated by a competent legislator for the attainment of the common good. If the ultimate objective of the law is the common good, then lawlessness is the absence of good laws and or failure to obey good laws. When the state is more powerful than the citizen, the state itself becomes the primary agent of lawlessness, its functionaries will steal and oppress. Many who live within such a state practice an anthropology of domination in the survival of the fittest. Ethnocentrism, which is another name for racism, is the vice of malicious solidarity substituting the virtue of ethnicity, the noble act of loving your ethnic affiliation. Ethnic affiliation is used as a hideout for the lawless. The same is true of the use and abuse of political and religious affiliation to camouflage lawlessness. In the final analysis, ethnocentrism, not ethnicity, intolerance in politics and religion, the enthronement of mediocrity are symptoms of pervasive lawlessness. We must avoid an intellectual laziness that attacks the symptoms while we fail to treat the cause.

This lawlessness is itself rooted in the tendency of a human nature wounded by sin to neglect and exploit, no doubt. In the peculiar situation in Nigeria, this lawlessness is firmly rooted in an illegitimate constitution. A constitution is the *grundnorm* of legitimacy in a polity. But where the constitution is itself illegitimate then Nigerian need to go back to the drawing board. Our constitution is illegitimate for a number of reasons. First, it was not produced by "we the people" but by a military junta. It would have been a people's constitution if it had been written by representatives of the people and if it had been subjected to a referendum. Instead, it was written by those whom the military chose and imposed by military fiat.

Secondly, that constitution fails to provide adequate answers to three fundamental questions, namely, what ought to be the relationship between the state and the citizen? What ought to be the relationship among the three arms of government—the executive, the legislature and the judiciary—as well as the relationship among the three tiers of government—federal, state and local? What ought to be the relationship between a citizen and a fellow citizen? That failure creates a polity where the state violates the rights of the citizen, and where rights of the citizen are violated by his or her fellow citizen.

Thirdly, the constitution fails to differentiate between country, state and nation. A country is a piece of land, a territory; a nation is an association of peoples sharing common core ideals; the state is a conglomeration of institutions established by their constitution to protect the land and its peoples as they go about in pursuit of their shared core ideals.

Politics is the intelligent regulation of the common life of a people with shared core ideals for the attainment of their common good. And the common good is "the sum total of social conditions which allow people, either as groups or as individuals, to reach their fulfillment more fully and more easily."[9] In the absence of an adequate understanding of politics and of the common good, we shall continue to be exposed to the exploitation of the citizen by the state personified in its functionaries—senators, governors, presidents and their advisers and special advisers—and the exploitation of the citizen by his or her fellow citizen.

The understanding of politics and of the common good in this essay is influenced by Catholic social teaching. That Thomas Aquinas influenced Catholic social doctrine is not in doubt. Again, as is well-known, the writings of Aquinas come out of reading Plato and Augustine in the light of Aristotle to account for the intelligibility of his religious convictions. His writings are not only relevant to religion they are also relevant to politics. He was not one who would separate religion and politics, not one who would make politics into a religion either, not one who would reduce politics to a set of operations intended to acquire and retain power. He was a thinker who would show how religion can positively motivate our political options even in a society of religious diversity.

Included in his political philosophy is a philosophy of law to which one can subscribe even without sharing in the Christian faith of Aquinas. Underpinning this philosophy of law is a natural law theory that believes in the human capacity to know what is good for a life lived in the society even through rational means. Included in this notion of natural law is a notion of common good as the objective of politics rightly understood. Even though he was not a democrat, implied in this notion of common good is respect for the dignity of the human person by way of respect for his rationality, his capacity to know by moving from the known to the unknown. The acknowledgement, promotion and protection of human dignity necessitates solidarity and subsidiarity. We cannot have one without the other. And here we touch on four pillars of Catholic social doctrine identifiable in the social encyclicals. From *Rerum Novarum* of Leo XIII to *Laudato Si'* of Pope Francis, passing through *Populorum Progressio* of Paul VI, *Sollicitudo Rei Socialis* of John Paul II, and *Spe Salve* of Benedict XVI, to mention but these, can be identified human dignity, common good, the principle of solidarity and the principle of subsidiarity.

At the heart of Catholic social teaching is a strong affirmation of the dignity of the human person from the womb to the tomb. Catholic social teaching recognizes that development is about the dignity of the human person. It is a question of sacred reverence for the dignity of conscience, freedom of choice, freedom to fulfill one's legitimate aspirations, and freedom to actualize one's God-given potentials. Where this dignity is violated or abbreviated, where countries have abysmally low standard of respect for human dignity there cannot be authentic development. What is at stake in the task of development is the recognition, respect, and promotion of human dignity as a transcendent value gifted to us by the Creator. Pope John Paul II, apostle of Christian humanism, repeatedly made this point in all his social encyclicals. Since this dignity cannot be promoted outside an intelligently regulated common life, Catholic social teaching also espouses respect and work for the common good, that is, the fulfillment of the human person in our collective fulfillment, the actualization of the potentials of each person in the actualization of our collective potentials.

Solidarity as a pillar of Catholic social doctrine is "a firm and persevering determination to commit oneself to the common good, that is to say, to the good of all and of each individual, because we are all really responsible for all."[10] It is solidarity that ensures that no one seeks his or her fulfillment at the expense of others, and that no one actualizes his or her own potentials by hindering others from actualizing theirs. It takes a solid commitment to the common good to overcome the mindset of rugged individualism that makes victims of others. As John Paul II puts it,

> The exercise of solidarity within each society is valid when its members recognize one another as persons [...]. Solidarity helps us to see the "other'—whether a person, people or nation—not just as some kind of instrument, with a work capacity and physical strength to be exploited at low cost and then discarded when no longer useful, but as our "neighbor," a "helper" to be made a sharer, on a par with ourselves, in the banquet of life to which all are equally invited by God.[11]

But solidarity goes together with subsidiarity. Subsidiarity is the principle which states that

> A community of a higher order should not interfere in the internal life of a community of a lower order, depriving the latter of its functions, but rather should support it in case of need and help to coordinate its activity with the activities of the rest of society, always with a view to the common good.[12]

In practical terms, especially in terms of relationship between various levels of government in a polity, the issue of true federalism in Nigeria is the issue of respect for the principle of subsidiarity. By virtue of this principle, the federal government ought not to take over functions that state governments can and must assume. And, by extension, state governments should not take over the functions of local governments. Respect for the principle of subsidiarity is respect for the initiative of the citizen. To disregard this principle is to leave the citizen at the mercy of a leadership that disables and makes it impossible for the citizen to actualize his or her potentials. When the federal government in a country of such size and diversity disregards or is ignorant of the principle of subsidiarity what you have is not a federation but an empire dressed in the stolen robes of a federation.[13]

In terms of the relationship between government and the people, the former should not take over functions which the latter can perform. The alternative will be an activist government which becomes big, corrupt, and inefficient. We have seen this in the history of Nigeria. The criminal seizure of government by soldiers inaugurated an era of illusion when government took over the functions of individuals and voluntary agencies in the education sector. It led to a civil war, it led to the collapse of institutions, it marked the beginning of the end of good education, the collapse of education at all levels in Nigeria, and the sum total: societal collapse. The violation of the principle of subsidiarity is symptom of a government that has become more powerful than the people. A government that is more powerful than the people is irresponsible, that is, incapable and or unwilling to be accountable to the people. It will rig elections, its functionaries will steal, and its agents in uniform will intimidate and brutalize the people they are paid to protect as our experience in recent memory teaches us. Such a government, if at all it can be called government, is a huge obstacle on the path to authentic development.

So far, this essay has concentrated on the relationship between politics and the common good. The relationship between politics and holiness now needs to be examined.

Politics and holiness

If the goal of politics is the common good, understood as the good of the citizen in the good of the city, and the good of the city in the good of the citizen; and if the supreme good of the human person is God, there certainly is a relationship between politics and desire for God, between politics and love of God above all things.

Holiness is in the love of God above all things which is manifest in love of neighbour. The manner in which the human person relates with God is manifest in the manner in which the human person relates with his or her neighbour and vice versa. The goal of politics can, at least in this sense, be said to be God. That may not be what is seen in politics in contemporary times, indeed in the history of the human race. Indicatives and imperatives are, quite often, miles apart, and history is the narrative of the huge gap between what is and what ought to be. The theological dimension of politics is often forgotten, often ignored, because God is himself forgotten and or ignored.

Jesus was describing the vocation of the Christian citizen in the Matthean version of the Sermon on the Mount when he said to his disciples, using two metaphors: "You are the light of the world [...]. You are the salt of the earth" (Matthew 5: 13–14). Light puts an end to darkness, and salt adds flavour to food, putting an end to tastelessness. The citizen who is a disciple of Christ must be a positively transformative agent in the city, working for the good of the city by working for his own good, and working for his own good by working for the good of the city. He or she can attain holiness by being such an agent.

The Second Vatican Council spoke in the same vein when it explained the participation of the baptized in the three-fold office of Christ. The Church is a communion of members whose dignity and equality flow from a common baptismal grace. In the light of this common baptismal dignity, every Christian participates in the salvific mission of the Church by sharing in the priestly, prophetic and kingly office of Christ.

The baptised share in Christ's priestly office when all their prayers, works and apostolic undertakings, family and married life, relaxation of mind and body become spiritual sacrifices acceptable to God through Christ. They share in the prophetic office when they bear witness to the Gospel in their daily family and social life. To be well noted here is that the Council singles out the married state as a special way of sharing in the prophetic office, and, ipso facto, in the salvific mission of Christ.

> The state of life that is sanctified by a special sacrament, namely, married and family life, has a special importance in this prophetic office. Where the Christian religion pervades the whole structure of life with a continuous and ever more profound transformation, there is both the practice and an outstanding school of the lay apostolate. In it the married partners have their own proper vocation: they must be witnesses of faith and love of Christ to one another and to their children. The Christian family proclaims aloud both the present power of the kingdom of God and the hope of the blessed

> life. Hence, by example and by testimony, they convict the world of sin and give light to those who seek the truth.[14]

The lay faithful share in the kingly office when they work for holiness, justice and peace in the world, when they "recognize the inner nature, the value and the ordering of the whole of creation to the praise of God." This ordering is to be done by the laity under the guidance of Christian conscience such that in temporal activities, nothing is withdrawn from God's dominion.[15]

The Conciliar emphasis on marriage as a special way of sharing in the prophetic office of Christ is not to be read in passing. For marriages make homes, and, in the commonsensically wise observation in Aristotle's *Politics*, homes make cities.[16] Etymologically, the economy (*oikonomike*)—understood here as intelligent ordering of affairs of the home and not the productive, purchasing and consumptive capacities of the human person—has consequences for politics (*politika*). The condition of the city is a reflection of the homes that make up the city, and the condition of the homes is a reflection of the condition of the souls of those who make up the home. Here we touch on the parallel discussion in Plato's *Republic* on the just city and on the just soul.

Politics, which is ordering of life in the city, when integrated into the desire for God that is in human beings, becomes a way of seeking God, a way of attaining holiness. The Christian, who is, at the same time, a disciple and a citizen, by virtue of his or her participation in the threefold office of Christ, ought to be able to understand that involvement in politics is a way of participating in the salvific mission of Christ, the Head, and of his body, the Church.

Like prophets in the Bible, the baptized have a political vocation, and that is, to bear witness to the word of God in the affairs of the city. But they can only bear witness to the Gospel they have received and internalized. For "nemo dat quod non habet." Like prophets in the Bible, the vocation of the baptised is to constantly provide a prophetic critique of prevailing political options. Rightly understood, and one must emphasise this, the role of prophets in the Bible was not to predict the future but to provide a critique of the politics of their era. To play this role, they used the monotheistic faith into which they entered when God made a covenant with their ancestors. The persistently stinging critique of politics and religion the prophets offered in the Bible was triggered by infidelity of the people and their king to the God of the covenant.

There are genuine concerns about the propriety or otherwise of bringing religion into politics in a multireligious world or country. Some would rather separate the two. In societies where there is an ideological civil war, Christians run the risk of being coopted or conscripted into contending armies confronting each other even within the Church. Real and present is the temptation to identify one ideology or candidate as Christian or Catholic, and another ideology or candidate otherwise. The Church would then become a battlefield in which her members are fighting ideological proxy wars. For this, and for other reasons, there are those who argue that there should be a separation of religion and politics. To such people, speaking of the role of Christians in the society may sound like mixing politics with religion. But I propose a distinction and not a separation because politics is a moral project. I shall explain.

Since morality is about understanding the good and striving for the good way of life, since every human being is in search of the best way to live, since the human being who is in search of the best way of life does not live in isolation but with others, the moral project of striving for the best way to live is a striving for the best way to live together.

Since the Christian ought not to separate politics from morality, and, since the moral life of a Christian is informed and formed by his or her religious beliefs, a Christian cannot afford to do politics without God, provided that such a Christian knows and believes that God is love. What is to be avoided is the imposition of God on others. Politics, in the true sense of the word—and I do not speak of politics of Machiavellian inspiration—is an act of love. Since politics is the intelligent ordering of common life for the sake of the common good, and, since working for the common good is an act of love, the Christian, by virtue of his or her vocation to love God and neighbour, has an obligation to be involved in the political process, and the political process is the task of working together to attain the common good. Assuming this obligation is fulfillment of the greatest commandment—love God above all things and love your neighbor because of God. Yet, there is need for a caveat.

While different shades of political opinions may be found in the

Church because of divergent political affiliations of her members, the Church must not become the propaganda organ of any political party. She has neither a favorite political party, nor an army, nor any anointed candidate. Her role is not to form an army but to shape public opinion by forming consciences, using the Gospel. If at all she is to have an army, it must be an army of disciples whose consciences have been formed by the word of God authentically interpreted by the Church's teaching office, as Vatican II teaches.[17] Her role is not to campaign for any candidate or political party. Her role is to lead people to make responsible choices in the arena of politics. This does not have to involve imposing the Gospel on people. This is about making the values of the Gospel present in every sphere of human endeavor, in every sector of the society, especially on the political terrain. It is about witnessing to the Gospel by the way we live in the city.

The love that the Christian must manifest in managing the affairs of our common life for the sake of the common good is the love of the triune God eloquently expressed on the cross by the crucified Christ. For a Christian to be light of the world and salt of the earth, the Christian has an obligation to participate in managing the affairs of our common life, which is what politics is about. Since the love that the Christian must manifest in politics is the love of the triune God, politics, for the Christian, ought to be understood and practiced as concretization of trinitarian love in the affairs of the city, the affairs of our common life.

Politics without religion is politics without God. Politics without God is management of the affairs of the city, of our common life, without God. While it is not impossible, it can be dangerous. At the same time, the mixture of corrupt politics and corrupt religion is poisonous. It brings about confusion, corruption, uncertainty, poverty and insecurity in the land.

The Catholic Church—in her clergy and lay faithful—is in a position to avoid this anomaly. She has the Gospel, and the rich corpus of her social doctrine, a doctrine which applies the Gospel to issues of politics and society. These can and should provide a guide in our involvement in the political process. The social interventions of successive Popes, especially from Pope Leo XIII's encyclical *Rerum Novarum* of 1845 to *Gaudete et Exsultate*, the Apostolic Exhortation of Pope Francis, and

Laudato Si', the Encyclical on the Environment by the same Pope, these call for answering the call to holiness of life in the political arena.

Conclusion

It is an imperative of moral theology to differentiate between politics as love of power for the sake of riches and pleasure, and politics as love of and commitment to the common good. It is equally an imperative to differentiate between love of politics and politics of love.

With the mutual inclusion of politics and morality as my premise, I draw the following conclusion: after all is said and done, involvement in the political process of searching for the best way to live together is a matter of striving for holiness of life, and striving for holiness of life is inseparable from striving for the common good. Striving for the good is striving for the Highest Good, and striving for the Highest Good is striving for God. For God is the Highest Good. Politics, rightly understood as striving for the good, is striving for God, and striving for God is striving for holiness of life.

Holiness is about love of God and love of neighbour, and it is the one who loves his or her neighbour who strives for the common good. Striving for the common good is the project of holiness and morality. That is why politics is not to be separated from the religious and moral obligation to strive for the common good even on the treacherous political terrain. Contrary to what we see, and contrary to what many believe, politics is a way of seeking to become a saint. In Africa, Julius Nyerere, former President of Tanzania, whose cause for beatification and canonization began in 2005, may be an example of a politician who fits into the description of a saint.

Chapter 4

Aquinas, Balthasar, and African Tradition: Christian Conversion of Individuals and Cultures

Melanie Susan Barrett

While recently traveling out-of-state visiting family, I attended a local parish for Sunday Mass. During the homily, which exegeted the parable of the weeds among the wheat, the priest asked the congregation whether they identified themselves more with the wheat (the good seed, who will attain the kingdom of heaven) or with the weeds: who are destined to be thrown by the Son of Man "into the fiery furnace, where there will be wailing and grinding of teeth" (Mt 13:42). He then proceeded to warn the congregation that by nature all of us are weeds, not wheat, and that it is only through our relationship with Jesus (initiated in Baptism) that we can be transformed from weeds into wheat. He justified this interpretation by connecting the parable's identification of Jesus (the Son of Man) as the sower of good seed (Mt 13:37), to Jesus' later declaration (to the rich young man) that "there is only One who is good," namely God (Mt 19:17): thereby implying that absent a living relationship with Jesus, initiated in Christian Baptism, we are not good but evil. He then proceeded to reframe the moral life *not* as exerting effort to acquire virtues and do good acts, but rather as receiving the work of Christ who recreates us in his image.

While I appreciated the priest's pastoral strategy of moving congregants in an upper middle-class, suburban, American parish away from common pitfalls—the sin of presumption and the heresy of Pelagianism—I worried that the anthropology undergirding this theological vision was more Lutheran or Calvinist than Catholic, given its emphasis on the utter depravity of our fallen state and the passivity with which we ought to approach the Christian moral life. By contrast, the reputable, thirteenth-century, Catholic theologian Thomas Aquinas contends that original sin destroyed entirely *only* the gift of original justice; "the principles [upon] which human nature was constituted, and the properties that flow from them, such as the powers of the soul" were "*neither destroyed nor diminished* by sin," and "the natural inclination to virtue" was *merely "diminished*" by sin: not destroyed.[1] Accordingly, Aquinas explicitly states—in his treatise on grace—that "because human nature is not altogether corrupted by sin, so as to be shorn of every natural good, even in the state of corrupted nature it can, by virtue of its natural endowments, work some particular good" even though "it cannot do all the good natural to it, so as to fall short in nothing."[2] More precisely, healing grace is needed to love God above all things, and to fulfill the commandments not only in "substance"—performing good acts externally—but also in "mode": being motivated interiorly by charity.[3] Thus for Aquinas, without grace, human beings can perform some good some of the time, but not perfect good all of the time.

Furthermore, advancement in the moral life necessitates human effort: not only to acquire natural virtue, but also to deepen infused virtue. Accordingly, the baptized person in a state of habitual grace must cooperate actively with grace—so as to perform good acts—in order to merit an increase in grace. The Catholic moral life thus may be described as active cooperation with Christ, to transform partial goodness into perfect goodness: rather than passively being re-created by Christ from evil weeds into good wheat.

From a Thomistic standpoint therefore, Christian conversion is not a matter of annihilating all that exists in non-baptized human nature—and the cultural traditions created by it—and replacing it with something entirely new, but rather sifting out the genuinely good aspects of nature (and culture) from the bad ones, and then transforming what is already good into something more perfect. But how does such a process take place? What are its necessary parameters? Building upon this Thomistic anthropological foundation, I will elaborate upon the insights of Paulinus Ikechukwu Odozor in his analysis of how Christianity intersects with—and rightly appropriates—aspects of both African tradition and Traditional African Religion. I then will mine the theological insights of the twentieth-century,

Catholic theologian Hans Urs von Balthasar, to discern the means by which Christian conversion can occur within a person's interior life. Equipped with Balthasar's aesthetic and Christ-entered approach to conversion, I will conclude with some constructive suggestions regarding how Christian discipleship could root itself more deeply in the African cultural context along the lines Odozor proposes.

I. Paulinus Odozor on African Christian Theology

In his book, *Morality Truly Christian, Truly African: Foundational, Methodological, and Theological Considerations*, Odozor contends that African Christian ethics, in its current form, lacks sufficient coherence and depth to confront and resolve Africa's most pressing moral and social problems, especially in the context of globalization, religious pluralism, secularization, and urbanization. Citing the Second African Synod, Odozor enumerates a list of issues including: "migration; the flawed use and exercise of political power; economic mismanagement and abuse of funds at all levels of public life; the debt burden"; destabilizing attitudes, values, and lifestyles imported from the outside; challenges to the stability of family life; "drugs and arms trafficking, environmental degradation, and war."[4] What all of these issues share in common, despite obvious divergences, is that they constitute "threats to the human person" because they "conspire [either] to negate life or to make it less human."[5] Although African cultural traditions and African Traditional Religion possess some truthful conceptions about the human person as such—conceptions that are "largely sound" in Odozor's estimation—they are "severely limited" and hence ineffective in combating present threats to human flourishing on the African continent.[6] Because African Christianity remains largely beholden to these limited perspectives however, Odozor's proposed solution involves not only evangelizing non-Christians but also evangelizing African Christians: whose reason still needs to be perfected by the Gospel faith, notwithstanding their self-understanding as Christians. Such a task needs to be undertaken with great delicacy however, lest such theological renewal be misinterpreted as a covert attempt at European ideological colonization, or as the imposition of Western values aimed at eradicating a culture treasured by its inhabitants for being rich in communal solidarity, artistic expression, and openness to divine transcendence.

Cognizant of the need for delicacy, Odozor offers concrete guidelines for theological inculturation in Africa, coupled with an assessment of the existing strengths and need for renewal in several areas: doctrine of God, anthropology, moral reasoning, and ecclesiology. After summarizing Odozor's proposed guidelines and their underlying rationale, I will focus my exposition on the first two areas—God and the human person—to which Balthasar's account of conversion will prove especially complementary.

a. Guidelines for Theological Inculturation in Africa

Acknowledging that all theology is contextual—necessarily "conditioned by its time and situation"[7]—Odozor declares that his overarching goal is to establish "firm foundations for an African moral theology that is both Christian and African."[8] He lauds traditional African ethics for its communitarian ethos in which: everyone is related (all human beings—both living and dead—God and the cosmos), we become human through fellowship with others, solidarity is necessary for effective action, and open dialogue among all members of the community (who actively endeavor to attain consensus) is upheld as a privileged form of conflict resolution.[9] But as with every historical tradition, praiseworthy strengths persist alongside glaring weaknesses. For example, solidarity to those outside one's clan was not always extended in practice; some villages raided others to support the global slave trade, and perceived ethnic superiority of some Africans over others led to deadly strife in Nigeria, Sierra Leone, and Rwanda.[10]

Also, communal discourse as a method for discerning moral truth can be hijacked by demagogues, distorted by biases (on the part of either individuals or groups), or manipulated by bad actors who cleverly disguise their own selfish agendas as community interests. Odozor astutely observes that process alone—without explicit moral principles—cannot insulate a community from arriving at bad decisions, such as jointly agreeing to violate the human rights of neighboring clans.[11] Even the anamnetic requirement to remember—and thus consult—one's dead ancestors might not improve the outcome, if the community fails to differentiate between those ancestors who lived saintly lives, and those who lived sinful lives (perhaps by voluntarily participating in the slave trade, or by personally benefiting from European colonialism at their countrymen's expense).[12]

But how does one discern which aspects of one's culture are moral versus immoral from a standpoint within one's culture itself? Is not *some* external vantage point required? But if so, then how could such an external critique be regarded not only as plausible but as persuasive to those on the inside, especially those who are spring-loaded to interpret all external challenges negatively, as furtive attempts at control and domination by colonial oppressors?

To meet this challenge, Odozor proposes seven overarching guidelines for theological inculturation. First, inculturation must be built on strong Christian theological convictions. Because revelation perfects human reason, faith must shape human attitudes and dispositions. Culture should not be prioritized automatically in the culture-faith dialogue, because not all things in one's culture are good or even adequate. Only by evaluating culture through the lens of Christian faith can we assess genuine cultural strengths versus distortions. Second, moral theology should be grounded in a comprehensive understanding of God. Monotheism is helpful but ultimately insufficient if the deeper Trinitarian reality is ignored or dismissed.[13]

Third, cultural critique cannot be undertaken without a "deep knowledge" of the culture in question, which Odozor defines as "a deep appreciation for its strengths and honesty about its weaknesses."[14] Fourth, anyone undertaking such critique also must know the Christian tradition thoroughly and deeply. Only the person who comprehensively understands both the culture and Christian tradition will be empowered to dialogue effectively with culture creators (those who set the current ethos for their society). Fifth, it is the present culture with whom one must dialogue, not the past. Although the past can inform, illuminate, or even guide the present, the past is not sacrosanct and ought not to be upheld uncritically as the true, pure, or ideal expression of one's culture.[15] Odozor states explicitly that African traditions (like all human traditions) are living traditions: extended arguments about the good. They are an ongoing construction, even if certain aspects within them persist over time. It is by means of tradition that we "make sense of reality and by which we determine what actions are rational and right or irrational and wrong."[16] Consequently, dialoguing with what no longer persists as a worldview would not be constructive.

Sixth, inculturation is a limited enterprise. Given that human beings are created in the *imago dei*, and that seeds of truth are present in all human cultures (to varying degrees), it would be imprudent for the Church to engage in dialogue from a standpoint of condescension and arrogance, with the aim of completely replacing a given culture. Not only would this likely foment resistance rather than reception of the Church's teaching, such a strategy ignores the fact that cultures evolve; that present cultures should not be judged by their actions in the past; and that Catholic tradition also is developing and should be open to receiving truthful insights from diverse human experiences. Accordingly, Odozor recommends that in helping a culture to navigate practical moral questions, the Church should restrict itself to what is true to the gospel, convergent with Catholic tradition, and based upon sound human experience; and should be willing (in principle) to interrogate not only the culture but also its own tradition (in cases where development is needed).[17]

Seventh and finally, inculturation can take different forms depending upon the subject matter. For example, liturgy naturally can incorporate more "colorings of the host culture" than dogmatic or moral theology, both of which are firmly grounded upon "the mind of Christ" and as such are more likely to challenge culture than to be colored by it. Such challenges arise because even when human beings are well-intentioned and endeavor to act according to reason, cultures can settle for what is easy and practical rather than what is truly good. Accordingly, faith is needed to help reason "lift itself up to the truth that is life—the Lord Jesus himself."[18]

b. Doctrine of God in African Christianity

Equipped with these guidelines, Odozor then proceeds to undertake the difficult but delicate work of theological inculturation by placing the Catholic Christian faith into dialogue with African Christianity (as it currently exists), especially where it builds upon both African culture and African Traditional Religion. The first area that he interrogates is doctrine of God. Odozor maintains that traditional (pre-Christian) ethics in Africa presupposed faith in God, but that its understanding of God was limited, and those minimalist assumptions largely have persisted in contemporary African Christianity.[19] Although Africans possess a sense of God, certain aspects of their belief need correction or completion from Christian revelation, especially regarding God's nature, God's relationship with human beings and the created order, and the universalism of God's love. According to Odozor, in African Traditional Religion, God is distant, withdrawn, and worthy of being feared rather than trusted. For example, the Igbo caste system is maintained because the people fear retribution from the gods (toward their families or descendants) if they choose to marry outside their caste.[20]

Odozor acknowledges that fear of God, in and of itself, need not be problematic, for even Christianity conceives God as a judge who eventually will call everyone to account for their sins. But Christianity does not conceive the high God as someone who regularly enters into human affairs to cause evils; and Christianity also opens up the possibility for atonement and forgiveness by God. Contra African Traditional Religion, God loves everyone—as demonstrated by his sacrificial death on the cross for all human beings—and God gives everyone—including sinners—a second chance. Accordingly, divine retribution does not take place in this world instantaneously simply because God is angry; rather, it occurs only in the eschaton in response to someone's deliberate choice to act against God.[21]

Odozor blames the dearth of catechesis partly on Christian missionaries, who "in a bid to plant the faith in Africa [...] quickly dislodged African divinities from their groves or quickly baptized them with Christian names without a corresponding change in the meaning they mediated."[22] To remedy the deficiency, Odozor conjectures that African Christianity should explain the true nature of God—who God is and how God relates to human beings—to those still embedded in African Traditional Religion, "by providing a careful and loving portrait of the God whom Jesus called Father [...] [emphasizing] that Jesus is Emmanuel, that God is for us, that God is our Father, [and] that God so loves the world that he sends his Son for our redemption."[23]

Additionally, "God is not the vengeful Other. God is love" and God's love is universal, as depicted in the parable of the Good Samaritan.[24]

Although African Traditional Religion possesses a deep sense of God's reality and presence, it lacks the knowledge that Jesus is not just another wise sage; he is God incarnate.[25] Odozor recommends that corrective catechesis begin with Jesus' parables, all of which depict God's kingdom as large, and God as a living God who acts concretely in the world and in history, and who is doing so right now with profound generosity.[26] That generosity extends even toward sinners, as illustrated by Jesus' encounter with the Samaritan woman at the well. By means of this narrative, Odozor argues, "Jesus presents an alternative option to the dominant praxis of his day regarding women, the sinner, and the marginalized. He presents us with the goal of the kingdom of God where, with God in charge, everyone is treated with inclusive respect and with equal regard, gender, social status, or lineage notwithstanding."[27]

c. *Theological Anthropology in African Christianity*

Catechesis also is needed in the area of theological anthropology. Odozor notes many concepts within Traditional African Religion that converge with a Christian understanding of the human person. Most notably, African creation myths regard the human being as the highpoint of God's creation, African Traditional Religion conceives the human being as open to transcendence and accountable to the divine, human life is regarded as sacred and as a gift from God, the communitarian ethos in African culture avoids excessive individualism, and the African family is considered foundational for society.[28]

However, as with its doctrine of God, the African understanding of the human person also suffers from some fundamental deficiencies that necessitate the more comprehensive vision of Christian revelation. To begin with, Odozor queries why many Africans could engage voluntarily in the slave trade, without moral qualms, given their communitarian ethic and its laudable commitments to solidarity and hospitality. His answer is this: Good as it is, praiseworthy as it is, the African communitarian ethos is inherently limited. Not only did Africans engage in the slave trade; they also struggled to construct modern states that protects the rights of all citizens, regardless of tribe or ethnicity. The common denominator in both cases was a failure to view those outside of their family, tribe, or ethnic group as equally human.[29]

The solution to this limitation, Odozor avers, is not political but spiritual. African Christians must equip themselves with the rich theological insights about the human person found in scripture and Catholic tradition and share them with non-Christians, in the context of discussing their own experience of God and the earthly reality.[30] A more comprehensive doctrine of God would provide the foundation for a fuller theological anthropology. In the Bible's creation narrative, the human being is unique among creatures as *imago Dei.* To image a God who is Trinitarian implies more than just rationality, however. God's nature as a communion of persons implies that human persons can receive God and dialogue with God. It also implies that human beings are meant to be in communion with one another, and to relate to one another as equal persons with distinct identities, thus establishing a social-political basis for equal human rights.[31]

Human dignity, or intrinsic human value, is further deepened by the fact of the incarnation. Odozor confidently declares, "The incarnation is God's profound statement about the goodness of being human," thus "there is something of Jesus in everyone [...]. Everyone is equally loved and lovable before God."[32] The basis for human dignity becomes even stronger in light of Jesus's sacrificial death, undertaken voluntarily out of love for all human beings: "Through his redemptive work on the cross Jesus takes humanity several notches higher [...]. Human worth can be gauged by the fact that God. Creator of the universe, gave his only Son so that human beings should not perish but have eternal life."[33] This spiritual reality is so profound, so significant that "the mission of the Church [...] is to proclaim this conviction and help bring about an authentic humanism," namely one "that has Christ at its center."[34]

Creation in the image of a Trinitarian God, coupled with Christ's incarnation and work of redemption, establishes a robust foundation for human dignity. The theological recognition that God is love then establishes the parameters for responding to this dignity by actively helping other human beings rather than harming them, even those beyond one's social group. For as Odozor points out, "Christian morality is a response ethic," one that responds to God's love through love of neighbor.[35]

Other key anthropological insights pertain to the meaning of marriage, and to human freedom. The Genesis account of creation reveals that man and woman complement one another and are radically equal in marriage, a theological framework that can strengthen, preserve, and protect the African family against contemporary challenges, while also purifying it of any sinful inequities.[36] As to freedom, Odozor points out that "Catholic moral tradition has always insisted on the supremacy of individual conscience," even while acknowledging the possibility of subjective error, and the ongoing need to form one's conscience according to the wisdom found in the Church (and to some extent in human communities as well).[37] In African tradition, by contrast, individual freedom to judge moral truth, and to shape one's destiny in accord with that truth, is substantially more limited. A certain amount of determinism exists—as evidenced by the widespread belief that a person's lot in life and moral character is given to them prior to birth—and communal discourse typically is prioritized over individual discernment, which can result in communal pressure regarding one's choice of marriage partner. Here too, Christian anthropology can offer a helpful corrective: by affirming African cultural impulses to avoid excessive individualism, while also modifying any excessive communitarianism that limits the legitimate free moral agency of individuals.[38]

How might these rich theological insights—pertaining to Catholicism's understanding of both God and the human person—be inculturated on the African continent, according to the general guidelines that Odozor proposed? Aside from dialogically emphasizing what is good and worthy of preservation in African culture, how can these new concepts be introduced without unwittingly cloaking them in European cultural attire, thus re-awakening long-standing fears of Western cultural imperialism, resulting in rejection rather than reception and integration?[39]

The solution, in my estimation, involves enabling a fresh engagement with the New Testament: neither by providing intellectual summaries of the ideas therein, nor by rehearsing abstract theological arguments derived from the Bible by well-regarded theologians in the Western tradition, but rather by facilitating an *aesthetic* encounter with the person of Christ as portrayed in the gospels (and to a lesser extent, in the lives of the apostles and the saints). Not only would such an approach avoid the dreaded European attire that can render theology unattractive; it would holistically engage the whole person (both mind and heart) while also communicating the needed concepts regarding both God and the human person due to its Christ-centered focus. To this end, I propose the aesthetic and Christ-centered account of conversion found in the theology of Hans Urs von Balthasar as well-suited to this task.

II. Balthasar on the Dynamics of Conversion

In an essay entitled, "Conversion in the New Testament," Balthasar differentiates conversion in general—"a freely willed change in man, a change in his moral attitudes and in the actions that follow from these"—from Christian conversion in particular.[40] Unlike certain other conversions, he argues, Christian conversion is neither superficial (a purely extrinsic concern), nor a mere "means [to] bring peace to the human heart, or release from restlessness, unhappiness, and earthly insatiability."[41] Rather, "it is a personal call, issued by the absolute," which "frees and satisfies the human heart."[42] Through the encounter with Jesus, one becomes aware of one's own reality; "stripped from [...] all disguises in which the 'I' has cloaked itself, and which have alienated it from itself [...] the soul [now] stands naked before God," as a sinner called to reconciliation with God (and with his fellow human beings as well).[43] The sinner who is reborn in God and empowered by baptism becomes "a 'new creation' (2 Cor 5:17; Gal 6:15) who lives a 'new life' (Rom 6:4)" and creates the Church anew through his relationship to God in Christ.[44]

At first glance, this account of Christian conversion sounds hardly unique; it could have been penned by any number of Christian theologians, either Catholic or Protestant. Upon closer investigation however, Balthasar's perspective is undergirded by an aesthetic orientation that renders his understanding of both the encounter with Jesus, and subsequent Christian formation, incomparably unique. The metaphysical foundation of this aesthetic orientation is the classical doctrine of the circumincession of the transcendentals, which Balthasar reads as implying that truth, goodness, and beauty are related not only in God, but also in their worldly expressions. Accordingly, an experience of authentic beauty can enable human beings both to grasp the truth about the good, and to be motivated to pursue it.

What does beauty's relationship to both truth and goodness imply for Christian conversion? As I have argued elsewhere, for Balthasar, it is the enrapturing beauty of God's love in Christ—and of Christ's love for us while we were still sinners—which makes possible our own faithful and loving response: (1) perceiving the truth that Jesus is God; and (2) becoming enraptured by and increasingly attuned to God, as we allow ourselves to be impressed by Christ's own form, which is the form of love.[45] When subsequently we express that form through loving acts toward God and neighbor, the inherent beauty of such acts can inspire others in turn: perhaps facilitating their conversions as well.[46]

a. Aesthetic Contemplation: Perceiving Jesus as God

How does the *beauty* of God's love in Christ enable human beings to perceive the *truth* that Jesus is God? Balthasar's theory of theological perception is set forth in his multi-volume series on theological aesthetics. Drawing especially upon the first volume, *Seeing the Form*, and the last, *Theology: The New Covenant*, I will explain how contemplation of Jesus' form in terms of two aesthetic dimensions—harmony and uniqueness—reveals Jesus' essential character as an expression of divine love. Balthasar uses the term "Christ-form" to designate that concrete person who was both Jesus of Nazareth and the second person of the eternal Trinity, and who is disclosed to us fundamentally in the Christian scriptures (and indirectly in Catholic tradition, the sacraments, and the lives of the saints). To contemplate the Christ-form aesthetically means to come to know Jesus through his beauty: to experience Jesus' beauty in such a way that one comes to recognize him as God.

In the Old Testament, the living God becomes present to the people of Israel in events that illumine God's glory so powerfully that those who behold it become overwhelmed. These theophanies (described in the scriptures as *kabod-Yahweh*) manifest God's lordliness and sublimity, thereby disclosing God as wholly other: albeit an "other" who freely, mercifully, and lovingly chooses to enter into a covenant with the people of Israel.[47] God subsequently reveals himself even more definitively in the Incarnation, for the person of Jesus is "not a mere sign [of God], but a form," in fact, "*the* definitive and determinant form of God in the world."[48] Unlike the prophet who hears God's word and then filters it through his own cultural and conceptual framework, Jesus is the Word of God itself, now visible in human form. Accordingly, we can come to know God not only by meditating upon Jesus' message, but also by contemplating his very form (as it appears to us in the Christian scriptures).[49]

Balthasar specifically recommends that we contemplate the Christ-form *aesthetically*. By experiencing Jesus' beauty, he avers, we can come to know Jesus more fully, and thereby recognize him as God. Such theological perception requires an openness on the part of the subject (the perceiver), but the greater burden lies with the object itself—the form being perceived—which must supply its own evidence by "giving itself" to the subject.[50] While all worldly forms give themselves to human perception, the Christ-form does so in a way that illuminates its distinctiveness. For it is not just the radiance of being that shines forth in Jesus, but God's own glory.[51]

Aesthetic contemplation proceeds as follows. First, we come to recognize Jesus as God by contemplating the Christ-form's *harmony*: its interior rightness, the beauty of all its proportions.[52] The perception of interior rightness arises from three aspects: unity, simplicity, and love. By *unity* Balthasar means that every aspect of Christ is related to every other aspect; nothing is contradictory, inconsistent, extraneous, unnecessary, or even imbalanced.[53] More precisely, Jesus' existence perfectly accords with his mission. Nothing he says or does or suffers (his existence) ever contradicts or even interferes with doing his Father's will (his mission): in contrast with earthly prophets who carry out a divine mandate but not in every moment of their lives.[54] This is evidenced not only in the Synoptic gospels (via the complete coherence between Jesus' words and behavior), but also in the gospel of John (who portrays Jesus not just as the one who fulfills the law, but as the measure itself) and the epistles of Paul (for whom Jesus is the justice of God).[55]

The Christ-form also appears as harmonious on account of its *simplicity*. By simplicity Balthasar means both effortlessness (Jesus knows how to do things without having learned them) and humility (the kinds of lowliness declared blessed by the Beatitudes, which Jesus exemplifies par excellence in the various trials and suffering that he undergoes); and Balthasar surmises that such simplicity is possible only for one who uniquely participates in God's own simplicity.[56]

Love reveals the harmony of the Christ-form as well. In *Seeing the*

Form, Balthasar contends that we recognize the Christ-form as authentic because it does no violence; it allows for our freedom and overpowers us with the evidential power of love. Indeed, its very meaning is love.[57] In a small book entitled, *Love Alone: The Way of Revelation* (the more recent English edition, published by Ignatius is entitled, *Love Alone is Credible*), Balthasar illuminates two aspects. First, the form of love particular to Jesus involves service to others, even to the point of self-sacrifice.[58] Second, Jesus' love is depicted by his perfect obedience to the Father's will.[59] A third aspect of this love-evidence is mentioned in *The New Covenant*, volume 7 of *Glory of the Lord*. There Balthasar asserts that Jesus demonstrates his love by making space for the Father: emptying himself so that the Father can work in him and through him, a fellowship of love between Father and Son whose dazzling glory seizes us with its beauty and draws us in.[60]

These three aspects—self-sacrifice, perfect obedience, and making space for the Father—arise within the context of Jesus' claim to authority (which involves not mastery or domination but a radical handing over of his entire existence to God); his utter poverty (which enables God's love to flow out of him and into the world, to those most in need); and his self-abandonment (throughout the entirety of his life—having renounced the form of God to assume the form of a slave—and then culminating in the final moments on the cross, where he thoroughly empties himself so that he can be filled by God alone).[61] As Balthasar explains in his books, *The Moment of Christian Witness* and *Word and Revelation*, the essential beauty of the cross as an act of love is hidden temporarily, but it becomes illumined when examined from the vantage point of the Resurrection: for Easter glory is present already in the veiled glory of Good Friday.[62] By means of this love, coupled with Jesus' simplicity and unity, the Christ-form appears as harmonious.

Aesthetic contemplation of the Christ-form reveals a second major respect as well: uniqueness. Compared to all other religious forms, Jesus is incomparably unique. In *Seeing the Form*, Balthasar cites several examples: (1) other religious founders point to a way, whereas Jesus consistently presents *himself* as the way; (2) Jesus' effortlessness, and the unity between his life and mission, render him unique among religious figures; (3) only in Christianity is death *itself* salvation; (4)

compared to non-biblical religions and philosophies, Christianity is eminently historical; and (5) the doctrine of the Trinity embodies a novel relationship between God and the world.[63]

To summarize: In contrast to all other worldly forms, the Christ-form (which is the "form of all forms") presents itself to us in a way that allows us to recognize Jesus as God. We come to recognize Jesus' essential character as an expression of divine love not by relying on signs or by trusting blindly, but by aesthetically contemplating his "form" in terms of its harmony (simplicity, unity, and love) and its uniqueness vis-à-vis all other religious forms. In this contemplative process, the Paschal mystery is the central moment and God's incomprehensible love is the central meaning. For Balthasar, one only needs to open oneself fully to the mystery that the Christ-form discloses to one's perception—and allow oneself to be guided by the light of faith that emanates from his form—and the truth of what Jesus claims will validate itself.

However, conversion of one's mind and heart—and the concomitant transformation of one's life—is in no way guaranteed. One possible response to this theological perception is resistance, even outright rejection. Balthasar explores this possibility at length in his *Theo-Drama*, especially volume 3, *Dramatis Personae: Persons in Christ*, and 4, *The Action*. In *Persons in Christ*, he decries the influence of positivism on modernity.[64] By restricting truth to scientifically verifiable statements, he avers, the human spirit is crushed because it is discouraged from asking questions that cannot be answered logically or empirically. The very drama that constitutes human life is thereby suffocated.[65] Furthermore, because the non-verifiability of religious statements renders them unwelcome in the public sphere, religion is relegated to private life, where it can no longer be experienced as a living reality. Amidst such oppression, one might revolt against society at large, or ascribe religious significance to mere social practices, or become mired in the conflict between different world religions.[66] Or, one might simply be spring-loaded to reject Christianity in advance: due to having been brought up in a different religion, or according to a secular worldview; or having never encountered any individual Christians who are serious about their faith and credibly witness to it.[67]

In *The Action*, Balthasar argues that freedom is the highest form of power, but it easily can be smothered by worldly power, or misled and overtaken by evil cloaked in some attractive good: to the point that evil becomes a commanding reality in human history, permeating both the broader society and an individual's personal life.[68] Accordingly, despite living "in a state of permanent tension"—constantly searching for absolute meaning but unable to construct it or even anticipate it—when that meaning is finally manifested (in the Incarnation), one's response might be rejection: thereby transforming the pathos of the world stage into something "grotesque, grimacing, and demonic."[69]

As Balthasar explains in his preface to *The Action*, "God's glory, as it appears in the world—supremely in Christ—is not something static that could be observed by a neutral investigator. It manifests itself only through the personal involvement whereby God himself comes forth to do battle and is both victor and vanquished."[70] Rather than the world proceeding from God and elegantly returning to God, we witness "a titanic rejection on man's part [as] he resists being embraced by [the] mystery of the Cross," as the Book of Revelation makes clear.[71]

b. Rapture, Imprinting, and Attunement to God in Christ

Another possible response is existential acceptance of the truth that Jesus is God, and subsequent Christian formation. Despite the many obstacles just delineated, one could allow oneself to become overwhelmed and enraptured by the sublime beauty of the Christ-form. As Balthasar explains (in *Seeing the Form*),

> Before the beautiful—no, not really before but within the beautiful—the whole person quivers. He not only "finds" the beautiful moving; rather, he experiences himself as being moved and possessed by it. The more total this experience is, the less does a person seek and enjoy only the delight that comes through the senses or even through any act of his own; the less also does he reflect on his own acts and states. Such a person has been taken up wholesale into the reality of the beautiful and is now fully subordinate to it, determined by it, animated by it.[72]

In aesthetic rapture, one is taken up into the beautiful, captured by it. The more intense the experience—the more one allows oneself to be moved, even possessed by it—the more one forgets about oneself. One who is truly enraptured does not wish to possess that which is beautiful, as one seeking self-gratification, but rather to give oneself to it, to submit to it. As in the case of both courtly love and majestic mythical beauty, one is gripped by the beautiful and willingly devotes oneself to it.[73]

Such a response is possible because the beautiful always "demands" the response of the whole person. This happens with all beautiful things, but especially with human love and even more so with divine love, which is the fullest possible kind of love.[74] Balthasar even goes so far as to claim, in his book *Heart of the World*, that our natural longing for true love "is so strong" that "it is a miracle that we do not love: love is the watermark in the parchment of our existence. It is to love's melody that our limbs respond. Whoever loves is obeying the impulse of life in time; whoever refuses to love is struggling (uselessly) against the current."[75]

In his essay "Movement Toward God," in the book *Creator Spirit* (volume three of *Explorations in Theology*), Balthasar stipulates that the human being's longing for true love is first awakened in the natural sphere of the family. The mother smiles, and the child smiles in response; her love calls forth his own. Love awakens love.[76] The child does not stop to consider whether he will reply; his own love is awakened naturally and effortlessly, just as a plant is awakened by the rays of the sun. As his own love is awakened, the child has an experience not only of his mother, but also of himself. The logic of love is also the logic of self-realization: I give myself, therefore I am.[77]

Because love is not wholly alien to human experience—but in an important sense is constitutive of it—a person's encounter with Christ's love is not completely unfamiliar.[78] However, prior to a definitive encounter with divine love in revelation, human beings have only a vague idea of love, and thus a limited ability to respond to love's beauty. Accordingly, the unparalleled intensity of Christ's love—a love that extended even to the cross—is so un-familiar that it appears as a scandal. Reason finds itself groping to grasp it, and the perceiver is thrown into an existential crisis. For in encountering Christ, one encounters God's love, and thereby experiences true love. But at the same time, one also experiences the fact that one's personal love is not merely inadequate; it is so vastly inadequate that it is not really love. The person realizes that he or she is not a lover but a sinner and an egoist. The beauty of God's love in Christ is so far beyond what the person commonly understands as love that it is "too beautiful to be true."[79] And yet, this love is *so* beautiful that it shakes the person at their foundation and they know that it *must* be true. The person ultimately is persuaded by what Balthasar calls the "evidential power of love," the fact that when all other things are in disarray, only love can be believed.[80]

If one arrives at this point existentially, it is not by one's own power, but by the power of grace. One's response is a response of the whole person, but it is a response that is empowered by God.[81] For to arrive at this point, a radical conversion of both heart and mind are required. One's heart must admit that in the light of this love, one has never really loved. And one's mind must realize that it needs to start over in order to re-learn what love really is. Because God bestows grace but also bestows genuine freedom, there is no guarantee that such a conversion will take place. The person can resist it in a million ways, for a million reasons. For God's grace is irresistible here only in the way that a beautiful painting is irresistible.[82] The power of conversion comes from God, but the perceiver retains the freedom and agency to refuse this conversion if he or she so chooses.[83]

On the other hand, if one allows oneself to become fully enraptured, and one's heart and mind to be converted, then an even deeper transformation will be initiated. For once a person genuinely has been moved by God's act, one cannot but act in response.[84] The person responds with faith, a faith that accepts what one sees as true. And faith's response is love, for the heart of faith is a personal encounter.[85] As Balthasar puts it, "Love is my response to the love that has sacrificed itself for me."[86] As with the mother and her child, God's love awakens love in the human perceiver. The person responds with his or her own love and thereby initiates a journey of self-realization. As one continues to trust God, as one allows God's love to awaken one's own loving response, God becomes ever more deeply implanted at the center of one's ego. One gradually becomes the unique person that one always was meant to be.

Balthasar consistently maintains that in the aesthetic rapture inspired by the Christ-form, the object of perception not only makes itself seen and comprehended; it also transforms the perceiver. In his *Glory of the Lord* series, Balthasar describes this transformation utilizing two aesthetic metaphors—being "imprinted" with Christ's own form, which is the form of love; and becoming increasingly "attuned" to God in Christ. These metaphors serve to illustrate the conferral of grace and the believer's cooperation with it. In *Theology: The New Covenant*, he writes:

> What is seen (the Word-image-light of the Father) not only determines the power of sight in the one who sees, but determines him as a whole and *imprints* himself on him. What is seen not only gives illumination, but also gives form and transforms by configuring to itself. The Word-image of God which has form and shows itself as light and life in a manner that transcends form (and thereby demands faith) has precisely in this the highest power to give form; the quality of form proper to absolute love displays itself in the transformation [...]. Thus it is possible finally to speak without any prefix of a "shaping of Christ" in the Christians (with the help of the labor pains of the apostle: Gal 4:19), and this means nothing else than the self-realization of the innermost disposition of Christ (Phil 1:8, 2:5) and thus of his life in them (Gal 2:20; 2 Cor 13:3,5; Col 1:27, 3:11).[87]

Balthasar goes on to argue that this shaping process, resulting in transformation, is not "primarily the result of one's own endeavors" but involves "permitting" God's shaping power (in Christ) to work within oneself: a trajectory described elsewhere (in *Seeing the Form*) as "active receptivity."[88]

What specifically does Balthasar mean by his assertion that, in this shaping process, the Christ-form *imprints* itself on the perceiver? It seems reasonable to conclude that Balthasar borrows this concept from Bonaventure, whose theology he explicates at length in volume 2 of *Glory of the Lord*, on *Clerical Styles*. There he contends that the fundamental experience for Bonaventure is "being overpowered by God in the act of the wondering ecstasy": an experience crystallized in St. Francis's being imprinted by the stigmata on Mount Alverna when the "beauty of Wisdom appears to Francis in the form of the crucified seraph," who is "not only the object of contemplative loving meditation" but is also an "active" agent who "expresses himself by impressing himself" on Francis.[89] Such an event is fitting because the Son of God is not merely the archetype upon which all worldly images of God are based; "he is God as expression."[90]

Notably, in his analysis, Balthasar emphasizes not the stigmata *per se*, but rather the soul of the man who received it. He writes, "The stigmatization is like a sign of [Francis'] *inward* resemblance to the crucified, a sign that demands a bodily visibility; and the inner resemblance, no less than the body resemblance, was the work of the crucified God whose love sought to express itself."[91] In other words, God's love expresses itself on Francis in two ways: first, by imprinting Francis' soul, and second, by imprinting Francis' body.

In this imprinting process, God's agency is primary, but Francis' active receptivity to God's love is indispensable: "The man's love makes the wax of the heart soft, and God's love imprints the seal."[92] Balthasar further underscores the fact that this trajectory pertains not only to Francis—who is relatively unique in receiving the stigmata—but to all Christians, for he immediately adds: "And so every Christian may be urged," (and here he quotes Bonaventure), "'Like a seal in soft wax, so print Jesus the Bridegroom on your soul.'"[93] Balthasar then further accentuates the Christian's active participation in this process by pairing this quote with another one from Bonaventure: "Likewise," says Balthasar, "'Long more forcefully for resemblance to God, through an explicit (*expressam*) following of the crucified Jesus.'"[94]

While Balthasar does not always use the same concepts as Bonaventure, the general trajectory is the same. For both thinkers, contemplating the cross can lead to an ecstatic experience in which one actually becomes like the crucified Christ. This process unfolds in the following way. The believer's own love (which is fundamentally not one's own but is rather a gift from God) allows one to actively receive God's love. The imprinting of God's love yields knowledge and enables the believer to express God to the world. Further, this imprinting is not a momentary event, in which God stamps the believer and then promptly removes himself, but an ever-flowing, continual, living relationship with God, one that is profoundly personal. And both thinkers are insistent that the believer ought to respond not with a half-hearted love of God but with a total emptying of self. For Balthasar, the kind of transformative, mystical experience had by Francis is but a more radical version of "ordinary" Christian experience: the process by which the believer gradually becomes more and more "attuned" to God.

Balthasar develops the concept of attunement in *Seeing in the Form*. The Christian becomes "attuned" to God, or "consonant" with God, when "the impressing of the Christ-form by God upon the believer" is coupled with "the believer's offering of himself to God."[95] Philosophically, this self-offering connotes an openness to the totality of reality—including God—in both knowledge and love: an "ontological concordance" in which one affirms Being and experiences the joy of Being.[96] Because God is the ground of Being, "the creature is ontologically resonant to God and for God," to whom he "is radically ordered" and was created to actively receive.[97]

Theologically, this self-offering is a response to "the distinctly Christian fact [...] that God, in the form of his Son, has sacrificed himself to the world": a form that grace has empowered the person to perceive and become so enraptured by that it inspires his or her loving submission in response.[98] After all, the proper response to such sublime beauty is to put one's whole existence at its disposal, so that one can be shaped into its image.[99] As Balthasar explains,

> All our senses are engaged when the interior space of a beautiful musical composition or painting opens itself to us and captivates us: the whole person then enters into a state of vibration and becomes responsive space, the "sounding box" of the event of beauty occurring within him. This is all the more so where human eros is concerned, and yet more in the encounter with divine eros!...It becomes clear at once that faith in the full Christian sense can be nothing other than this: to make the whole man a space that responds to the divine

> content. Faith attunes man to this sound; it confers on man the ability to react precisely to this divine experiment, preparing him to be a violin that receives just this touch of the bow, to serve as material for just this house to be built, to provide the rhyme for just this verse being composed.[100]

In faith, and through faith, the person is "made open and dispossessed of self."[101] Balthasar thus sets forth an aesthetic definition of faith as "the attunement and adaption of [one's] whole existence to God."[102]

Notably, because one who radically opens oneself to God becomes attuned not merely to God but to God in Christ, such attunement necessarily involves Christ-specific content. For it is "Christ's continuing action [that takes] shape in the believer," Balthasar asserts, citing Paul's characterization in Galatians 4:19 ("until Christ be formed in you)."[103] The upshot of this is that "Christian experience can mean only the progressive growth of one's own existence into Christ's existence."[104] As Balthasar perceptively remarks in his commentary on Bonaventure's theology,

> The superabundance of light that remains incomprehensible demands faith, the superabundance of love in the crucified demands pure humility and surrender of oneself, and finally the superabundance of the divine prodigality imperiously demands total poverty, which, as the human gesture of giving away everything, is the most exact answer possible for man to God's act of total abandonment even to the cross.[105]

The interior fulfillment that results from allowing oneself to be shaped in this way further confirms the Christ-form to be true, a stipulation that Balthasar makes explicit in *Seeing the Form*.[106] By authentically living as a Christian, the believer receives "a new form of Christian certitude," thereby confirming his or her original decision to convert.[107]

The more a person continues to contemplate the mystery of God's love, the deeper this process of formation becomes. Both one's intellect and will continue to be shaped by that which one contemplates. As to intellect: more concentrated attention to the Christian mystery yields more precise knowledge about what discipleship entails. In particular,

Christ's filial relationship to the Father becomes the model for one's own spiritual life. By "seeing" Christ empty himself to do the Father's will in loving obedience, one learns that love for God properly takes the form of self-surrender. As to will: the more one reflects on the beauty of trinitarian love (self-giving love between Father and Son, expressed as Spirit and poured out on humankind), the more one is motivated to surrender oneself.

The knowledge that one should surrender oneself, coupled with the motivation to do so, culminates in an act of self-surrender: promising oneself to God, putting oneself at God's disposal.[108] If one's love for God were perfect already, then one could make a total gift of oneself and all that one possesses to God (and also to one's neighbor for God's sake).[109] But even while one's love still is imperfect, one can cultivate the virtue of love by adopting an attitude of total self-surrender and then striving to live in accord with it. Ideally, the virtue of love then enlivens—but is also enlivened by—three secondary virtues demarcated by the spirit of the evangelical counsels of poverty, chastity, and obedience. This trajectory can be found in two of Balthasar's books, *Christian State of Life* and *The Laity and the Life of the Counsels*; and in my book on Balthasar, I explicitly develop it as providing the foundation for an aesthetic theory of virtue ethics.

Although the process of sanctification is ongoing throughout one's life, Christian conversion may be considered completed when it begins bearing fruit in the world for God's kingdom. Balthasar situates such fruit-bearing squarely within the Ignatian and Johannine category of "mission." However, he explains *how* individual missions bear fruit in part by extending the aesthetic frame of formation. Having been informed with the form of God, the Christian now expresses that form in subsequent loving acts toward God and neighbor: the beauty of which then can inspire others in turn.

III. Deepening Christian Discipleship on the African Continent

How might Balthasar's account of individual conversion further some of the goals set forth by Odozor in his proposal for theological inculturation? Three aspects are especially helpful here. First, because it is

Christ-centered, the content helps to correct the afore-mentioned deficiencies both in doctrine of God and theological anthropology. Second, Balthasar's aesthetic approach engages the heart as well as the mind; by impacting the whole person, the likelihood of reception is greatly increased. Third, because Balthasar upholds the personal encounter with Christ in the gospels as primary—rather than relying on theological arguments *about* Christ to facilitate one's conversion—this emphasis would prevent theological inculturation from being rejected out-of-hand as an external imposition handed down from a culture that regards itself as intellectually and morally superior.

To root itself more deeply in the African cultural context, therefore, the New Testament first needs to be read by African Christians with fresh eyes, so as to deepen their own discipleship. By contemplating Jesus aesthetically, with open hearts and minds, they can perceive the harmony between his existence and his mission, his effortlessness, his utter humility, his unwavering obedience to the Father, and the radicality of his love: the contours of which are not sentimental but sacrificial, not self-aggrandizing but self-emptying, and poured out for all human beings, not just some of them. Taken together, all of these aspects can cohere in an experience of sublime beauty, enabling the perceiver to recognize Jesus as God, and to cooperate more fully with the imprinting power of God's grace.

Continued reflection on the scriptures will engender cognitive reframing to see the world as Jesus sees it, and internal motivation to act according to Jesus' example. Such an interior transformation can illuminate their minds and strengthen their wills to confront soberly and courageously any aspects within African Christianity that need to be expanded or changed. For example, an African Christian who was been formed interiorly with the heart and mind of Christ, and who subsequently engages in communal discourse—to discern moral truth in a particular case confronting his village—will possess the necessary intellectual acumen and willpower to resist the distorting influence of charismatic demagogues, personal/cultural biases, and bad actors motivated by self-serving agendas so as to defend objective moral truth publicly and prevent human rights violations of neighboring clans that otherwise his village might be inclined to support.

Furthermore, his existential commitment to Christ, undergirded by prior aesthetic contemplation of Christ in the scriptures, will enable him to see the Christ-form where it appears in the lives of the saints, according to the instruction set forth by St. Paul: "Be imitators of me, as I am of Christ" (1 Cor 11:1). Not only do the saints serve as moral exemplars—as "guiding stars for others" to use Balthasar's phrase—they also function as dynamic spiritual aides, for "having surrendered themselves to the Redeemer's fruitful love, they intercede for us and become our chosen helpers."[110] Accordingly, when the African Christian's village proceeds to consult their dead ancestors, he can guide them prudently to distinguish ancestors who lived saintly lives from ancestors who lived sinful lives, so as to accept guidance from the former rather than the latter. By means of such interventions, African communal traditions can be purified and elevated rather than simply replaced with Western-style processes and procedures: thus enabling the African Christian to remain both African and Christian simultaneously. Such transformations also would establish a compelling cultural foundation from which to spread the good news of the gospel to non-Christians on the African continent, by inviting them to read the New Testament with similar openness of both mind and heart.

Chapter 5
The Importance of Anamnesis for Moral Life

Jana M. Bennett

The title of Fr. Paulinus Odozor's book *Morality Truly Christian, Truly African* might lead some erroneously to think the book's discussions only apply to moral theologians in Africa. Yet in my estimation, such readers would be the poorer for not having engaged with Fr. Odozor's work. In this essay, I examine one of many ways Fr. Odozor's work might engage moral theology done in the context of the United States.

The particular moral question is the place of Christian practices in Christian moral life, especially the sacraments. Christian practices have been identified by some scholars as crucial means by which Christians can respond to a secular worldview. Stanley Hauerwas and Sam Wells argue that part of the current problem in ethics is ethics is cut off from the theology and practice that made moral life make sense. They suggest that in the Enlightenment era (18th century), in the aftermath of the previous centuries' wars of religion, ethics came to be understood as that which "can be acknowledged by 'anyone.'"[1] The wat humans can live together in harmony and avoid the disastrous wars of religion (or indeed, any war) was to come together over that which unites them. Enlightenment thinkers like Immanuel Kant divested themselves of religious belief and sought a morality that could stand alone. Kant argued that what unites people are reason and freedom to choose (and autonomy to make those choices). Only individuals could make ethical decisions, and societies could make laws and ethical norms that would enable all to participate. On this view, we can and should, therefore, separate what seems "ethical" and therefore shareable by many from the more divisive aspects of Christianity, such as the particularities of worship, prayer practices, habits of hospitality, and more. As Hauerwas and Wells claim, such a division between a presumed private belief and a public ethic makes it seem "as if Christian theology could be divorced from the ecclesial context necessary for theology to be intelligible."[2]

Instead, in Hauerwas' and Wells' view, Christian belief and practice go hand in hand: belief in Christ shapes the ways we respond to others and vice versa. For example, Hauerwas is known for advocating non-violent practices as acts of Christian witness because violence does not make sense for someone who believes that the violent death on the cross of Jesus, Son of God, changed the world. Similarly, distinctly Christian prayer practices like the sacraments can form people in faith, as can counter-cultural practices that witness to God as the God who acts on behalf of the poor and the marginalized. For an example, William Cavanaugh's book *Torture and Eucharist* describes the ways that Chilean Catholics, via Eucharistic practices, could critique both the despotic regime of Augusto Pinochet as well as those church leaders who supported him.

Other scholars argue against Hauerwas', Wells', and Cavanaugh's views of Christian practices, seeing those views as a kind "sacramental optimism"[3] that overlooks the damage Christian practice can cause. Scholars such as Katie Grimes and Lauren Winner argue that the sacraments form people away from Christ. For example, in Winner's view, "[d]eformations of Christian practices are part of the practices themselves."[4] Sacraments are a problematic vehicle, then, for learning about, and witnessing to, God's coming reign. Her claim raises other questions, including the extent to which such practices enable aspects of moral life, such as virtue formation, Christological vision of the world, and the ability to take a stance against the relativizing and secularizing tendencies in the contemporary world. Ultimately, there is an impasse regarding the relationship between sacramental practice and the moral life, between those who argue the sacraments are capable of bearing witness to God's vision of the world, and those who argue the sacraments most often fail to witness to God's view and, instead, support sinful human worldviews.

This essay will focus on the question of Christian practice and its importance in Catholic moral theology, with some attention to the broader implications mentioned above. The discussion about sacramental optimism will take place in relation to Fr. Odozor's development of African anamnetic ethics. I argue that his vision of anamnetic ethics would helpfully further the conversation about sacramental/moral formation. Anamnesis is a term used in liturgical theology to speak about the ways Christians ritually remember Jesus in the bread and wine. As such, the term both directly and implicitly connects to the question of moral formation in the Eucharist. Remembrance is also key for moral life: what we remember and what we forget figures in what we understand as moral living.

I will extend Fr. Odozor's discussion of an anamnetic ethic in order to show how it provides some helpful resources for US Catholic moral theology. I do this first by reflecting on the work of African theologian Bénézet Bujo, who developed the term in relation to African ethics. Then, I discuss how Fr. Odozor expands the use of anamnetic ethics. Finally, I consider the ways his anamnetic ethic enables more fruitful conversation for thinking about contemporary US Catholic moral theology.

I. An Antecedent: Fr. Bénézet Bujo and Anamnesis

Fr. Odozor's specific term anamnetic ethic develops from Bénézet Bujo's work on anamnetic ethics, and so Fr. Odozor's development of the term requires that we first have a clear sense of Bujo's work. Bujo explains/defines the concept in this way: "the ancestors' words and deeds, the norms they set, are made available to the current generation so that it has life and continues to look after the deceased, and so that it prepares the future of the not-yet born."[5]

Bujo's use of anamnesis itself has an antecedent in philosopher Walter Benjamin's work on memory. Benjamin wrote against the common trope that history is always written by victors and oppressors. On the contrary, Benjamin wondered if historical accounts could actually be used to promote social justice and solidarity with the oppressed. As Benjamin suggests: "To articulate the past historically does not mean to recognize it as 'the way it really was' [...]. It means to seize hold of a memory as it flashes up at a *moment of danger* [...] [emphasis mine]. In every era the attempt must be made anew to wrest tradition away from a conformism that is about to overpower it."[6] Historians have a crucial role in seeking justice, which is to maintain the memories of those whose remembrance is threatened—especially of those who have stood up for the powerless. As he says: "The present generation redeems the past in an anamnestic solidarity with all who suffered at the slaughter-bench of history."[7]

For Benjamin, such dangerous history is definitely imbued with theological overtones (though Benjamin himself was secular). We humans have "been endowed with a weak messianic power,"[8] Benjamin claims, that enables transformation, perhaps even eschatological revolution, of the past. "[R]edemption becomes possible in arresting the historical continuum by blasting 'a specific era out of the homogeneous course of history.'"[9] Grand historical narratives that recount tales of the wealthy victors/oppressors must be shown to be dependent upon the "anonymous drudgery of [great geniuses'] contemporaries."[10]

Benjamin's work has attracted theologians who see, similarly to Benjamin's historians, God as acting decisively on behalf of those who suffer injustice. Such a view is allied with Mary's proclamation in her Magnificat that God rescues the lowly, the ones who are not remembered in history but are forgotten:

> He has scattered those who were proud in the thoughts of their hearts.
> He has brought down rulers from their thrones,
> And has exalted those who were humble.
> He has filled the hungry with good things,
> And sent the rich away empty-handed. (Luke 1: 51b–53, NABRE)

For example, Johann Baptist Metz takes up Benjamin's vision to propose a more theologically-centered view where the concept of solidarity is "expanded into an anamnestic solidarity, a solidarity of memory with the victims of history"[11] but also to the dangerous memory of Jesus Christ, crucified. Death might seem to be the victor, but in God's salvific vision, Christ conquers death and sin through his own death on the cross. The dangerous memory of Jesus enables Christians to respond counter-culturally and creatively to a world that does not recognize that suffering and death might, in fact, be means for the greater and more glorious reality of the resurrection.

Bujo is one theologian who follows Benjamin's work, but with a view toward how memory relates to African context. Bujo argues that Benjamin's view of history and memory is far too constrained: "In connection with the African model however, it should be mentioned that such an interpretation of anamnestic solidarity is too narrowly defined. African ancestral worship is not restricted to the victims of history but intends to keep the memory of those to *whom those left behind owe their existence*"[12] [emphasis mine]. That is, it is not only the victims of history who matter, the ones whose memories are in danger of being forgotten, but all of the ancestors. Bujo states: "The fact that for the African, life cannot bloom and develop in its multiple dimensions unless the descendants stay faithful to their ancestors, keeping their *memory* alive."[13] From Bujo's point of view, anamnesis means not only retelling history, perhaps not only propelling Benjamin's "weak messianic power" of telling stories about those who would otherwise be forgotten—but in fact recognizes a strong messianic power, that of "keeping memory alive."

Bujo emphasizes the importance of remembering ancestors, which is linked directly to ethical response. Ancestors are those whom he names as having "led exemplary lives fulfilling what the community holds to be the ideal lifestyle. After their death they are in the 'village of happiness.' The decisive standard of judgment to be retained as ancestor is a life of virtue according to the prescription of the founder, the original ancestor."[14] Bujo describes rituals of remembrance, which "[aim] at reinforcing the life and repeating the deeds of the ancestors and remembering their sayings [...]. The ancestor is thus contemplated as *model* and *guarantor* of the moral life of the community."[15] Members of the community "search for and point toward ways of solving today's problems" through conversation with past traditions, including prayers, past rituals, laws, and sayings. In part, this leads to "palaver," Bujo's sense of the way Africans consider problems in community, rather than as individuals. Past exemplars are brought into the present via memory and remembrance as upholders of the community, and such exemplars are also named as part of the tradition for future perpetuation.

Bujo sees in this sense of time a way to articulate both an African anamnesis of ancestors and a Christian anamnesis of God Incarnate:

Jesus Christ as the "Proto-ancestor," an ideal model that guides us, and we remember Christ in the Eucharist. This is no mere "memorializing" but an anamnesis that is "communicating life in full."[16] We must share in this "life-giving force" which itself sustains our moral activity, for "[m]oral action concerns above all the domain of interpersonal relations with reference to the ancestors. By reference to the ancestors, moral action in Africa has a character of anamnesis [...]. Black African ethics is centered on the good of the human being (life) insofar as he is member of a three-dimensional community: the living, the ancestors, and the not-yet-born."[17] For Bujo, this anamnetic character of Christian ethics on his view enables both remembrance of Jesus, the ancestor par excellence, and questioning elements of African life that may not be in concert with "Jesus Christ Proto-ancestor."

By naming Jesus Christ as Proto-ancestor, Jesus becomes the key exemplar in a particularly African ethics that is focused more on community than on the individual, and so stands in contrast with key strands of Western moral thought. It is the communally-engrained anamnetic character of African community, with its palaver, that Bujo sees as a way to do Christian ethics without focus on what he sees as Western-centered ethics, especially ethics as grounded in natural law.

One commenter on Bujo's work, Fr. Ghislain Ndondji-Tshiwisa-Adidem, further helps clarify Bujo's development and distinction between traditional African and Christian views of anamnesis: "African anamnesis [...] turns radically towards an ancestral past which it tries to reproduce in the present."[18] In an African anamnesis, the present reiterates the past. By contrast, Christian anamnesis "reveals the identity of Jesus [...] anamnesis results in faith, and faith tends toward eschatology (when you come into your throne)."[19] Seeing Christ as Ancestor shapes time in a bit different way. We remember Jesus who was incarnate in the past, who now propels peoples' faith in the present, but that faith aims toward a future in which Jesus Christ will come again. That vision of Christ as exemplar shapes peoples' moral life, as they seek to emulate Jesus themselves.

To sum up, we see then that Bujo's account of memory takes a decisive shift away from Benjamin's (and Metz's) "dangerous memory" of the poor and outcast, those whose stories are often not told in history.

Instead, Bujo focuses on remembering ancestors, which connects to a moral vision that emphasizes African ancestors as people to emulate because they are examples of virtue and community. In this moral worldview, Jesus Christ is the ancestor par excellence. The shift toward African ancestors enables Bujo to make at least two additional moves related to moral life. The first is to critique Western ideals about life that quite simply don't work in African contexts, especially the individualism of many European and US Catholics that ignores communal considerations. The second is to bypass aspects of Catholic ethics that seem mostly Western and therefore antithetical to many African stances on moral life. For example, Bujo rejects natural law, a sense that "truth 'may be grasped by one kind of methodology, via a 'one-way' street.'"[20]

II. Fr. Paulinus Odozor, C.S.Sp.

Fr. Odozor takes up Bujo's concept of anamnetic ethics, though with some crucial changes and developments. While Odozor mentions anamnetic ethics directly on only a few pages in *Morality Truly Christian, Truly African* (chiefly on164–65 and 269), nevertheless the concept is apparent throughout the book. In his various descriptions we can discern both the ways Odozor is making use of the concept while simultaneously rejecting, fine-tuning, or adding to Bujo's discussion. Chiefly, Odozor finds Bujo's account to be insufficiently Christological. Christ cannot be merely the best of all possible men, the chief exemplar, the Proto-Ancestor. Anamnetic ethics, instead, draws Christ in other ways.

Anamnetic Ethics is Inclusive

For example, Fr. Odozor writes: "African Christian/Catholic ethics must also be anamnetic—in a more inclusive way than that identified by Bujo as being the case in African traditional ethics."[21] Odozor directly inculcates anamnetic ethics but refuses to make the emphasis solely one of African culture and what it has to communicate about Jesus Christ. Odozor states, rather: "the subject of remembrance must begin with Jesus Christ and the saints of all ages and places, including of course the African ancestors whose lives and deeds are worth remembering."[22] Odozor's account of what it means to remember thus places African

Christian moral life in *connection* with Christian tradition broadly speaking. Moral exemplars of the faith cannot only be African, but may be drawn from, for example, lives of non-African saints. At the same time, he clearly notes that Christian moral exemplars must include African saints, and including African saints is not only on behalf of African Christians who are witnesses of Christ. The inclusion of African saints is for the whole Church because what it means to be a person who witnesses to Christ—that is, to be one who bears the memory of Christ—is to be a member of the Body of Christ, which is geographically unlimited. To be more inclusive means to recognize and be part of the whole of the Christian saints.

Yet in making this Christological move, Odozor is not rejecting the particularity of African Christian witness. Rather, he intends that African Christian life and witness enables correctives for the whole Church, especially when and where people have taken up positions which he worries are antithetical to the Gospel. These include ethical concerns that arise from focusing African Christian ethics too much toward traditional African views without allowing Christ to shine light on the question. For example, Odozor writes about Jesus' parables as a way of offering a strong point of contrast to Bujo's use of traditional African religious concepts. Odozor observes that a central characteristic in African traditional religion is a focus on fear, yet the parables demonstrate that God is love, such as in the Good Samaritan:

> the radical equality between himself [the Samaritan] and the man who had been beaten by brigands. This equality cuts through every other classification that separates the two men—race, class, and other circumstances of life [...]. The lesson of this parable is clear: The God of Jesus is universal as creator, sustainer and redeemer, and his love is inclusive and blind to ethnic and racial or class considerations.[23]

We cannot live out of fear and still include and love others.

The result of Odozor's focus on the love of Christ is that his more inclusive Christological concept of anamnesis critiques both Bujo and Western individualism. Bujo raises important points, but so too does

Western culture (very broadly speaking). For example, Odozor discusses the way that African Christian anthropology emphasizes a wide range of familial relationships. He notes that African thought:

> provides resistance to any attempt to reduce an individual person to an atom or a monad—'an individual substance of a rational nature.' The web of relationships that characterizes the personhood of the individual in Africa is sometimes beyond imagination. It is like a vast network stretching literally (horizontally) in every direction, to embrace everybody in any given local group.' In essence, every individual 'is a brother or sister, father or mother, grandmother or grandfather, or cousin, or brother-in-law, uncle or aunt, or somebody else, to another person else.'[24]

Odozor is of course referencing family. Yet readers should also note that this African-centric focus shows an account of the family that is so much more broadly understood than often happens in many Western contexts.

The care and deftness with which Odozor treats the question of individual and family, broadly understood, shows in how he extends the discussion. Odozor argues that familial inclusivity requires that African ethics take seriously theological anthropology as centered in Christ, especially the notion of "creatureliness as a basic characteristic of the human *individual* [emphasis mine]."[25] Odozor is decidedly not trying to pit the individual against the community or negate individual in favor of communal relationships. Instead, what he aims to show readers is how both individual and community become something "beyond imagination" in Christ. The individual human being must be understood and respected as not merely a "monad" or a singular entity, but as one who by nature exists in relationship. In addition, the community Jesus gives demonstrates a much bigger web of relationships, past, present, and future, that link each individual to each other and to the Body of Christ. Jesus Christ. The multiple saints and witnesses of Christian faith become part of our Christian family, which is large, and remarkable, and even almost unimaginable, especially in a Western world that figures kinship ties in terms of father, mother, and children. The broader African understanding of kinship and family enables Christians to see the new community, that Jesus offers, the Church, precisely because it is broad. In Christ's family, we have new ties to each other because of our life, our baptism, our ties, to Him.

Odozor speaks about the ways that too much of a focus on communitarianism in African ethics can be too dismissive of the individual to the detriment of both. Thus, "the challenge for African Christian moral theology is to be on guard against communitarian imposition that makes light of human individuality as the basis for free moral agency, while on the other hand avoiding excessive individualism."[26] Odozor argues that such an ethic of discipleship stands in contrast to some of the ways traditional African communitarianism operates, in which the openness and hospitality of the community that Bujo describes is often "limited to the known other."[27] That is to say, communitarianism will not necessarily lead us on Jesus' pathway, any more than individualism does. Jesus offers a way to critique both individualism and communitarianism.

Odozor's discussion of the human being is connected to natural law, which Bujo rejects.[28] But for Odozor, natural law should not be rejected, for it "affirms the very thing Bujo is trying to affirm, which is that human beings everywhere are capable of coming to know the truth" which must include the significance of being human and drawn into Christ's life and love.[29] However, Odozor notes that natural law cannot be the sum total of Christian ethics because Christian ethics is "especially an ethics that is drawn from the revealed word of God in the Bible. At the center of this ethics of course is Jesus, his life and his teaching."[30] Bujo's account of human beings is not inclusive enough precisely because it does not account for natural law which draws all human beings together. Additionally, Bujo's failure to develop natural law also means his ethic is not Christological enough because his account is not centered deeply in Christian concepts of law. A Christological focus would be centered on the fact that Jesus is the Law and the Lawgiver.[31] We human creatures are drawn into Christ's own life in part because the Son is the Lord of Creation who shows forth the law that is written on our hearts.

Anamnetic Ethics Requires Remembrance of Sin

Second, Fr. Odozor also develops the concept of Bujo's anamnetic ethics by arguing that anamnetic ethics must involve memory of sin. Like the

Christian exemplars that come from many times and places, sin is evident in many times and places. So Odozor writes that we must "recall in shame the deeds of those African ancestors whose ruinous neglect—the 'particularist greed'—manifested in four exhausting centuries of bloody exportation of their kind and in four centuries of political disorientation and social disorganization in the face of European incursions into Africa."[32] Simply because there are ancestors to whom we owe gratitude for life and for a particular ethical vision, that does not give them a pass from their grave misdeeds. Rather, the misdeeds place the ancestors alongside all Christians who recognize that one of the characteristics of human life is that it involves sin (our own and others) as well as a failure to forgive sins.

Anamnetic ethics, if well done, will not only expose misdeeds of the past, but will also highlight misdeeds of the present. That is, Odozor considers that in order to do inculturation properly, "the theologian [...] must also be aware of some deep-seated assumptions, a carryover from the community's history as it were, which continue to inform the societies of the present day for good or for ill."[33] The Gospel can critique cultures even as it celebrates aspects of those cultures that help us see Christ more clearly. This is again why much of Odozor's focus is on Jesus, who is mercy. Anamnetic ethics requires that we look squarely in the face of this utter mercy and know it, not just as offered historically to the ancestors we have in the People of God, but as offered to us here and now. Odozor therefore sees a contrast and important distinction between African Christian ethics and African traditional ethics—a contrast that is not evident in Bujo's work. Odozor suggests that African traditional religion focuses on fear, but Christian understandings focus on mercy.

In light of the encounter with God's mercy, Odozor names that "African Christian ethics as an anamnetic ethics must not stop at merely exposing the misdeeds of the past. It must also be a constructive ethic of reconciliation."[34] In this way, we again come face to face with Benjamin's dangerous ethic, for surely naming misdeeds and seeking reconciliation is difficult work. Many Africans have been wounded by "historical wrongs, real or imagined," and it is the "task of Christian ethics as theology to help find ways of healing memories in Africa through conflict resolution."[35] This is no mere seeking justice in the sense that Benjamin might have wanted, but it is instead a direct call to live the Christian life, which must be a life filled with forgiveness and mercy. Seeking both fuller understanding of sin as well as reconciliation requires an understanding of human conscience and human freedom, which in turn requires a fuller understanding of the individual alongside the community.

Such forgiveness and mercy, as lived in the community, must be sustained by a theology of sin that recognizes both individual sin and social sin. This connects us, again, to the first point about anamnetic ethics, which is that it must be inclusive. So, rather than sin remaining private, between the self, the priest, and God, Catholic moral theology has recently recognized that social sin involves both "group blindness and inactivity."[36] There are also "dehumanizing trends built into the various institutions—social, political, economic, religious, and others—which embody people's collective life."[37] Yet most damning is the way in which social sin shapes individuals with malformed consciences, especially by creating a communal ethos in which "destructive actions" appear instead to be the right thing to do.[38] Odozor's view of social sin and conscience is important in the face of certain American conceptions of freedom that emphasize each individual's lifetime of choices.

The discussions of sin are especially occasions when Odozor speaks against Western conceptions of individualism, freedom, and family. Where the West needs to recover more of a sense of community, African Christians need to hold on to conceptions of family and community but also enable a broader vision of kinship as wrought in baptism and Eucharist.[39] In order to seek reconciliation, a community, as well as its individual members, will require opportunities to come face to face with both the sin done that would be fairly readily recognized as sin, *and also* the sin done that wouldn't be recognized as sinful. Of course, the latter is the more difficult component of doing ethics.

Anamnetic Ethics Means Discipleship

Finally, Odozor argues that "African ethics as Christian ethics must be an ethics of discipleship," which means we "take seriously what Jesus took seriously."[40] Discipleship stems from the forgiveness we receive from God and neighbor in mercy. As Odozor names it, our life of discipleship understands

> love as the center of Christian ethical life; attention to the poor and marginalized; recognition of the equal humanity of all persons irrespective of ethnicity, gender, or religion; and continued vigilance over culture to make sure it does not harbor, condone or nurture any tendencies harmful to the welfare of the human person integrally and adequately considered.[41]

Odozor's focus on discipleship names multiple actions that focus on remembering, the emphasis of anamnetic ethics.

For example, "attention to the poor and marginalized" should bring to minds and hearts that plights of those easily forgotten and overlooked by societies that privilege wealth and position. Similarly, Odozor's mention of ethnicity, gender, and religion should be shorthand for recalling multiple moments when these aspects of human life have been a means of forgetting people, thereby cutting them off from the mainstream of society. One such case is in the immediate contemporary context of war, violence, and immigration crises that might push Christians to focus on refugees in Syria and Sudan, or on Jews, Christians, and Muslims in the Middle East who target each other or are targeted by nation states beyond the Middle East. Finally, the focus on "continued vigilance over culture to make sure it does not condone [...] any tendencies harmful to the welfare of the human person" bring to mind all those who are caught up in contemporary throw-away culture, whose lives are seen as expendable, including the pre-born, the elderly, and people with disabilities. Discipleship, when done with an anamnetic vision, asks us to remember all these people, and many others, in past, present and future.

In sum, Fr. Odozor's developments of anamnetic ethics involve the following: first, recognition of anamnetic ethics as significant for African ethics; second, that anamnetic ethics must display greater inclusion than indicated in Bujo's work; third, anamnetic ethics is also about remembrance not only of the blessings of particular cultures but also the shame of the past and the present; fourth, we seek out reconciliation as a response to uncovering these misdeeds; and fifth, having done the work of anamnetic ethics and seen Jesus, we then respond in loving discipleship to God by caring for our neighbors, especially those who are marginalized. In light of Odozor's developments, again I wonder: is this a dangerous ethic, this ethic in which we follow Christ? I have suggested above that recalling our misdeeds and seeking reconciliation are actions that might be particularly dangerous, especially in times and places when people are prone to conveniently forget their pasts. But I believe, as I suggested earlier, that we are indeed in such a moment today.

III. *Anamnetic Ethics in US Catholic Moral Theology*

Having discussed Fr. Odozor's development of African anamnetic ethics, we can now reflect on whether and how anamnetic ethics helps with the impasse about Christian practices that I described above.

Before focusing on Odozor's account, however, we must first understand how the concept of *anamnesis* in the West links to the Eucharist as a sacramental practice. In liturgical theology, anamnesis typically refers to the way the Church remembers and memorializes "God's salvific deeds in history (especially in Jesus)."[42] This happens in such parts of the Eucharistic rite as the recounting of the Last Supper but it also extends far beyond the simple components of prayers and gestures. Jesus, made known to us now in the Eucharist is anamnesis, a way of recalling Jesus in the past, but also in the present and the future. In the Mystery of Faith spoken in each mass, we recognize that past, present, and future moment of anamnesis, all at once: "We proclaim your death, O Lord, and profess your resurrection, until you come again." Jesus died and rose again, but in the resurrection is present now, and will be present in the future as well. In the broader understanding of *anamnesis*, remembering Jesus Christ's action for us in the past requires also knowing and receiving Jesus Christ in the present, which then also means that we are looking to the fulfillment of Jesus Christ in the *parousia*. What we live in the Eucharist (and in other sacraments) is in a sense Christian life as caught up in Christ, who is the Lord of time. The concluding prayer that sends Catholics out from Mass links our praise of Christ in the Eucharist to our daily (moral) life, for example:

"Go in peace to love and serve the Lord." The Eucharist is therefore intimately connected to Christian ethics, as Christian ethics is both about living a life in Christ and making a response to Christ. Our liturgy enables and requires both of these: that we live in Jesus Christ, and that we respond to Jesus Christ who has given himself to us in the Body and Blood. Receiving the Eucharist enables that which we remember, receive, which we are, and which we become.

Anamnesis: Truly Moral?

The theology of anamnesis as described above demonstrates how remembering Christ in the Eucharist connects us to moral life. However, anamnesis as I have laid it out here is open to vocal and difficult critiques, including the charge of sacramental optimism that I mentioned above. The concern is actually long-standing. Saint Augustine himself says: "To bless God in word and curse Him in deed is by no means to bless Him in the churches."[43]

More recently, Xavier Montecel's presentation at the 2023 meeting of the Catholic Theological Society of America: "Liturgical Vice: Unfreedom and Injustice in Christian Worship,"[44] makes a case that there are some moments when liturgy not only doesn't shape us in Christoform ways, but in fact shapes us in very evil ways. Katie Grimes' book *Christ Divided: Anti-Blackness as Corporate Vice* shows Montecel's concern in more specific ways. She argues that while it may be the case that Catholics say the Eucharist is a sacrament of unity in Christ, she worries that human practice of the liturgy has in fact "allowed Whites to be bound too tightly together in ways that have strengthened a segregated White Christian body."[45] For Grimes, because the Church is not closed off from the world, the habituation of white supremacy and antiblackness can mean that the poorly-habituated "corporate body will assimilate the cultic meal to itself at least as much as it is assimilated by it."[46] Grimes argues that all too often racism is not only not questioned in the Eucharist, but is ritually enacted in the Eucharist. Grimes therefore argues that theologians like William Cavanaugh and Stanley Hauerwas are overly optimistic because they both overplay the extent to which the Eucharist actually helps us resist evil; she proposes instead what she names a "sacramental realism."

Liturgical theologian Tony Alonso argues similarly that the problem with "sacramental optimism" in Hauerwas and Cavanaugh is "not that they completely fail to acknowledge a lack of correspondence between their eucharistic ideals and Christian witness in the world but that when they do acknowledge that lack, it merely serves as evidence that the Eucharist has been corrupted by forces like secularism, individualism, or consumerism; or as evidence of a lack of sincerity or conviction among its participants; or that the liturgy is not being celebrated as it ought to be."[47] But Alonso's point is that when we put all the blame on external forces, we fail to see the sinfulness that we ourselves bring out in and through the sacraments. Oras liturgical theologian Edward Phillips puts it, "How do we identify what is normative for Christian ethics in worship if the actual worship is not always consistent with Christian ethics?"[48]

These critiques are important because they articulate concern with the way US Catholics perpetuated sins of slavery and racism even as they have celebrated the sacrament of unity. While I think Grimes and Alonso overlook key aspects of both Hauerwas' and Cavanaugh's arguments and are overly selective about what they choose to emphasize about Hauwerwas and Cavanaugh, the point still remains: what do we do when we bless God in our worship, yet "curse Him in deed"?

In the remainder of this essay, I reflect on this question by bringing it together with Odozor's three points about anamnetic ethics.

Christian Practice Must Involve Inclusive and Christological Anamnesis

Fr. Odozor's critique of Bujo was that the latter was not inclusive enough, precisely because he was not Christological enough. The ancestors that we name as examples for living Christian faith cannot be restricted to African ancestors, for in Christ we must find that we have many more examples in faith. Surely a similar critique also falls on those who have emphasized white skin and commit other acts that exclude those who should be part of the Body of Christ.

The Eucharistic liturgy enacts such inclusivity, even if those gathered for the prayers do not live in a way that demonstrates that inclusiveness. For example, there are multiple intercessory prayers in the

Eucharistic liturgy that ask for prayers from the whole of the Christian community, both those ancestors from the past as well as those in the present. In the intercessions, we remember the Church, the Pope, the local bishop, and "all your clergy," "brothers and sisters who have fallen asleep" and indeed "us all [...] that with the Blessed Virgin Mary, Mother of God, with the Apostles, and all the Saints who have pleased you throughout the ages, we may merit to be co-heirs to eternal life." The whole church in time and space is drawn together, because of Christ.

Christ's inclusivity as proclaimed in prayer may fail to be present, however. In pointing this out, Grimes, Winner, Alonso, and others are entirely correct. What we pray may not match what we live. Odozor would, I think, agree with them. Without Christ at the center, the benefit of African exemplars may in fact remove us from the faith. Even all witnesses from the whole cosmic Church cannot not unite us, unless we come together in Christ.

Christian Practice Must Involve Attention to Sin, Redemption, and Reconciliation

Thus far, I think that Odozor might be in agreement with those who critique sacramental optimism. But it is his second admonition, his concern to recognize sinfulness, where Odozor's discussion of anamnetic ethics offers the kind of corrective needed. Memory requires remembering what we would rather forget. Part of Odozor's concern with Bujo's version is exactly that communities become too insular and hence replicate sinful practices that serve to reinforce insularity, all in the name of community and unity. Odozor gives the example of twin hunters who kill twin babies, which showcases one way in which a community's insularity perpetuates wrongs.[49] Or as another instance, he mentions the complicity of insular African communities that perpetrated slave trade against other Africans.

So here too, Grimes' accounts of slavery and Catholic complicities helps us to remember those who have been forgotten, who have suffered at the hands of members of their own communities. At the same time, among those who critique sacramental optimism there does not seem to be recognition of the ways remembering sin mitigates the optimism. On this point, Odozor would find himself in agreement with Hauerwas and

Cavanaugh. For example, Cavanaugh is not, in fact, wholly optimistic about Eucharistic and other Christian practice as somehow solving the political problems in Chile or bringing about some unfettered glorious future. Cavanaugh knows that many people in the Church failed, utterly, to critique torture and abuse of fellow Christians at the hands of the state. Many in the Church themselves instigated such abuses, such that Cavanaugh observes that the Church had simply relegated itself to a supposed "spiritual realm" removed from the physical realm of the Chilean government. The supposed distinction between spiritual and physical realms "can function to augment the power of the state by eliminating the interference of the church."[50] That is because the social imaginary often sees the spiritual as being private and interior, while the physical is public and external. The Church loses power to form people, since what is interior and spiritual ends up ultimately seeming to be the purview only of the individual, and the state ends up with control over the physical.

Cavanaugh sees, in some communities, that the Eucharist became visible and so the Church became visible. He writes, "Care must be taken not to reduce the Eucharist to a celebration of some politics derived from worldly sources. But if the Body of Christ is not to be [...] hovering above the real suffering and bodily lives of his members, then we can, I think, make bold to allow Christ to order our in the here and the now."[51] Part of the way the Church became visible in Pinochet's Chile was through practices of confessing sin and seeking specific ways to redress those sins.[52] Cavanaugh's vision is no false or quick and easy optimism; rather it requires real work, real attention to, and movement in, relationships, real mercy, and—if no reconciliation occurs—real judgement.

As we have already seen in his discussion of sin, Odozor makes a point of critiquing the ways Western individualism as well as communities can negatively form people in faith. We can be shaped in ways that make it seem like the "destructive" practice is the one that seems best to do. Odozor is aware that such communities actively work against a Christologically-focused life and indeed can cause us to fail to see our own sins as well as others. This point once again underscores the importance of his Christological emphasis that necessarily requires greater inclusivity.

Odozor's concern for speaking truth about sinfulness, and seeking forgiveness and reconciliation, also make it apparent how important it is that there are multiple—even constant—opportunities for people to be brought face-to-face with themselves and their own sins. Because we live in a world where we are always in danger of seeing ourselves wrongly—and in a US context particularly because our individual desires are privileged against others'—the place of mercy and forgiveness in the Eucharistic prayer is especially apt. Forgiveness and mercy are threaded through the entirety of the prayer, from the Kyrie Eleison, to the Our Father and the Agnus Dei, the "Lord, I am not worthy to receive you under my roof," and more. Furthermore, just as anamnetic communities need to seek reconciliation with each other, so we in the liturgy seek reconciliation in saying the Our Father and in the sign of peace, among other moments. Finally, we receive God's mercy in the Eucharist, especially as evidenced in the Body and Blood, and we make a response to the gift of God. At least, we are directed to do so in words and actions. There is always a chance—more than a chance—we shall miss the point, as well as God and each other. So, each week, and even daily, there is opportunity in the Mass (and in other practices) to come face-to-face with our failings.

I argue that this is not an overly optimistic view of the Eucharist nor of confessing sin and seeking forgiveness. Rather it is a starkly realistic view, one that understands human beings as both created in God's image and yet living in this fallen world as people who fail to see the glory of God's kingdom. The constancy of Christian practices like the Eucharist allows for that realistic vision to be put before us, as often as possible, so that we might remember, as often as possible.

Christian Practice Must Involve Discipleship

Fr. Odozor's third point is that anamnetic ethics involves discipleship. We who encounter God's love and mercy respond in love and mercy to others. That means, as. Odozor reminds us, we hold before us the people who are in danger of being forgotten, especially in the US, with its failure to attend to the disabled, the elderly, the unborn, the poor and marginalized, and all those who are victims of injustices.

The ones who might be forgotten become remembered in our

anamnesis. US Catholics can certainly stand to remember many people who are forgotten. The Jesuit priest Bruce Morrill reminds us, in his book *Anamnesis as Dangerous Memory*, that Western Christians need to be caught up in the "dangerous memory" of Christ, because only Jesus can run counter to the ways European and American societies are caught in instrumentalizing human beings and over-privileging market forces, efficiency, and technology use. By remembering Jesus, our Paschal sacrifice, in the Gospels and in the Eucharist, we can also come to remember "all victims of humanity's inhumanity."[53] So he argues that "Christian memory, then, functions not only for the purpose of correcting believers in their lapses in remembering the content of the faith, but also as the means whereby communities and individuals receive further riches of the mystery of redemption."[54]

The difficulty with an underdeveloped understanding of anamnesis for Christians is that Jesus Christ *is* the Eucharist, fully man and fully divine. The Eucharist is source and summit of our faith, it is a foretaste of God's kingdom even as, here and now, that banquet may be very poorly realized. We shall be a collection of bodies not as attentive or praiseworthy as we ought to be, but more than that, we are people who fail to do what God in Jesus Christ requests us to do and be. Thus Lauren Winner observes, "Sacramental practice is tensive. A constitutive part of practicing Eucharist—and of an account of that practice—is the tension between acknowledging that, on one hand, the Eucharist has, and inevitably sometimes will go, wrong, and on the other hand, articulating the reason to go on doing it."[55]

Here is when the anamnesis of the Eucharistic liturgy becomes ironic, for in fact we humans fail to remember properly what it is that God does for us in the Eucharist, and therefore we fail to make a proper response. Winner wonders,

> Perhaps another characteristic deformation of the Eucharist is human participants' failure to remember that we are not the Eucharist's agents. At the altar, Christians are being inscribed into the agency of God. We think we are celebrating the Eucharist in memory of—in memory of Jesus' death, resurrection, and ascension; in memory of the Last Supper. But

> maybe it is fundamentally not we but God who is remembering.[56]

If we focus too much on ourselves and our response to God's gift of Eucharist, we, in our sinfulness and forgetfulness, run the risk of forgetting God and emphasizing the benefits *we* might gain. Rather, the point and purpose are Christ and the gift that *God* has given to us.

Finally, what the Eucharist asks us to do, even in poor ways, is to remember God's love and mercy, and to fall on God's mercy. If we aim in moral life to be people who remember and we seek always to remember, in the broad way that Odozor suggests, we will at the least be holding forth Christ and proclaiming the Gospel. Remembering becomes dangerous work, not necessarily because we have set off a revolution toward direct social justice in the ways that Benjamin or Morrill suggest. Rather, the act of remembering Christ itself shall run counter to much in our culture. It is dangerous memory because it reminds us humans of who we are, which is to say, *not* God, *not* perfect, *not* removed from sin, *not* existing in some kind of imagined okay-ness or sinlessness, or so forth.

Yet in this time and place, I do not know any other way to be than to be people who remember. That is the Gospel message and God's promise, and I thank Fr. Odozor for the opportunity to reflect on anamnetic ethics.

Chapter 6
Abominations and Absolute Prohibitions: Killing the Innocent According to Anscombe and Odozor[1]

John Berkman

> "Pharaoh summoned Moses and Aaron and said, 'Go sacrifice to your God within the land.' But Moses replied, 'It is not right to do so, for what we sacrifice to the LORD, our God, is an abomination to the Egyptians. If we sacrifice what is an abomination to the Egyptians before their very eyes, will they not stone us?'" (Exodus 8:24–28)

> "There is no story that is not true. The world has no end, and what is good among one people is an abomination with others." Uchendu in *Things Fall Apart*[2]

Introduction

In his book *Morality Truly African, Truly Christian* (henceforth MTATC), Paulinus Odozor sketches a connection between absolute prohibitions[3] and abominations. The former is a key but contested concept within Catholic moral theology. The latter is, according to Odozor, a key but also contested concept in African traditional religion.[4]

In this essay I analyze how Odozor brings these two concepts into conversation, and present my understanding of their relationship. Towards these ends, I draw on an authoritative source for each of these two concepts. For an understanding of absolute prohibitions, I turn to the work British philosopher Elizabeth Anscombe.[5] For an understanding of abomination, I draw on the work of Nigerian novelist Chinua Achebe. Our key sources date from the year 1958, that being the year Anscombe published her article 'Modern Moral Philosophy,' and Achebe published his novel *Things Fall Apart.*

2. Elizabeth Anscombe and Absolute Prohibitions

Elizabeth Anscombe was one of the most important of 20th century philosophers, who made seminal contributions to action theory and moral philosophy. While Odozor's discussion of natural law and absolute prohibitions draws explicitly on the work of Joseph Boyle, Boyle was himself heavily influenced by Anscombe, considering her an intellectual mentor and guide.

Odozor begins his chapter on moral reasoning in *MTATC* by discussing a critique of the legitimacy of absolute prohibitions (and natural law more generally) by the moral theologian Bénézet Bujo, who characterizes natural law (and absolute prohibitions) as "not being open to intercultural dialogue." Odozor challenges Bujo's characterization of natural law, arguing that while there have been many problematic and ideological appeals to the natural law in the Church's history, African Christian ethics can and should engage in a careful and nuanced appropriation of the notion of natural law "as guide and conversation partner in the arduous task of the search for moral truth."[6]

Contrary to Bujo and following Odozor, I argue that the existence of absolute prohibitions is essential both for an adequate Catholic morality and for productive intercultural dialogue. According to Anscombe, if there are no absolute prohibitions (and an adequate understanding of the principle of double effect for making the necessary judgments about these prohibitions) "anything can be—and is wont to be—justified, and the Christian teaching that in no circumstances may one commit murder, adultery, apostasy (to give a few examples) goes by the board."[7] If there are no absolute prohibitions, then everything is open to negotiation. In a sinful world, this more often than not results in the wealthy and powerful manipulating and/or orchestrating matters to get what they want.

Anscombe notes that while absolute prohibitions by no means exhaust Christian ethics, they are absolutely indispensable, "and without them the Christian ethic goes to pieces."[8] What does Anscombe have in mind in terms of an absolute prohibition? Since both the natural law and a distinctively

Catholic morality have to be ordered to the common good of all persons, are any absolute prohibitions necessary? For Anscombe, the most fundamental presupposition of any society which upholds even a limited conception of justice is the absolute prohibition of murder, namely that it is always and everywhere wrong to intentionally kill innocent human persons.

While "Thou shall not kill" is a fundamental divine command, divine revelation is not required to recognise the fundamental wickedness of the killing of innocent persons.[9] To give only one obvious example, in the current war in Ukraine (this is written in 2023), peoples of any nation and faith tradition recognise that the intentional targeting and massacre of innocent civilians constitute war crimes, crimes against humanity. The injustice of killing innocent persons is a truth of natural law, a universal truth that all reasonable persons are capable of recognizing. While those who order the intentional targeting of civilians in a war may deny the wrongfulness of what they do, the same persons almost universally condemn similar attacks when they themselves or their loved one are the subject of such attacks.

Anyone who knows anything about World War II knows that it was the most murderous war in human history. Non-combatants ('innocents') were intentionally targeted in unspeakable numbers throughout that war. As a 20-year-old student in England at that start of World War II, Anscombe (along with her friend Norman Daniel) published a pamphlet arguing that the British government intended to target civilians during the war.[10] She further claimed that according to Catholic just war principles, any Catholic who found their argument that their government intended to target non-combatants claims of their pamphlet persuasive could not, morally speaking, fight for Britain during the war. In retrospect, the young Anscombe's claims about what the British government intended to do in terms of targeting non-combatants was proven to be even more true than Anscombe likely could have imagined. This will not be a surprise to many who experienced British colonial rule in the first half of the 20th century.

In May of 1956, Anscombe opposed a proposal at Oxford university to grant an honorary degree to Harry Truman, at the time a former President of the United States. Anscombe objected to this honour because she considered Truman a mass murderer of innocent civilians.[11] In ordering the atomic bombings of Hiroshima and Nagasaki, Truman rejected the fundamental moral tenet of the natural law, namely that justice requires that one never intend to kill innocent persons.[12]

While Anscombe understood the prohibition against killing the innocent to be a natural law moral truth, it was also a divine command clear to all Christians. While it would have been bad enough for an irreligious person—a Stalin, a Hitler, or a Genghis Khan—to have massacred countless innocent civilians, for Anscombe the fact that Truman claimed to be a Bible-believing Baptist made it all the more morally horrendous.

Anscombe's protest was overwhelmingly rejected, but Anscombe did not give up. She continued her protest in a series of articles and letters in newspapers, in a talk on BBC radio, in her 1957 book *Intention*, and it culminated a year later in Anscombe's writing what would become arguably the most famous article in 20th-century moral philosophy, entitled "Modern Moral Philosophy." This article was the beginning of the recovery of Aristotelian approaches to the moral life (sometimes inaccurately called "virtue ethics") and it profoundly influenced many philosophers who would think about the morality of killing the innocent, such as Philippa Foot, Thomas Nagel, Michael Walzer, and Alasdair MacIntyre.

In "Modern Moral Philosophy," Anscombe argued that if a society does not maintain a prohibition on certain kinds of heinous actions, its ethic and rule of law will crumble. Anscombe gives the example of a judicially sanctioned execution of an innocent person for ulterior ends.[13] According to Anscombe, if a society could justify the judicially-sanctioned killing of an innocent person, then it could justify any evil action. As she noted, once the notion of any absolute prohibitions is dispensed with, the powerful will always find ways to change their moral principles and/or to change the laws to fit what they want to do.

In discussing Oxford University giving Truman an honorary degree, Anscombe concludes her pamphlet trying to convince her colleagues not to attend the ceremony honouring Truman. She writes "It is possible still to withdraw from this shameful business in some slight degree; it is possible not to go to Encaenia [...] I, indeed, should fear to go, in case God's patience suddenly ends."[14] While some might see this as a rhetorical flourish, this is only one of numerous examples where Anscombe make reference to the possibility of divine judgment on those who participate in wrongful actions.[15]

Having briefly outlined an example of an absolute prohibition, knowable both by the natural law and by revelation, I will now focus on untangling the concept of an abomination.

3. Odozor on Abomination

In his chapter on moral reasoning, Odozor devotes a short section to the notion of "abomination," indicating briefly how it functions in what he calls African traditional religion. An abomination is not only a sin, it is a grave sin, and moreover, it is a *particular kind* of grave sin. In his crisp analysis, Odozor presents three key characteristics of an abomination.

The first characteristic of an abomination is that it is "absolutely non-negotiable."[16] By 'non-negotiable' Odozor has two things in mind: *first*, an abomination is non-negotiable because "to attempt such an act would incur the wrath not only of human beings but that of the gods as well";[17] and *second*, an abomination is non-negotiable because functions in a way *analogous* to what the Catholic moral tradition refers to as an absolute prohibition.

The second characteristic of an abomination is that when it becomes publicly known, it *contaminates* relationships more broadly in that community. These contaminated relationships can only be purified through a public process of atonement and reconciliation.[18]

The third and final characteristic of an abomination is that it is difficult to clearly account for the vehemence with which an abomination is seen as wrong in African culture. Odozor says that it is "part of a stock of moral insights which go into making [Africans] the type of moral agents they have become. [...] [And that Africans] 'see' with more than just one 'eye'—including their faith, their emotions, and their experience as human beings."[19]

4. Abomination in Achebe's *Things Fall Apart*

Having outlined Odozor's characterization of an abomination as a part of African traditional relogion generally speaking. I now illustrate the meaning and function of this notion in a specific context. To do so, I turn to Chinua Achebe's novel *Things Fall Apart*—a novel which Odozor mines brilliantly— because "abomination" is so often on the lips of Africans in that novel. Indeed its importance cannot be overstated, functioning as it does to connote the strongest form of what I shall call a '*religio-moral*' condemnation.[20]

Odozor's use of Achebe is not accidental. For Achebe, like Odozor, is a member of the Igbo people of Nigeria, and the characters in Achebe's novels are members of the Igbo people. More importantly, Achebe is universally recognized as a truly pioneering novelist. As Chimamanda Adichie puts it, "*Things Fall Apart* was pioneering not in its subject [i.e. Africa], but in its African point of view."[21] Hence, Achebe's novels are an authentic and reliable source for understanding the notion of 'abomination' in African traditional religion, or at least in the traditional religion of the Igbo people of Nigeria.

In *Things Fall Apart*, the term 'abomination' (*aru*) has both noun and adjective forms. Whereas an individual or group may act abominably, individuals or groups that perform such proscribed acts become abominations.

As noted earlier, abominable acts are a small sub-class of wrong acts. On the one hand, abominable acts are those that are considered particularly detestable, odious, or loathsome. That is, they are the kind of actions that arouse particularly strong subjective emotions. On the other hand, they are perceived objectively as violations of the commands of, or obligations to, one or more of the gods.

In Achebe's novel, there is another aspect of abomination not highlighted by Odozor. It is that an individual or group can be or become an abomination *without performing any action whatsoever*. For example, one may be or become an abomination through having a certain characteristic, such as by being 'unclean', either ritually or through contracting a particular kind of illness. To take another example from *Things Fall Apart*, a person may be or become an abomination simply by one or more of the gods deeming one so. In this situation, an abominable person or group is then viewed as polluting or infecting the community. As such, an abominable person (or persons) becomes a danger to the community, and the community must take some form of action to protect itself from the threat posed by the abominable person(s).

Ultimately, abominable acts and/or abominable persons are a religious affront to the community, and as such they constitute a bad omen. Abominable actions anger the gods, who when affronted will bring calamity or destruction either on the particular individual, or on that individual and their closest kin, or in some cases on the whole society.

5. Christianity as an Abomination

Having presented the nature of an abomination in Achebe's novel, I now turn to the paradigm example of abominable actions and abominable people in *Things Fall Apart.* In the novel, the paradigm examples of abominations are both individual Christians, and Christians as a group. But before I examine how and why Christians are the paradigm examples of abominations in *Things Fall Apart*, something else needs to be said about the novel, something not highlighted by Odozor.

Things Fall Apart is fundamentally a story of the initial Christian evangelization of the Igbo people of Nigeria. Historically, this evangelization by Anglican missionaries began at the end of the 19th century.[22] Since this is a story of Christian evangelization of the Igbo people primarily from the perspective of one Igbo man, a man who is not at all sympathetic to 'the white man's religion,' it constitutes an excellent source for understanding the view of a practitioner of a particular African traditional religion when confronted by Christianity. It is also a good place to begin to understand how a society that worships many gods and ancestors understands abomination.

In the novel, the individual who uses the term 'abomination' most frequently is Okonkwo, the novel's protagonist, a leading warrior and oft-appointed representative for his village in its dealings with outsiders. Okonkwo is strong, hardworking, and decisive, a fiery warrior who praises violence as a sign of manliness. He is an Igbo with a healthy dose of *machismo*. Okonkwo is tightly bound to an honour-based culture. The particular honour-based culture in which Okonkwo lives is one in which a) social and gender roles are rigid, b) a man is expected to rise to a place of honour in that society, and c) the process and requirements for rising to the highest places of honour in Igbo society are clearly delineated. Okonkwo is also proud, rigid, and domineering over his family and in most village relationships. His quick and violent temper is his achilles heel, repeatedly getting him into trouble, and at times leading him to violate the very social norms he is otherwise so rigid in defending.[23]

While Okonkwo's use of 'abomination' (and its use more generally in the novel) is diverse, the terms employment falls into one of *three* general categories. First, there are *cultic or ritual* abominations, those whom for generally unknown reasons the gods deem as outcasts.[24] Second, there are social abominations, a label given those individuals who fail to conform to the social roles expected of them.[25] Third, there are religio-moral abominations, which function to undermine the whole way of life of the clan.

When referring to both individual Christians and the Christian Church as abominations, Okonkwo generally has in mind religio-moral abominations. Thus, I will not comment further on the first two types of abominations, and focus on the third, which I understand to be the most serious or worst abominations.

A good example of a religio-moral abomination in the novel is a situation where a Christian does something so inconceivable to the clan's way of thinking, that it has never occurred to the clan to decree a penalty for its violation. Achebe describes the situation as follows:

> [An *osu* who had become a Christian] brought the church into serious conflict with the clan a year later by killing the sacred python, the emanation of the god of water.[26]
>
> The sacred python was the most revered animal in Mbanta and all the surrounding clans [...]. If a clansman killed a royal python accidentally, he made sacrifices of atonement and performed an expensive burial ceremony such as was done for a great man. No punishment was prescribed for a man who killed the python knowingly. Nobody thought that such a thing could ever happen. [...] The rulers and elders of Mbanta assembled to decide on their action. [...] Okonkwo, who had begun to play a part in the affairs of his motherland, said that until the abominable gang was chased out of the village with whips there would be no peace. (111–112)

Faced with this abomination, the leaders of Mbanta are divided as to whether the appropriate response is to "fight for our gods," or to allow the gods to take their own revenge. In the end the decision is to ostracize the Christians in Mbanta, so that "we would then not be held accountable for their abominations" (112).

The attack by a Christian on the python is an example of the rejection of the clan's gods. According to how Okonkwo sees things, one has an obligation to reverence both the gods and one's ancestors, offering sacrifices and so forth, for in doing so Okonkwo keeps one's ancestors alive. What Okonkwo fears most is that his descendants will convert to Christianity. For if his descendants convert, they will no longer reverence and offer sacrifices to him and their other ancestors. Okonkwo and the other ancestors will be abandoned and forgotten. For Okonkwo, to be forgotten in this way constitutes the complete annihilation of both him as an individual and his culture more generally.

Hence, it is not surprising that Okonkwo erupts into fury when he finds out that his oldest son Nwoye is associating with the Christians. Okonkwo attacks Nwoye violently, strangling him. Nwoye survives only because Okonkwo's uncle aggressively intervenes. After this attack, Nwoye leaves home permanently, throwing in his lot with the Christians, who send him to receive an education in a Christian school. Achebe describes Okonkwo's reflection after Nwoye leaves:

> Now that he had time to think about it, his son's crime stood out in its stark enormity. To abandon the gods of one's father [...] was the very depth of abomination. Suppose when he died all his male children decided to follow Nwoye's steps and abandon their ancestors? Okonkwo felt a cold shudder run through him at the terrible prospect, like the prospect of annihilation. He saw himself and his fathers crowding round their ancestral shrine waiting in vain for worship and sacrifice and finding nothing but ashes of bygone days, and his children the while praying to the white man's god. (*Things Fall Apart*, 108)

Okonkwo is not the only leader of Mbanta who foresees the danger posed by the abominable Christians. At a banquet given by Okonkwo, one of the elders of Mbanta says much the same thing:

> I fear for you young people because you do not understand how strong is the bond of kinship. You do not know what it is to speak with one voice. And what is the result? An abominable religion has settled among you. A *man can now leave his father and his brothers*. He can *curse the gods of his fathers and his ancestors*, like a hunter's dog that suddenly goes mad and turns on his master. I fear for you; I fear for the clan. (117)

Having given a brief description of how and why for the clan leaders the Christians constitute an abomination, I now turn to an analogous characterization from the ancient world in which we see Judaism similarly characterized as an abomination.

6. Judaism as an Abomination

In this section, I characterize African traditional religion as portrayed in *Things Fall Apart* as polytheistic.[27] In doing so I am aware that I diverge from what is apparently the dominant characterization of African traditional religion.[28] As I understand it from Odozor's work, the currently dominant view is that behind the apparent polytheism of African Traditional Religion there is in fact a belief in monotheism. In this view, the various gods are understood to be emissaries of the one true God.

In this essay I focus *only* on the transcendent in *Things Fall Apart*. In that novel the transcendent is only represented by the oracles and the various gods. I find no evidence of a latent 'monotheism' lurking behind a polytheistic 'front.' Therefore, I am only asserting that there is at least one African traditional religion that is polytheistic, that being the gods as portrayed in *Things Fall Apart*.

Let me lay out the argument upfront. As I see it, abomination takes on a fundamentally different character in a polytheistic society (a society which worships many gods and/or ancestors) from the character of an abomination in a monotheistic society (i.e. how an abomination is characterized in the Old Testament). The argument is this: in a polytheistic society, an abomination is first and foremost a rejection of the gods and/or ancestors. In a monotheistic society, abominations are first and foremost idolatries, the worshipping of false gods, idols, and/or man-made objects.[29]

I now proceed to my analogous characterization from the ancient world, in which another polytheistic religion characterizes Judaism as an abomination. In an article written in the 1980s, Anscombe recounts how the Roman historian Tacitus describes the Jews[30]:

> Most authors agree that when there was a disfiguring disease in Egypt, King Bocchoris consulted the oracle of Jupiter Ammon to find a remedy and was told to cleanse his kingdom and expel *that race of men as hateful to the gods*. The people were collected and dumped in the desert; they were sunk in weeping, but one, Moses, advised them to expect no help from gods or men[31], as they were deserted by both [...] gave them *religious rites which were new and contrary to the rest of mankind.*[32] *Everything sacred to us is profane to them* [...]. They kill the ram, as if to insult Jupiter Ammon. They also sacrifice the ox, because the Egyptians worship Apis. [...]
>
> They instituted circumcision of the genitals so as to be recognised by their difference.[33] *Their converts do it too, and the first thing they learn is to despise the gods, to shuck off their fatherland, to count parents, children and brethren cheap.*
>
> The Egyptians venerate several animals [...] the *Jews by their mind alone think of only one divinity* [...]. Therefore no images are set up in their cities, let alone in their temples."[34]

The question now is, what similarities can be seen between Tacitus' criticisms of Jews, and Okonkwo's criticisms of Christians? What are the shared characteristics of Christians and Jews that make them abominations in these two particular contexts?

1. They are 'hateful' to the gods, because the first things converts are taught is to "despise the gods," and emphasize there is only one God.

2. They reject or abandon their ancestors, family, and kinsmen.
3. They take on contrarian practices—e.g. sacrificing the animals holy to the polytheists.
4. They emphasize their visible differences.

In summary, monotheists and polytheists have contrasting views of what constitutes an abomination.

In her article discussing polytheism in the ancient world, Anscombe claims that compared to monotheism, polytheists are relatively uninterested in the particularities of their beliefs. Rather, what is of great importance are their religious practices, their customs and rituals, their sacrifices, etc. In contrast, Jews and Christian in the ancient world are often referred to as being 'credulous', in that they take the specifics of their beliefs about God very seriously. In other words, it is important that their beliefs about God be in fact true, since they understand themselves to worship *the* true God. Anscombe further argues that polytheism generally does not have a problem with other societies having different or other gods. In this sense polytheism is assimilative, in being able to respect if not incorporate the gods of other polytheists. In the ancient world, Jews and Christians were often referred to as atheists, because they were thought to be rejecting—and rejecting vehemently—all the gods of the polytheists.

7. The Appeal of Christianity for the Igbo People

A criticism that Odozor makes of African traditional religion is that its sphere of moral concern is generally limited to one's particular clan or people.[35] While I do not wish to challenge the veracity of this claim, I believe there is a different reason why, in *Things Fall Apart*, Christianity has appeal to some of the clan. My argument is that the towns of Umuofia and Mbanta (the two towns in which Okonkwo lives in *Things Fall Apart)* fail at the level at which they—as practitioners of a communally oriented African traditional religion—are supposed to be strongest. What do I mean by this claim? As we learn in *Things Fall Apart*, long before the arrival of Christian missionaries, these towns are internally rent with divisions.

In Achebe's narrative, we periodically get glimpses of many townspeople who are in various ways marginalized, excluded, or outcast, many of whom are considered abominations through no actions of their own. We read of Okonkwo's father who, afflicted with a kind of swelling that the gods identify as an abomination, is exiled to die alone in the Evil Forest.[36] Another abomination are babies born in those towns who happen to be twins, who are similarly abandoned in the Evil Forest. Furthermore, a woman who repeatedly had twins would herself be deemed deeply suspect among the clan. We read at times about the *efulufu*, those men who are considered worthless. There are also the *osu*, the outcasts, who are members of inter-generational families dedicated to the gods. They too are excluded from most of the ordinary privileges of members of the clan. At times the *osu* could be sold into slavery by a clan, or also serve as human sacrifices when demanded by the gods in order the town to avoid greater evils. If African traditional religion is supposed to be such a communitarian faith, why are so many of the community marginalized or excluded?

Christianity Creating the Possibility of Unity: Salvation for the Marginalized

When the Christian missionaries arrive in the towns, we learn that it is precisely the lowest people in the town—such as the *osu* and the *efulefu*—who comprise most if not all of the initial converts to Christianity. For those who have been marginalized or excluded by the clan, the Christian message will obviously have greater appeal. For the fate of most of the excluded of the clan is a result of the decrees of the gods, mediated through numerous oracles. The Christian missionaries emphasize that their God is the true God, and that this God loves and accepts all people who seek him.

The Christian message offers a radically different conception of God to that experienced by members of the clan. As Odozor points out, in African traditional religions generally, and certainly in these villages, the fundamental attitude of clan members to the gods is unrelenting fear. If the demands of the gods are not met, terrible things will happen to the villagers. It seems to me that various demands by the gods are the typical source of the exclusion of these marginalised members of the clan.

In contrast, according to the Christian missionaries, none risk exclusion apart from their own wicked actions or their abandoning this God. For persons in the villages who are considered abominations, once they become Christians they no longer consider themselves unclean, they are no consider themselves unworthy of God, they no longer consider themselves inferior to the rest of their village.

Ultimately, for these marginalized villagers, Christianity takes away their status as abominations. From the perspective of their new Christian faith, what was previously an abomination, is no longer an abomination. They have been given a new account of themselves and as such are becoming a new people. As Uchendu puts it, "What is good among one people is an abomination with others."

However, if the above characterization of polytheism as being more concerned with practices than with beliefs is correct, then it follows that the preaching of the missionaries will not initially constitute a significant challenge to the townspeople. Rather, as we see, what both impresses and scandalizes the townspeople of Umuofia and Mbanta are the diverging practices of the Christian missionaries.

Such practices as building a Church in the Evil Forest, and going further into the Forest to rescue the babies that are abominations, and accepting the *osu* as full participants in their Church—they meet with a combination of incredulity and puzzlement.[37] Expecting the Christians to be summarily killed by the spirits of the Evil Forest, the villagers find it challenging to explain how it is these interlopers are still alive, having violated particular taboos.[38]

But as long as this goes on in outside of the places where the townspeople live and function, this is understood by the townspeople as harmless.[39] As Achebe puts it, "The white, man had indeed brought a lunatic religion, but [...] there was a growing feeling that there might be something in it after all [...]. This growing feeling was due to Mr. Brown, the white missionary, who was very firm in restraining his flock from provoking the wrath of the clan" (126).

Here we see the Christians as abomination being the source of salvation. Were the Christians *actually* an abomination?

8. How Odozor Morally Evaluates Killing the Innocent

> "it is *aru* to spill a kinsman's blood knowingly or unknowingly." (Odozor, 263)

Early on in the novel, we see that one of the deepest customs of the clan is the abomination of killing another member of the clan. If one kills another deliberately, one must be killed. If one kills another clan member inadvertently, the one who kills must go into exile for seven years to avoid being put to death by the clan.

In this section, I will bring together the earlier discussions of a) absolute prohibitions and of b) the meaning of abomination by examining two examples Odozor analyzes of killing in *Things Fall Apart*.

The first example is a killing understood by the Umuofians to be a religious sacrifice. The background of this example pertains to keeping good relationships between two different clans. Members of the clan of Mbaino had murdered a daughter of Umuofia. This led the men of Umuofia to meet and decide that either Mbaino would pay a ransom to expiate this murder, or that Umuofia would go to war against Mbaino. Since Umuofia was a strong and feared tribe, there was little doubt that Mbaino would pay the ransom, whatever ransom Umuofia might demand. The ransom demanded by Umuofia was twofold: a young women, who would be given to the man whose wife was murdered as a replacement wife; and a young man, who would belong to Umuofia as a whole, and whose fate would be determined by the gods of the Umuofians. As an expiation for a murder, the outlook for this young man was not encouraging.

Okonkwo was elected as Umuofia's emissary to the people of Mbaino. He thus went to Mbaino to present the Umuofians conditions for avoiding a war, namely the above-mentioned ransom. The people of Mbaino quickly assented to the ransom, and Okonkwo soon returned to Umuofia with the two young persons in tow. At that point the leaders of Umuofia delivered the young woman to the widower. They also instructed Okonkwo to take custody of the young man, whose name was Ikemefuna.

Okonkwo looked after Ikemefuna for three years, and Okonkwo came to love him as a son, and thought that Ikemefuna indeed had the admirable characteristics of a young man that Okonkwo wished his own son had.

After being in Okonkwo's care for three years, one day the Oracle of the Caves and Hills decrees that Ikemefuna should be sacrificed. At that point, one of the village elders goes to see Okonkwo. Soon after the oracle declares Ikemafuna's fate, a party of men is gathered to take Ikemafuna a long way from the village to perform this deed. When the time comes, one of the party suddenly stabs Ikemafuna with a machete. At that point Ikemefuna cries out to his father Okonkwo for help. In response, Okonkwo himself delivers the death blow to Ikemefuna. Upon returning to the village, Okonkwo does not eat for the next two days, and has trouble sleeping for three nights.[40]

The second example finds Okonkyo accidently (though arguably negligently) killing a member of his own tribe. The accidental killing occurs in the aftermath of the funeral of a tribe member, when in a celebratory moment, Okonkwo fires his gun into the air. When the bullet comes down, it kills the 16-year-old son of the deceased whose funeral has just concluded. In this case, because the killing is accidental, the dead teenager may only be avenged for up to a period of seven years. Therefore, if Okonkwo flees from the tribe for seven years, then he may safely return.

Odozor thinks that the sacrificial killing of Ikemefuna, or at least the killing of Ikemefuna by Okonkwo is wrong. He says the communal decision-making, the palaver, "shows us everything that is wrong with the process of palaver." He thinks that the rationale for the killing of Ikemefuna was an "eye for an eye" is wrong in this case, because Ikemefuna was in no way involved in the killing. This raises the underlying question of the ransom paid to avoid a war, and what would be the right way to resolve the situation?

An individual from one tribe killed a person from the other tribe. Rather than allowing the situation to become a feud where a sense of retribution leads to a large number of killings, the solution is that one person from the offending tribe will send to the aggrieved tribe an individual who is in some sense recompense for the killing.

Odozor says the killing is wrong because—from a natural law perspective—Ikemafuna is an innocent person. From the perspective of the Catholic moral tradition, Okonkwo's killing of Ikemafuna can be known to be wrong both from the natural law and from divine revelation.

However, from Okonkwo's perspective, he was obeying what he understood to be the command of one of the gods. According to the oracle, it was necessary that Ikemefuna be sacrificed, presumably as an expiation for the murder of one of the daughters of the Umuofian clan. In one sense, the sacrifice of Ikemefuna was simply the necessary follow-through of an earlier determined ransom for the daughter of Umuofia who had been murdered. We might say that the primary injustice had been done then. Why had Umuofia not demanded that the murderers be held accountable? Why instead had two innocent young persons been demanded by Umuofia. The novel does not tell us?[41]

On the other hand, we are also told in *Things Fall Apart* that the goddess who is primarily responsible for the moral conduct of the Umuofians had not sanctioned the killing of Ikemefuna. Here, we find a quandary for the polytheist. What is one to do when one of the gods requires a particular sacrifice, but another more important god, by that gods silence, seems to deny its legitimacy? Who of the gods is the polytheist to obey? At least at the theoretical level, this quandary is one that is either resolved or resolvable more easily in a monotheistic tradition, especially when the religious and moral expectations of God have been provided in revelation.

Thus, I would argue, Okonkwo's dilemma—how he might know clearly what he should do—can only be resolved with a different understanding of the divine.

Odozor has noted that the tendency of African traditional religion to give full humanity only to one's own kinsmen (e.g. the example from the novel of robbing people from other clans) shows that to the extent this perspective shows that Africa needs a more adequate basis for its anthropology, that it needs a theological anthropology that gives full dignity and humanity to all human beings. From this example, it would seem that to give full dignity and humanity to all human beings also requires a more adequate theology, namely one that recognizes that there is one true God and that God commands us *never* to kill the innocent.

9. Conclusion

So, is the killing of Ikemafuna an abomination? According to Okonkwo's view of god and the world, it is not an abomination. On the contrary, it is a requirement of the gods, and necessary if one does not want the gods to bring death and destruction to one's family and/or one's kinspeople.

On the other hand, we might look to the perspective of Nwoye, Okonkwo's son. In the novel, according to Nwoye's emerging moral sensibility, the killing of Ikemefuna, who was not only a friend but effectively a dear elder brother, struck him as something akin to an abomination, even if that time he does not have the language to articulate it. But there was surely an inkling in Nwoye's soul, an inchoate sense of the natural law and of the nature of God, that led Nyoye to accept the Christian God, which would give Nwoye the religio-moral resources to know that the killing of Ikemefuna was indeed an abomination.

Chapter 7
African Theology and a Classical Theory of Inculturation

John C. Cavadini

Father Paulinus Odozor's book *Morality Truly Christian, Truly African* lays down some premises about what a genuinely African Christian theology might look like. We can find them stated in different ways throughout his book, but they all tend towards the same conclusion. First of all, as a first premise,

> What would be unacceptable as African Christian theology would be to water down the universal and absolute significance of Jesus as Lord and Savior or to put African Traditional Religion on a par with Christianity as means of salvation. To proclaim Jesus as 'the way, the truth, and the life' (Jn. 14.6) is to acknowledge that 'in this name and in no other is salvation offered to human beings' (Acts 4.12).[1]

He notes further that, "Any African theology that is Christian must start with this faith, even though it must also listen to insights from African Traditional Religion about the divine presence in Africa and in our world."[2] Here we find, along with the first premise (that we must start with the Christian faith), a second premise, namely that a Christian theology that has a claim on being African must listen to insights from African Traditional Religion. Why is this true? As he had put it earlier in the book, "there are many reasons for taking African Traditional Religion seriously. One such reason [...] is that it supplies the most important substratum for the African as a religious being in his or her encounter with Christianity."[3] In another passage, Fr. Paulinus notes that one of the "sources" of African theology as such is "African tradition." "African theology tries to take the lived experience of Africans into account,"[4] and in this way takes seriously the need for the inculturation of Christianity in African contexts.

The crucial element in African tradition, for the purposes of the discussion of the inculturation of Christianity in Africa, is African Traditional Religion. I find the following passage, the context of which is a discussion of tradition in the terms that Alasdair MacIntyre suggests, to be very clarifying:

> [H]owever we look at it, the arrival of Christianity on the African continent and the acceptance of Christianity as an alternative scheme of reference to the one provided by African Traditional Religion amounts to an acceptance in some ways of the inadequacy of the latter as an explanatory schema. A new narrative has emerged, therefore, which arises in some way from the fusion of Christianity with elements of African tradition. What emerges from this fusion still has to be recognizable to both the Christian community to be acceptable as "Christian," and to the African community to be acceptable as "African." This is the issue at the heart of the discourse on inculturation in African theology today.[5]

Thus, "there are many reasons for taking African Traditional Religion seriously," and "one such reason [...] is that it supplies the most important substratum for the African as a religious being in his or her encounter with Christianity."[6]

In responding to Fr. Paulinus's admirable achievement, in both this book and in his many articles, I had thought to try to enter his ideas into conversation with some element of the patristic heritage that we have received in many ways as normative, even now, for the universal Church. But then I thought, if African Traditional Religion were the main element to be considered in thinking about inculturation of Christianity in Africa, the Fathers are not a likely source of encouragement. Both the Greek and the Latin Fathers present a fairly negative attitude towards the polytheistic cults of the Roman Empire. Justin's *First Apology* sets the trend. The gods worshipped in polytheistic rites are demons, the angel of darkness parading as angel of light. The myths in which these so-called gods figure are actually deliberate demonic distortions of Christian mysteries in an attempt to divert people's worship away from Christ and towards the demons, although for Justin this does mean that they contain a grain of truth. Justin appeals to those who believe, for instance, in the ascent of Bellerophon to the heavens on Pegasus the flying horse. If you can believe in that, surely you can believe in the Ascension of Christ.[7] In this case, the myth does indeed contain an element of truth. Nevertheless, the cult based on this myth and the others is to be completely abandoned[8] since it is a distortion of true worship. Justin also thinks of the rites of the mystery religions, with their lustrations and ritual meals as deliberate demonic distortions of the sacraments, mainly, of Baptism[9] and Eucharist.[10] You can use the similarities to attract people to Christian worship, but the rites of the mystery religions themselves must be completely abandoned because they are devices the demons themselves use to divert worship from the true God onto themselves. Origen certainly follows suit when it comes to polytheistic rites.[11]

Augustine, in the *City of God,* if anything, is more negative than even Justin. He believes that any so-called god who desires worship, especially in the form of sacrifice, for him or herself, as *ipso facto* an evil demon and not a good angel. The angels, by contrast, are always trying to help us to be formed in the newness of our minds, as Paul had exhorted, so that we turn away from idolatry of any sort towards the true worship of the true God. To the extent, then, that the gods of Roman civil religion desire, or tolerate, worship for themselves, to that extent they are hardly divine, but are evil demons. Augustine is suspicious not only of the cult, but of the myths themselves and of philosophically inspired attempts to interpret the myths allegorically, since, from his point of view, the allegories serve to make the myths acceptable to the more squeamish scholarly establishment, and that, in turn, serves only to bolster the cult, now that we have an enlightened understanding of it as only a symbolic acting out of general philosophical truths that the allegory has discovered and articulated.[12]

But as I read Fr. Paulinus's book, and, in particular, his descriptions of African Traditional Religion as well as the traditions of belief that flow from it, I began to see a more promising approach opening up. At one point Fr. Paulinus notes that, "As I have stated repeatedly here, in Africa religion is the culture and the culture is religious. Although this does not mean that everything is explicitly stated as religious, it does show that religion permeates every aspect of life. It is faith informed by reason […]."[13] How so? We begin to see how as Fr. Paulinus unpacks this statement, bringing forward descriptions by various scholars of some of the presuppositions of ATR as they have been drawn out by reason. Summarizing the views of one scholar, Fr. Paulinus notes that, "Africans came to believe in God by reflecting on their experience and through observation of the created universe. Specifically, by reflecting on the wonder and magnitude of the universe, they came to the conclusion that God must exist: they posited the existence of God to explain the existence and sustenance of the universe."[14] God is the "Creator,"[15] and as such is the origin of all things and beings, visible and invisible. God's Providence guarantees order in the universe, and in particular the laws of nature. The universe is administered partly through lesser spiritual powers who are regarded as God's "intermediaries."[16] Not only is there natural order, but there is, in the second place, moral order: "Secondly, there is moral and religious order. […] Africans believe that God has ordained a moral order for humans, through which they came to understand what is good and what is evil, so that they might live in harmony with one another and safeguard the life of the people. This order […] is knowable to humans, by nature."[17]

This sounds in part like ancient Stoicism, and in part like ancient Platonism. In other words, African Traditional Religion sounds, at least in part, like ancient philosophy. And, while the Fathers were very suspicious of polytheist rites and rituals, they were much more attracted to and willing to deal with ancient philosophy, especially in its Stoic and Platonist forms, and these, in their own way, unlike contemporary analytical philosophy, were religious. They did not involve rites, but they certainly involved beliefs about God, the natural order both physical and moral, Providence, the goodness of the world, the unity of the cosmos, various spiritual beings, etc. The Platonists in particular believed in a hierarchy of spiritual beings, and writers like Apuleius inquired into their nature. Christians like Augustine were prepared to accept even some of these invisible spiritual agents. They were what Christians call not gods, but angels — IF and only if, they did not claim or accept worship of themselves, that is, were not the objects of any cult of worship.

I started thinking of one of the most well-known works of St. Augustine, his *De doctrina christiana*, *On Christian doctrine,* to translate it literally but, for all that, misleadingly. "Doctrina" means "teaching," and in a variety of senses. It includes what we call in English "doctrine," that is, teachings or doctrines particular to Christianity, but it also includes not only what is taught, but the act of teaching, and the relationship between the two.[18] Was there a distinctive Christian approach to teaching that was tailored to its content? The baseline meaning of "doctrina" is communication[19] itself: is there a Christian way of communicating? And one could sum up all of these meanings, as with the somewhat similar Greek word "paideia," with the word "culture."[20] Is there a Christian kind of education, which is predicated upon Christian beliefs and which generates a certain style of communication, or teaching, or formation, akin to the passing on of Greek culture that is *paideia*. And, if there is a specifically Christian *doctrina* or *paideia*, how is it related to the various classical claims on culture and education? Is it totally new? Does it entail rejection of what went before? Or some kind of transformation, so that these ancient forms are, we could say, inculturated in a new way, into a Christian way of communicating with a particular Christian aim? This is not precisely the way discussions about inculturation are set up now. Nowadays we think of Christianity as floating free of culture, waiting to be incarnated or embodied in the given cultures of humankind. But Augustine poses the question as though there were, in fact, a specific Christian goal, method and practice of teaching, a "culture" in that sense, available to inculturate other pre-existing forms. I think this is an interesting way of posing the question. I also think it is, in a way, what Fr. Paulinus offers us, which I think is something new in the theology of inculturation.

I will explain what I mean by a closer examination of the *De doctrina*, even if it is only a preliminary one for our purposes here, necessarily constrained by time and scope. Augustine begins his treatise by saying "There are some rules (*praecepta*) for treating Scripture, which I consider can be not inappropriately passed on to students, enabling them to make progress not only by reading others who have opened up the hidden secrets of the divine literature, but also by themselves opening them up to yet others again."[21] From this opening sentence we learn that a Christian *doctrina* is, in the first place, Scriptural, and, in the second place, not just an affair of private study but an educational culture of receiving and in turn giving, a community of seeking to understand so as to be able to engender understanding the obscurities of Scripture, which are often an indication of riches below the surface of the text. As he begins Book 1, Augustine divides his treatise into two phases or modes, the *modus inveniendi,* or the mode of seeking understanding, of research, or discovery, and the *modus proferendi*, or the mode of communicating to others what one has understood, the mode of preaching or proclamation of the message of the inspired text.[22] The norm for interpretation is the rule of faith "which [we] have received from the plainer passages of scripture and from the authority of the Church."[23] Augustine discusses extensively, in Book 1, the "things," or "*res*" that Scripture teaches boldly and plainly, and the discussion there follows the order of the rule of faith, which is in this case something like the Apostles' Creed as it was known in North Africa.[24]

Returning to the Prologue, it is well known that Augustine defends his approach, namely, that there even *is* a Scriptural culture or *doctrina*, against those who would say one doesn't need rules for treating the divine letters, because the Holy Spirit, through a divine gift, "makes possible the praiseworthy opening up of the obscurities of this sacred literature."[25] Augustine's irritation with this otherwise unnamed group is pronounced and pointed. While knowledge of the precepts for seeking and engendering understanding of the divine literature is not a guarantee of results, those who deny the usefulness of cultivating a disciplined conversation of seeking and receiving and offering understanding have a much more limited prospect of getting anywhere. Augustine reminds these charismatic hardliners, if that is what we may call them, that they at least learned the alphabet and letters from going to school. And, should someone have the boldness to mention that St. Anthony did not even know how to read, let such a person, Augustine wryly observes, remember that he did not teach himself how to speak or invent the language he speaks—unless, adding insult to injury, he believes he should wait for his little children to receive a knowledge of language from the Holy Spirit directly, instead of teaching them to speak himself.[26]

In fact, God does occasionally thunder from the sky, through the intermediary of angels of course, as happened to Paul and the centurion Cornelius, but both of them were sent to the Church to be instructed and to receive the sacraments, even though God could have done it all Himself through the angels, presumably. But then, Augustine comments in earnest, "no respect would have been shown to our condition as humans, if God appeared to be unwilling to have his word administered to us by other human beings." Paul claims that *the temple of God, which is what you are, is holy* (1 Cor. 3.17), but it would seem an idle claim "if God never gave any answers from his human temple, but only thundered out his revelation from the sky and by means of angels."[27] In fact, this is one of the primary ways of building up charity, for "pouring minds and hearts together with the knot of unity," namely, by human beings learning from each other.

Augustine diagnoses the reluctance to learn from other human beings, and, in particular, from the Church, as a refusal of charity that for him always constitutes pride, the refusal, in this case, to be humble enough to receive instruction from others and, in that way, to build a culture of love. The apostle Philip, in Acts 8.27–35, did not send the eunuch, who was reading but not understanding the prophet Isaiah, to an angel. Rather, Philip was sent to him by an impulse from God, "and sat with him, and in human words and human language (*humanis verbis et lingua*) opened up to him what had been concealed in the passage he was reading."[28] And still hammering the point home, Augustine notes that since his critics "read and understand without any other human being explaining the text to them, why are they so eager to explain it to others, instead of referring them back to God, so that they too may come to understand it through his teaching them inwardly, and not through the teaching of other men." But they don't go that far, but rather "they communicate (*produnt*) to others what they understand, by speaking or by writing."[29] It is this activity of learning and teaching, seeking to understand and helping others to understand by preaching or lecturing or writing, that we can recognize as *doctrina Christiana*, an ecclesial culture of communication focused on the interpretation and proclamation of Scripture.

Ultimately, this *doctrina* is governed by the Incarnation, which is itself a kind of *doctrina,* since Paul calls it the *folly of preaching, folly* because *the foolishness of God is wiser than men* (1 Cor. 1.21, 25).[30] The Wisdom of God came to us in mortal flesh, just as a thought, without any change in itself, takes the form of a sound, a spoken utterance (*formam vocis*) called speech.[31] The Word, in other words, in becoming flesh, doesn't *just* become flesh, but speech, language, and gesture, with the connection of these to texts, communities, to received wisdom, to education and the passing on of various kinds of learning and understanding. "Flesh" implies all of this, and thus an extreme degree of "foolishness," of self-emptying on the part of divine Wisdom, a self-emptying which ultimately is a kind of entrustment. The Word does not become flesh by creating His own divine language and His own divine culture, but empties Himself into our *doctrina*, our seeking and speaking, our language, our texts, vulnerable as these are to distortion through translation, copying, etc. This entrustment builds a new *doctrina* or teaching or speaking in which the bond of charity may be built up as, honored with the most important Word or message there is, human beings teach and learn this to and from each other, drawing on the authoritative proclamation of the Word made flesh in the preaching of the Apostles and its reception in tradition (the "rule of faith") and, especially, its transmission in the Scriptures, the "divine letters." And, while this does not mean a new, separate sacred and revealed language or heavenly culture, it does mean a conversation initiated by and inspired by the entrustment of the Word of God to *our* language and *our* words and texts. Scripture as divine initiates a new conversation, unique because it *transforms* our speaking with the gift of a message, a revelation, an entrustment out of love, that we could not have given ourselves and did not give ourselves. It is this which is the distinctive Christian *doctrina*, this enfleshed, entexted Word that transforms the *doctrina* received from the culture we have inherited. Buying into this conversation means entrusting oneself back, entrusting oneself to the Wisdom of God as expressed in God's Word, and that means entrusting oneself to Scripture as received by and in the Church. Ultimately it means an entrustment to the Church.

It is this dynamic of *doctrina Christiana* as transformative of already existing *doctrina,* already existing cultures of teaching and learning, broadly speaking, that prompts me to think of *those cultures* as what is inculturated into and by this new *doctrina*, distinctive in its focus on the study, interpretation and proclamation of Scripture in the context of the ecclesial community.

Augustine goes on to make his famous distinction between "signs" and "things": "All teaching (*doctrina*) concerns either things or signs, but things are learned about (*discuntur*) through signs."[32] "Signs" are the product of any significatory activity by which a rational creature tries to make its intentions, its will, its mind known to another, the preeminent one being language. One could think of cultures as systems of signs, as sign systems, and one could think of *doctrina* as a particular culture in the mode of handing itself on. Augustine clarifies that signs, as he is talking about them, are entirely conventional, invented by human beings without any particular instruction from God. There is no special, revealed sacred language. The Word does not come enfleshed in a special language but enmeshed in one that is entirely conventional, that must be learned or translated if people from other cultures are to understand what is signified, one that has a resonance in the same human soul and the same human reason at work in any culture or sign system. But, if I am interpreting Augustine correctly, I would not regard this as the "inculturation" of the Word, but rather the transformation of the culture in which He takes flesh, a kind of reverse inculturation.

Augustine spends Book 2 thinking about what sign systems, what *doctrinae*, can be "inculturated" by or into *doctrina christiana*. There is no avoiding this move, precisely because the Word has entered into our sign making, our cultures, our *paideia* and has done it in a way that will transform the very way we engage in culture and in the signifying activity from which culture arises and which is, *tout court,* culture itself. That is why Augustine says that the "*first thing*" (emphasis added) one has to discover in Scripture is oneself, "as tied up in love of this world, that is of temporal things, and far removed from such love of God and such love of neighbor as scripture itself prescribes."[33] This compunction, as it were, is not culturally specific but applies to all of us whose primary bond to each other transcends all cultures, namely, the original sin of pride that not only transcends all cultures but in the end breaks all cultures or at least corrupts them all and produces structures of domination instead of structures of charity. The first stage of *doctrina christiana* is fear of the Lord: "What is needed above all else [...] is to be converted by the fear of God to wishing to know his will, what he bids us seek and shun. Now this fear of necessity shakes us with thoughts of our mortality and of our death to come, and so to say nails our flesh and fixes all the stirrings of pride to the wood of the cross."[34]

The next step is *pietas*, piety or humble devotion: "What is needed next," that is, after conversion by fear of God, which in a way means fear of our own pride, "is to grow modest with piety, and not to contradict the divine scripture, whether we have understood it when it lashes our vices, or whether we have not understood it, as though we could be wiser or teach better ourselves. Instead, we should rather think and believe that what is written there is better and truer, even if its meaning is hidden, than any good ideas we can think up for ourselves" (2.7.9). The very idea of the hiddenness of Scriptural wisdom is intended to wear down our penchant for reading into the text the seemingly obvious, the fashionable and the self-justifying superficialities we are content to accept in our prideful desire to seem as though we have mastered the divine wisdom.[35] But who masters "foolishness?"—it is a contradiction in terms. This is not a *doctrina* that invites mastery so much as a culture of response of the heart, of gratitude expressed in faith, hope and love. It is a *doctrina* that is inherently dialogical. To understand the text is to understand *someone*, whose "foolishness" is so magnificent that He "became the pavement under our feet," in Hill's dramatic translation,[36] so as to be the Way as well as the goal of the journey to God. You don't inculturate Him; He inculturates you, and all of your studying, speaking, thinking and self-expression, in other words, all human culture.

The student of Scripture, of *doctrina christiana,* has to be willing to master all of the various elements of human culture which have already been taken into the divine letters and inculturated in them. This includes languages—no escape from language study if one wants the best chance of clarifying the meaning of the biblical text—as well as logic and dialectic, history, rhetoric and mathematics, the natural sciences, and even astronomy. The Word of God cannot be studied independently of the world of signs and things into which He emptied Himself, which He took up in taking up our "flesh," our way of living and being in the world. Nor yet can it be reduced to the terms of any secular study. Augustine counsels, on the one hand, boldness: "all good and true Christians should understand that truth, wherever they may find it, belongs to their Lord."[37] So, even if knowledge of music is mixed up with idolatrous veneration of the mythological muses, one should not shun the study of music, since music itself has been "inculturated" in the sacred books, in Christian *doctrina*, in the foolishness of preaching.

On the other hand, Augustine counsels caution: "it seems to me that the most salutary advice I can give to eager and bright young people who fear God and are seeking the happy life is that they should not impetuously and unconcernedly pursue any teachings (*doctrinas*) that can be had outside the Church of Christ, as though these could ensure them a happy life."[38] Augustine warns specifically against any *doctrina* or learning that cultivates "superstitious arts," by which he means the arts of augury, any magical arts, soothsaying, incantations or amulets for healing, astrology, "anything established by human beings which refers to the making and worshipping of idols, or the worshipping of creation or any part of creation as God."[39] These sign systems are not able to be "inculturated" by *doctrina Christiana*; they are language systems that cannot be converted because they form various kinds of human community with demons: "all such things only have the value that has been agreed upon by presumptuous spirits as forming a kind of common language with demons."[40] These signs, this language, cannot be spoken to any other effect or lifted into any higher meaning without at the same time destroying them. All the other disciplines can be taken up into *doctrina Christiana* and in fact in being taken up, in being "inculturated" by Scriptural speaking, they find the ultimate truth for which they had all, in one way or another, been seeking.

Augustine goes on to consider one last, and very special, case of learning, and that is philosophy, which is the love of wisdom:

> If those, however, who are called philosophers happen to have said anything that is true, and agreeable to our faith, the Platonists above all, not only should we not be afraid of them, but we should even claim back for our own use what they have said, as from its unjust possessors. It is like the Egyptians,

> who not only had idols and heavy burdens, which the people of Israel abominated and fled from, but also vessels and ornaments of gold and silver [...] which the people secretly appropriated for their own, and indeed better, use.[41]

Augustine further explains,

> In the same way, while the heathen certainly have counterfeit and superstitious fictions in all their teachings [...] which everyone of us must abominate and shun as we go forth from the company of the heathen under the leadership of Christ, their teachings also contain liberal disciplines which are more suited to the service of the truth, as well as a number of most useful ethical principles, and some true things are to be found among them about worshiping only the one God. All this is like their gold and silver, and not something they instituted themselves, but something which they mined, so to say, from the ore of divine providence, veins of which are everywhere to be found.[42]

Christians can use these for preaching the Gospel, and this can even include institutions that the non-Christian elites have established. Moses himself was educated in all the wisdom of the Egyptians, as it says in Acts 7.22. But all of these, Augustine says, and I am using my own words, must be inculturated by the culture of the foolishness of divine Wisdom, that is, by the culture of the Cross, the final standard and arbiter of *doctrina Christiana.* Those who come to the study of the Scripture immersed in human culture, in human *doctrina*, in human learning, even of the most exalted sort, namely that about God and about ethics, "should never," Augustine says, "stop reflecting on that maxim of the apostle's, *Knowledge puffs up, love builds up*" (1 Cor. 8.1).[43] Coming forth from Egypt, one must celebrate the pasch. But, Augustine reminds us, "*our Passover, which is Christ, has been sacrificed* (citing 1 Cor. 5.7),"[44] and it is that sacrifice that relieves us of the heavy burden of saving ourselves by our own *doctrina*, our own human wisdom, instead of offering it all, with a gentle and humble heart formed by devotion to the *foolishness of preaching* that is the cross, in order to see more deeply into that preaching and continue it ourselves as we teach others what we have learned. "This sign of the cross" is the ultimate sign of Christian *paideia*, of *doctrina Christiana,* forming the heart in a new way of seeking and speaking and enabling us to "revoice" previous *doctrina* with the spirit of love revealed on the cross as God's own clear, sweet and persuasive rhetoric, His communication to us, His *doctrina.*

To me this seems to fit what Fr. Paulinus has drawn out as the contours of genuine African theology. The quote with which I began seems to come back newly illuminated:

> What would be unacceptable as African Christian theology would be to water down the universal and absolute significance of Jesus as Lord and Savior or to put African Traditional Religion on a par with Christianity as means of salvation. To proclaim Jesus as 'the way, the truth, and the life' (Jn. 14.6) is to acknowledge that 'in this name and in no other is salvation offered to human beings' (Acts 4.12).[45]

Even more explicit are passages we find later, in chapters dealing more explicitly with moral theology:

> African tradition has its myths and stock of ancient wisdom expressed in various symbolic forms. It has its stock of sages and philosophical and historically enlightened figures. To deny this is to deny that Africa has had its great civilizations.[46]

In Augustine's terms, Africa is teeming with the gold of Egypt (in fact, Egypt is *in* Africa). Yet "in the face of this great constellation of persons and despite this venerable tradition, Christianity, as in all situations, makes a bold assertion about Jesus Christ: [...] [T]hat he is God incarnate [...] the one who definitively and absolutely reveals God's intention and purposes for the world."[47] This includes the "spiritual and cultural" riches of Africa, its "treasures," as Pope Benedict XVI referred to them in a speech that Fr. Paulinus cites.[48] "The fact is," Fr. Paulinus continues, "the gospel is new in every culture, and African theology must explore its meaning and show how it can renew African societies."[49] This is what, I think, in Augustinian terms, is inculturation. Not, in the first instance, inculturation of the gospel in a given culture, but an inculturation of that culture itself, with all its spiritual wisdom, *especially* its spiritual wisdom, in *doctrina Christiana*, the unique and irreducible "culture" of foolishness, the foolishness of God, which is, after all, *wiser than men*. This unique cultivation of seeking to understand the foolishness of preaching that is the Incarnation, Passion, Death and Resurrection of Jesus, and of seeking to engender understanding of it, lifts all cultural expressions, all the gold of Egypt, into a new conversation focused on the sign of the cross.

This brings us, by way of conclusion, to the second phase of *doctrina Christiana* as Augustine sees it, namely, the *modus proferendi*, the mode of speaking forth, of engendering understanding and conviction at the same time, the mode of proclamation and preaching. The purpose of eloquence is threefold, Augustine reminds the reader, namely, to instruct, to delight, and to persuade.[50] But this always means knowing the audience, knowing what they need to learn, what kinds of speech will delight them, and what sort of grand eloquence will move them to tears,[51] if that is what is necessary to persuade them to act on the truth they have come to understand. Augustine assumes that *doctrina Christiana* involves a mode of preaching or proclamation that is able to mobilize the rhetorical resources of the culture of the preacher and put them to good use in preaching, especially where this involves preaching that is intended to affect peoples' behavior.

Augustine gives examples of Christian preachers who have used everything they had learned in the secular schools to create a biblical eloquence that is at home in their own cultural situations. He mentions Cyprian and Ambrose in particular.[52] Fr. Paulinus gives a great example of this in his discussion of what African Traditional Religion calls "aru," or "abomination." The phrase "intrinsic evil" does not do justice to the particularly disruptive and malicious evil known as "aru." The preacher wanting to persuade his audience of the depth of the evil of certain crimes, and the need for conversion and reparation, can "inculturate," now in the more traditional sense of the word, his preaching of the Biblical ethic and his exhortation not to violate love of God and neighbor. Fr. Paulinus suggests that "Christian ethics in the Western churches has largely lost this dimension of some kinds of wrongdoing, but this is something African traditional ethics has to help the Church recover."[53] It would be, he says, particularly pertinent in preaching and teaching about the sexual abuse scandals that have caused so many to fall away.[54] Part of *doctrina Christiana*, of the learning and teaching culture that is uniquely Christian, is the deployment of words and categories that do not come from revelation in the first instance and strictly speaking, but can be used very efficaciously in engendering, really in creating, a deeper understanding of the biblical ethic and its broad ramifications. In the process one could also say that the African Traditional ethic has found its true voice, its truest voice, its ultimate reference, as it serves to proclaim the ultimate truth that is Jesus Christ.

Christian preachers, if they are to speak both eloquently and wisely, must in the first instance "see into the heart of [the Scriptures] with the eyes of their own hearts."[55] They must be able to see the love revealed on the Cross which is the heart of Scripture and be able to make that heart so known and loved by their listeners that they are moved to respond to the heart of Scripture with their own hearts. But this means that the preacher must be able to speak the language of the hearers and all that that language contains in terms of customs, stories, spiritual sayings and wisdom, and put all of that "gold" to the use of the *modus proferendi*, of proclaiming the love of God revealed in Jesus Christ, engendering an understanding of it, a love of it and the appropriate response to it. The elevation of traditional *doctrina,* the traditional wisdom of any culture, into *doctrina Christiana,* its "inculturation" by the Gospel, must, if it is to be effective, be spoken making use of all the traditional language and wisdom, laid at the foot of the Cross.

It is this clothing of eloquence in the language the culture speaks, constitutive of the second mode or phase of *doctrina Christiana,* that is what is more commonly referred to today as inculturation, as enfleshing the Christian message in cultural terms. But this presupposes that in phase one, the *modus inveniendi*, these very terms have already been through the celebration of the Passover from Egypt. They represent a *paideia* or *doctrina* already transformed in the attempt to understand more deeply *what is the breadth and length and height and depth* of the Lord's Cross, of the life *rooted and founded in love* (Eph. 3.17–18).[56] In their transformation we see what the ultimate truth, meaning and reference of anything that was true in previous *doctrina* of any kind and from any culture, was all along both reflecting and seeking.

Chapter 8

Catholic Comparative Theological Ethics: Elements of an Approach to Tradition, Ethics, and Dialogue (with Odozor and Clooney, in the Church)

David A. Clairmont

To what extent is a comparative spirit, and the practices that spring from it, integral to the life of the Catholic Church?[1] It is easy to see this question as the sole province of theologians, work delegated to those paid to spend their time thinking about differences: religious, historical, cultural, political, ritual, sexual, spiritual. Perhaps those who work in full time ministry also have something to say about difference. The faithful come from different families with different histories, resting from different journeys and recovering from different tragedies. Each person in the Church compares: their youth with their old age, their freedom with their limits, their hopes with their fears, their belonging with their alienation. Only the dead are beyond compare, and yet to the living they find a way of staying with us, as we measure ourselves against them—our standards of success and failure, of sin and redemption.

It is of the gravest importance that we keep these small works of daily comparison in mind when our comparisons expand beyond person and family, to the Body of Christ and to that Body's gestures to the world. The Body of Christ undertakes an inner dialogue, and the Body of Christ enters conversations with the world. That Body does not cease to think, to question, to wonder when it turns to speak; the Body walking the road to Emmaus glances to the horizon—nervous, unfocused, at times supremely overconfident and undermerciful—arms and legs hurrying to catch up with the Head. Theologians run the risk of taking the place of the Head, in their urgency to catch up to, and even anticipate, where the Head leads. They are no less at risk in their reticence to be surprised by the Head, and even the Body, as the people of God—the Church—often leads theologians where they do not wish to go.

In this essay, I propose to examine the comparative spirit and practices of theologians in the Catholic Church, with primary reference to two directions where that comparative spirit might lead: deeper within and engagingly beyond. One theological direction (deeper within) finds the comparative spirit drawing all members of the Body of Christ deeper within the life of the Church to recognize, appreciate, and live transformed by the internal diversity of Church. The other theological direction (engagingly beyond) finds the comparative spirit moving from the life of the Church to explore similarity and difference among humanity's variegated seekings of God, as the human heart yearns to gaze upon and root itself in the truth, like a young plant sinking its roots into good soil and bending its face to the sun.

The "deeper-within" comparative spirit is like a contemplative farmer, who seeks to understand the land more deeply in order to bring forth its fruits in greater abundance. This spirit commits to the stability of the Church in each time and place, seeking to disentangle the weeds from the wheat and thereby to provide more reliable sustenance for the community (Mt 13:24–30), but it also seeks to draw forth the values and lessons, preserved or specially exemplified in one part of the Church, and pass them on as nourishment to other parts of the Church that are hungry.[2] The "engagingly beyond" comparative spirt is like an apostolic gardener, who seeks to bring the beauty of the Gospel to all people and who wonders at the beauty of other ways of life. They return home to their gardens bearing those beauties, to share with their faith family and friends what they have seen and learned about these new seedlings of foreign faiths. They will give them a new home in the garden, not to supplant what is already there but to try to understand the possibilities for harmony among these many beautiful creations. The gardener's lessons are hard won: not all plants will survive in new homes; some plants will not thrive next to their new neighbors; and some invasive kinds will overrun their new residence. The comparativist as apostolic gardener is neither a collector of bare novelties nor a secret agent of ecological destruction. Rather, the comparativist aims at understanding the what and why of real differences and harmonious relations, the substance of beauty but also the process of its creation.

When I speak of a comparative spirit, I do not mean to elide the inspiration to compare—emerging from the life and thinking of one committed to the mission of Jesus and the life of the Church—with the work of Spirit in the Church or in the world. I mean only to suggest that there are different comparative spirits at work in the Church, that each comparative spirit emerges from the distinctive way that the individual Christian encounters the Gospel in light of their particular family, cultural, social, and educational backgrounds, and that we would do well to think about their distinctive expressions and how they relate, one to another. In this essay, I draw from the work of two prominent Catholic theologians—Paulinus Odozor, C.S.Sp. and Francis Clooney, S.J.—to explore these two comparative spirits and their contributions to theological ethics.

In addition to exploring these two comparative spirits, I also argue for a particular form of comparison that I think is both underdeveloped and supremely important in the life of the Catholic Church, what I will call *comparative theological ethics*, which requires attending to both of the comparative spirits noted above. In order to develop this account, I highlight the importance of the different ways that tradition and culture function in the work of Odozor and Clooney. Specifically, I consider how Odozor's particular approach to comparison—a variation of Catholic theologies of inculturation—relates to other approaches to comparison in Catholic theology and how it relates to ethics. My central topics will be the accounts of culture and tradition that appear in Odozor's work and to show how his particular views of culture and tradition allow him to articulate a different approach to comparison than we find in the work of many contemporary Catholic comparative theologians, especially but not only in the influential work of the Indologist Francis Clooney.

I develop this essay in four parts. First, I sort through some important terminological issues to isolate what I mean by theological ethics and why I think this formulation is important in positioning the two kinds of comparison I discuss. Second, I examine Odozor's accounts of culture and tradition as these appear in his influential 2008 *Theological*

Studies article on inculturation and moral theology and in the second chapter of *Morality Truly Christian, Truly African*. Third, I place these accounts into brief dialogue with the description of comparative theology offered by Francis Clooney, offering a few remarks on why and how their different comparative anchors matter for their comparative methods. Fourth, I conclude with a few thoughts on the relative strengths and weakness of these respective approaches, offering a preliminary formulation of how these two approaches help describe what is involved in a Catholic comparative theological ethics.

I. The Role of Comparison in Catholic Theological Ethics

Before proceeding to the place of these two comparative spirits in Catholic theological ethics, it is important to make some terminological clarifications. In Catholic theological settings (especially but not only in Catholic seminaries), the study of "life in Christ" (the label given to the third part of the *Catechism of the Catholic Church* which discusses topics pertaining to living a good life, one characterized by self-gift and obedience to God's commands) is called moral theology.[3] The logic of this word pair is that there are definite moral implications to what the Church believes: if I make a profession of faith in the Catholic Church, this means that I am professing not only what I believe about God and the Church but also a kind of commitment about how I should live.

The problem is that the terms "ethics" and "morality" (or "ethical" and "moral") have taken on different meanings in the history of philosophy and theology. Morality is sometimes taken to mean how a community thinks it ought to live (*mos*, the Latin word for custom, as in a Catholic morality), but it is also taken to mean that which is obligatory in all cases at all times, irrespective of what one's community thinks about this form of life—a form common to many modern uses of the word morality. Immanuel Kant, for example, wondered what makes a particular set of obligations *moral* rather than simply customarily affirmed? So too "ethics" is taken to have various meanings. In one sense, ethics can be taken as a substitute for morals, or it can mean not only what is approved of in a community—the community's standards of right and wrong—but also the stable traits of a person's character (*ἠθικός* in Greek is sometimes translated as character). Among some Christian theologians, ethics is understood to mean a critical reflection on a way of life (on the *mos* of a community), wherein sources for ethics include but are not limited to what the community understands to be the right way to live.[4] It is this understanding of ethics—ethics as critical reflection on a way of life—that I use here. For that reason, when I refer to a Catholic ethics, I mean to include, but not limit ethical reflection to, the morality of the Catholic Church.

For reasons I develop further along, I claim that the term "moral theology" does not actually reflect the kind of ethical thinking that occurs most often in the Church—even in its official pronouncements through the statements the Councils, popes, and bishops' conferences—and that Catholic *theological ethics* is probably a more appropriate, though certainly not perfect, formulation. What Odozor (and many other Catholic theologians) are doing is not simply unfolding the logical implications of the Catholic profession of faith rooted in the Church's credal formulae. They are doing ethics: they are critically reflecting on how people live—both Catholics and non-Catholics—in conversation with Catholic moral teaching but their sources, their approaches, and their forms of reflection are critical.[5] They want the lives of Catholic Christians to become better, more deeply reflective of their humanity and the message of the Gospel, and that standard for measuring what is better and what is worse is not to be found only in the Church's history or in its present teaching. Another way to put this point is to say that Catholic theological ethics is a kind of comparative activity in the sense that the process of critiquing involves a comparative spirit.

To return to the earlier agrarian analogy, in some cases that comparison will be expressed in the mode of the farmer as noted above, who delves deeply into the soil of the past, or of a particular local Church community, to see what can be planted and harvested for the benefit of all. The theologian may develop a criticism of how the community is living now based on the past, comparing the context and social conditions of the historical community with the context and social conditions of the present community. This is a kind of deliberate historical comparison that can highlight what the community has gained or lost in its present form of life based on how it responded to developments in previous eras. Alternately, the theologian may examine how the Church is living in one part of the world and compare it with how the Church is living in another part of the world, highlighting patterns of behavior or even elements of Church teaching that have given rise to violence, neglect, or abuse. After all, the farmer plans, clears, plants, weeds, fertilizes (and sometimes even cooks!) from what she or he can draw from the distinctive place and history of the land. Yet in so doing, the farmer also knows what will not survive on this particular land, what conditions are necessary for certain plants to flourish and what will cause them to wither, what can devour the crops and what is the best way to prevent such disaster. As the farmer is concerned with the physical health of the community, so the theologian is concerned with the social and spiritual health of the community.

In other cases, the comparison will be expressed in the mode of the gardener. Like the farmer, the gardener must be familiar with the local soil, must be knowledgeable about what grows well in a particular place and why, but the gardener has a different focus. The gardener is not responsible for feeding the people (although the garden's produce may certainly nourish the body), but the people do look to the gardener to present the full array of beauty that the garden can sustain. The gardener is likewise concerned about the land in which the plants of the garden take root. Like the farmer, the gardener must know about the plants, about the soil, about the climate, but the garden has other aims too. Unlike the farmer's cultivation of the field, the garden's cultivation aims at beauty, repose, the integration and coordination of similarity and difference for the sake of harmony. This is a kind of critical work too, since there certainly exist poorly designed gardens, neglected gardens, styles of garden that do not fit the location, and gardens that bring together plants that ultimately cannot be reconciled. In either case, the point of the agrarian analogy is that it helps us to think about different comparative spirits and how these might be brought together in a productive way in the work of Catholic theological ethics.

II. Odozor's Contribution to Comparative Theological Ethics

Paulinus Odozor develops an ethical project rooted in both Catholic moral theology and Catholic inculturation theology.[6] It is through the relation of Catholic moral theology traditionally understood, and Catholic inculturation theology as it has developed since the middle of the twentieth century that Odozor's comparative theological ethics emerges. To understand Odozor's approach, two terms must be clarified and related: culture and tradition.

In his article "An African Moral Theology of Inculturation: Methodological Considerations," Odozor draws on Catholic theologies of inculturation in order to critique to work of Congolese theologian Bénézet Bujo.[7] "My concern with Bujo's presentation on the role of African communities and cultures in the search for moral truth," Odozor writes, "is that it is a bit one-sided. This fact is evidenced by idealizing Africa's past and giving insufficient attention to the current structurally negative and damaging elements in those traditions."[8] This article is the basis for his comments he makes in his book *Morality Truly Christian, Truly African*[9] on both inculturation and tradition and even supplies the books title—solid initial evidence, I think, of the article's central place in the Odozor's thinking about these issues.

The article begins with a discussion of Catholic inculturation theologies, wherein Odozor differentiates three senses of inculturation: (1) "the attempt to preach the gospel of Jesus Christ in any human situation," (2) "a process in which the faith embodied in one culture encounters another culture and becomes embodied in it," and (3), quoting Pedro Arrupe, "The incarnation of Christian life and of the Christian message in a particular cultural context, in such a way that this experience not only finds expression through elements proper to the culture in question (this alone would be no more than a superficial adaptation) but becomes a principle that animates, directs and unifies the culture, transforming it and remaking it so as to bring about a 'new creation'."[10] Odozor here develops the inculturation theology of Aylward Shorter, who differentiates inculturation from enculturation ("the cultural learning process of the individual, the process by which a person is inserted into his or her culture"), acculturation ("the encounter between one culture and another" whereby people "possess the collective freedom to modify their particular cultural tradition through contact with people of another culture") and transculturation (or cultural domination, "the unwelcome transfers of foreign cultural traits: symbols, meanings, values and behavior, from one culture to another.").[11]

Since Odozor does not clarify how, if at all, he departs from Shorter on understandings of culture and inculturation, we are left to assume that he finds the remainder of Shorter's account satisfactory. For Shorter, a culture is "what a human being learns, or acquires, as a member of society. It comprises learned aspects—as opposed to the inherited aspects—of human thinking and human behavior [...]. Culture is therefore essentially a transmitted pattern of meanings embodied in symbols, a pattern capable of development and change, and it belongs to the concept of humanness itself. It follows that, if religion is a human phenomenon or human activity, it must affect, and be affected by, culture."[12] Commenting specifically on Shorter's discussion, Odozor agrees that "faith cannot exist 'except in a cultural form.' It is this reality and not just geography that makes it possible to speak of 'American Catholicism,' 'African Christianity,' 'Asian Christianity,' etc. It means that to speak of inculturation is to speak of dialogue between a culture and faith in cultural form."[13] This is important because it establishes a baseline for thinking about how Odozor relates culture to tradition.

What does Odozor have to say about tradition? In the earlier article, Odozor uses MacIntyre's discussion of tradition to challenges what he takes to be Bujo's uncritical reliance on African culture (particularly the palaver tradition) to critique what Bujo takes to be the culturally insensitive or inhospitable aspects of the natural law tradition. Odozor says that "What Bujo has not sufficiently adverted to, however, is that African traditions as living traditions are extended arguments about the good and are, as such, an ongoing construction. This is not to say that there are no constants in African traditions and cultures. Indeed, there are numerous benchmarks that give African traditions character and identity."[14] While Odozor agrees with Bujo that there are clear and internally coherent patterns of thought and practice in African culture, he diverges from Bujo in his judgment about the importance of and means for immanent critique within African cultures. "My concern with Bujo's presentation on the role of African communities and cultures in the search for moral truth" Odozor says, "is that it is a bit one-sided. This fact is evidenced by idealizing Africa's past and giving insufficient attention to the current structurally negative and damaging elements in those traditions."[15] There are, in other words, elements in African cultures that require critical assessment—

ethics—and the mode of critical assessment will come through a comparison of Christian life in Africa and the life of African traditional religions.

Although Odozor continues to reference MacIntyre in *Morality Truly Christian, Truly African*, he adds several other perspectives to develop his understanding of tradition further. "Tradition," he says, "can be understood in a variety of ways: as the transmission of particular beliefs; as that which his transmitted, an object or content; as the source of particular transmission; as memory of the past. The term tradition could thus imply conservatism, community, and/or continuity." Odozor adds, with Edward Shils, that "tradition often involves changes that are unrecognized by its recipients, because between generations 'changes by variations so small as not to be perceived as significant changes' occur."[16] He further notes, following Yves Congar, that tradition "involves something like a 'back-and-forth movement' that happens in a genuine conversation. It involves 'an ability to listen, to reflect, to correct, to speak to the point,' all in the effort to understand, to know, and to seek truth."[17] Tradition is, Odozor says, "the embodiment of an ethos in a living community of human beings, a community of shared values which is nonetheless always on the quest for meaning and for deeper understanding of its nature, goal, and purpose."[18]

Tradition is important for Odozor not only for his discussion about inculturation but also for his assessment of the place of African Traditional Religions (ATR) in African Christian theology. Odozor affirms Adrian Hastings's claim that "'the chief non-biblical reality with which the African theologian must struggle is the non-Christian religious tradition of his own people."[19] Similarly, he follows Kwame Bediako's assessment that African theology is "something of a dialogue between African Christians and the primal religions and spiritualties of Africa.'"[20] For Odozor, African tradition means not only the pre-Christian beliefs and practices of African people but, as a source for theological thinking, is to be understood as the "lived experience of Africans,"[21] which means, interestingly, that African tradition is itself reflective of the multiplicity of religious life and discourse in Africa. In this sense, a tradition is not so much something one studies, and about which one has conversations; a tradition is the confluence of historical events, present realties, and the living reflection on past and present experience.

To understand Odozor's theology, which is clearly an ecclesially-rooted theology, it is worth noting that his enumeration of the sources of African theology is somewhat different than the usual Catholic reference to Sacred Scripture and Sacred Tradition: (1) the Bible, (2) "the uniqueness of Jesus Christ as the revelation of God," (3) African tradition, and (4) and "received Christian tradition."[22] As a "lived experience," both African tradition and received Christian tradition are passed down not only in terms of the content of African and Christian life, but the nature of the passing down as experiential. Put differently, one cannot be an African or a Christian except through participation in the life of the African or Christian communities. Yet his enumeration of the sources of African theology are noteworthy for another reason as well. By articulating "the uniqueness of Jesus Christ as the revelation of God," connected to but not subsumed into either the Bible or received Christian tradition, Odozor highlights the position of the person of Jesus and the uniqueness of divine revelation in Jesus as central to the project of African theology. It is not surprising then that Odozor will, in his African moral theology of inculturation, preserve the critical power of Jesus as unique divine revelation over certain interpretations of the Bible, over certain expressions of African tradition, and over certain expressions of the received Christian tradition. What I think this means for Odozor's account of tradition is that a tradition—African or Christian—may always be analyzed and evaluated in light of the uniqueness of Jesus Christ and so, although in certain senses traditions may appear as rivals or at points either meld or splinter as a result of certain unresolved historical tensions (as MacIntyre would have it), for Odozor whatever might be viewed as a tradition—as a lived experience, composed of both content and a history of life—stands before the person of Jesus as God's unique arbiter of life and judge of all cultures, including African culture and Christian culture.

This brings into somewhat sharper relief the particular comparative spirit animating Odozor's work (what I described above as going "deeper within") which I am here describing as critical but in a way that calls the tradition of African culture and Christian culture to account for the ways that each both respects and enhances to human good and also disrespect and diminishes that good. It is a Christian critical reflection (a Christian ethics) because it is rooted in the person of Jesus Christ, and it seeks to articulate a way to live in light of the critical light that Jesus shines on both African and Christian cultures.

III. Clooney's Contribution to Comparative Theological Ethics

Francis Clooney does not describe his work as ethics, but as with Odozor I would like to offer an argument for how it might usefully be interpreted as a resource for theological ethics in the sense noted above. Clooney's approach to comparative theology is deeply grounded in his own work as an Indologist (focusing primarily but not exclusively on premodern Sanskrit and Tamil texts), his teaching in both Catholic theological and secular university contexts, and as a Jesuit priest. For Clooney, comparative theology is an individual and largely autobiographical endeavor which may, if done well and its results presented at timely points in the history of the Church, have a powerful role to play in the life of the Church.

It is of particular significance to Clooney himself, and to understanding Clooney's approach, to know what comparative theology is not. It is *not theology of religions*, if by that we mean in Clooney's words "a theological discipline that discerns and evaluates the religious significance of other religious traditions in accord with the truths and goals defining one's own religion."[23] Neither is comparative theology the detached comparative study of religion, in which the "ideas, words, images and acts, historical developments—as found in two more traditions or strands of tradition" are studied from the perspective of "detached inquiry by which the scholar remains neutral with respect to where the comparison might lead or what it might imply religiously."[24] Neither again is comparative theology to be confused with inter-religious dialogue which Clooney says refers to "actual conversations, sometimes formal and academic, sometimes simply interpersonal conversations among persons of different religious traditions who are willing to listen to one another and share their stories of faith and values."[25] Comparative theology, by contrast, is both "*comparative* and *theological* beginning to end" and "marks acts of faith seeking understanding which are rooted in a particular faith tradition but which, from that foundation, venture into learning from one or more other faith traditions. This learning is sought for the sake of fresh theological insights that are indebted to the newly encountered tradition/s as well as the home tradition."[26] In a later article, reflecting on his own approach to comparative theology, Clooney says that "While I am not quite anti-theory, I am skeptical about the value of theory that is not richly and deeply supported by knowledge of more than one tradition. My work is then 'micro-comparative,' zooming in 'on very specific items such as certain individuals or groups, certain texts, certain objects, certain practices, etc.'"[27]

Clooney goes on to explain that comparative theology can take several different forms and be undertaken for a range of viable purposes. Situating his own work on comparisons between early Indian religions and Christianity, he embraces three comparative aims. (1) "*Thematic comparison*" that "clarifies concepts by looking at them from different angles [...] improves on them by interreligious learning; disabuses believers of inaccurate claims about uniqueness; in my case, it also engages theologians who do not do comparative work, highlighting the advantages of learning more widely simply by highlighting productive ideas that arise."[28] (2) "*Comparison for a performative, transformative purpose*" which "proceeds by the study of texts that are notably transformative, with intense attention to the engagement of the scholar, in both traditions. In such projects I still build on and draw attention to certain Hindu materials that I have been reading and have found personally compelling. Then, to draw in Christian readers, I seek analogous Christian texts that famously draw readers into practice and worship."[29] (3) "*Difficult comparison*" which he describes as "my effort to slip the Western hold on the vocabulary and methods of the study of religions by drawing intensively on the highly developed categories of another tradition, in engagement with a primary text or texts of that tradition, read in the original language, for the sake of noting the technical vocabulary of the tradition. Such comparisons introduce difficult comparands that thwart or make all the more difficult the very project of comparison, even breaking settled discourses."[30]

Considering these three comparative aims, the critical dimension of the comparative spirit appears. Explicitly inter-religious comparisons disabuse the comparativists of false claims of religious uniqueness, which includes the ways in which Christians might be tempted to think that life in Christ is entirely different from other forms of life. These comparisons may also help us to see ways that elements of our ethics—for example, our account of the virtues, or the distinctiveness of a Christian moral anthropology—may be helpfully developed in ways we could not have foreseen. Certainly, one engaged in Christian theological ethics need not in every instance begin with a comparative spirit of outwardly directed engagement with religious difference, but if we recall the image of the gardener we can begin to appreciate the importance of this comparative spirt. For Clooney, the comparative theologian has an important role to play in the life of the Church not only in the cautions cultivated by her or his comparisons but also in a deepening appreciation of what is different but beautiful and worthy of care in another tradition.

To give one example from Clooney's work, on a number of occasions and in several different comparative theology projects, Clooney has studied the Jaiminīyanyāyamālā (the Garland of Jaimini's Reasons), a Sanskrit text written 14th century scholar Mādhava. Clooney relates that he had already worked on the text for one project comparing Hindu and Christian ways of communicating divine absence and was wondering if it might be useful for a new project.[31] Part of what puzzled Clooney was the motivation behind his own efforts to read a commentary on Hindu ritual. His was not a practicing Hindu, and he realized that while the practice of reading this text could be beneficial to him as a scholar, he was under no illusion that his reading of the text or what he shared with his readers about that experience would be immediately translatable of useful to others. So why bother? What Clooney learned was that his own particular reasons for reading the text, and then reading that text with other Hindu texts and with a selection of Christian texts, might be of some use to others who did not share either his particular knowledge of these Hindu texts or his particular Catholic history in the parochial grade schools of New York City where he first learned his Catechism to his work as a Jesuit scholar of ancient Indian religious texts. "Our texts instruct, and they disclose truth. But traditions intent upon knowledge and truth want more than the intellectual assent of their readers. Rather, instruction and doctrine are meant also to draw readers into the communities they visit in their reading, become participants who reenact as their own the words they read. This eventuality becomes all the more apparent when spiritual classics actively draw readers into participation by words that appeal to heart as well as mind."[32] There are some things that can only be learned from entrusting oneself to the slow process of learning the unfamiliar, and yet what one learns from those exercises can be profoundly reorienting to what we assume is most familiar. What we see about a previously unfamiliar religious text, or ritual, or community, or set of beliefs will not be exactly what we see in the traditions closest to us, but what we cannot avoid is that the process of learning about religious difference will draw us into our home traditions along different paths, simultaneously more acutely appreciative and also more humble about what we know and how we learned that in which we have such confidence.[33] What kind of ethics does this comparative spirit yield?

IV. Elements of a Catholic Comparative Theological Ethics

At the beginning of this essay, I set forth two images—the farmer who digs deep to feed the Church and the gardener searches widely to adorn the Church and show the potential harmonies that come from the gathering of difference—to envision two kinds of comparative work (or spirits motivating comparison) that I view as central to Catholic theological ethics: going deeply within one's own tradition and going engagingly beyond that tradition. I further argued that each form of comparative work promises a certain kind of harvest for the good of the Church, even as each comparison also contains within it a critical expression. In Odozor's joining of theology of inculturation to traditional Catholic moral theology, we noted the emergence of a distinctive kind of comparative theological ethics that drew forth examples of religious life—in the Catholic Church in Africa and in the life of African Traditional Religions—as instance of living well that could benefit the whole Church even as each stood in need of the critical power of Jesus Christ. In Clooney's exercises in comparative theology, we noted important ethical insights that arose from the theologian's search for truth, beauty, and goodness in other religions, but the critical work took place not only in what the comparativist holds up for consideration but also in how the comparativist arrived at what she now displays.

The shape of Catholic comparative theological ethics is still forming, drawing insights for different kinds of comparative work around different encounters and challenges in the Church. I conclude with three observations about this emerging comparative theological ethics. First, a central task for the future of Catholic theology is charting the relation between those comparisons that emerge from identity, cultural values, and long-standing practices embedded in the life of local church communities and those that emerge as deliberately inter-religious from scholarly, ecclesial, or personal urging. Of the first kind of comparison, the work of Francis Clooney offers a primary model. Of the second kind of comparison, the work of Paulinus Odozor offers a primary model.

Second, if we were to try to draw out a central insight from each of these models, they would look something like this, and each of the models comes with a corresponding cautionary note. The central insight of Odozor's model is the ecclesial theologian of inculturation's conviction that the fullness of the Gospel message, while historically and permanently linked to Hebrew, Greek, and Roman cultural practices and modes of thought, is not fully expressed or shared unless its particular encounter with each cultural and each ecclesial community is recounted, examined, and interpreted for all other local communities of the Church. The cautionary note can be formulated this way. The inculturation model tends to deemphasize those areas where Church culture might not only be illuminated but also be appropriately critiqued either by another tradition's thought and practice—precisely because of the different encounters the rival tradition has undergone the historical social, political, economic, and scientific developments—or by modern critiques of power structures rooted in and defended through religious discourse. By contrast, the central insight of Clooney's model is the comparative theologian's hard-won conviction that one cannot fully understand one's own tradition unless one has taken the time and expended the effort to learn another tradition to the degree that its truth, beauty, and goodness become real challenges counseling the true but provisional nature of our God-talk, our tendency to see certain beliefs and practices in our home tradition as unique without doing the requisite work to make such judgments, and our incomplete transparency of belief and action. The corresponding caution that the comparative theologian must keep in mind is this: comparative theology tends to deemphasize the local and the long-lived realities of the religious communities examined.

Third, if we were to return to the terms that we examined earlier, especially tradition and culture, I think we would see that inculturation theology—at least as we have it from Odozor's pen—develops with more nuanced accounts of tradition and culture than we find in comparative theology—at least as we have it from Clooney's pen. For example, Clooney tends to view tradition as a more or less clearly historically demarcated conversation among those who share a certain set of beliefs and practices. Many of these beliefs are refined through practices ranging from ritual to commentary, but they understand themselves—historically and now—as part of a coherent conversation. The comparative work depends on clear definition of each tradition's coherence, and that coherence is set and defended by religious specialists (scholars of those traditions or those within the traditions who have a certain level of social power to pronounce what is and what is not part of each tradition). We also have in inculturation theology different accentuations of the comparative moment which incline to a different understanding of what counts as a tradition. In Odozor's inculturation theology, what is and what is not part of a tradition depends on the everyday practice of the local community, which although it will certainly be in dialogue with the religious specialists or cultural guardians of that community depends on how the culture is expressed and changes over time in light of particular challenges faced by people living and working together over a long time in the same place. Inculturation theology as a form of comparative engagement, it seems to me, requires a kind of textured and terrain-sensitive historical memory that is not required for comparative theology (although comparative theologians may certainly attempt to access such memories as part of their work).

To be fair to the comparative theologians, there is a certain freedom of exploration afforded them which may allow to them to wander into territory and bring back fruits of their comparative plantings that the community and ecclesial foci guiding the inculturation theologian renders difficult or even prohibitively uncomfortable. In my own thinking about these matters, I have found that it is sometimes easier to consider the conscience-dulling and corrupting effects of power, even ecclesial power held by the best of people with the best of intentions, if we begin with another religious tradition and then work our way back to our own, allowing what we see in another tradition's power dynamics to focus us in a way that it becomes difficult not to see what we do not want to see in our own traditions. The challenge for the comparative theologian, of course, is to maintain an actual relationship with her or his home tradition as she or he explores other traditions, since unlike the inculturation theologian there is no requirement that would link the comparative theologian to the life and well-being of an actual Church or other local community in any way but through the tenuousness of textual interest.

Chapter 9

The Legacy of the African Church Fathers to St. Thomas Aquinas' Account of Virtue Growth and Spiritual Practice

David Elliot

It is an honor to celebrate the many contributions of Fr. Paulinus Odozor to moral theology, from his important historical work *Moral Theology in an Age of Renewal*, which navigates the recent history of moral theology, to his more recent *Morality Truly Christian, Truly African*, and many other works. Over a decade ago I was his student at Notre Dame where he helped to introduce us to the craft of moral theology and the sweep of its modern history. He conveyed a powerful sense of the major authors not just as names but as real people, helping to make the field come alive for us, and showing generous hospitality to us students. I would like to thank him for his many years of scholarship and teaching, and offer this essay in his honor.

My point of departure in this essay will be a passage in Odozor's *Morality Truly Christian, Truly African*, where he refers to Tertullian, Cyprian, and Augustine being spoken of at times as a kind of early "trinity" in African theology and as "ancestors" of African theology more broadly.[1] I will take up this thought in connection with my own area of research, which is focused on virtue ethics and the moral theology of St. Thomas Aquinas. In particular, I will describe the truly vast impact which early African theology had on the vision of moral practice which St. Thomas offered as an aid to growth in virtue, perfection in holiness, and discipleship in Christ. Since the influence of "the common and universal Doctor of the Church" upon the universal Church is itself incalculable, this distinctly African contribution to St. Thomas' moral and spiritual itinerary should be better known and celebrated.

Over the past few years I have been struck by this powerful but neglected legacy of early African theology to medieval theories of virtue growth and spiritual practice. That impact is particularly true of St. Thomas' Aquinas, and most especially of his later work. Nor is this African factor limited to the great influence of St. Augustine. It includes, for example, an important supplemental role for St. Cyprian of Carthage, whom Pope Benedict XVI praised as "the first Bishop in Africa to obtain the crown of martyrdom."[2] And behind St. Cyprian stands the well-known influence of Tertullian, of whom Pope Benedict wrote that, despite various concerns, he "inaugurated Christian literature in the Latin language" and "His work brought decisive benefits which it would be unforgivable to underestimate."[3]

In this legacy the African ecclesial and cultural background often plays a major role in the theological foreground. It is not just the case that Augustine and Cyprian impacted St. Thomas and the tradition, and that they happened to be Africans. Rather, they impacted Thomas and the wider tradition in distinctly African ways, in ways that already struck early Christians from places like Italy saw as distinctly African. Thus when Peter Brown stresses that certain doctrines of Augustine and Cyprian must be understood with reference to the early African Church and its history, it is many of these particularly African features that will go on to shape Thomas and the Catholic tradition.[4] This fact is all the more remarkable in that the history of the early African Church was very little known to the high medievals.

Of course, the early African Church cannot simply be equated with the contemporary African Church, for all kinds of reasons. Yet Odozor has written about, for example, "the Kampala declaration of Pope Paul VI, in which he insisted that the African church must develop its own brand of Christianity and even went on to suggest how this could happen."[5] Among various suggestions, Paul VI pointed to the enduring value "of African writers, such as Tertullian" as well as "Cyprian and Augustine."[6] In fact, intriguing parallels between the ancient and contemporary African Churches are not lacking.[7] But without conflating the two or pushing the point too far, I will proceed with the assumption that early African theology is one potent and local "resource" (as Paul VI called it)[8] for contemporary African theology.

Specifically, I will suggest that St. Thomas late theory of virtue growth represents an African patristic homecoming of sorts in ways that were unique among his medieval contemporaries. Given the importance of virtue theory to moral theology, and St. Thomas' prominence within both, I suggest that this African connection is deeply significant. The first half of this essay will lay out the relevant medieval and Thomistic terrain, and in the second I'll discuss the distinct African contribution to it.

Growth in Christian Virtue

The Second Vatican Council urged that students of theology should "learn to penetrate" the "mysteries of salvation" with "the help of speculation, under the guidance of St. Thomas."[9] In moral theology a Thomistic interest was further encouraged by rising discussions of virtue and character. As Odozor has noted, "recent Catholic theology" involves a "turn to virtue ethics,"[10] and here as elsewhere in moral theology St. Thomas Aquinas has been a critical influence. As is well-known, the topic of virtue is central to St. Thomas' entire account of the moral life. Both virtues and vices are called "habitus" by him, but despite the persistent effort to translate this word as "habit," the differences between the two are striking:

> While "habit" suggests a pattern of mindless or unconscious repetition, *habitus* supplements natural capacities through deliberate and diligent practice. If the paradigmatic example of habit is drug use, especially in American vocabularies, the equivalent examples of habitus—for figures as chronologically disparate as Aristotle, Boethius, Isidore of Seville, and Thomas Aquinas—are knowledge and virtue, *scientia* and *uirtus*. While habitus and habit are [...] capable of describing propensities for either good or bad acts, classical and medieval treatises on habitus tend to concentrate on acquiring the former.[11]

Thomas famously distinguishes between natural or 'acquired' virtues and supernatural or 'infused' virtues. The former roughly track virtue as described in Aristotle's *Nicomachean Ethics* and as proportioned to good citizenship and natural happiness; the latter track virtue as portrayed in the Gospels and as proportioned to supernatural beatitude and eternal life. The acquired virtues are obtained by practicing at them in a long process of habituation analogous to musical or athletic training.[12] By contrast, the infused are gratuitously 'poured into' (*infunduntur*) the soul by God with habitual grace at conversion.[13] Yet precisely as virtues they are moral qualities by which we act and may grow in Christian discipleship. This is possible because grace cooperates with our agency rather than bypassing it. The Christian who performs an act of faith, hope, charity, for example, could not do so without God's grace. But because grace cooperates with him it is truly his act.

We are told to "Be perfect as your heavenly Father is perfect" (Matt 5:48) and through grace our acts of infused virtue can "merit'" from God the reward of further growth in virtue.[14] By this means we may move closer to Christian perfection. To articulate the process, St. Thomas embraced a traditional 'degrees of charity' (*gradus caritatis*) scheme of 'beginners–proficient–perfect' according to which beginners focus on eliminating sin, proficients on progressing in virtue, and the perfect on union with Christ.[15]

Ascending the heights of perfection is clearly no easy task. It is true that the baptized have 'put on Christ' and been regenerated into spiritual life. The presence of the infused theological and cardinal virtues as principles of operation reflects this change. But unlike the acquired virtues, the infused do not come about through the accustomization process which makes good conduct pleasant and natural.[16] Moreover, the wound of concupiscence which descends from the Fall morally weakens us and cannot be fully healed in this life. Thus while the infused virtues represent a real transformation, the fact remains that baptized infants, reformed sinners, and Christians in general have a long moral struggle ahead of them to grow in virtue and holiness.

This growth in virtue does not happen all at once: we must first be 'disposed' for it by virtuous acts, like a stone being hollowed out by rain drops.[17] The problem is that mere routine or mediocre virtuous conduct fail to sufficiently dispose us for moral growth. Increase in virtue will be delayed, Thomas says, until we 'break out in acts of more fervent love and strive to advance in charity."[18] But this is hindered by impediments to infused virtue's operation, such as the "contrary dispositions"[19] remaining from past sins (*reliquiae peccatorum*).[20] The time and effort required to overcome the accumulated effects of our past sins may be staggering,[21] and the ease with which we sink into comfortable mediocrity in the moral life is only too familiar. The result, Thomas concludes, is that steady moral progress tends to prove elusive even among the virtuous.[22] This helps to explain why so few Christians attain perfection in charity and the virtues: in other words, why so few are saints.

Spiritual "Training" in Virtue

If all Christians are "called to the fullness of Christian life and to the perfection of charity,"[23] how can we overcome the tendency to flatten out or plateau in the spiritual life? Measures are clearly needed to help us keep virtue on an upward path. But in practice what will this look like? The answer is partly what we would expect. Christian virtue grows amid fervent acts of love for God and neighbor along with acts of justice, the other infused virtues, and gifts of the Holy Spirit as sustained by prayer and the sacraments. But in addition to these there is a key but neglected ingredient which fuels moral growth that St. Thomas describes as spiritual "training" or "exercise" (*exercitium, disciplina*).[24]

The notion of spiritual discipline or training (*exercitium*) has been a staple concept of Christian moral literature from its beginnings. The terms suggests that just as physical health requires exercise, so too does the moral or spiritual life. Common examples from the tradition include concerted prayer, fasting, vigils, recitation of psalms, manual labor, examination of conscience, vigilance over thoughts, mortification, reading Scripture, meditation, and so forth.[25] St. Thomas continually refers to spiritual training when discussing means to growth in virtue and holiness,[26] and points to practices such as prayer, fasting, vigils, and meditation on Scripture. Such exercises, he writes, enable us to "to ascend to a high degree of charity: perfection does not consist in them; but they are, so to speak, instruments whereby perfection is acquired."[27] This is an enormous claim to make for them, and St. Thomas' own Dominican life in the thirteenth century was powerfully shaped by them.[28]

Patristic and medieval literature long overflowed with the theme of spiritual training or discipline. Like its Greek equivalent *askēsis* ("exercise, practice, or training," origin of "asceticism"), the Latin literature at times describes spiritual training in athletic terms, reflecting scriptural uses such as to "run the race" (2 Tim. 4:7). But in Latin works the military associations tend to predominate. As Katherine Breen explains:

> The general meaning of *exercitium* is exercise or practice, in the sense of a concerted attempt at self-improvement. Etymologically, however, *exercitium* is closely related to *exercitus* (army) and frequently signifies military training either directly or in a transferred sense. Thus the formal devotional exercises of monks and other religious were called *exercitia* specifically to emphasize their practitioners' status as soldiers of Christ.[29]

Yet this was far from limited to monks and religious. Scriptural references to putting on 'the armor of God' (Eph. 6:11) and laboring as 'a good soldier of Christ' (2 Tim. 2:3) were widely embraced.

The literature on spiritual training in Western Christianity is greatly indebted to African sources. For example, Tertullian's 202 *Ad Martyres* was written to imprisoned catechumens (many think it was the distinguished group that included Sts. Perpetua and Felicity)[30] facing martyrdom and he exhorted them that:

> No soldier comes out to the campaign laden with luxuries ... even in peace soldiers inure themselves to war by toils and inconveniences: marching in arms, running over the plain, working at the ditch, making the testudo, engaging in many arduous labours ... In like manner, O blessed ones, count whatever is hard in this lot of yours as an exercise (*exercitationem*) of your powers of mind and body, for you are about to pass through a noble struggle (*agonem*).[31]

In their case the *agon* was martyrdom, but the idea of needing to train for whatever moral struggles would come one's way became generalized and is ubiquitous in the literature. The soldier imagery does not commend mindless aggression but the opposite: it underscores our stressing our moral vulnerability and therefore our need to cultivate discipline. Thus a few generations later, Tertullian's fellow African St. Cyprian of Carthage sought to "arm" his congregation like soldiers against the false persuasions of sin. But what he armed them with was meditations from Scripture on love of neighbor which they should "exercise" in themselves in to overcome jealousy and envy.[32] Far from self-indulgent aggression, the soldier of Christ's application of force is against sinful tendencies that endanger love of God and neighbor, and this is a pervasive trend in the literature.

By Thomas' time spiritual training under names like *exercitium, exercitatio,* and *disciplina,* was a major fixture with venerable associations and centuries of usage behind it. In the literature example a monk's cell, for example, may be described as a "workshop" or "factory" (*officina*) of spiritual training, with its exercises like a "thousand shields" hanging from the wall of the *castra Dei*. The goal of the Christian life is said to become like a "water mill" which never ceases turning, but day and night grinds the "wheat" of prayer, psalmody, reading Scripture, meditation, fasting, and so forth. St. Bernard of Clairvaux in an Alpine image calls such practices the *semitae*: the narrow paths which the soul must travel to love God perfectly, as though by this foot-path one ascended a spiritual Mount Blanc. Such remarks are all over patristic and medieval collections such as the *Patrologia Latina* and the Library of Latin texts.[33]

Although the fact is widely overlooked,[34] Thomas himself saw spiritual *exercitium* as crucial to infused virtue growth. If anything he is more adamant about this than most of his contemporaries, and in this he defies the stereotype of scholastics (*scholares*) that was already current in his time.[35]

In St. Thomas' view the purpose of spiritual training is to facilitate perfection in charity and infused virtue. Broadly speaking, this can happen in two different ways. The first we might loosely call the 'remedial' task of conducing to fuller and freer exercise of infused virtues by removing impediments to it. Thus we should go beyond just countering individual temptations and seek to counteract the "contrary dispositions" or *reliquiae peccati* ('remnants of sin') from past sins which foment temptations.[36] Instead of being like someone who just swats mosquitoes, we should drain the swamp that breeds them. To overcome major moral weak spots, one should apply opposed *exercitia* to the contrary dispositions of our past sin so as gradually to overcome them. To this end Thomas prescribes exercises that are contrary to a given impediment as though by way of remedy. For example, fasting is opposed to tendencies of lust and gluttony, almsgiving is opposed to avarice, and so forth.[37] These remedies operate on the 'contraries are healed by contraries' principle identified by Aristotle.[38] The hope is that the more charity commands the elicited acts of infused temperance, fortitude and the other virtues into remedial action, the more the impediments to infused virtue growth should be eliminated, helping to 'dispose' us for further growth.

In addition to this "remedial" side of spiritual training there is a more "constructive" task which involving practices which seek to kindle greater fervor as a stimulant to charity and infused virtue, ideally leading to more 'intense' acts of them and fostering growth.[39] For example, Thomas repeatedly identifies spiritual 'reading' (*lectio*) and 'meditation' (*consideratio* or *meditatio*) as premier exercises for stimulating the growth of charity and the infused virtues. Meditation causes devotion and feeds charity (and by extension all the infused virtues)[40] like 'fat' (*pinguedo*) feeding a fire.[41]

> For if we hear good things about someone, we are fired up to love him. So when we hear the words of God, we are fired up to love him (Ps 98:140): 'Your word is fire-tested, and your servant loves it'. The second requisite is continual thinking about good things (Ps 38:4): 'My heart became hot within me'. So if you want to acquire divine love, meditate on good things.[42]

Those in religious life undertake spiritual training as, so to speak, 'full-time professionals'. Yet Thomas insists that spiritual training is possible and deeply desirable for all Christians, and that it transfers across all vocations in suitably modified forms.[43] He even has his chosen lay exemplars of holiness and perfection, such as the biblical Abraham[44] and his own contemporary St. Louis IX.[45] Quoting St. John Cassian, Thomas wrote that 'Fastings, vigils, meditating on the Scriptures' and so forth 'are not perfection but means to perfection' and we should 'endeavor to ascend by these steps to the perfection of charity.'[46] The same and similar claims are paralleled in any number of passages across is corpus.[47] As these texts make clear, Thomas does not value these *exercitia* for their own sake but only insofar as directed by charity, and they all track the mean of charity and infused virtue into which they further train or 'drill' us.[48]

The African Legacy

I turn now to the specifically African legacy to accounts of growth in virtue and perfection in holiness. Few would deny that early African theologians had a towering influence upon all subsequent Western Christianity. For example, we might say with pardonable exaggeration that the entire Catholic theology of grace is but a series of footnotes to St. Augustine. But this is far from the only African influencc.

> Three of the most influential theologians of the early Christian period — all of them decisive for Latin Christianity — were Africans. Tertullian was the first to write in Latin and left an extensive body of work that covered nearly the entire creed and many practices, both ritual and ascetic. Cyprian's justifications of the sacramental practice of his church and the role of its officers set the terms of debate for the following millennium... A century later, Augustine drew upon both of these predecessors to develop a theology characteristic of Western Christianity. Not only did Christians first begin to speak Latin in Africa, but there the translation of the scriptures into Latin began.[49]

The influence of early African writers on Western Christianity's model of ascetic spiritual practice was also vast, as already hinted above. But the theology of grace championed by St. Augustine and the African Church was seismic in its impact, like the shifting of tectonic plates. It changed Western Christianity's whole conception of the moral and spiritual life, and became a dominant theme in St. Thomas Aquinas. This African impact on him has especially to do with his mature reception of St. Augustine's later works, but it also includes an important supplemental role for St. Cyprian of Carthage.

So what precisely is the further African influence on St. Thomas model of virtue growth? The account of spiritual training sketched above may sound very technique oriented, though I noted that such efforts should depend upon God's grace. This may seem like a commonplace observation but it seems that later in his career St. Thomas was seized far more forcefully by this reliance on grace, and that in light of this overhauled his account of moral growth in radical ways. In particular, he came to place far more emphasis on human vulnerability and the constant need for divine help, and vastly increased the need for prayer in the moral life, altering his basic model of virtue growth and spiritual training. This is best seen by contrast.

Thomas' major early work was his *Scriptum super Sententiis*, his large commentary on Peter Lombard's *Sentences*, the great theology textbook of the period. In it Thomas addresses virtue growth in detail, implying that it takes steady application but is not especially difficult. Specifically, the early Thomas taught that Christians in a state of grace can grow and persevere in infused virtue *without* the help of any further form of grace.[50] To be sure, this demands that we avoid mortal sin and use our grace-enabled freedom well. Nevertheless, as Joseph Wawrykow notes, with the influx of habitual grace "the onus in salvation passes to the human person," so that "once grace is obtained, it does not seem all that difficult for a person to keep on the way." Such views of grace were utterly mainstream in Thomas' time.[51]

But a major shift began in Thomas' later work and was complete as of his *Summa theologiae*. In his later work he taught that habitual grace and infused virtue are not sufficient for us to act well and grow in discipleship. As Odozor notes,[52] he asserts that we also need a continual supply of further graces which act as specific divine motions or divine interventions "here and now." Thomas calls this form of grace divine "auxilium," the Latin for "help, aid, assistance, support."[53] Whereas the virtues are *habitus* or resilient character traits, this further grace of *auxilium* refers to a motion (*motio* or *motus*) of grace rather than to another habit of grace. It is a specific divine intervention impinging upon the human powers to assist moral action.[54]

We need this "divine assistance" (*auxilium*) to persevere in a state of grace and not lapse into mortal sin amid temptation. Whereas in

Thomas' early work habitual grace alone sufficed for us to do this, he now argues that the Christian needs this further grace "the Divine assistance (*auxilium*) guiding and guarding him against the attacks of temptations."[55] Greater stress on divine reliance is paired with a greater emphasis on the damaging effect of sin.

But even apart from sin, Thomas held that we need this divine assistance to "actualize" the infused virtues as supernatural potencies and thereby to enable us to perform the acts of the infused virtues themselves. Hence the sense of this grace as a divine "motion" bringing potency into act. Later called "actual" graces (in the sense of "actualizing" the state of grace and the supernatural virtues), Thomas' mature teaching is that we need this divine aid or *auxilium* for every act of infused virtue.[56]

To return to spiritual training or *exercitium*: the above points modify Thomas' moral growth account by making clear that spiritual ascetic exercises cannot be self-reliant but must prayerfully depend on a continual flow of 'helping' (*auxilium*) graces to be fruitful. Even the best *exercitium* still leaves us morally vulnerable and in need of those further graces. Yet we cannot command these graces, we can only pray for them. The cause of virtue's progress moves from a focus on human moral capacities once in a state of grace to continual dependency on further graces which we should pray to receive. The result is to shift the center of gravity in the moral and spiritual life, a shift best captured in Augustine's phrase that "man is a beggar before God."[57] While the use of Augustine in Thomas's time was ubiquitous, *this* use of him was extremely rare.[58] These may sound like obvious points to us now, but they were not in St. Thomas' time. If they sound obvious to us it is thanks in part to his labors, and to the early African theology which he helped to recover.

"The African Temperament"

We must avoid the impression that St. Thomas discovered these points as a solitary genius. Rather, in making them he was a keen and attentive student of early African theology. As the historical scholarship suggests, behind this shift was an increasingly Pauline turn to Aquinas' theology of grace encouraged by his reception of late works of St. Augustine from the so-called semi-Pelagian controversy, works in which citations from St. Cyprian play a crucial role.[59] Thomas in line with St. Cyprian sees the petitions of the Lord's Prayer as asking for such divine aid through entreaties such as *fiat voluntas tua* and *ne nos inducas in tentationem*. As Augustine incisively asks, in a passage Thomas endorses: "Why is perseverance besought of God, if it is not bestowed by God? For is it not a mocking request to seek what we know He does not give, and what is in our power without His giving it?"[60] These late works of Augustine rarely circulated in their entirety in the thirteenth century, but alongside his own theoretical advances, Thomas appears to have tracked down and read them in full during his fruitful stay in central Italy in the 1260s, and heavily revised his earlier views.[61] For my purposes the precise contours of that story matter less than the end result, which McGrath describes as a "growing pessimism concerning man's natural faculties" and concomitantly increased role for divine grace to bridge over human inadequacy.[62]

In Thomas' mature work a stress on human frailty and neediness comes to the fore. Sin's effects are viewed as more damaging and moral struggle as more of a problem, leading to an increased role for grace to bridge over human inadequacy.[63] The question "how does infused virtue grow?" is held increasingly alongside the question "and how does infused virtue *survive*?" Some might regard this as pessimistic, but I think it can be taken as a realistic reminder that moral growth is a long and difficult process which poses many snares and reversals, so that we do not lull ourselves into complacency with false expectations of rapid progress or moral invincibility even after we advance in virtue.[64]

This focus on divine assistance and perseverance is very much an early African legacy to Thomas' mature theology—one *not* shared for the most part by his own contemporaries—and it was clearly mediated to Thomas through Augustine with Cyprian in a key supporting role.[65]

Conclusion

Odozor suggests that "inculturation is a two-way process. While it is true that, through inculturation, [quoting Pope John Paul II] 'the Church makes the Gospel incarnate in different cultures,' it is also true that, through the inculturation of the gospel in various local churches, 'the universal Church herself is enriched with forms of expression and values in the various sectors of Christian life.'"[66]

We see a very powerful early example of this in the early African Church. It was the African Church that woke the West up to the threat of the Pelagian heresy, and led the charge against it.[67] This galvanization did not simply emerge from nowhere. As Peter Brown notes, there is a distinctly early African stamp to this theology of grace and perseverance:

> Augustine claimed that this doctrine had always been proclaim in the church. In a limited sense, he was right: for in Augustin's attitude… we can feel the arctic current of specifically African views of the church. Cyprian had already presented the church as a group of 'saints', whom God alone could enable to survive the bitter hostility of the 'world'. Augustine will fall back on this idea. For him, also, the most difficult task that faced a man was simply to survive [and]… the gift of perseverance… was the greatest of God's gifts to the individual.[68]

Something of this sensibility animated the major shift in the Thomas' later moral anthropology and doctrine of grace. In that sense we might that the Thomist tradition was itself inculturated into African Christianity.[69] What Brown calls "the African temperament"[70] has deep roots fostered by early persecution as unforgettably rendered in works like Tertullian's *To the Martyrs* and *The Passions of Saints Perpetua and Felicity.*

I think these points accord well with what Odozor speaks of as hallmarks of inculturation in the best sense, such as a focus on Scripture and on the uniqueness of Christ, on which the early Africans staked their faith, and also with Odozor's insistence on a respect for the best African traditions. As Pope Benedict XVI says, St. Cyprian "Before Rome… staunchly defended the healthy traditions of the African Church." One scholar notes that Augustine had to endure "lingering elite scorn for Christian [African] Punic culture" from the Italian-Roman Julian of Eclanum, the famous Pelagian apologist, who claimed to want to save the Church "from abduction into Africa."[71] This drew a very pointed response from St. Augustine, who wrote: "Are we, then, brigands come out of Africa against you, because against you, a pest come to us from overseas, and a pest to be conquered by Christ the Saviour, we oppose one martyr from here, Cyprian, through whom we prove we are defending the ancient Catholic faith against the vain and profane novelty of your error?"[72] Augustine invoked Virgil's great epic the *Aeneid* to imply that he, Augustine, is like the hero Aeneas slaying the villain Turnus. But whereas Aeneas slays Turnus through Pallas, so Augustine defends the theology of grace and slays the Pelagian heresy through the African figure of Cyprian.[73] We can detect here a potent sense of African distinctiveness and *esprits de corps*.

St. Thomas' late grace teaching marks a significant reconception of the moral life. Since we cannot merit *auxilium* but can only pray for it, the cause of virtue's progress moves from a focus on human moral capacities once in habitual grace to a constant and prayerful dependency on a continual flow of graces to the very end.

This does not undo the crucial role of spiritual training but gives it far better theological foundations. Thomas continued to view spiritual training (*exercitium* or *disciplina*) as a key driver of infused virtue growth. Through cooperative grace, practices such as prayer, fasting, vigils, meditation on Scripture, and so forth, help to preserve us from sin, purify us from its effects, and detach us from lesser goods; on the one hand, and they help with the constructive task of kindling fervor and greater moral dedication; on the other. As such they help to prompt growth in charity and infused virtue. To really shape our moral agency, such exercises should not be done "every now and then," but undertaken with seriousness and consistency. Here the analogy to physical training is most obvious. Someone who jogs once a month is not getting into shape by doing it; but jogging twice a week would be a real exercise regimen. Thomas and his sources have the same assumption with spiritual training: whatever precise form it takes, it should be a concerted effort worked into our regular routines and rhythms of life to be truly formative, to be real *training*.

But the early African tradition qualified this ascesis with the cautionary point that no effort of ours can produce a morally impeccable spiritual elite. Even those with sanctifying grace, when they undertake spiritual practice, must constantly rely on a continual flow of further graces for it to be fruitful and not a mere exercise in pride. This reinforces humility and prevents the idea that spiritual training could become a technique, self-help program, or spiritual technology. The African legacy made clear that moral progress cannot be regarded as a matter of human efficacy or spiritual athleticism, but only as a grace-enabled effort in which growth itself is ultimately a gift.

This shift in St. Thomas' mature work was eventually hailed as a major advance in theology, and ultimately it is a legacy of the early African Church. It was born of the "current of specifically African views of the Church"[74] which the later Thomas appropriated with relish. In that sense we might that the Thomist tradition was itself inculturated into early African Christianity, and that this would go on to have important consequences for the universal Church. Odozor notes that Tertullian, Cyprian, and Augustine can be seen as important "ancestors" of African theology, and St. Thomas was markedly indebted to the latter two.[75] We should acknowledge their major influence on one of the Church's greatest and most influential theologians, and appreciate the fact that Thomas Aquinas' mature theology of moral growth represents a certain African homecoming for theology.[76]

Chapter 10

Facing Up to the Challenge of Moral Formation in African Catechumenates Today: Drawing on African Catechumenates of the Past and Paulinus Odozor's Seven Guidelines for Inculteration

Dennis Kasule

Introduction

In *Method in Theology*, Bernard Lonergan points to a distinction, articulated by the French Jesuit, Joseph de Finance de Clairbois, between "a horizontal and vertical exercise of freedom."[1] A horizontal exercise of freedom involves choosing or deciding within an established horizon. A vertical exercise of freedom involves choosing or deciding by moving from one horizon to another.[2] In this sense, a "horizon," is the maximum field of experiencing, understanding, judging, deciding, and acting available to a subject in his or her historical situation. In this essay, I argue that the challenge of moral formation lies in attempting to accomplish two objectives. The first is forming/shaping new horizons to provide a sound basis for valuing and doing good. The second is cultivating or empowering the individual, as an integral subject, for "vertical" exercises of freedom in his or her daily choices or decisions.[3] To develop the argument, I consider the African catechumenates in antiquity and the late nineteenth century. Then, I develop the application of the seven guidelines for inculturation proposed by Fr. Paulinus Odozor in terms of their potential for contributing to the revitalization of catechumenates in the twenty-first century in African contexts in line with the two objectives of moral formation identified above.

What is the rationale for such a project? At first glance, one may see catechesis or the catechumenate as a distant enterprise from such lofty theological discussions as those developed by Odozor. However, when we recall that in the early Church the most important work of a *didaskalos*, that is, a teacher-theologian, was to instruct others in the Christian way, then we realize that it is problematic to overemphasize the differences between theology and catechesis. The great African Fathers, such as Cyprian, Origen, Athanasius, and Augustine, and all the illustrious Doctors, indeed knew themselves primarily as re-echoers of Christian faith and living. The great Franciscan Doctor, St. Bonaventure, in particular, emphasizes that theology has as its intention *"ut boni fiamus"* (that we become good).[4] In this vein, I sense that underlying Odozor's theological endeavors, especially in his work, *Morality Truly Christian, Truly African*, is a quest to provide a sound basis and frame of reference for moral values, as well as instruction on choosing or deciding as authentic Christian disciples who are also authentically African.

At the heart of the challenge of Christian moral formation in African contexts is the formation of the very identities of personal subjects as Christians and Africans. This is so because, at the end of the day, ethical and moral systems aim at shaping identities. The primary school for the formation of Catholic identity is the catechumenate. In line with this reasoning, the first part of this essay examines the African catechumenates in Christian antiquity and the late nineteenth century, considering how they re-oriented the catechumens' religious and moral horizons vis-à-vis the established religious and moral frames of reference, and how they empowered them to choose or decide on the then "new" Christian religious and moral horizon.

Before going further, it is important to give reasons for linking the African Church in antiquity with the African Church in the modern age. Among other reasons, three are highlighted. First, a certain continuity between the African Church in antiquity and the African Church in the modern age has been recognized by the Catholic magisterium. Consider these words of Paul VI at the canonization of the Ugandan Martyrs in 1964:

> The African martyrs add another page to the martyrology—the Church's roll of honor—an occasion both of mourning

> and joy. This is a page worthy in every way to be added to the annals of that Africa of earlier times which we, living in this era and being men of little faith, never expected to be repeated.
>
> In earlier times, there occurred those famous deeds, so moving to the spirit, of the martyrs of Scilli, of Carthage, and of that "white-robed army" of Utica commemorated by Saint Augustine and Prudentius; of the martyrs of Egypt so highly praised by Saint John Chrysostom, and of the martyrs of the Vandal persecution. Who would have thought that in our days we should have witnessed events as heroic and glorious?
>
> Who could have predicted to the famous African confessors and martyrs such as Cyprian, Felicity, Perpetua, and—the greatest of all—Augustine, that we would one day add names so dear to us as Charles Lwanga and Matthias Mulumba Kalemba and their twenty companions? Nor must we forget those members of the Anglican Church who also died for the name of Christ.
>
> These African martyrs herald the dawn of a new age. If only the mind of man might be directed not toward persecutions and religious conflicts but toward a rebirth of Christianity and civilization![5]

Although aspects of discontinuity can be easily identified between the African Church in antiquity and the African Church in the modern age, there are also aspects of continuity as Paul VI has shown.

Second, during the patristic age, one could not only refer to the Church in Africa but also to the Church "of Africa." There were aspects distinctive to the African Christian experience, practice, doctrine, and theology. In other words, the Church in Roman North Africa and its teaching had significant links with its African context.[6] Notable features included (1) never lacking controversy and usually some form of persecution; (2) bilingual locality; (3) a Latinizing tendency and resistance to it in some areas; (4) the preacher-catechist as a reincarnation of the *grammaticus* and small-town lawyer; (5) functioning as the intellectual powerhouse of the Latin Christian world; and (6) the memory of the

African martyrs. These features gave the African Church of antiquity a certain self-confidence and independence. To give one example, the Creed of the African Church, while so similar to that of Rome, had this specific affirmation: "*Credo in .... sanctam matrem Ecclesiam.*"[7] Perhaps this is why the African church fathers, including Tertullian, Clement, Origen, Cyprian, and Augustine often invoked the image of the Church as Mother. Similarly, in the contemporary age, one must not only recognize the African Church as "the Church in Africa" but also as "the Church *of Africa*." As in antiquity, today, some characteristics distinguish the African Church. These are rooted in the lived experiences of African Christians and subsequently the resulting doctrinal emphases. For instance, in terms of ecclesiological doctrine, African theology today tends to emphasize the image of the Church as "family of God." Two examples relating to ecclesial practice include the non-implementation of the "permanent" diaconate after it was restored by Vatican II, and the forbidding of the application of the declaration, *Fiducia Supplicans*, by most African bishops for contextual reasons.

Third, and specific to Christian formation, catechumens and catechumenates were often at the center of controversies because they were at the core of the process of formation of identities both within the Catholic group and competing Christian sects. The kind of Christian group one espoused depended on the kind of catechetical formation he or she received. Thus, debates on initiation into the Church were not peripheral to the concerns of bishops of the African Church in antiquity. A well-known example was the controversy relating to the reincorporation of lapsed Christians. It is an issue that lingered from the time of Tertullian at the beginning of the third century to that of Augustine in the fifth century.

The African Catechumenate in Christian Antiquity

Alan Kreider has posited that evidence from the first six centuries of the Church shows that Christians initially gave priority to Baptism, and only later in the period from the Didache to Augustine did catechesis precede Baptism. By the fifth century, the pre-Didache order prioritizing Baptism was restored and then the catechumenate largely disappeared after the sixth century.[8] The precedence of Baptism over catechism in the biblical narratives is quite evident. The impression one gets from Acts is that Baptism was done speedily and resocialization into the community came later. On the day of Pentecost, for instance, following his sermon, Peter called upon those who had been "cut to the heart" to "repent and be baptized" (Acts 2:28). Thereafter, "they devoted themselves to the apostles' teaching and fellowship, to the breaking of bread and the prayers" (Acts 2:42). This report does not indicate that those who were baptized following Peter's preaching underwent a lengthy period of instruction before Baptism. The Great Commission also mandates "baptizing them" and then "teaching them" (Mt 28:18–20). Overall, Scripture is generally silent on the details of the process leading to Baptism and even the way it was conducted. However, there are clear indications that Baptism followed acceptance of the apostles' teaching about Jesus Christ and assenting to the demand for repentance. Also, it is implied that some further instruction in the teaching of the apostles and commitment to Christian living followed Baptism.

By the beginning of the second century, however, clear guidelines and clues were provided regarding the process of instruction and preparation (in the forms of prayer and fasting) before Baptism. The seventh chapter of the *Didache*, for instance, shows that Baptism was to be done after a period of instruction.[9] Chapters 1–6 of the Didache detail the kind of instruction that was given. The instruction was structured on the "two paths … one of life and one of death" with an emphasis on the great difference between the two paths.[10] The content of the instruction was essentially scriptural and morally oriented. Similarly, Justin Martyr's *First Apology* indicates that Baptism was preceded by a period of listening to the word and instruction that included doctrinal and moral content. Justin reports that the ones to be baptized had been persuaded and freely consented to Christian teaching as true.[11]

Baptism carried with it a commitment to a manner of life, and one had to be instructed in this manner of life prior to receiving Baptism.[12] In many cases, instruction continued after receiving Baptism. The backbone of the instruction was the two paths already mentioned in the *Didache* or the "way of light" in contrast to the "way of darkness."[13] The process of preparing candidates for Baptism became known as catechesis and the framework in which it was conducted was the catechumenate.

As the original meaning in Greek of the term catechesis signaled, the teachings heard in the catechumenate were to be re-echoed in one's mind and moral conduct. Thus, catechesis focused on forming those who wanted to join the Christian community in the beliefs and moral conduct of Christians. It was intended to result in a kind of resocialization by inculcating a new identity in Christ, committing to a different path of life, and abandoning ways of life that are disagreeable with the new path and the new community. For this to happen two things had to take place. First, the shaping of an alternate religious, social, and ethical horizon; and second, empowering converts to choose or decide upon the alternate horizon. Next, we examine each of these factors.

Shaping an Alternate Religious, Social, and Ethical Horizon (Frame of Reference)

Persecution, imprisonment, and martyrdom characterized the third century Christian experience in North Africa. In that environment, Christianity was a religion not of the weak of heart, but of the tough, the persevering, the unyielding, those ready to endure the prospect of execution for who and what they believed. The catechumenate of the third century took up the task of forming those to be baptized not just for the sacramental reception of Baptism but also to be ready to face these types of existential circumstances. This is evident in the writings of Tertullian, Cyprian, as well as Origen. They make frequent references to catechumens and hearers (*catecumeni* et *audientes*), and to the catechists and lectors, who were their teachers.[14] Often, the authors had themselves been catechumens in their early adulthood.[15] Thus, they were familiar with the catechumenate from being catechumens as well as being catechists as priests and/or bishops.

A dominating feature of the catechumenate was the requirement to reject the world or the worldly frame of reference (i.e., being in the world, but not of the world). As a catechumen, one was introduced to a different hierarchy of relationships. The emperor and imperial order were displaced by God and the ecclesiastical order. With God placed centrally in the hierarchy of relationships, the circle of relationality was extended to include those who were previously not part of one's in-group. The relationship with Christ became the criterion of inclusion or exclusion, what was to be obeyed or disobeyed, what is proper behavior or improper.

Those caught up in the world, and thus, choosing on the worldly horizon were characterized as being in darkness. The catechumenate was a process of becoming purified and enlightened to choose on the alternate (Christian) horizon. Thus, catechumens were to learn to choose suffering over pleasure, poverty over wealth, and care for the poor over personal comforts. Catechists had to ensure that those who entered the Church at Baptism had learned perseverance, to keep and not fall away from the Christian way of life. This is evident, for instance, in Cyprian's *Ad Quirinus*.[16] In book three of this catechetical manual, there are 120 moral precepts drawn from across the New Testament.[17] These precepts were to be learned and lived. Above all, the curriculum was Christ-centered. The catechumens as hearers had to acquire a good grasp of the gospel and to memorize the essentials of the Christian story.

Those who finally made it to Baptism had to first undergo a rigorous process of formation in Christian behavior. Rigorous training continued after Baptism. At its height, the ancient catechumenate in Africa involved three stages. The first stage, which was for ordinary catechumens, involved hearing the Bible read and commented on. This exposition to salvation history and Christology often took place in church and was often offered daily. The second stage, which was for the elect or the competents, involved the *traditio symboli*, i.e., hearing the Creed commented on article by article by a catechist who often was the bishop. This culminated with the *redditio symboli* i.e., the profession of the Creed before Baptism. The third stage involved post-baptismal instruction or mystagogical catechesis aimed at familiarizing the recently baptized with Christian symbolism and inculcating the living of the Christian symbols in one's life.[18]

Empowerment for Vertical Exercises of Freedom

A striking feature of the ancient African catechumenate was the strong connection between catechesis and exorcism. As mentioned already, the catechumenate involved a rejection of the worldly horizon, especially elements in the culture that were deemed contrary to Christian morality and identity. The exorcisms experienced by the catechumen were to assist him or her on the journey of rejecting the way of darkness and embracing the way of light. Exorcisms were therefore a means of purification. There was a sharp awareness that the struggle of reforming one's life involved overcoming various forces whether psychological, physical, cultural, cultic, or spiritual, vices, gods, and the devil and his minions. But purgation was only one side of the coin. Exorcisms were performed for the Holy Spirit to enter. This was why the unholy spirits and ways of living had to be expelled. Thus, the catechumenate not only involved the labors of the catechist but also the exorcist. Catechumens had to throw off all ways, ideas, and desires contrary to the Christian ideal as it was understood.

In Tertullian's time, for instance, catechumens had to renounce going to circus games, athletic competitions in stadiums, and irreverent plays in the theater. Women were not to dye their hair, wear expensive jewelry, or don fashionable seashells. Christian soldiers were discouraged from wearing victory crowns or swearing oaths of allegiance. Men and women were to forsake or forgo professions that would in any way compromise their Christian living including teaching in secular schools because the curriculum involved teaching about pagan gods, and the school calendar revolved around pagan feasts.[19] Coupled with this movement "out from the world," ascetical practices, such as fasting, and frequent prayer were required to facilitate the indwelling of the Spirit and complete entry into the Church.

Further, orthodox communities were distinguished from heretical ones based on how they handled their catechumens. In his *Prescription against Heretics*, Tertullian contends that "To begin with it is doubtful who is a catechumen, and who a believer; they have all access alike, they hear alike—even heathens, if any such happen to come among them. …Their catechumens are perfect before they are full-taught."[20] In other words, heretics (as understood by Tertullian) tended to fully incorporate even those who were not yet fully mature as Christians. In contrast, in his work *On Baptism*, Tertullian maintains that among orthodox communities, "they whose office it is, know that Baptism is not rashly to be administered… This precept is rather to be looked at carefully: 'Give not the holy thing to dogs, nor cast your pearls before swine'" (Matthew 7:6).[21] Tertullian argues against a hasty Baptism because of the kind of life Baptism implied. The ones to be baptized had first to become well-instructed in that life and purified of all that would prevent the indwelling of the Holy Spirit in their souls and bodies.

In short, the catechumenate was a time of rigorous moral and identity formation. As Tertullian put it, *fiunt non nascantur Christiani* (Christians are made not born).[22] The making of Christians took place in the catechumenate in which one was exorcised from the powers and ways of the world and re-socialized into the Church. The catechumenate was a process of empowering one to choose life according to the Spirit and reject life according to the flesh. It was rigorous. It contained a strain of sectarianism and rejection of the world. Very importantly, the catechist was an experienced Christian with developed abilities in teaching and high marks on character. Think of Tertullian, Cyprian, and Origen!

Much of all that would change gradually with the conversion of Constantine, his edict of Milan in 313, and the subsequent installation of Catholic Christianity as the only legal cult in 392. This turn of events brought Catholic Christianity from the peripheries to the center. It also changed "the social function of conversion."[23] Alan Kreider highlights four changes.[24] First, conversion was no longer to a deviant group. Second, there was "a legal impetus for conversion" since Catholic Christianity had become the only legal cult. Third, conversion to Catholic Christianity could be beneficial since the emperor favored it. Fourth, the sheer number of converts made it difficult to prepare them well, to ensure that they were ready to embrace the convictions and lifestyles that had been impressed upon catechumens in previous centuries. Besides, infant Baptism became more normative.

By the time of Augustine, the catechumenate was still well-established, but it was different from the catechumenate of Tertullian, Cyprian, and Origen. Christianity was by now, essentially, the established horizon. Instruction prior to Baptism became considerably shorter and less rigorous. For instance, in *On Faith and Works*, Augustine's list for scrutiny includes prostitutes, actors, or other disrespectable persons, especially the adulterous.[25] After passing this scrutiny, one was admitted into the *competentes*, who could request for Baptism. The training that followed before and after Baptism contained morals primarily based on the Decalogue, which was oftentimes approached mystagogically, but overall, by Augustine's time, there was a shift to focus more on belief, the Creed, or the Christian story in general, along with the Lord's Prayer. Compared to the previous centuries, the material devoted to Christian morals became relatively shorter vs. the material devoted to belief.[26] Moreover, it is arguable that the Decalogue only became established as the mainstay of Christian moral instruction with Augustine.[27] The previous centuries had focused primarily on the teachings of Jesus structured on the paradigm of the two paths and empowering catechumens to choose the path of light vs. the path of darkness.

The African Catechumenate of the Late Nineteenth Century

For purposes of specificity, in this section, I use the catechumenate in Uganda as a case in focus, particularly, the catechumenate in Buganda under the leadership of the Missionaries of Africa (White Fathers).[28] It must be noted here that Catholic missionary activity in Uganda was conducted by at least three missionary groups including the Missionaries of Africa (White Fathers) in Western Buganda and other Western parts of Uganda, the Mill Hill Fathers in the Eastern Buganda and other Eastern parts of Uganda, and the Verona Fathers (Comboni Missionaries) in the Northern part of Uganda. Of the three major missionary groups, it is arguable that the Missionaries of Africa were the first to establish the catechumenate and the most effective evangelizers (as a group) in the early years of Catholicism in Uganda. Their catechumenate is the focus of this exploration.

To shed light on the context of nineteenth century catechumenate, it is important to briefly explore the advent of Christian presence and activity in Uganda. Christian evangelization began in Uganda in 1877. The first group of missionaries to arrive were the Anglicans—members of the Christian Missionary Society based in Britain. They arrived in 1877. In 1879, French Catholic Missionaries, called the White Fathers (later Missionaries of Africa) arrived. The two groups competed with one another for converts. This atmosphere of competition elicited creativity as well as efforts to show the distinctiveness between Protestant Christianity and Catholic Christianity.

In their early evangelizing efforts, the Protestant Missionaries emphasized the Bible. As the late Ugandan Church historian, Fr. John M.

Waliggo, noted in his article "Bible and Catechism," in the Protestant missionary approach, "the achievement of a missionary or preacher is determined in terms of the number of Bibles distributed or sold (the number of local languages into which the Bible is translated), the number of Bible-correspondence courses or Bible-study groups instituted, the number of Christians who profess to reading the Bible daily, and above all, the number of those who can quote Bible verses which brought about their instant conversion to Christ."[29] This description is a bit of a caricature, but it represents the essential orientation of Protestant Christian formation.

Early Catholic evangelization spearheaded by the Missionaries of Africa (White Fathers) was based on catechisms. The missionary catechumenate of the late nineteenth century required a minimum of four years of "gradual and continual religious instruction."[30] Given this length of time and the level of rigor that was required, for the first 25 years, Catholic Christianity was a venture of the young in Buganda. This is why most of the Ugandan Martyrs were between the ages of 15 and 30.

The catechism from which St. Charles Lwanga and companions and the first converts learned the faith was published in 1881 just two years after the arrival of the White Fathers. It was intended for those preparing for Baptism. Another catechism appeared in 1888 for both catechumens and neophytes. The objectives of these catechisms can be understood using similar categories as the objectives of the African catechumenate in Christian antiquity. Next, we explore these objectives.

Shaping an Alternate Religious, Social, and Ethical Horizon (Frame of Reference)

Many parallels can be made between the ancient African catechumenate and the missionary catechumenate of the late nineteenth century in Buganda. There are six areas where similarities can be discerned. They include 1) redressing aspects of the established religious/moral horizon, 2) rigor, 3) a multi-stage process, 4) an emphasis on Christian living and Catholic identity, 5) the catechumenate as the primary identity formation process, and last 6), the chances of suffering martyrdom or other forms of persecution for one's faith and moral choices were high.

The horizon of Catholic Christianity was formed by distinguishing it from the established horizon of traditional religion and from Protestantism. Through the catechumenate Catholic identity was shaped linguistically, liturgically, pastorally, and devotionally. This was primarily achieved through catechisms and other Catholic literature of the time. For instance, whereas Protestants used "Yesu Kristo" for Jesus Christ, the Luganda Catechism and other Catholic literature used "Yezu Kristu." Whereas the Protestants used "Kanisa" for church, the Luganda Catechism used the word "Ekelezia."[31]

In the first 15 years of the arrival of Catholic Christianity in Uganda (1879–1894), as many as seven different catechetical books in Luganda were printed and made available to seekers and new converts. These books were the literature available to the heroic generation of early converts including the Ugandan Martyrs. The early Luganda Catechism for Beginners, which was first printed in 1881 and revised in 1890 concentrated on basic truths—God, the Savior, man, sin, grace, prayer, and Baptism. They also included a prayer section and a section on how to read and write the Luganda language. The most well-developed and focal chapter of this Luganda Catechism for Beginners was the chapter on God. It built on what the Baganda previously knew of God—*Katonda* (Creator) and then went on to present that God as Trinity.[32]

The Luganda Catechism for Neophytes (the already baptized), which was first printed in 1888 and revised in 1891, included instruction on the work and gifts of the Holy Spirit within the life of the Church and every Christian, the importance of grace, and constant prayer, the nature, and use of each sacrament, and explanations of the Mass. They also included a section of devotional prayers for Catholics. Other books included a book of ordinary Catholic prayers and prayers of the Mass published in 1891. A year later, a book on biblical salvation history and the development of the Church through the centuries was printed. The latter contained two parts. Part one included edifying stories from the Old Testament. Part two focused on the teaching of Christ, explanations of various heresies, and the councils.

In 1894, a kind of *summa* of theology in Luganda was published with the title *Edhiini ya Katonda* (the Religion of God). It was meant for mature baptized Catholics. It promoted a vision that all baptized

Catholics are capable of the loftiest religious knowledge. The result of understanding the teaching in this catechetical *summa* was twofold—a) that the Christians of Buganda "will learn how to live well according to the demands of faith"[33] and b) that "those who will have studied this book will be able to defeat the arguments of the heretics who teach false religion."[34] It contained answers and explanations based on the Bible, theology, and philosophy. The 1898 edition of this Luganda catechetical *summa* was as long as 544 pages. It elaborated on the errors of Arius, Nestorius, Eutyches, Wycliffe, Luther, Henry VIII as well as Calvin. It provided explanations on ecclesiastical structures, and canon law rulings relating especially to marriage, apostasy, excommunication, and other subjects. Also, in 1894, a Catholic Luganda translation of the Gospel according to Matthew was published.[35]

Evidently, the early catechumenate in Uganda was rigorous. The missionaries insisted on a four-year catechumenate. The catechumenate was both an evangelizing and moralizing project that prepared early converts not just for Baptism but for Christian living and evangelizing. The two aspects were well captured in the four-point summary based on which baptized or Christian catechumens would give Baptism to those in danger of death. The one to be baptized in danger of death would have to consent to the following:

1. God is one. He punishes the bad but rewards the good in the eternal life.
2. In one God there are three persons: Father, Son, and Holy Ghost.
3. The Son of God became man to redeem us, his name is Jesus Christ.
4. Christ commanded us Christians to observe the commandments of God and especially never to marry several wives.[36]

All Catholics, whether baptized or catechumens, were strongly encouraged to evangelize. It was stressed that everyone has the missionary duty of converting others.

Empowerment for Vertical Exercises of Freedom

From the get-go, the nineteenth-century catechumenate in Buganda was a religious as well as a personal and social empowerment program. As much as the missionaries were tasked with bringing the Catholic faith and practice into Buganda, they were equally tasked with building up the Christian individual as well as his or her community. This was the direction Cardinal Lavigerie, the founder of the Missionaries of Africa (White Fathers), invited his confreres to take. He insisted that "Christianity is not merely a matter of religious belief and practice, but it is the foundation of a whole social order."[37] He based this conviction on his understanding of the socio-cultural transformation or "civilization" of Europe in the fifth century. For him, civilization was Christianization. As Jay Carney states, "For Lavigerie, a society was only cultured to the extent that it was Christian; Europe was therefore becoming less cultured as it turned away from Christianity, with Africa appearing as a possible successor as the heart of Catholic civilization."[38]

Following the direction of Lavigerie, the Missionaries of Africa in Buganda were required to adapt as much as possible to the exterior habits of the people they were evangelizing. This adaptation would create a bridge between the evangelizers and the evangelized. They were first to be "Christians" and "apostles" rather than French or European. They were to learn the culture and habits of the people they were evangelizing and use their local language. The provision of education was to aim at enabling the individual to build up his or her local community. Ecclesial offices were to be adapted to the prevailing needs of the community.[39]

The directives to adapt the Church to Africa, as can be seen above, were complemented by the directives to adapt Africa to the Church. This would involve elevating all aspects of the material life of the evangelized through education, leadership training, and combating forms of slavery. The Missionaries of Africa therefore adopted a "civilizational model of mission"[40] in which civilization meant Catholic Christianization.

The four-year catechumenate played a key role in empowering individuals for their sakes and for their communities. In the catechumenate, as catechumens read the Catechism for Beginners, they also found in it a section of prayers and a guide to reading and writing the Luganda language. A second book printed at the same time as the Catechism for Beginners contained reading and arithmetic lessons, as well as stories from Genesis all in the local language.[41]

The Luganda Prayer Book of 1891 comprised prayers adapted to the devotions and spirituality of the local people. These included what to pray when genuflecting, what to pray before Mass, etc. During Mass, which was presided in Latin, those attending used the Luganda translations of the *Confiteor*, *Kyrie*, *Gloria*, *Credo*, *Sanctus*, and *Agnus Dei* all contained in the Prayer Book. As the presider said the collect in Latin, the Catholics in the assembly had prayers to say as well. Thus, throughout the Mass, there was active participation of the young Catholic community through prayer and action.[42] This enablement to participate in the Mass in word and action was highly empowering for the emerging Catholic community.

Finally, the newly evangelized Baganda Catholics were encouraged and empowered to evangelize and baptize. This empowered posture of the early Catholic movement in Buganda has been depicted for posterity in the stained-glass windows of St. Charles Lwanga baptizing the teenage St. Kizito. Because of this posture of the early Catholic movement, the Church in Buganda produced some of the earliest modern indigenous African Catholic priests. These were Bazilio Lumu and Victoro Mukasa Womereka ordained to the priesthood at Villa Maria on June 29, 1913.[43] Also, the first modern indigenous African Catholic bishop, Joseph Kiwanuka Nakabaale, was consecrated in St. Peter's Basilica, Rome, by Pope Pius XII on October 29, 1939.

All in all, following Lavigerie's direction, many Missionaries of Africa tried to make it evident to the Baganda that one did not have to give up his or her heritage, language, and values to become a Christian. At the same time, they distinctly formed the early converts in the Christian way, empowering them to choose this way in their moral decisions as well as to bring the gospel to their communities. These early evangelizing endeavors of the Missionaries of Africa were far from perfect. Many missionaries did not understand the values underlying many local customs; the earliest catechisms that they produced in Luganda were fraught with linguistic and even theological mistakes, and at times Lavigerie's idea of civilization as Christianization was displaced by the idea of civilization as Westernization. However, their labors were not fruitless or entirely off the mark. St. Charles Lwanga and his companions remained truly Africans as they became truly Christians and so did the heroic pioneers Bazilio Lumu, Victoro Mukasa, and Archbishop Joseph Kiwanuka Nakabaale. The catechumenate, with all the challenges it involved, was the principal center of indigenizing the Church, as well as Christianizing Baganda.

The Potential of Odozor's Seven Principles as Structural Benchmarks for Shaping African Catechumenates as Centers of Moral Formation in the Twenty-First Century

Thus far, we have undertaken a double return to the sources. First, we have shone a light on the African catechumenate in Christian antiquity. Second, we have sketched the African catechumenate in the late nineteenth century in Buganda. We have shown that in both cases when Catholic Christianity was peripheral to the established religious/moral horizon (frame of reference), the catechumenate played a central role in the formation of Christian identities. The challenge of moral and identity formation was approached by shaping alternate religious and ethical horizons and empowering individuals to exercise freedom by moving from the established horizon to the new. Next, we turn to Odozor's work, *Morality: Truly Christian, Truly African,* specifically his suggested guidelines for inculturation in the African context.

Based on the title, *Morality: Truly Christian, Truly African* presupposes a kind of fusion of two horizons or fields of experiencing, understanding, judging, deciding, and acting concerning the good, one Christian, the other African. Odozor refers to the process of bringing together the Christian and the African ethical horizons theologically as "engaging in inculturation in African ethics."[44] He proposes that this process requires adherence to seven guidelines.[45] These are:

- Building on strong Christian convictions
- Based on very clear assumptions about God
- Having a deep knowledge of the culture
- Having more than a fleeting knowledge of the Christian tradition
- Being conscious that inculturation is not only about the past but more about the present
- Limiting the work of inculturation considering present realities

- Keeping the work of inculturation subject-specific

These seven guidelines for inculturation in African ethics are the focus of the remainder of this essay. The concern is not to assess or critique these guidelines. Rather, it is to attempt to apply them to a concrete aspect of the Church's ordinary life, namely, the realm of catechesis, specifically the shaping of the catechumenate. One could wonder as to how inculturation and catechesis can be related. The reasoning here is as follows. If inculturation relates to the transmission of the faith, and the catechumenate is where the Christian faith is transmitted to men and women undergoing the process of Christian initiation, then, inculturation does or could have a significant role to play in the catechumenate.

With this understanding, I attempt to apply the seven guidelines that Odozor offers for inculturation in African ethics toward developing key structural benchmarks for shaping the catechumenate in Africa today as a center of cultivating the Christian worldview, behavior, and identity. In this context, structural benchmarks are to be understood as unquantified goals or reference points to be met by catechetical programs, even though they could go about achieving these goals in different ways. Similarly, they can be seen as reference points by which the outcomes of catechetical programs could be measured in relation to shaping the religious/moral schemes of reference for African Christians and empowering them for vertical exercises of freedom.

Before proceeding to apply the guidelines, we must recognize the emerging context in which many Christians find themselves today, and how it relates to the experiences of Christians in the centuries already discussed above. Various parts of the world with ancient Christian roots are inching toward a post-Christian horizon. This does not so much mean the complete disappearance of the Christian frame of reference as its displacement in determining the day-to-day lives of people. In some places, the process of post-Christianization is well-advanced, in others, it is coming along. Characterizing the situation of the Church today, the Guinean Cardinal, Robert Sarah, in a recent interview, has stated, "The profound crisis that the Church is experiencing in the world and especially in the West is the fruit of the forgetting of God. If our first concern is not God, then everything else collapses. At the root of all crises, anthropological, political, social, cultural, geopolitical, there is the forgetting of the primacy of God."[46] He has decried what he calls a "poison of which we are all victims: liquid atheism. It infiltrates everything, even our speeches as clergymen. It consists in admitting, alongside faith, radically pagan and worldly ways of thinking or living."[47]

If there is some measure of soundness in Cardinal Sarah's view, then, the experience of Christian living today, in many parts of the world, is not so different from that of Christians in the 3rd and 4th centuries in North Africa or the nineteenth century in most of Sub-Saharan Africa. Once again, we have a situation in which the Christian frame of reference competes with another frame of reference, which as Cardinal Sarah points out, is not so different from that of the so-called "pagan" worldview. If that is the case, then questions relating to Christian initiation and ongoing formation take on greater importance. The ensuing discussion of benchmarks for shaping the contemporary African catechumenate, which draws from Odozor's seven guidelines, is based on this view of the emerging situation of the Christian experience in the twenty-first century.

(i) Benchmark One: Centering the Christian Story as Life's Interpretative Lens

The first guideline proposed by Odozor is building "on strong Christian theological convictions."[48] By this, he means putting on Christological lenses to view life and reality, or personally being engaged in the Christian story in a way that gives priority to it over cultural patterns or other norms and making the Christian story the criterion of the soundness of other sources or norms. Put in another way, this involves making the Christian story the interpretative lens of one's day-to-day experiences.

As discussions in sections II and III have shown, the success of the African catechumenate in antiquity and the late nineteenth century largely depended on re-orienting the core convictions and relationships of catechumens—moving them toward experiencing the meaning of their lives on a new Christocentric horizon. Whether one considers the life story of Cyprian of Carthage or Charles Lwanga, one recognizes a shift in their core convictions attendant to the shift in their religious and moral frames of reference. The catechumenate was at the center of shaping and reshaping fundamental beliefs, convictions, and interpretations of experiences to align with the Christian way and frame of reference. The rigor and length of the catechumenates in antiquity and the nineteenth century aimed at that goal.

A key avenue through which the catechumenates in antiquity and the nineteenth century shaped the frames of reference and identities of their catechumens was immersing them in Christian literature, symbols, and rites. These devices were tapped for their transformative power. To give an example, in the ancient African catechumenate, exorcisms were performed regularly. They signaled the expected transformation of the individual as he or she progresses in the process of Christian initiation. Similarly, in the catechumenate of the nineteenth century, there was an emphasis on active participation in the ritual and symbolic world of Catholicism. The emphasis on active participation was meant to enhance the transformation of convictions, behaviors, hopes, and aspirations of the catechumens, as well as build up a sense of Christian belonging among them.

In the twenty-first century, African catechumenates face a similar challenge to those faced in antiquity and in the nineteenth century, namely, how to make the Christian story determinative to how the men and women, boys and girls undergoing Christian initiation interpret their day-to-day experiences and give meaning to them. Thus, catechetical programs must be oriented to immersing their audiences into the Christian story so that it becomes the determining framework for making sense of their everyday experiences and decisions. Achieving this objective requires a Christ-centered and pneumatologically rich approach. The core content of the catechetical material must reflect the Christian story and engage it aesthetically to reach the hearts of those undergoing Christian initiation. To this end, immersing catechumens in the Christian/Catholic literary, symbolic, and ritual world must have a central place in catechetical programs.

(ii) Benchmark Two: Enriching Assumptions About God Based on Christian Revelation

For his second guideline, Odozor urges that the inculturation of ethics in Africa must be based "on very clear assumptions about God, as revealed by Jesus Christ and attested to in the longstanding theological tradition of the church,"[49] rather than "on minimalist assumptions about God found in African culture as in all other cultures,"[50] and so failing to attend to the newness of the God of Jesus in every culture. One may not entirely agree with Odozor on his blanket assertion of "minimalist assumptions" about God found in African cultures given that he has not surveyed all African assumptions about God. Nevertheless, he points to the uniqueness of the revelation of God in/by Jesus Christ. As seen above, presenting this uniqueness of the revelation of God as Trinity and what that implies for faith and life were central and essential to the catechumenates in antiquity and the nineteenth century.

For example, as pointed out earlier in the discussion on the African catechumenate of the late nineteenth century, the first chapter of the Luganda Catechism for Beginners, which was printed just two years after the arrival of the Missionaries of Africa, first affirmed what the Baganda knew about God. However, it did not stop there. It introduced to the early converts the uniqueness of the God of Jesus Christ as Trinity. On this point, Fr. Waliggo noted that the Trinity was presented as a mathematical puzzle, which created the greatest difficulty in understanding the doctrine.[51] Nevertheless, this unique Christian conviction and experience of God was established for the catechumens from the start.

Teaching the early converts the Christian doctrine of God was critical for shaping a new frame of reference for them and so for shaping their moral choices. This is because one's assumptions about God are foundational for determining his or her orientation to the world, relationships, and behavior. On this correlation, consider these words of St. Paul: "For I have told you often before, and I say it again with tears in my eyes, that there are many whose conduct shows they are really enemies of the cross of Christ. They are headed for destruction. Their god is their appetite, they brag about shameful things, and they think only about this life here on earth" (Phil 3:18–19). The Christian way is specified and shaped by Christian assumptions about God revealed by Jesus Christ and not merely those accumulated by a culture.

The African catechumenates of the twenty-first century in attempting to shape the behavior of catechumens must endeavor to centralize the Christian revelation of God as Trinity and so as Love. Practically, in many contexts, this does not require minimizing African concepts of

God but enriching them and using them to arrive at an enhanced experience of God, which in turn frames attitudes, relationships, and behaviors. This is not so different from what Jesus undertakes in his parables relating to the reign of God. His teachings about God and God's reign buttress expectations concerning Christian relationships, attitudes, and day-to-day behavior.

(iii) Benchmark Three: Critical Cultural Appropriation

The next guideline proffered by Odozor is having a level of cultural analytical expertise to be able to recognize the strengths and weaknesses of the culture in which one is working vs. the gospel. A culture is a multilayered reality. Odozor maintains that a theologian engaging in the inculturation of ethics must have "a deep knowledge of the culture in which he or she is working."[52] This ability for cultural criticism saves the theologian from succumbing to culturalism.

One way in which this guideline could be applied to catechetical programs is in the choice of explanatory instruments or vehicles for transmitting doctrinal elements. The selection of illustrations requires a more than fleeting knowledge of the overall context of men and women, girls and boys undergoing catechetical formation, including the history, culture, social dynamics, and relationships in which they are embedded. To give an example from the nineteenth century, as the Missionaries of Africa conducted their early catechetical work in Buganda, they were required to take into consideration the communal ethos of the Baganda. In his directives, Cardinal Lavigerie insisted that the missionary catechizing must recognize that the catechumen is a part of a community.[53] Following Lavigerie's directive, beyond the transmission of religious knowledge, the catechumenate of the late nineteenth century was designed to build up young men and women so that in turn they could build up their communities. Thus, the goal of the catechumenate was not simply to transform the individual but to make him a "transformer"—a catalyst for the transformation of his or her community. In practice, often the missionary catechists fell short of understanding and appreciating the local culture and its ethos. Nevertheless, the directive of their superior remained a worthy standard that was embedded in the overall programming of the catechumenate.

Further, specific to moral formation, it must be acknowledged that whereas there are objective moral principles that must be transmitted to catechumens, the morality of personal decisions involves bearing in mind the contexts or circumstances in which those decisions occur. Thus, moral formation must be attentive to the cultural contexts or the personal-social-existential dimensions of the catechumens to empower them to make moral decisions with appropriate discernment as integral subjects.

In the nineteenth century, moral formation in African catechumenates or catechetical programs must be adapted to local contexts—the languages, the cultures, the historical experiences, and the socio-economic dynamics that contribute to the formation of the religious and moral horizons in which catechumens make decisions. In this vein, it is also important to recognize that most localities are no longer largely isolated cultural contexts as was sometimes the case in the nineteenth century. Rather, considerations must be made relating to the cross-culturalism that has been engendered by the internet and higher social mobility.

(iv) Benchmark Four: Familiarizing Catechumens with the History of the Christian—Catholic Tradition

Odozor's next guideline is the requirement of "more than a fleeting knowledge of the Christian (Catholic) tradition."[54] He argues that having sufficient knowledge of the Christian tradition avoids the risks of "chasing after red herrings, reinventing the wheel, or even engaging in outright heresy."[55] This guideline is easily applicable as a benchmark for structuring African catechumenates today.

In discussing both the African catechumenate of antiquity and the missionary catechumenate of the nineteenth century, it was pointed out that a strong emphasis was placed on familiarizing catechumens with the Christian tradition. Some of the most learned expositions in the Catholic tradition were catechetical treatises composed for the African catechumenate in Christian antiquity. Similarly, as indicated earlier, the 1894 Luganda Catechism produced by Streicher and introduced by Hirth was nothing short of a *summa* of theology in Luganda made available to catechumens and graduates. It did not shy away from including extended discussions on the errors of Arius, Nestorius, Eutyches, Wycliffe, Luther, Henry VIII, as well as Calvin.

The above are strong indicators that in both the African catechumenate of Christian antiquity and the missionary catechumenate of the nineteenth century, heart and mind were not separated. The transformation of the heart was understood to go hand in hand with immersion into Christian sacred texts, Catholic worship practices and symbols, devotions, and spirituality. These elements of the tradition and experiences coalesced to shape the emerging theological and moral horizon of the catechumen. Moreover, there was little hesitation about clarifying how the Catholic faith and practice are different from the views and practices of other denominations and sects.

The African catechumenates of the twenty-first century must become once again vital centers of Catholic "traditioning," that is, handing on the riches of the Catholic intellectual and moral tradition. Very importantly, catechists must have more than a fleeting knowledge of the Catholic theological tradition, devotions, and spirituality. This requirement calls for strengthening training programs for catechists and their associates.

(v) Benchmark Five: Selective Appropriation of the Past for Resourcing the Present

The fifth guideline suggested by Odozor urges the theologian attempting the inculturation of ethics to "be conscious that inculturation is not only about the past. It is especially about the present,"[56] or what he calls "the breathing and living form" of a culture, and how it is informed, illuminated, and guided by its past. Odozor sees inculturation as a form of dialogue taking place here and now between the gospel and the living form of a local culture. The past form of a culture can be brought into the dialogue, but not at the expense of the present.

An application of this guideline as a benchmark for catechetical programs is tapping into traditional African initiation rites. These rites (of birth, adulthood, marriage, eldership, and ancestorship) were established long ago to link the individual to the community and the spiritual world of the ancestors. Although many ceremonies were often involved and the rituals were often long and complex, at the core, the initiation rites were processes of virtue formation and growth as a member of the family, and the community, corporeally and spiritually, in this life as well as in the next. It could be beneficial to tap into these rites to bring them to bear on the present task of Christian moral formation. However, any appropriation of the rites would have to be selective and thus involve much discernment. Developing holistic alternatives to the traditional initiation rites could draw from what was of value in the traditional rites transposed through the lens of new insights about the human person illuminated by Christian doctrine and values.

The African catechumenate of the twenty-first century must be shaped as a space of dialogue between what is truly of value and worthy of preservation in the African rites of initiation and what the gospel reveals about the human being—the self (body, mind, and spirit), others, family, community, the world, God, and humanity's eschatological destiny in Christ. In this way, the catechumenate becomes a space of empowerment for men and women, boys and girls undergoing Christian initiation. This approach requires avoiding the extremes of the displacement model that was sometimes employed by the missionaries, involving a blanket rejection of all African traditional customs and practices. It also avoids the extremes of the cultural restorationist model that involves a blanket sacralization of all African customs and practices and has little regard for the present and negative aspects of certain traditional customs.

(vi) Benchmark Six: Relevancy to Concrete Present Realities

Building upon guideline five, Odozor's sixth guideline for inculturation in African ethics emphasizes the present over the past. Odozor maintains that the theologian engaged in inculturation should limit the work of inculturation because of present realities and people's current lived experiences.[57] The theologian should work within the present realities rather than imagined ideas and obsolete ways of living left in the past due to the dynamic evolution of culture and human experience.

Relating to the catechumenate, it is not an uncommon occurrence that religious and moral formation focuses too much or spends too much time on topics that the catechumens think they do not need or will not need for their lives. Too often this occurs due to wide social and generational gaps between catechists and learners. The two groups often inhabit one geographical space, but they live in different worlds socially, linguistically, psychologically, and in their aspirations. Perhaps this is one explanation as to why too often when catechumens graduate from religious education or receive Confirmation, the next step is to depart from practicing the faith and aspects of the morality that they have been learning about. Such distancing is practical feedback that they do not recognize how what has been taught to them is needed for their lives now.

Catechetical programs that are attentive to "today" must be shaped as spaces of accompaniment.[58] Attention to today does not simply mean "keeping up with the times." Rather, this means that, as the *Catechism of the Catholic Church* states, "It is in the present that we encounter him (the provident Father), not yesterday nor tomorrow, but today."[59] With this focus, the catechetical programs of the African Church today should prepare the men and women, girls, and boys undergoing the process of Christian initiation for a deeper prayerful engagement with God regarding the daily events happening their lives as well as the broader contextual and societal circumstances (socio-economic, cultural, political, familial and ecclesial realities) in which they find themselves. This approach also allows for the recognition of the uniqueness of everyone's faith journey and so their personal relationship/path with God in Christ.

(vii) Benchmark Seven: Adaptive Continuous Program Improvement

Last, Odozor recommends that the theologian engaged in inculturation in African ethics should keep the work of inculturation subject-specific because what is required, let us say, in liturgical inculturation could be different from what is required in ethical or dogmatic inculturation.[60] This is perhaps one of the most delicate of all the guidelines because it involves successfully engaging in the other guidelines discussed above. As such, it calls for much discernment, prudence, and courage. Engaging in the process of inculturation does not require everything to be culturally undressed and redressed. It should not result in a wholesale rejection of everything that seems to bear the legacies of a foreign culture. At the same time, it calls for the courage to re-examine and, if required, let go of certain "inherited" ecclesiastical customs and arrangements, which are not at the heart of the gospel and could hinder its communication or get in the way of the evangelizing mission of the Church in a new locality.[61]

In the catechumenate or for catechetical programs in general, the seventh guideline calls for moderation and continuous programmatic adaptation so that everything remains guided by the overall mission of catechesis, namely, "initiating the hearers in the fullness of Christian life."[62] In their efforts, catechists and the program coordinator can benefit from this exhortation of Pope Francis:

> The Church has rules or precepts which may have been quite effective in their time, but no longer have the same usefulness for directing and shaping people's lives. Saint Thomas Aquinas pointed out that the precepts which Christ and the apostles gave to the people of God "are very few." Citing Saint Augustine, he noted that the precepts subsequently enjoined by the Church should be insisted upon with moderation "so as not to burden the lives of the faithful" and make our religion a form of servitude, whereas "God's mercy has willed that we should be free." This warning, issued many centuries ago, is most timely today. It ought to be one of the criteria to be taken into account in considering a reform of the Church and her preaching which would enable it to reach everyone.[63]

On the need for adaptation, we can find examples from the African catechumenate in antiquity that we discussed above. Before 392, the catechumenate was generally characterized by a strain of sectarianism and an emphasis on rejecting the world. That was in line with the posture of the Church at the time as it faced centuries of severe persecution. After 392, the posture of the Church shifted. Outright persecution at the imperial level had died down and a reversal had taken place following the institution of Christianity as the imperial cult. It became normative to become a Christian. The new atmosphere allowed for a greater fusion between the Christian and the Roman North African horizons. The catechumenate of the time reflected this shift. Moreover, it also reflected the shift of emphasis from Christian morals to Christian doctrine due to the prevailing debates relating to the doctrine of God, Christology, and sacramental theology.

Today, African catechumenates should embrace continuous adaptation in view of initiating men and women, girls, and boys in the fullness of Christian life within the contexts in which they are embedded. As pointed out earlier, ethical systems and moral principles shape identities. They do so by interiorly clarifying differences and drawing boundaries between the moral value of this conduct vis-à-vis that conduct. Moral formation in the African catechumenates of the twenty-first century should serve that purpose. However, since the recipients of Christian initiation are integral subjects, catechetical programs must be continually adapted and improved to reach and transform the hearts of men and women, girls, and boys in the process of Christian initiation and open them to the love and mercy of God in Christ.

Conclusion

This essay has been an attempt to show that Christian moral formation involves 1) shaping a sound Christian basis for choosing/deciding and 2) empowering individuals, as integral subjects, to choose/decide on that basis. The African catechumenates in Christian antiquity and the late twenty-first century have been shown to have involved efforts aimed at both objectives. Going back to these catechumenates was an exercise in returning to the sources as a means of retrieving certain elements that could be vital for shaping African catechumenates today. At the same time, the essay has attempted to appropriate Odozor's seven guidelines for engaging in inculturation in African ethics to the task of preparing candidates for Christian initiation and the institutions involved in that task—the catechumenate and catechetical programs in general. The seven guidelines have been used to propose benchmarks for structuring catechumenates and catechetical programs in African contexts. In the end, the essay has attempted to place Odozor in the lineage of outstanding African catechist-theologians.

Chapter 11

Natural Law in Bénézet Bujo, Paulinus Odozor, and Stephen L. Brock

Matthew Levering

In his 2016 study *Black Natural Law*, which focuses on natural law in the political philosophy of Frederick Douglass, Anna Julia Cooper, W. E. B. Du Bois, and Martin Luther King, Jr., the theologian Vincent Lloyd argues the following:

> The black natural law tradition addresses the same problems addressed by other natural law traditions, but it offers more coherent and compelling responses. Where other natural law traditions start with accounts of human nature that only partially capture our humanity—for example, understanding humans as directed toward natural ends in the same way as animals or other elements of the physical world, or understanding human nature as essentially rational—black natural law appreciates the mix of reason, emotion, and imagination that makes up our humanity, and black natural law concludes that human nature is ultimately unrepresentable. Where other natural law traditions focus on the individual human being who discerns and implements natural law, the black natural law tradition appreciates the influence communities have on individuals and the need for political change to happen through social movement organizing.[1]

Due to his focus on American figures, Lloyd does not attend to important recent engagements with natural law within the broader context of African Catholic ethics. Intriguingly, however, the above paragraph has affinities with the position taken by the African Catholic theologian Bénézet Bujo in his *Foundations of an African Ethic*, against reliance upon (European) natural law reasoning. Bujo emphasizes the imaginative and non-verbal dimensions of moral reasoning, as well as the centrality of community-building and dialogue (expressed in the African cultural tradition of the palaver) for discerning and negotiating moral norms and resolving moral conflicts. Bujo's work, in turn, has prompted a significant response by Paulinus Ikechukwu Odozor in his *Morality Truly Christian, Truly African*. Odozor defends the place of natural law reasoning within a God-centered and Christ-centered ethics. For Odozor, natural law and its commitment to universal human nature and universal moral norms help to ensure that ethics does not become a matter of the strongest voice running roughshod over the weaker. At the same time, Odozor consistently rejects the view that Christ (and faith and Scripture) is only needed in Catholic moral theology "as an explication and confirmation of what is already knowable and known by natural law."[2]

In the present essay, I compare Bujo's perspective to that of Odozor. I introduce a third figure as well, representative of Thomas Aquinas's understanding of natural law: the philosopher Stephen L. Brock. Brock's *The Light That Binds* supports Odozor's perspective on natural law and also demonstrates that much of what Bujo values has a place within Aquinas's understanding of natural law.[3] In my discussion of Brock, I focus on two elements that Odozor and/or Bujo identify as central desiderata for Catholic moral theology. The first element is that human reason knows moral precepts that apply in all circumstances—a key concern of Odozor's. The second element is the importance of community and the counsel of the wise for correctly apprehending and applying natural law precepts—a key concern of Bujo's (shared by Odozor). I hope to show that natural law does indeed belong to an ethics that is—in the words of Bujo, laying down a challenge that Odozor takes up—"at the same time both truly African and truly Christian."[4]

I. Bénézet Bujo

In *Foundations of an African Ethic: Beyond the Universal Claims of Western Morality*, Bénézet Bujo, who taught moral theology at the

University of Fribourg and who was trained in the 1970s and early 1980s at the University of Würzburg, warns that "modern technology creates a *monoculture*."[5] Non-Western cultures risk being swallowed up by the technological culture created by the European West. The resulting globalization would destroy non-Western cultures in their own distinctiveness and integrity. Bujo argues that the mass media, controlled by the West, has "spread ideologies that destroy the good in the non-Western cultures," on the assumption that Western culture represents progress and the future.[6]

Bujo identifies democracy as an instance of this monoculture. It is not that democracy in itself is bad, but democracy depends for its functioning in the West by numerous institutions and traditions that are not necessarily present in non-Western cultures. Bujo has African countries specifically in mind. Writing in the 1990s, he states, "Democracy is transposed to the black continent without question, and promoted vis-à-vis a largely illiterate populace by means of modern media such as television and radio. This new culture… destroys the world in which Africans have traditionally lived."[7] In particular, Bujo mourns the loss of community governance through "the palaver." While affirming that there are varieties of palaver—such as for instance the palaver that takes place between a traditional African doctor and a sick person, within the context of the family and the community (as well as the invisible world of ancestors and spirits), with the aim of identifying and expurgating the problems or sins that lie at the root of the illness—Bujo pays particular attention to the public palaver presided over by "the king or chief or a member of the council of elders."[8] In such a palaver, the presider aims to discover the wisdom embedded in each speech made by a participant; and it is common for proverbial speech and parables to play an important role. Silence, too, has weight. The truth emerges gradually through "many questions and counterquestions."[9]

The community thus stands at the heart of moral thinking, in the palaver model articulated by Bujo. Particular problems, dealt with existentially (in terms of the real life and the real flourishing of the community, provide the matter of the palaver. When violence and conflict threaten to consume the community, the palaver functions to restore harmony—not only among the people involved, but also with the whole cosmic order.[10] Unlike Western Aristotelian-Thomistic ethics, says Bujo, the palaver model does not neglect the community through a focus on the virtues needed for individual flourishing. The goal is the fullness of life for both the community and the individuals within the community. According to Bujo, African ethics characteristically "finds its starting point not in nature or in Being but in the community, which is life-giving in both its visible and its invisible dimensions."[11]

Bujo argues that the palaver model is firmly at odds with natural law ethics. He remarks, "Unlike many of the principles of the natural law… the Black African palaver model does not begin with abstractions. It takes up contextual questions and proceeds by way of discourse, without, however, narrowing down participation in this discourse to an exclusively intellectual performance alone."[12] By means of various examples, he contests the idea that certain actions can be known as such to be "intrinsically evil," so that no situation can ever arrive in which performing such an action could be morally licit. His point is not that there necessarily are no actions that are outside the pale; rather, his point is that every dispute must be brought to the community for adjudication in light both of "the experience of the ancestors" and new contexts.[13]

The palaver model also shows the ethical ramifications of aspects of Christian life that we might not consider to have such ramifications. For instance, Bujo contends that the celebration of the Eucharist through wheat bread and grape wine not only involves non-African food and drink, but also burdens Africans with importing this food and drink largely from Europeans, another situation of economic exploitation that needs to be addressed by an African local church palaver.[14] But the main elements that Bujo has in view are well-known moral teachings such as the ban on contraceptive sexual intercourse reaffirmed by the encyclical *Humanae Vitae*. Citing Josef Fuchs, Bujo maintains that "even Jesus in his moral teaching did not venture to lay down universal norms that would be applicable to all times and cultures."[15] What is needed, says Bujo, is a palaver involving the whole Church and, specifically, between the papal Magisterium and the moral theologians.

In the African context, Bujo criticizes a number of practices and beliefs, including female circumcision, the invalidity of childless marriages, polygamy, belief in sorcery (and the corresponding accusations and persecutions of women and men thought to be witches or sorcerers), the practice of killing or shunning twins, the abuse of power for personal enrichment by heads of state, the refusal to work and the choice instead to live off others, the practice of retaliation and mob (in)justice, and so on.[16] Bujo calls for people to be "persuaded to love and commit themselves to universal peace," which will require "the dismantling of envy, hatred, lustfulness, all kinds of discriminations, baseless suspicions, and so on."[17] At the same time, he also maintains that the fundamental directions of African traditional practices are preserved and enriched by inculturated Christianity.[18] In this view, to reject the above sins is to support the goal of communal and individual flourishing in life that African traditional practices aimed (even if at times in faulty ways) to support. At the heart of the matter for Bujo is the insistence upon community and thus upon an ethics of the palaver. He comments, "Africans understand freedom not only in the sense as freedom 'from.' It is at the same time freedom 'for,' but most importantly of all, it is freedom 'with.' Freedom does not only exist for me: it is for everyone, since I myself am free only when everyone is."[19]

Although Bujo rejects the notion of intrinsically evil acts and challenges the teaching of *Humanae Vitae*, he does not embrace an individualistic ethics based solely on a person's conscience in a particular situation. He rejects making a moral absolute out of one's own opinion, even one's opinion in conscience. He affirms the existence of "objective" truth, insisting that "the individual does not establish this truth for himself: it exists antecedently and must be given a place in his reflections."[20] Indeed, he emphasizes that the individual alone is simply inadequate, as we would expect given his advocacy of the palaver model. He states that "a Christian ought not to make any ethical decision without bearing in mind the ecclesial fellowship of those who believe in Jesus Christ. In general terms, it does not matter how the individual understands a given norm" because what matters is how the community understands it and how it reflects the experience of others.[21] The community, not the individual, must have the central place. But it must be a community rooted not in the universalism of the (Europe-centered) Magisterium but in the particularity of communal dialogue taking into account the relation of a specific norm to "the interpersonal, historical and social context" of believers at particular times and places.[22]

Moreover, this communal dialogue must have a place for the experience of the ancestors who established the norms. This applies, even if in somewhat different ways, both to the whole Church and for African local churches. It requires the palaver in order to work rightly. Bujo maintains, "The norms established in the palaver reflect the experience of the community and represent a continuous summons to the individual, in his ethical conduct and decisions, to interpret the norms on the basis of the community."[23]

Bujo's critique of natural law ethics is developed in light of Pope John Paul II's 1993 encyclical *Veritatis Splendor*.[24] According to Bujo—and I disagree with him—Thomas Aquinas's understanding of natural law rejects the notion of intrinsically evil actions or universal affirmations that a particular kind of action cannot be licitly done.[25] Bujo argues that only the most general principles of the natural law are universally binding, as for example "do good and avoid evil." With regard to more specific precepts (which extend and specify the general principles by a process of moral reasoning), there is not only the possibility that erroneous thinking has entered in, but also there is—in Bujo's view—the fact that "the general law, even the natural law, cannot a priori determine what *bonum, malum, just, unjust* mean in one specific context."[26] When it comes to condemning a specific kind of act, says Bujo, such natural-law condemnations can apply only to the majority of moral cases; one cannot rightly claim that the condemnation applies to all possible cases.

Indebted to Fuchs, Bujo sums up what he believes to be the key mistake in *Veritatis Splendor* by remarking that the encyclical "employs a Western doctrine of natural law; but the precepts deduced from this doctrine are based on human reason, which does not necessarily exclude errors."[27] Put otherwise, the point is that in a particular context the community, gathered in the dialogue of the palaver, may apply the general principles of natural law along lines that do not cohere with any universalized precept. Morality, too, must be inculturated and cannot be assumed to be universalizable on European terms. Bujo states, "*Veritatis splendor* fails to do justice to this fact, since it asserts a priori a claim to universality *in moralibus*."[28] Bujo expresses the wish that Pope John Paul II had perceived more clearly his Eurocentric perspective and had exhorted moral theologians to seek to listen to voices from other cultures.

On issues of sexual morality, Bujo attempts to mark out a distinctive, African Christian stance. Procreation, he argues, is not the defining moral center of human sexuality, and neither is individual pleasure. Rather, it is the community and its flourishing that must be central. Bujo contends, "The goal of sexuality is to keep together the community entrusted to us by our ancestors and to bestow ever new life on this community."[29] This requires a harmonious marriage, contributing to the community's harmony. Bujo notes that the 1992 *Catechism of the Catholic Church*, while claiming to be a universal catechism, reveals its Western grounding by continuing "to employ natural-law arguments in the area of sexuality," as for instance by appealing to the procreative "end" of marriage and thereby to the illicitness of frustrating that end.[30] Bujo thinks that such natural-law language cannot do justice to broader contexts beyond the encounter of the two individuals. What is needed is the palaver-model with its broad appeal to the wisdom of the whole community, including the ancestors and those still to be born. Bujo underscores his point, "Let me repeat: a moral theology that rigidly argues on the basis of natural law becomes irrelevant since it fails to recognize the dynamic and anamnetic character of African ethics, which is realized through communitarian and communicative action."[31] In his palaver model, ethics also involves symbolic dance and art (such as masks), and so African ethics is neither a universal ethics of natural law nor a merely academic or intellectual achievement.[32] He maintains, "The entire community must participate in sociopolitical, economic, and indeed even ethical life. This takes place and is realized by means of the African palaver."[33]

Bujo appreciates that Aquinas himself sometimes reasons in terms of the good of the community rather than strictly in terms of bodily teleology. An example is the question of whether the patriarchs of Israel committed adultery when they practiced polygamy. Aquinas answers no on the grounds that the community needed to grow. Aquinas also holds that natural law reasoning is often difficult, with the result that revelation is often needed to pinpoint the truth about a matter of morality.

In fact, Bujo thinks Aquinas is closer to traditional African moral reasoning than is the contemporary Catholic Church. In African ethics, it is consistently the case that "the decisive and convincing argument will not be an abstract one, drawn from natural law: it is only the community dimension that supplies lasting justification" for a particular moral position.[34] The Catholic Church today, by contrast, continues to rely upon abstract natural law arguments, thereby betraying its Eurocentrism. The problem consists largely in placing human nature, not the community, at the center. For instance, the *Catechism* teaches the immorality of homosexual acts on the grounds that they are opposed to nature. Bujo considers this argument to be flimsy because it presumes a normative account of human nature as heterosexually oriented, whereas modern science shows that a homosexual orientation is relatively common in human beings. I think Bujo has missed the point here, but nonetheless the argument that he goes on to mount *against* the licitness of same-sex sexual acts is a strong one. For Bujo, the keys are the community's ordering toward future children and the importance of the male-female bipolarity. He proposes that "the dialogue between ecclesiastical moral theology, based on natural law, and African moral theology, based on the community, would be made easier if the church paid more heed to the Thomistic distinction between *ius naturale* and *ius gentium*."[35] It is the latter that can soften and contextualize (by attending to the historical particularity of communities) the abstract absolutes of the former, as is the case when Aquinas reasons about the polygamy of Israel's patriarchs.

With respect to intrinsically evil actions, Bujo's concern consists in how we can know with absolute certainty and universal application which actions fall under this rubric. For example, he observes, "people in Black Africa agree with the doctrine of natural law that adultery must always be condemned, without any exceptions; but the question is, to what form of marriage this rule applies."[36] He adds that we cannot rule out the possibility that we might condemn people for actions that later we realize are morally acceptable, or, to put it another way, "the *status quaestionis* in moral judgments [is] something always preliminary, since it is related to and determined by the community."[37] Given this position, it is no wonder that African moral theologians, according to Bujo, "will need to maintain a critical distance vis-à-vis an ethic that speaks of the *intrinsece malum*."[38]

When Bujo spells out his position, he raises examples such as African cultures in which, given the societal approval of polygamy, a man commits adultery only when he had sexual intercourse outside his marriages. Adultery is strictly condemned in these cultures, but a man can have more than one wife. In other African cultures mentioned by Bujo, adultery is strictly condemned but polite hospitality requires the husband freely to give his wife to his male guest, so that the guest can have sexual intercourse with her. In still other African cultures, again adultery meets with condemnation, but a wife who cannot satisfy her husband sexually is expected to bring him another woman, who stands in for the wife. Bujo recalls that Aquinas himself argues that the prophet Hosea's adultery was not a violation of the natural law, on the grounds that God commanded it. As another example, Bujo remarks upon the African tradition of "marriage by stages": the couple is expected to have sexual intercourse with each other in order to test for compatibility prior to sealing the marriage finally.[39] Another example is incest, where Africans traditionally are in some ways stricter than Western societies. Marriages between cousins are absolutely forbidden. On the other hand, a widow is expected to marry an in-law, so as to remain faithful to her husband's family.

Bujo's point is not to approve all the above.[40] Rather, his point is that natural law ethics does not allow for the more extensive and contextual inquiry that would be needed in order to be able to determine "when prohibitions are valid *semper and pro semper*."[41] Even when the overarching good is agreed upon (such as that sexual intercourse "outside" marriage is a sin), the contingent goods in which the overarching good is found can lead different people and different cultures to contrasting moral judgments. Put simply, *pace* the absolutes of natural law reasoning, African ethics requires the contextual elements of the palaver, including narrative (parable) and so on.[42] Bujo states, "The natural-law argumentation gives the impression of looking for the absolute 'ultimate justification,' whereas African ethics is content with a less ambitious goal—not an absolute 'ultimate justification' but only an 'ultimate justification' until a better argument turns up."[43] Even when a palaver results in a determination, that determination is always open to revision, at least in theory. Bujo sums up, "The theories with universal claims must be brought down to earth by particular practices which concretize the universal; more than this, they must also expose themselves to questioning and demonstrate their worth."[44]

Of course, African ethics also knows of universal principles, which are brought to bear upon particulars. But for Bujo the challenge moves not only in the direction of allowing the universal principle to judge the particular case; the particular can also cause the universal to be judged and revised. This is done not only by formal reasoning but also by narrative. The main point is that it makes a difference which cultural framework one takes as normative for grounding moral reasoning. Bujo comments in this vein, "The question is not whether one *theoretically* acknowledges the absolute claim to validity of the *intrinsece malum*, but how, by whom, and according to what rationality this is established or asserted."[45] Western or European versions of rationality cannot be presumed a priori to be superior to African versions of rationality. Both European and African contexts must be included and tested in the process of putting forth moral arguments, and this will require a profoundly dialogic ethical framework. Bujo identifies the palaver as a superb starting point for such a framework.

II. Paulinus Ikechukwu Odozor's Response

In two sections of his *Morality Truly Christian, Truly African*, Odozor engages with Bujo's perspective in *Foundations of an African Ethic*. Odozor first treats Bujo in the context of inculturation. As Odozor notes, Bujo is motivated by concerns about globalization and the production of a monoculture, as the West spreads its culture as though it were unquestionably and universally normative. Odozor sums up Bujo's position in this regard: "The imperative for inculturation arises… from the fact that Western culture does not have either the last or necessarily the superior word on what it means to be human and/or on how to construct the *humanum*; nor does the expression of Christianity with which it is identified constitute the only or best possible expression of the Christian faith."[46] As Odozor sees it, then, Bujo's goal is to bring forward elements of traditional African culture and ethics in order to challenge Eurocentric Catholic ethics and thereby to push forward toward a truly African Catholic ethics.

Odozor points out that it is not only the retrieval of traditional African culture and ethics, however, that shapes Bujo's approach. Importantly, much of what Bujo identifies as inculturated African Christian ethics turns out to be in accordance with the German Catholic theological ethics in which Bujo was trained. Odozor notes that Bujo's reading of Aquinas and of "natural law" ethics shows the strong influence of "the work of the 'autonomous ethic' theologians, especially Alfons Auer" and Fuchs.[47] The view of this school of moral thought was that the content of Christian ethics is no different from the content of any ethics grounded in the natural order. Christian ethics is simply human ethics. The difference that Christ makes, on this view, consists in stimulating and integrating human ethics—in making it stronger and purer. Recall that Bujo argues that traditional African ethics is fundamentally on the right track, but can be purified by Christianity.

Odozor suggests that the impact of German "autonomous ethics" upon Bujo is twofold. First, it leads him to hold that what Christianity does is to simply question, purify, and strengthen traditional African ethics. Second, it leads him to be doubtful about the teaching of moral norms by the Church's Magisterium. After all, if "human beings as creatures of God are capable of generating norms that guide their lives without receiving any other explicit norms through revelation," then it follows logically that "the involvement by the church's magisterium in the search for norms is not necessary and might sometimes be no more than an authoritarian imposition."[48]

Odozor attends to Bujo's constructive account of a palaver-based African Christian ethics, replacing or at least strongly supplementing natural law reflection. Fundamentally, says Odozor, Bujo wishes to place the community and its modes of relational inquiry—inclusive of the ancestors, those to be born, and God himself—at the heart of Catholic ethics. Put another way, the heart of ethics should be relatedness: "human beings become human only in fellowship with others."[49] The others here are obviously not only other human beings, let alone only members of one's family or tribe. Instead of being grounded in natural law reasoning, then, ethics should begin with solidarity. Whether solidarity is strengthened or weakened should be a crucial factor in evaluating a moral norm. To discern what strengthens solidarity is itself a social task, accomplished through some version of the palaver.[50]

Odozor sums up, "Bujo's African ethic is an 'autonomous ethic' where people, created in the image and likeness of God, in open dialogue with each other, search for the way to respond to the summons of conscience by 'palaver' or the 'word.'"[51] Through the palaver, the community and individuals within it discern their identity and moral norms. All persons are welcomed into the palaver. Contributions to the discernment that takes place therein can be made in various ways, whether spoken or through non-verbal communication. Furthermore, "God and the world of the ancestors are an integral part of palaver."[52] Odozor describes the ethics grounded in the palaver as seeking consensus through dialogue and the sharing of experiences, and thus also as always open to revision through the incorporation of new voices and experiences. It is a contextual ethics rather than an ethics received from authorities. It denies that the European Catholic tradition has a privileged status that enables the Magisterium to produce moral dictates for all cultures. It does not reject moral norms, but it rejects their imposition without dialogue. It "acknowledges that the right of specific communities to formulate obligatory norms impels them to dialogue with other communities in the search for moral truth."[53]

After this summary, Odozor lays out some concerns that he has about Bujo's perspective. First, he worries that Bujo has idealized traditional African cultures. For example, it is contestable that traditional African ethics really took an all-encompassing view of the human community. Certainly, African hospitality and care for friends and family are real and profound. But, in Odozor's view, the fact remains that "many traditional African societies do not appear capable or willing to extend to persons beyond their immediate purview the recognition of full personhood and hence the same hospitality and friendship they would show to members of their families and clan."[54] An example of this, he thinks, is the participation of some African tribes in the slave trade. Another example is the deeply violent and at times even genocidal ethnic strife in contemporary Africa, which mirrors ethnic strife from the African past. These realities cause Odozor to think that a richer appreciation of the metaphysical unity of the human race and of the universal character of the norms of natural law would serve Africa well. Odozor states, "I cannot accept Bujo's claim regarding the lack of metaphysical or natural law grounding for either African ethics in general or even for African solidarity."[55]

Secondly, Odozor deems that Bujo has idealized the palaver. In fact, says Odozor, there are elements of the demonic that play a role in palaver. He describes a town meeting (or palaver) in Eastern Nigeria that he himself witnessed. In this palaver, which was held to address a spate of robberies, the community almost accepted a suggestion by one of the wealthier participants that robbery could be forbidden in the town but *allowed* in other towns outside the clan. He also cites an Igbo tale that describes a town meeting or palaver in which the gods demanded an animal sacrifice in order to be appeased, and the one animal who had not attended the meeting was chosen to be sacrificed. The lesson that Odozor draws is that "palaver is not a foolproof approach to determining moral norms, because it is open to being hijacked by demagogues and to distortion by community and individual biases."[56] In a palaver, it can in fact at times be easy to choose the wrong path for wicked reasons, if the community's interests are thereby upheld.

For this reason, Odozor urges that natural law must receive an important place in African Christian ethics. Bujo's criticism of natural law reasoning as too abstract and universal does not strike Odozor as persuasive. He grants Bujo's point that natural law is certainly not the only way that moral truth can or should be ascertained. He also grants that natural-law reasoning can be done poorly, and that it has at times been done poorly. African moral theology therefore needs to discern carefully what is the core of "natural law" and how such natural law can be valuable in moral inquiry. For Odozor, paragraph 16 of *Gaudium et Spes* contains a description of natural law that gets to the heart of the matter: "deep within their consciences men and women discover a law which they have not laid upon themselves but which they must obey. Its voice, ever calling them to love and to do what is good and avoid evil, tells them inwardly at the right moment: do this, shun that. For, they have in their hearts a law inscribed by God."[57]

Clearly, this passage from *Gaudium et Spes* on conscience and natural law takes its inspiration from Romans 2:14–15, "When Gentiles who have not the [Mosaic] law do by nature what the law requires, they are a law to themselves…. They show that what the law requires is written on their hearts, while their conscience also bears witness." In conscience, we discover fundamental moral norms that brook no dissent.

When we refuse to obey them, we feel guilt. All humans have a basic moral knowledge. It is not simply from the community or the family that we learn our moral knowledge. Instead, we have within us an understanding of basic moral norms. If this were not so, then each community would get to establish its own moral norms; something that the example of genocidal communities tells us cannot be the case. People know basic right and wrong, and people are free to choose what is good, even though this may prove costly. There are in fact "moral standards that are exempt from cultural determination."[58]

Of course, Odozor is aware that the natural law in us (like the voice of conscience) can be obscured. But he aims to show that "Africa not only has standards for moral reasoning but also has managed to arrive at some of these standards based on natural law."[59] These standards or norms are universal, and need to be recognized as such. In a palaver, Odozor points out, the fundamental goal is to arrive at a course of action that meets the approval of the community and that therefore often bears the hallmark of a compromise. But since there are universal moral norms from which any declension by compromise involves evil or sin, it is not possible that a contextual palaver unguided by universal precepts of natural law (as illuminated by revelation) will be sufficient. Moreover, Christian ethics involves going beyond the self's and even the community's self-interest. The self-sacrificial actions required by Christian ethics are not merely the result of the local community arriving at a solution that makes the members of the community comfortable. Moreover, it is not enough to appeal to communal conscience, formed by the palaver. The person's individual conscience, in which the natural law resounds, stands against "the danger of communal coercion and demagoguery," and should not be subordinated to communal conscience.[60]

In Odozor's view, Bujo also needs to be more critical of traditional African cultures and, likewise, of the ancestors. Many of these ancestors, after all, participated actively in four centuries of political disorder and enslavement of fellow Africans. In the present day, too, a ministry of reconciliation is needed on many fronts. In this context, Odozor calls for a different approach to inculturation than that taken by Bujo. He urges that the primary identity of the theologian must be that of a Christian, not that of an African. At the heart of African Christian ethics must be Jesus Christ and the God he reveals. The Christian story, not the African story per se, must be paramount. The African theologian must be confident in the truth of Christianity. Odozor underscores that for the Christian, "the primary criterion for measuring the soundness of any other source" will be Christ and the Christian story.[61]

In Odozor's view, Bujo does not devote sufficient attention to the uniqueness of the God of Jesus Christ. Instead, Bujo seems to "assume total commensuration between the notion of God in African religions and Christianity."[62] But the God of Jesus Christ died for all humanity on the Cross, loving sinners with the "prodigal" love of the Father in the parable, and calls us to share in his eternal Triune life. Odozor maintains, "African ethics cannot be built on minimalist assumptions about God found in African culture as in all cultures. Rather, African ethics can be an effective transforming ethos only when it takes into full consideration the implications of God's stunning deed in Jesus."[63]

Thus, African Christian ethics for Odozor should not only include the universal moral norms ascertained by the natural law tradition at its best and illuminated by divine revelation, but also shouldinvolve a strong call to repentance and conversion of mind and heart in configuration to Christ. Traditional African cultures cannot be the starting point for African Christian ethics, since cultures are a mixed bag, ever changing and only partly good. The Catholic Church values cultures, but not as a substitute for the teachings of divine revelation or of reason illumined by faith. For African theologians, says Odozor, it can be tempting to take a stand primarily on traditional African culture on the ground that the Church's tradition developed largely in Europe (and the ancient Near East)—and therefore it might seem appropriate to develop African Christianity, as it were, from scratch or at least not on the basis of European developments. Odozor emphasizes that knowing the Catholic tradition is crucial, since otherwise theologians are hampered by an ignorance that may bring theological disaster and do no good to Africa. For Odozor, Bujo's argument that African theologians should start their doctrinal reflections with traditional African culture is a serious mistake, since it presumes that Christian catechesis should take second place to affirmation of traditional African culture. The likely result will be ignorance of Christianity as well as failure to perceive "how much the gospel can challenge the aspect of culture in question to take on 'the mind of Christ.'"[64]

These criticisms are amplified by Odozor in his chapter on "Moral Reasoning in African Theological Ethics." There, Odozor summarizes again Bujo's critique of natural law morality in favor of a contextual and communal ethics as exemplified by the palaver, including palaver's welcoming of the modes of narrative and symbol. For Bujo, as we saw, the rigid universal moral norms of natural law reasoning give way to norms that are inherently flexible or revisable due to the palaver's openness to new voices. Odozor notes that for Bujo, the fundamental moral standard for African ethics is whether something "builds or destroys community,"[65] a standard that is contextual indeed, since it seems possible that something that now fosters a community's growth and life might later, in a new context, imperil it.

Odozor again pushes back strongly against the privileging of the palaver as the determinative body that defines moral norms. Odozor's central worry is that particular cultures would then get the final say, through the inevitably local or particular process of the palaver, about what counts as a moral norm for the community. This would be problematic because it would open the door to particular cultures defining their own abusive practices as normative. The doctrine of natural law, in Odozor's view, is not blind to the role of cultures and traditions in morality, because natural law doctrine affirms that God is at work in every culture—since all people, through their God-given rationality, have access to the core principles of natural law. But natural law doctrine also imposes a check upon cultures, ensuring that there is a recognized standard that stands above every particular culture, rather than a particular culture being the normative conduit of moral truth. Natural law doctrine, says Odozor, has the authority to hold "everyone and every culture accountable for what they do in this world."[66]

Bujo's model subordinates natural law to the communal process by which moral norms are negotiated and worked out at the practical level. In Odozor's view, once the palaver becomes a "moral method"—standing in contradistinction to "European" natural law morality—then one has elevated "what can be a means for moral discernment in some situations into a principle."[67] Odozor is not denying the value that the palaver can have in particular situations of conflict within a community. But Africans themselves use plenty of other approaches, just as do persons from other cultures. Fundamentally, Odozor's criticism is that "[t]o base the judgment of right and wrong on the principle of community building can be a two-edged sword, lofty as the idea sounds.... When or where do we draw the line between demagoguery, the imposition of the will of some powerful people over others, and a legitimate goal that really serves the common good?"[68] Such a line requires a complex mode of discerning true human flourishing and the true common good, and this will require not only prudence (and not only the particular communal dialogue) but also fundamental norms that constitute a basis for properly pursuing the ends of human life. The alternative to this is inevitably some form of "utilitarian relativism."[69] Odozor indicates that Bujo's ethics ends up on a utilitarian or consequentialist line insofar as it makes community-building into the fundamental standard.[70]

In the end, Odozor's main problem with the palaver model is that it risks turning African ethics into something that holds for Africans (or for particular African peoples) but not necessarily for other human beings. Insofar as "ethics" names something about the good for humans, it is crucial not to accept the division of humanity into particular ethnic enclaves, each with its own local ethics. African ethics must take fully into account the fact that human beings share a common human nature that has theocentric and teleological ends. This common human nature and the natural law that it entails is what gives Africans, like all other peoples, a full place at the table in global discussions of Christian morality. It is also what gives Africans a set of universally true moral norms that can guide the moral casuistry undertaken in the palaver. Both Bujo and Odozor recognize that Africans, like other humans, possess such norms. As Odozor says, "African societies generally hold that certain things are wrong always and everywhere. For example, they generally consider infidelity to one's spouse as adultery and morally wrong. African societies know that unjust killing of an innocent human being is wrong."[71]

Like Bujo, however, Odozor considers natural law to be insufficient by itself. Without doubt, although natural law provides core moral truths, it can be difficult for fallen minds to reason from these broad principles to more concrete precepts. Odozor grants that, as Bujo says, the conclusions of natural law reasoning "can sometimes be distorted by sin, laziness, bias, or lack of knowledge."[72] In fact, Catholic ethics should not rely solely upon natural law, but rather should center itself upon Jesus Christ's life and teaching, as presented and interpreted by the whole New Testament (and indeed by the whole of Scripture). Christians must seek to acquire "the mind of Christ" (Phil 2:5). Odozor observes, "Christian ethics in the Catholic tradition is therefore not simply an ethics of natural law. It is also, and especially, an ethics that is drawn from the revealed word of God in the Bible."[73] By contrast to Bujo, furthermore, Odozor argues that the light of revelation does more than illuminate (and thereby clarify and refine) the moral norms found in human ethics. Christ reveals the depth of the divine love, and ethics becomes a matter of configuration to Christ rather than simply being a matter of norms.

Odozor underscores that the two key sources of African Christian norms must be "the direct words of Jesus, and the teaching of the church drawn from these words down through the ages."[74] Not the local community in a particular time and place, but Jesus' teachings as handed on by the Church must be authoritative. Odozor explains, "The community of Jesus... is empowered to teach in his name (Matt. 28:19; John 20:22–23). Although this community has the authority to teach in the name of Christ it can teach only what Christ taught or what Christ would have taught had the question arisen or been brought before him."[75] The point is that Catholic ethics, including African Catholic ethics, rests upon Christ's authoritative teaching as mediated authoritatively by the Church over the centuries.[76] This is because Christ, with the Father and the Holy Spirit, is the sovereign Lord and Creator. It is Christ's Cross and Resurrection, not human cultures per se and not natural law by itself, that stand as the ground of Christian ethics.

Although Odozor's perspective differs in significant ways from Bujo's, let me note that there also are many points of convergence, as Odozor recognizes. For instance, Odozor well appreciates the value of African traditional religions in contributing to Christian ethics. He points out that African traditional religions recognize the fact that some sins are so damaging to the community that they "demand public penance and a public process of reconciliation," something which goes beyond simply confessing the sin to a priest in the sacrament of reconciliation.[77] He comments that an example of this is the sexual abuse of children and its ecclesiastical cover-up. Traditional African religions can help Christianity in all areas of the world appreciate that this sin cannot be resolved merely through the normal sacramental and legal modes, and neither can it be blamed solely on the perpetrators. In a real sense, the whole Church—the whole community—has failed and has been complicit. As Odozor remarks, "The fact is that because our members have sinned in such a big way, we are all implicated, either because we were in charge and did nothing when we should have, or because we are simply members of the same body."[78] What is needed is a communal process of repentance and reconciliation, and African traditional religion provides models here.[79]

Likewise, Odozor rightly agrees with Bujo (and John Henry Newman) that strict logical reasoning is not the only mode of moral reasoning. We have reasons that arise from the kinds of people we have become by participating in particular communities; and these deep reasons, even when we cannot articulate them, should not be dismissed as irrational. Odozor is well aware that our moral reasoning, therefore, will be community-specific—without denying the reality of natural law and universal moral norms. For Odozor, the West's Sexual Revolution offers a case study. He comments that in the West, unlike in Africa, sexual intercourse has been fully sundered in the popular mind from any necessary relation to procreation, with the result that the sexual difference of male and female no longer seems particularly significant as a moral reality. In his view, African culture has much to teach the West on this topic, since the truth (as the Catholic Church has always taught) is that sexual difference matters for marriage and also that the unitive and procreative dimensions of sexuality cannot rightly be sundered. Of course, the Catholic Church should not thereby be seen as merely ratifying African laws, given the existence (in, for example, Uganda and Zambia) of unjust laws that mandate the death penalty for male homosexual acts.

Like Bujo, too, Odozor argues that Christian ethics must be "anamnetic" in remembering and including the ancestors and those yet to be born. Odozor places the emphasis here, however, upon remembering and including Jesus and his disciples over the centuries (the saints). He sums up, "for the Christian, anamnesis is primarily an ecclesial affair."[80]

III. Stephen Brock's Account of Aquinas on Natural Law

In my view, Odozor has by far the best of the debate. He is right to contend that the palaver cannot suffice in the determination of the path to be followed in particular circumstances by the community. He is right to warn against ever-revisable moral norms, which would inevitably (even if not in every case) entail utilitarianism and, worse, the triumph of the powerful over the weak and vulnerable. The appeal to the palaver is similar to the appeal by postconciliar revisionist Catholic moralists to collective conscience.[81] It is necessary to note that, without the basic precepts of natural law known through synderesis, there is no conscience worthy of the name; conscience would simply be a rubber-stamp for what the individual or community deemed best at the time.

Odozor is right, too, to insist upon the distinctiveness of Christian morality, the fallenness of cultures, and the Spirit-guided role of the Magisterium, not as an arbitrary final court of appeals, but precisely in bringing forward and showing the implications today of the truth of divine revelation as communicated in Scripture and Tradition. Odozor is right to adhere to the wrongness of separating (via contraception) the procreative and unitive ends in marital sexual intercourse, and he insightfully adheres to the prohibition of abortion. He fully apprehends the goal of sharing in the Trinitarian life.

In this final section, I wish to enrich the Odozor-Bujo debate by briefly examining natural law doctrine more directly. For this purpose, I will turn to Stephen Brock's study of Aquinas's natural law doctrine, which is widely recognized as one of the most important recent treatments of natural law. My brief exposition will focus upon two elements: human reason's knowledge of moral precepts that are binding in every circumstance, and the community's role in the apprehension and application of natural law.

Natural Law and Knowledge of Universal Moral Precepts

At a basic level, natural law is never absent in human persons. Brock speaks of the "practical reason's *common* principles, which are the primary precepts of natural law and which require no instruction."[82] Aquinas holds that these primary precepts or principles are held in the human mind through the habit of synderesis.[83] Synderesis is receptive to what Aquinas calls the eternal law—that is, God's wise plan for human flourishing—due to the mind's created participation in the divine light. Natural law is promulgated by God precisely as the created light of reason. As Brock says, "It is God who promulgates natural law by instilling the light of reason into our minds and thereby making the law something that we naturally come to understand."[84]

In an important sense, then, everyone knows natural law. It is not an obscure body of knowledge accessible only to theologians and philosophers. It follows that natural law in human minds is quite distinct from *natural law doctrine* as known by scholars. To provide an adequate account of the doctrine of natural law, for example, scholars need to know that God has promulgated it. But human beings do not need even to believe in God in order to know natural law precepts. For Aquinas, as Brock says, "atheists have conscience too. They do so even if the deny it. And this is because they know the common precepts of natural law."[85]

Aquinas recognizes that fallen human beings are generally inclined toward vice. Given that humans arrive at rational inquiry via the path of the senses, it should hardly be surprising that humans tend to act on the basis not of reason but of what the senses desire.[86] Vice is "contrary to nature," therefore, not insofar as people generally act virtuously, but insofar as vice is not suited to rational nature. Human nature is rational nature, even though humans often act against reason, and even though humans certainly do not act in accordance with reason "by nature." Aquinas does not "think that the order of reason itself, whose principles are the precepts of natural law, is founded merely upon the ways in which people usually act or tend to act"—since this would entail that the order of reason "is founded, at least in part, upon things that are contrary to it."[87]

If the order of reason is not founded on the ways people usually act, then what does Aquinas mean when he so closely associates the natural law with "natural inclinations" toward certain human goods? For Aquinas, says Brock, the "good" which natural law commands us to pursue is a "good" because it is an "end" for us.[88] As an "end," it is something that we apprehend as serving our flourishing: it is a good that befits the perfecting of our nature. When we apprehend a good as an end for our nature, it can be said that we have a natural inclination toward that good. Brock underscores that this natural inclination is not pre-rational but rational, rooted in our apprehension of something as a good and an end for us. As Brock puts it, "What reason naturally apprehends as good, the rational appetite—the will—naturally desires.... Man, as man, is naturally inclined to certain things, *because* reason naturally apprehends them as good."[89] The point is that our natural inclinations toward life, life in society, childbearing, truth, and so on are not pre-rational inclinations but rational ones: reason identifies these things as goods and ends perfective of our human nature. Since there is a certain order of these goods and ends—some are more fundamental than others—"the order of the precepts of natural law is according to the order of man's natural inclinations."[90] Therefore, natural law does not arise from pre-rational inclinations which practical reason apprehends and builds upon. Rather, "the relevant inclinations derive from reason's natural knowledge of the goods themselves."[91]

Brock repeatedly returns to Aquinas's insistence that "the precepts of natural law are certain practical principles that are self-evident," and, as such, are the first principles of practical reason, principles perceived by the light of reason, which operates by making judgments of truth.[92] For Aquinas, again, these principles are "self-evident not only in themselves but also commonly or naturally to all men," which means that "the process of apprehending their terms requires no special instruction or effort, and... even the most uncultivated minds are apt to know them."[93] In sum, the most basic natural law precepts are known by everyone, even though the application of these principles in complex cases is difficult and, for fallen humans, often unsuccessful.

The Community's Role

Since human reason knows the core principles and precepts of natural law, there are universally knowable moral absolutes, just as Odozor emphasizes. These absolutes ground community deliberation about what is to be done rather than arising out of community deliberation. Nevertheless, for Aquinas, there is also a strong place for the community in understanding and applying natural law precepts. In this vein, Aquinas holds that there are things belonging to natural law that people generally come to know through receiving instruction from wise teachers or from God. For instance, Aquinas considers that in order to perceive that lying is wrong, people generally need instruction: natural law does not suffice, even though lying is a violation of natural law. Similarly, although people can generally see that committing adultery is wrong, Aquinas argues that "the prohibition of fornication… and even the prohibition of the so-called sins against nature [including same-sex acts] pertain to the instruction of the wise."[94] After all, Aquinas is aware that some pagan cultures did not consider fornication or male homosexual acts to be sinful. Yet in Aquinas's view, both fornication and the "sins against nature" are deeply harmful to human persons, families, and communities, and these sins are very much against the natural law.

In most cases of moral reasoning, Aquinas maintains that "without instruction, the matter is not immediately clear," even though "natural law (absolutely considered) does order toward all acts of virtue at least in a general, confused way."[95] Given the complexity of human action and of human flourishing—and given human fallenness—human beings may often be confused about what should be done in particular cases. Aquinas states that often "instruction is needed in order to clarify that order [i.e. the ordering toward the acts of virtue] or to specify its requirements."[96] Catholic ethics needs the instruction provided by the Magisterium and the doctors of the Church regarding the content of natural law.

Brock grants that the natural law "only provides starting-points, common principles," for the moral life that "human beings need for life in any community, divine or human."[97] He remarks, "For [Aquinas], law and obligation… always refer to life in community and to common good, and he does not think that even the whole set of conclusions that can be drawn from the precepts of natural law suffice to regulate any community, human or divine, to which human beings actually belong."[98] Natural law by itself is insufficient for the Christian community. As Brock sums up, it is the case that "under the conditions of sin, even many of the precepts that belong to natural law absolutely, and indeed the most important of them, seem to need divine help, not only for actual compliance with them—that certainly requires grace—but also for a more than tenuous, merely notional or theoretical hold on them."[99] This point should lay to rest the notion of natural law as sufficient in itself, or the optimistic notion of cultures without being able to gain a correct view of the moral life without the guidance of divine revelation.

IV. Conclusion

Brock's emphasis on the rational knowability of human goods and ends, and the first principles of the natural law retained by synderesis, grounds the existence of unrevisable moral norms that cannot be rightly violated in any circumstance. At the same time, Brock recognizes the importance of divine revelation and of the community in knowing natural law with firmness.

In this light, we can return to the debate between Odozor and Bujo. Their viewpoints are quite close in certain ways. For example, Odozor's call for a Christ-centered African ethics generally fits with Bujo's remark in his 1986 book *African Theology in Its Social Context*, where Bujo states, "I believe that a truly dynamic Christianity will only be possible in Africa when the foundation of the African's whole life is built on Jesus Christ, conceived in specifically African categories. Such an African Christocentric ethic does not of course exclude rational reflection."[100] Odozor would gladly agree with this combination: a Christocentric ethic inclusive of "rational reflection."[101] With Brock, however, Odozor maintains that to be a human reasoner is to know basic principles of natural law and to apprehend thereby some non-revisable moral precepts that hold in all circumstances. This is so even if in important ways we need the community's (and thus the Church's) help to apprehend and apply natural law precepts. Emmanuel Katongole, reviewing *Morality Truly Christian, Truly African*, rightly observes that Odozor fears that "without attending to the universal dimension of ethics, the African moral voice could easily lapse into relativism and the related social problems of ethnocentrism."[102] Odozor holds, as Katongole says, that "African conceptions of ethics need a boost from natural law to take them beyond mere blood ties to a universal vision."[103] Human reason is not simply context-dependent or community-dependent.

At the same time, Bujo's emphasis upon the community's role in the apprehension and application of moral precepts reflects the viewpoint of Odozor, Brock, and Aquinas about the necessity of human and divine instruction for successful natural law reasoning. As Katongole puts it, for Odozor, "the conclusions of natural law can be distorted. Natural law needs the light of revelation as well as the magisterial teaching of the church to 'bring out the truth that it sometimes reveals only dimly.'... [I]t is the church that is the locus for moral reasoning."[104] Bujo's repeated suggestion that natural law is Eurocentric and abstract (cut off from the narrative and contextual dimensions of the moral life) does not do justice to natural law. Aquinas's natural law doctrine, like that of the Church Fathers, draws heavily upon Scripture and recognizes the significance of cultural contexts in the apprehension and application of natural law. He attends carefully to Romans 2:14–15, with its teaching about the law inscribed on the heart.[105] For his part, Paul draws upon Hellenistic Jewish sources and also upon Israel's earlier scriptural witness to the moral law. Natural law is not a "Eurocentric" reality.[106]

As we saw, Bujo seeks to bring about a specifically African Christian ethics that takes fundamental starting points from African traditional religion and culture, especially the palaver. In response, I have suggested that Odozor is correct to hold that the starting points of African Christian ethics (like all Christian ethics) must be Jesus Christ and natural law's universal moral norms, which are not revisable by the community. Odozor makes clear that natural law's grounding of universally applicable moral norms must be affirmed in the African context, precisely in order to ensure that such things as the palaver function well. Moreover, the role of the Spirit-guided Church and the Christian saints and doctors over the centuries in teaching moral truth needs to be appreciated. Otherwise, emphasis on the African context can turn into an exercise in reinventing Christian ethics along lines that lose touch both with divine revelation and with the insights into life in Christ that have been gained over the centuries in the light of revelation.

Chapter 12

Paulinus Odozor and Joseph Ratzinger on the Question of Moral Objectivity: A Morality Truly African and Truly Christian?

Tegha Afuhwi Nji

I. Moral Objectivity—Why Does It Matter?

"How ought I act or live?" is the core ethical or moral question. The undergirding presupposition of this question, which can no longer be taken for granted today, is the claim that there is *the* right way to live or to act. In other words, that there is a universally shared ideal of rightness or wrongness (of actions) which in turn rests on a shared sense of objectivity, be it in terms of "duty" in deontological ethics, or "value" in axiological ethics, or "the desirable end" in teleological ethics. Put simply, there is assumed a shared sense of "truth." Was it not Immanuel Kant who, for all his rejection of metaphysics, still maintained that honesty or truth was an absolute moral obligation? "To be truthful in all deliberations" he said, "is a sacred and absolutely commanding decree of reason, limited by no expediency."[1] In today's pluralistic society, however, the very notion of moral objectivity or the absoluteness of truth is called into question. "Truth," as it were, stands trial anew before modernity's Pilates: "*Quid est veritas?*" (What is truth?). Coextensive with this pejorative interrogation of "truth" is the parodying of "good," "duty," and "value."

I recall an experience during one of my graduate courses in Berkeley, California. A debate had broken out in class regarding the morality of homosexuality. The contribution of a particular student, an ordinand, stayed with me, not because it impressed me, but because it was particularly irksome. Perhaps not wanting to offend the other students in the class, he said in words similar to these, "We cannot insist on there being an unshakable objective truth or standard of judgement. We should stop referring to Jesus as that standard. Truth is simply what we agree upon in conversation." With an irresponsible reference to the biblical text of the woman caught in adultery in John 8:1–11, he added, "Even Jesus did not condemn people by means of moral judgment."

That which stunned my moral sensibilities was not so much this student's opinion, with which I totally disagree. That comes secondarily. The first has to do with the fact that the student in question was a Catholic, and more so, a candidate for priestly ordination. But why should this be bewildering? Precisely because of the underlying presupposition that a Catholic is one who believes that Jesus is the Truth, the Way, and the Life (Jn 14:6); one who accepts and believes in the Church's teachings, and these teachings are clear on the debated issue. If this is true of a Catholic, it should be even truer for a soon-to-be priest. Paulinus Odozor says, following Paul Ricoeur, that "no one speaks from nowhere; people come to [any] debate laden with presuppositions that inform the positions they take."[2] This student was trying to speak from "nowhere," perhaps in order to be accommodating to non-Christian views. However, in reality, he negated his own supposed religious or Christian presuppositions that he could have brought to the discussion. Not just that, he ended up validating an anti-Christian presupposition. He came to the debate as a non-Christian. Now, at the secondary level, but equally crucially important, this student failed even to articulate the Christian view correctly. He mentioned Christ's non-condemning attitude toward the woman caught in adultery, but failed to mention that Christ did not confirm her sin either, but forgave her, lifted her up from her sin (wrongdoing), and said to her, "Go, and do not sin again."[3]

The axiological, and even deontological, nihilism couched in the affirmations of this student is symptomatic of the reality that is commonplace in today's neo-Nietzschean society. Jack Gist captures the situation quite correctly when he speaks of Nietzsche's radical individualism—the notion that there is no absolute truth—as germinating "the seed of relativism that was planted before him." The seed, now in full blossom, gives off fragrances that are anything but pleasant.[4] Nietzsche's ideal man is the *Übermensch* (Overman). Even as the name suggests, the overman stands beyond the constraints of good and evil (or what Nietzsche perceived as a servile Judeo-Christian morality). The overman alone is truly "free" and so creates his own values.[5] This sort of moral relativism, in vogue today, hinges on a distorted notion of freedom, makes it imperative for any serious *theos-logian* to reconsider the question of moral objectivity, with urgency and greater perceptivity. Questions of this nature can no longer simply be taken as givens: What is moral objectivity? Is it even possible to speak of an objectively moral way to act today? If so, what guarantees such a morality?

Engagement with these and many such questions lends a timeless relevance to works such as Paulinus Ikechukwu Odozor's *Morality Truly Christian, Truly African: Foundational, Methodological, and Theological Considerations.* Though arguing for moral objectivity, at the same time, the very title of this text—"Morality truly Christian, truly African"—raises a further question as to whether morality is culturally dependent, and if that be the case, would it not degenerate into cultural relativism? This essay offers two responses to this question. First, morality in a true sense is culturally dependent (or inspired) but not culturally 'determined.' Second, cultural plurality does not necessarily mean relativism. The latter is more at home in pluralism. Granting these distinctions as givens in Odozor's project, then, the even more important question to be considered is this: What in Odozor's consideration makes morality objective, while at the same time remaining both Christian and African?

The following quote from Odozor anticipates our discussions on this subject:

> If the African scholars' speculation on the lofty nature of human beings within God's creative intention and purpose is accurate, the inevitable question would be, what happened? Why is the human person in such a dire situation in Africa today? In his post-synodal exhortation, Pope Benedict XVI proclaims that 'Africa is facing an anthropological crisis.' In this situation, he says, 'Africa will have to rediscover and

> promote a concept of the person and his or her relationship with reality which is the fruit of a profound spiritual renewal.' I contend that, for this renewal to occur, African theology must rediscover Christian anthropology as an important contribution to the understanding of the human person as subject and moral actor in Africa.[6]

In the context of the above-quoted anthropological question, Odozor recognizes that the pursuit of authentic human existence within genuine African cultural value systems and scholarship, and the Christian counterpart, are one and the same, or at least, ought to be so. African theology, he posits, would benefit from an engagement with Christian anthropology, with specific reference to the understanding of the human person as a moral agent. Corroborating this claim, as we shall argue, the Christian vision of man likewise stands to benefit by drawing upon genuinely worthy local customs and values that promote human dignity.

In the discussions that ensue, this essay offers a validating reading of Odozor's work, by bringing his thoughts on the question of moral objectivity into an even more precise dialogue with one of Christianity's foremost scholar and theologian, Joseph Ratzinger (Pope Benedict XVI). Besides his personal and authoritative witness to the Christian faith, the choice of Ratzinger as a dialogue partner in this endeavor is likewise occasioned by Odozor's own lengthy engagement with the latter, even as evinced in the above-quoted text.[7] Both authors concur on the necessity of returning to the moral question today. In discussing how they each do this we arrive at interesting overlaps in their thought, and especially corroborative explications in Ratzinger's articulation of the Christian faith or theology that lend credence to Odozor's discussion of morality as truly African and truly Christian.

Arguably, Ratzinger's most precise and very widely known and referenced assessment of today's moral landscape is contained in that famous homily he delivered at the *Missa Pro Eligendo Romano Pontifice* (Mass for the Election of the Roman Pontiff) at St. Peter's on April 18, 2005. In prophetic style, he describes the central challenge facing today's Church and the world. Excerpting from that text, we read,

> The small boat of the thought of many Christians has often been tossed about by these waves—flung from one extreme to another: from Marxism to liberalism, even to libertinism; from collectivism to radical individualism; from atheism to a vague religious mysticism; from agnosticism to syncretism and so forth. Today, having a clear faith based on the Creed of the Church is often labeled as fundamentalism. Whereas relativism, that is, letting oneself be "tossed here and there, carried about by every wind of doctrine," seems the only attitude that can cope with modern times. We are building a *dictatorship of relativism* that does not recognize anything as definitive and whose ultimate goal consists solely of one's own ego and desires. We, however, have a different goal: the Son of God, the true man. He is the measure of true humanism… A mature adult faith is deeply rooted in friendship with Christ… that opens us up to all that is good and gives us a criterion by which to distinguish the true from the false, and deceit from truth.[8]

What ties together this quotation from Ratzinger and the earlier quote from Odozor is both theologians' assessment of the troubled condition of the human person in today's world vis-à-vis questions of truth, value, and moral action. They both conceive of the human person as a "moral actor," whether Asian, African, North/South American, Antarctician, European, or Australian/Oceanian. Presupposed here is the even more fundamental claim to a universal human identity and destiny, which should accord a specific nature and purpose to human actions, acknowledged or not. Furthermore, this general comparison of both quotes reveals a mutual recognition of the centrality of Christ in addressing the moral crisis of today. Odozor says the way out of the present predicament in Africa is to "rediscover Christian anthropology" while Ratzinger invites us to rediscover in *Christ* the "true measure of humanism." In other words, this initial comparison reveals a mutual interest and agreement on the necessity of what I like to call "*Christification*" of cultures. Such Christological convergence in the thoughts of Odozor and Ratzinger is among the many themes explored in this essay, whose overarching goal is to compare both theologians' thoughts on the question of moral objectivity.

To properly attain this goal, and for the sake of a more fruitful dialogue, it is expedient that we let both theologians speak for themselves. Accordingly, in the next section (II) of this essay, "Culture, Faith, and the Question of Moral Objectivity"—subdivided into four headings, under which are examined the sources of morality, and five guarantors of moral objectivity, viz., Christ, God, natural law, human nature, and conscience—the views of Odozor and Ratzinger are simultaneously engaged in a mutually reinforcing fashion. In each case, there is attempted a non-dialectic synthesis of their views. Additionally, as the discussion unfolds, it becomes evident how morality can be simultaneously African and Christian, without at the same time buying into the perils of a pluralistic relativism, thereby validating Odozor's thesis. In the final section (III), we conclude with a reaffirmation of a now fully reformulated version of Odozor's thesis, that "There is an objective morality that is truly African, and truly Christian, marked by five guarantors of moral objectivity."

II. Culture, Faith, and the Question of Moral Objectivity

a. Culture and the Sources of Morality

Subscribing to Robert Schreiter's characterization of theology as a contextual discipline, Odozor goes on to identify four sources of African theology, and hence of African morality, which reflect this contextuality. These include the following: i. God's Word (the Old and New Testament of the Bible); ii. The uniqueness of Jesus Christ as the revelation of God; iii. African Tradition;[9] and iv. The Received Christian Tradition.[10] Looking at these sources one would be right to say that from the outset, Odozor has in mind an "African-Christian Moral Theology." The hyphen between "African" and "Christian" eventually drops when he sufficiently explicates the 'unity' between the two. His very methodological preference in naming the sources of moral theology to include both African cultural values and Christian values, shows that he sees a possible unity in being African and being Christian. In his search for a moral theology, he is appealing to that unity rooted in that fundamental human reality, that which marks the human person with an undying openness to God. This openness to God ultimately becomes a configuration to Christ, who stands at the heart of the Christian message and hope. This assumption further aligns his thoughts with those of Ratzinger, for whom Christ is the "true measure of humanism," or put differently, "To be human is to be open to Christ."[11] We could imagine Odozor making the following addition: "To be African is to be open to the uniqueness of Christ within the context of one's Africanness." This addition is justified by Odozor's above-mentioned second source of African theology, namely, "The uniqueness of Jesus Christ as the revelation of God." He follows Edward W. Fasholé-Luke closely, who sees the task of African (Christian) theology as "to translate the *one faith of Jesus Christ* to suit the tongue, style, genius, and character of African peoples."[12] It is within this translation process that dialogue takes place, called by different names—inculturation, enculturation, or interculturality.

There arises from this translation the following challenge: How can one culture, say, the Christian culture, be translated into another culture, say, the African culture, without harm coming to either culture? It means, then, that the success of Odozor's project rests on how well he positively addresses this challenge. In my estimation, true to the practical nature of the goal of his project, Odozor performs this translation most successfully, even though he takes for granted the theoretical framing of the latter. This situation lends particular relevance to the task of this essay, since dialogue with Ratzinger lends us insights on how to theoretically frame the theological task of "translation" performed by Odozor.

In March of 1993, in a setting we could describe as one of contextual theology, Ratzinger, as Prefect of the Congregation of the Doctrine of Faith, speaking at a Meeting with the Doctrinal Commissions in Asia, in Hong Kong, begins by noting the seeming impossibility of inculturation with the following argument: Religion is an essential aspect of every culture and determines the very structure of its values (moral ones included) and therefore its inner logic. How then can a culture, living and breathing the religion with which it is interwoven, be transplanted into another religion without both of them going to ruin?[13] Put another way, if one were to remove from a culture, say, the African culture, its own religion which begets it, then, would one not be robbing that culture of its heart? And should one implant in it a new heart, the Christian heart, it seems inescapable that the organism (culture) which is not ordered to it (the new Christian heart) will reject the foreign body.[14] But as it soon becomes clear, this is only a provisional mismatch *à la* Ratzinger. Despite the difficulty to envision, *prima facie*, the success of this operation, that is, inculturating the Christian faith in a culture, Ratzinger masterfully demonstrates the congruity of the operation by means of the principle of "interior openness" of cultures, one to another. Included in the openness of culture is "its capacity to give and receive, its power to develop, to allow itself to be purified and become more conformed to truth and to man."[15] Ratzinger further hinges this argument on two other principles. The first is that every culture shares in what Ratzinger calls "potential universality" of culture; and the second is that in all cultures, the same "human nature" is at work.[16] Taken together, these three principles provide the theoretical basis presumed in Odozor's theological performance. Hence, the relevance of the dialogue between both theologians.

In a nutshell, inculturation rests on an anthropological presupposition, the openness of the human person to the truth, and ultimately, to God. In this reading, culture itself becomes a vehicle of man's own *purification* and *elevation*, a reaching out to the deepest yearnings of his *Geist.* Now, in the Christian registry, explicitly defended by Ratzinger, Christ is the Truth, and the perfect man, the exemplary man, the goal or end of humanity, and hence of culture. Therefore, this purification and elevation happens in and through the person of Christ. It is Christ who relativizes every cultural knowledge, value, or morals. Christ is the indispensable criterion for determining objective moral rightness or wrongness. This Ratzingerian logic holds good for every culture, whether African, European, American, or even the so-called culture of modernity. Granting this, it means that included in Odozor's "process of translation" is both the *distillation* or *purification* from the African culture that which stands opposed to the truth or to the dignity of the human person, and the *elevation* of that which does it honor.

For illustrative purposes, take the example of what Ratzinger considers the privileged moment of inculturation, namely, the encounter between Christianity and the Greek culture. This he calls the Hellenization of the Christian message. In this encounter, Christianity, for example, purified and adqpted the Greek ideas of *logos*, *ousia*, *homoousios*, etc. These purified and adqpted ideas enriched the Christian understanding of the faith, by offering it precise philosophical or reasonable terminologies with which to bolster its self-expression against heretics, thereby laying bare its authentic kerygmatic inner moment. Within this philosophical (*philo–sophia*) registry, the wisdom (*sophia*) of the faith came to be expressed as follows: Christ is the eternal *Logos;* the persons of the Trinity are consubstantial (*homoousios*) as opposed to *homoiousios* (merely similar); the Incarnate *Logos* is one divine person in two natures (*ousia*), divine and human. While such Hellenization has become normative for the universal Church, it does not reject, but rather demonstrates the relative validity of the inculturation of the Christian faith even today. The Christian faith continues to be enriched in its encounter with various and different cultures, while continuing to relativize and elevate these cultures. For example, Jesus is validly referred to as a Proto-Ancestor, a terminology from African ancestrology, which, once purified of all entanglements with pagan rituals, depicts the fact that "Jesus is the ultimate embodiment of all the virtues of the ancestors," or of human perfection, generally. He is the Pro-Life force who bears "[the] transcendent form of the primitive 'vital union' and 'vital force.'"[17] Or again, among the Asians, as Yonk-Bok Kim maintains, Jesus is best understood as "the Messiah of the Minjung." Minjung means "People of God, all people." There develops around this concept a corporate understanding of Christ as "the Minjung." Jesus is the Minjung and the Minjung is Jesus.[18] The examples of such inculturation initiatives are widespread.

Of course, no tradition is a *tabula rasa* with respect to the advent of the Christ. For if "all things were made through him and for him" (Col 1:16), then, it follows that all things are marked with a *predilection* for the *Logos,* in whom they have their being. It is this *Logos* (the Christ) who is for both Odozor and Ratzinger the prime guarantor of moral objectivity. Besides Christ, there are discernable four other guarantors of morality according to these theologians. Let us now examine these in greater detail, although first we must keep in mind that whether in

Hellenization or in African or Asian inculturation, no cultural language or symbol can exhaust the mystery of the Word it seeks to represent. There is always a Christological *more* that escapes our grasp.

b. Christ (and the Church) as Guarantor(s) of Moral Objectivity

Scripture itself offers us an originary example of what happens when the Word is encountered by a culture, in this case, the Jewish culture and its religious institutions. The result of this encounter was never an abolition of the latter, but rather its purification, transformation, and elevation. Read this way, the Jewish culture reached toward its finality in Christ, by opening up to the universal factor introduced into it by Christ. A particularly relevant example is how the Jewish moral valuations and praxis shift dramatically with the advent of Christ. For instance, in Matthew 5:43–45, quoting Leviticus 19:18, Christ purifies and perfects the law as follows, "You have heard that it was said, 'Love your neighbor and hate your enemy.' But I tell you, love your enemies and pray for those who persecute you, that you may be children of your Father in heaven. He causes his sun to rise on the evil and the good, and sends rain on the righteous and the unrighteous."[19] Christ goes on to extend the very notion of "neighbor" beyond its restrictive interpretation among the Jews for whom neighbor meant one's fellow Jew. The classical text here is the famous Parable of the Good Samaritan, a non-Jew who proved himself a neighbor to a wounded and abandoned Jew when his own fellow Jews passed by unconcerned.[20] Christ would ultimately exemplify in his very person this sort of universal love, which knows no boundaries: He loved his executioners by forgiving them, and by his very death, he drew unto himself *all* peoples.[21] In these texts, the most important biblical moral code, love, undergoes a significant Christological reconfiguration, without at the same time repudiating the "seeds" of this *Christific* love in the earlier Jewish culture and/or religion. Rather, these seeds were purified, elevated, and brought to fruition. This is indeed Christ's own example of "inculturation," *avant la lettre*, and it is paradigmatic of the sort of work theologians like Odozor are engaged in.

In fact, there is a very similar move in Odozor, in the rapprochement between African morality and the Christian faith with respect to the question of whom we should love or consider neighbor. Arguing against some other African theologians like Bénézet Bujo who, while invoking African communitarianism, have claimed that it is customary among Africans to extend love even to those who are not members of one's own group, Odozor thinks the truer picture is that "African communitarianism is often limited to the known other."[22] Without getting into the details of this critique, it behooves me to mention here that the very ethnic discriminations and inter-tribal and civil wars across Africa are more validating of Odozor's contentions than Bujo's. Granting then Odozor's observation, this 'restrictive love' shows a shared affinity between the pre-Christian African culture and the pre-Christian Jewish culture. It goes without saying, then, that the Parable of the Good Samaritan holds as much relevance for the African situation as with the Jewish. In fact, it is relevant for every other culture. This Christological reshaping of love, values, and morals across cultures is what I have referred to in another context as the *Christification of solidarity*:

> The needed purification… of African solidarity from all tendencies of ethnocentrism and other forms of 'hate' is fully realized in Christ, and this happens in what we have called the *Christification of solidarity*. Christ is that unique 'Good News' in every culture, the true principle and guarantor of perfect communion in every culture and across religious denominations, for it is in and through him alone that all are reconciled and made one.[23]

The point, therefore, is that it is in Christ that all moral ideals, including solidary or neighborly love, or the values of authentic African communitarianism, such as *ubuntu* ("I am because we are") or *ujamaa* (that African Socialism which does not consider one class as an enemy but always as a brother/sister) reach their perfection and most paradigmatic exemplification. Culture, indeed, becomes more perfectly itself when it reaches toward universality, both intra-culturally and inter-culturally. Therefore, the relativizing of culture by Christ is not a destruction of culture but a fulfilment of its potential for universality. This universality is achieved in and through Christ, since he is the very creative *Logos* in whom, through whom, and for whom all things were made and came into being (Col 1:16). Christ is the finality of all creation, human cultures inclusive. Assuming human nature, and like a craftsman, working from within, he has brought all human cultural aspirations to fruition.

Applying this to the moral standpoint, this "Christ-factor" serves both Odozor and Ratzinger as a safeguard against the danger of the otherwise rich culturally inspired morality from slipping into spirals of cultural relativism. They are both agreed that every culture—its customs, norms, values, morals, etc.—is judged with respect to its finality and the perfection of the human subject, and that it is in Christ that this perfection or finality is attained. One very significant instance where Odozor engages this Christ-factor in culture is found in the opening pages of Chapter Nine of the text under consideration, where he speaks of the anamnetic character of an ethics truly African, truly Christian. He begins with Bujo's claim that African ethics is necessarily anamnetic, that is, it keeps alive "the memory of the words and deeds of their ancestors [and so] ensures continuity between the past and the future of the peoples of the continent,"[24] but then makes an important Christological qualification. He speaks of a "more inclusive anamnesis" which goes beyond that proposed by Bujo. It is more universal in that it offers an ecclesial dimension to anamnesis, tracing this "memory" back to Jesus Christ, then his disciples and their successors, and to the believing community formed around Christ, traversing cultural boundaries and barriers. He writes,

> I [argue] that African Christian ethics must be anamnetic in a more inclusive way. It must be an ethic that begins with remembering Jesus, his teaching and his deeds. Further, this ethic must also take seriously the teaching of Jesus' disciples and of those other members of the community of Jesus who through the centuries in every part of the world have kept the memory of Jesus alive. In other words, for the Christian, anamnesis is primarily an ecclesial affair; Christian ethics is anamnetic but in an ecclesial way.[25]

The significance of this passage goes even beyond the context in which Odozor uses it. He does not say this, but what is immediately apparent here is the pulling together of all the four sources of African Christian Ethics which we noted above: God's word (OT and NT); Uniqueness of Jesus Christ as the revelation of God; African Tradition (here called ancestral memory); and Christian Tradition (here called ecclesial memory). At the center of this "pulling together" is Christ. It is Christ who validates the truth value of God's word; it is he who stands at the heart of the Christian memory and tradition; and it is he who relativizes and brings to perfection every other cultural memory of a people, by that principle of "interior openness" of every culture toward the transcendent, toward universality, since he himself is that transcendent universal truth.

As already intimated, but now in greater detail, the operation of these principles (of the "interior openness" and "universality") at the background of Odozor's work, even though he does not articulate them, is one of those areas in which, bringing Odozor's work into dialogue with Ratzinger's proves of the greatest benefit to the former. By means of these principles, Ratzinger supplies the finest argument for the "relativizing impetus of Christ" in every human culture. Ratzinger's argument could be situated within the broader context of his critique of the Enlightenment and modern reductionism: the reduction of faith to merely a disincarnated spirit ultimately void of reality, of culture to mere form, and of religion to inexpressible mere feeling or thought. *Sed contra*, for Ratzinger, "Faith itself is culture." There is no naked or disincarnated faith or mere religion. Faith (in Christ) creates its own culture as it carries within itself a way or form of life, telling man who he is and how he ought to be human. Through a long history of intermingling, Christian faith has formed its own structure of life, the interaction of man with himself, his neighbor, the world, and with God. This means too that faith is its own subject, a living and cultural community which he calls the "People of God."[26] This culture of faith—"People of God," or St. Paul's "Body of Christ," or simply, "Church"—is universal and stands over and above every individual historical or classical culture, be it Asian, American, African, European, etc. It is not one culture among other classical cultures. It is culture which has attained the desired universality and finality in Christ, which all cultures tend toward by their given interior openness toward the universal, premised on, and safeguarded by the very transcendent upsurge of the human person, the subject and agent of culture.

While standing over and above every individual culture, Christian faith exists, in concretum, within these different cultures; hence, we speak of African Christian, European Christian, etc. Therefore, there is a "doubling of cultures," such that "man now lives in two cultural worlds, his historic culture and the new one of faith, both of which permeate him." While noting the impossibility to achieve complete "synthesis" in this encounter, Ratzinger unequivocally states that the goal of this encounter is that man, living within whatever particular historic or classical culture, might "learn the transcendence toward wholeness and universality which is proper not to a specific people, but precisely to the People of God, which embraces all men."[27] With this, we arrive at the Archimedean point, the relativizing impetus, the standard or measure of true humanism, and hence, of human values and morals, namely, Christ.

This argument validates Odozor's claim that "The arrival of Christianity on the African continent and the acceptance of Christianity as an alternative scheme of reference to the one provided by African Traditional Religion amounts to an acceptance in some ways of the inadequacy of the latter *as an explanatory schema.*"[28] In this context, though, I would modify the final words of this quote to read, "as a *self-sufficient* explanatory schema," to emphasize the fact that the African schema is itself a relevant explanatory schema for moral valuations, but an imperfect one, whose fulfilment or perfection, as has just been noted, is in its tending toward universality in Christ. In fact, sounding a cautionary note against an exaggerated romanticization of the so-called traditional African values and customs, Odozor speaks of the necessary work to be done for a wholesome Africa, namely, "to unearth the deep structures of sin embedded in African tradition, as in any others—structures that need to be exposed to the saving effects of the gospel."[29] He argues his case with the example of the *osu* in Igbo land in Nigeria, through the mediation of Chinua Achebe's novel, *No Longer at Ease.* The character in this novel is Clara. She is an *osu,* that is, "a non-person, sacrificed to a local deity," to use the words of Romeo Igwebuike Okeke.[30] As an *osu,* Clara has no freedom nor any possibility of redeeming herself from this "enslaving role" till natural death. She is restricted to the shrine of the god and must thus call off her marriage engagements with the young man Obi Okonkwo.[31] With this story, Odozor successfully makes his point that the African cultural values are yet to be rid of all deformities, and this will happen only through Christ's purifying, perfecting, and universalizing impetus.[32]

It is important to note here how the universalization being spoken of differs, not just in degree but in kind, from Kant's own project of universal morality. Kant sought a deontological ethics that would make the duty of respecting human dignity, for instance, a "universal given," and that would likewise mandate the responsibility of all peoples to act only in such fashion that their actions could be universalized as a moral norm.[33] Fabolous as this might sound, Kant lacked the grounds upon which to make this stick, for he had already relegated God and the possible knowledge of God or God's will to the realm of the unknowable noumenon. Remember, Kant's God was merely a "postulate of practical reason." This automatically precluded the possibility of a revelation of God and God's moral will in Christ Jesus, and hence the unique universalizing impetus of the 'Christ factor' thus far discussed. Paradoxically though, it is only in Christ that even the lofty aspiration of the Kantian moral universe has any chance.

That said, the point Ratzinger further makes is that this tending toward the universal is an undying human tendency, which we find even in those cases when man tends to deny the truly transcendent, God and religion. Such is the case with the so-called universal brotherhood of the Enlightenment and the French revolution. Without anchoring this otherwise Christian value of brotherhood in the *Logos*, Christ who makes us all brothers, the truly transcendent guarantor of genuine universality of brotherhood and love, the modern quest for an egalitarian society, before long, and precisely due to this lack of an authentic foundation, degenerated into forms of unbrotherliness and struggle, as was the case with the Marxist utopia, and as has been seen in the horrifying wars and violence around the world. James Lee is therefore right to say that according to Ratzinger, the crisis of the present day is, in essence, a long-deferred resumption of modernism, which laid the foundation for that particular kind of relativism that remains the chief threat to humanity. The paradox here is that rather than preserving human freedom, such relativism effectively eliminates it and leads to the destruction of the ethical foundations of the past and to the dehumanization of society.[34]

Contrarily, the long-sought-for brotherhood is possible only by granting a moral responsibility of human persons and for human persons, one to/for another. This responsibility must be objective and guaranteed by that which is itself unmovable, unchangeable, and unreservedly self-gifting. Nothing finite fits this category. God's love alone, made manifest in Christ, fulfills this paradigm. How fitting, then, is Odozor's conclusion that without God, it is impossible to conceive of the human person, talk less of him as a moral subject. God, in other words, is the chief guarantor of humanity's very existence and of universal moral objectivity. In terms of that commonplace theological jargon, "the Fatherhood of God is the very basis of the brotherhood of men." It remains now to examine this claim in greater detail.

c. God as the Guarantor of Moral Objectivity: A Theocentric Ethics

The onetime president of the Baptist Union Theological Seminary in Chicago, George Washington Northrup, though speaking in a typically American Baptist context, different from Odozor's and Ratzinger's contexts, made the following irrefutable claim, which lends us a takeoff point for our discussions on God as the guarantor of Moral Objectivity. He said, *inter alia,*

> Similar to the conception of the central position of the sun in relation to our solar system is the idea of God in relation to the system of the moral universe. This idea is…the determinative principle of every system of theology—the principle in virtue of which the facts and truths of the moral universe may be understood and comprehended as a self-consistent whole. The fundamental idea of God is that of his absolute ethical perfection, which consists in holy love and is the essence of his fatherhood.[35]

A very similar affirmation comes from another onetime Chicago (and Yale) theological ethicist, James M. Gustafson, who proposes a theological ethics established on convictions about God and the world. However, while for G. W. Northrup such a theocentric perspective is determinative and prescriptive of the moral conduct that ensues from our relationship as "sons" and "daughters" to God as "Father,"[36] for Gustafson, a theocentric ethicist neither prescribes nor proscribes the conduct of others.[37]

We would be anticipating correctly by noting that Odozor's project aligns more with Northrup. In fact, he analyses Gustafson's six characteristics of a "theocentric ethics" for their merits and demerits, but ultimately rejects his above-stated conclusion. For Odozor, arguing from the premise that God is the foundation of ethics or morality, of necessity arrives at the prescription of moral objectivity. He agrees with Northrup that God is "absolute ethical perfection." Situating these affirmations within the context of African Christian Morality, Odozor makes the following argumentation:

> Knowledge of the moral law is neither based solely on any faith nor limited to any one tradition since it is disclosed through the order of creation which reflects the reason of God. The point then is that although the various traditions to which we belong shape our perceptions of the world and of the moral order, they neither have exclusive hold on our reasoning nor offer exclusive insights into normal moral dilemmas and problems. The corollary is of course that "the notion of a moral order must always be tempered by the understanding that 'objectivity' in this sense does not mean 'something out there' to which we must all conform irrespective of our particularities. It is an objectivity that is structured by our subjectivities but not held captive by them. The moral law does not exist independent of who we are and yet it is prior to us, to our traditions, and to our caprices and whims."[38]

Two important points are raised here: First, God and the law of reason which he embeds in creation relativize "individual" (personal or collective) moral judgement. Second, following the tradition that goes back to Augustine, Newman, and more recently, Ratzinger, Odozor signals to an a priori "in-dwelling of God's voice" or "the moral law" or "truth and good" in the human person. This latter point is taken up in the next section when we discuss in-depth the category of conscience. The important point to reiterate here is that, for Odozor, ethical or moral objectivity is rooted in God, his creative will and intellect. Or, as Laurentia Magesa, like John S. Mbiti before him, puts it, "Ethical commitment in Africa, as elsewhere, is anchored in the people's concept of the God they worship."[39]

Odozor is well aware of, and attends to, the urgent challenges or questions that such assertions call forth. The first challenge raised here is that the theocentric ethical framework seems to work well to guarantee moral objectivity only in a monotheistic system, since in a polytheistic system there are likely to be competing "divine legislations, and there are many instances of a rather polytheistic belief in Africa. Odozor's provisional solution to this challenge is the observation that even where there is polytheism in Africa, often, there is still a "supreme being that represents primacy."[40] Secondly, Odozor must still answer questions such as, "How does the African understand God? Is it different from the Christian idea of God? How does that affect the question of moral objectivity?" The urgency of these questions is even sharpened by the following assertion of Ratzinger, that "There is only one single, universal, and necessary morality, a true and clear light perceived by all persons, provided only that they open their eyes. This one moral truth comes from God, and every individual law and norm must take this truth as its point of reference."[41] In responding to these questions, Odozor does not shy away from repeating over and over again, that even the provisional solution of invoking a "supreme primal being" still falls short of capturing the idea of God as revealed in Jesus Christ.

The more lasting solution discernable in Odozor's corpus, I think, unfolds in three stages: First is to recognize the immense and deep theistic worldview of the African culture. Second, to acknowledge at the same time its insufficiency and at times even questionable theocentric ethic. Third, to open up this African conception of God to the clarifying and perfecting light of the fullness of God's revelation in Christ Jesus. This in my opinion is very distinctive of Odozor's style and method as an African theologian, his unique way of shortening the hyphen between African-and-Christian. Of course, presupposed in these three stages is the point we made earlier regarding the insufficiency of any historical culture as a self-contained schema of moral reference. Or put positively, as Ratzinger does, the point that every culture is interiorly open to the universalizing power of Christ, the revelation of God. For Odozor, therefore, what African Christians need today, as James Henry Owino Kombo puts it, "is not the African concept of God... [but] a clear picture of the Christian view of God." Corroboratively, Ratzinger, even as Odozor quotes him, speaks of Christ as "the way, and there is no way that is independent of him, on which he would no longer matter."[42]

Far from a repudiation of the genuine longings and aspirations of the African toward God, in Christ, these aspirations are taken up and perfected. The one true God, we could say, did not want to be invoked only in shades and shadows, but has drawn close to us definitively, so that all peoples might come to true, reliable and salvific knowledge of him. This he has done in Christ, the author of revelation to all the nations.[43] Now, therefore, all peoples know the will of God, and with this, the truth of our origin and destiny.[44]

The universality of God, which Jesus has revealed, is likewise a central thesis in Ratzinger's *Many Religions, One Covenant: Israel, the Church, and the World*. Through the one covenant God made with his elect, Israel, his love has extended to all the peoples of the world, as this covenant came to perfection in the "true Israel," Jesus, the Christ. In a very true sense, therefore, the peoples of Africa, Europe, Asia, America, etc., by this singular plan of God, can likewise find their fulfilment in this Anointed One of God, Jesus. Another payoff of such a theocentric ethics espoused by Odozor and Ratzinger, besides its universal appeal, is that it serves as a critique of the sort of Nietzschean ethical agnosticism or relativism in vogue today—a living *etsi Deus non deratur*. Of course, Nietzsche had already sung the "requiem of God" in *The Gay Science* (1882). "*Requiem aeternam Deo* (Eternal rest to God)," sang Nietzsche's madman as he forced his way into several churches after searching in vain for God, only to be silenced by the mocking garishness of the "gay" masters of knowledge/science (atheists), proclaiming rather jubilantly, "God is dead, and we have killed him."[45] Nietzsche is engaged here in a nefarious parody and a transmutation of the liturgical hymn at Christian Funerals which addresses God on behalf of the deceased, "*Requiem aeternam dona eis, Domine*" (Lord, grant them [the dead] eternal rest). A theocentric ethics such as Odozor's or Ratzinger's retorts to

Nietzsche quite sharply, "*Deus est!* (God is!)" with all the ethical implications thereof.

d. Natural Law, Human Nature, and Conscience: Three Interconnected Guarantors of Moral Objectivity

From the foregoing, it is at least implicit that moral objectivity, precisely as something based on God and on a certain universalization of moral values (even if this remains a mere aspiration in some contexts), in turn depends on the universality of human nature, in which nature is written, from the very beginning, a universal law. This reflects the teleological ethics espoused, for example, by Augustine and Aquinas. Even among the Greek philosophers, prominently Aristotle, this idea was already present. Aristotle, for instance, conceived of this kind of teleological ethics in terms of *eudaimonia*, that is, human flourishing. He saw this "flourishing" or "happiness" or "a well-ordered life" as the goal of human existence.[46]

In Augustine, this Aristotelian *eudaimonia* undergoes significant Christianization, precisely through the understanding that human nature receives at creation a divinely inscribed "law" of operation, which makes such a nature (Augustine uses "heart") "restless" until it attains fulfilment in a participation in God's very life.[47] This participation is begun here on earth in Christian hope for blessedness, but it is never perfect. In *De Civitate Dei,* Augustine demonstrates how the sought-for perfection is attained only in the bliss of the eternal city of peace, joy, and happiness, when the *Theos-tending* human nature (heart) possesses the *summum bonum,* its proper end, in a complete and permanent manner, lacking nothing and not threatened by change. It is this that constitutes the *vita aeterna* (eternal life), as Augustine will again articulate in *De Trinitate.*

Aquinas then builds on this Augustinian framework but makes very important additions. The most significant addition being to approach human nature and its end or goal from point of view of the universality of human reason and the natural law. Aquinas followed Aristotle in affirming nature's teleological arrangement. However, he added God to the picture. For him, therefore, nature was created by God, who rules the world according to divine reason. To this effect, Aquinas discusses four kinds of law: *i. Eternal law:* God's perfect plan, not fully knowable, governing animals, humans, and all creation. *ii. Divine law:* Revealed in scriptures. *iii. Natural law:* The light of reason placed by nature (and thus by the Creator God) in every man to guide him in his acts. The prime principle of natural law is that "good is to be done and pursued and evil avoided." Such reason, Aquinas states, is capable of revealing some particular natural laws about what is good (e.g., self-preservation, marriage and family, and the desire to know God) and what is evil (e.g., adultery, suicide, and lying). *iv. Human law:* Laws made by human beings (changeable and not absolute).[48]

Despite all the criticisms and limitations that some scholars like Bujo might want to impute on the theory of natural law in general, and Aquinas' articulation of the latter in particular, Odozor is right in affirming the necessity of natural law as a guarantor of objective morality. Bujo, for instance, rejected grounding moral justification on natural law because he claimed that it is more Western and so foreign to the African. He then calls for a legitimization of pluralism with regard to ethical praxis. What is surprising is that he also goes on to claim that such pluralism must not necessarily imply a lack of objectivity.[49] How this can be possible remains an unresolved question in Bujo's thought. Perhaps this challenge justifies the following rhetorical criticism of Bujo by Odozor:

> If it is indeed correct, as Bujo asserts, that the African sense of solidarity is devoid of any moorings in metaphysics and natural law, then we have arrived at some important reasons for the slave trade and for continuing African ethnic strife. For if people do not see any binding reasons—whether religious or humanistic—for treating others fairly, then all attempts at "solidarity" can easily become no more than ideological attempts to impose on another or to push an agenda. But even though I criticize the African traditional conception of hospitality as sometimes lacking in universal import, I cannot accept Bujo's claim regarding the lack of metaphysical or natural law grounding for either African ethics in general or even for African solidarity.[50]

Odozor is spot on! He is insistent that "African Christian ethics cannot afford to dispense with the natural law as a means for moral justification."[51] To push Odozor's argument even further, the problem is not with advocating for a context sensitive ethics, for ethics should actually take context into consideration, rather, the problem lies in the fact that Bujo wants an ethics without a metaphysical (rational) foundation. This begs the question of what undergirds or informs the burden of choice in each context. Or do we give up altogether on the question of right and wrong? It is hard to see how a dismissal of natural law does not lead to the sort of moral relativism that thrives in contextualism (or situation ethics), contrary to what Bujo would want us to think. It is like turning upon its head John Paul II's famous principle of "gradualness" to now become "graduality of the law itself."[52] In other words, the gradual contextual application of one and the same law gives way to the variation of the law itself according to circumstances or contexts. For example, this means willful killing of the innocent could be permissible in one case but not in another.

The following example, which Odozor draws from Chinua Achebe's *Things Fall Apart*, is both illustrative and enlightening. The context is the arrival of Ikemefuna (a fifteen-year-old boy) in the village of Umuofia. Ikemefuna was from a neighboring village, Mbaino. He was given to the people of Umuofia as an appeasement for the killing of Ezeugo, the wife of Ogbuefi Udo from Umuofia, by the Mbaino people. Once in Umuofia, Ikemefuna was then handed over to Okonkwo for "safe keeping." The boy grew up to regard him as a father. However, after many years, the people of Umuofia decided to kill Ikemefuna as an expiation for the blood of Ezeugo. The claim is that it was an act commanded by the Oracle of the Hills and Caves (that is, by their god). Ogbuefi, a friend to Okonkwo approached him with the warning not to have anything to do with such a gruesome act. "That boy calls you father. Do not have a hand in his death," he said, trying to reason with him. Okonkwo did not heed. He himself did the killing. After the deed, another friend of Okonkwo, Obierika, reprimanded him for such an act. "Yes, the Oracle said he should be killed," Obierika argued, "but the oracle did not ask you to do the killing."[53]

Odozor recounts this story to demonstrate, through the characters Obierika and Ogbuefi, the repulsiveness of the so-called command of the god and the decision of the community to go along with it. It shows a classic case of the failure of the "communitarian ethics" Bujo is pushing for. Also, there is epitomized in Obierika and Ogbuefi, a human consciousness that is alert to the natural law within the human person, which saddles him with an individual moral responsibility, regardless of external variables. This introduces us to the concept of conscience, a concept which Odozor engages at length. In the lines that follow, we are proposing that conscience functions in Odozor as guarantor of moral objectivity.

Generally, conscience could be understood as the interior ordinance of reason, an instantiation and clarification of natural law within each individual, prompting us to do good and to avoid evil in each given case, and convicting us of wrongdoing should we choose evil. The Christian tradition calls it the "voice of God within us." Thus understood, individual conscience trumps "community ethics." In fact, in the above scenario Achebe paints, community ethics is itself judged and evaluated on the basis of the conscience informed by natural law.

Conscience, Ratzinger shows, is not a matter of mere subjectivity, whereby "the subject has the final word vis-à-vis the claims made by authority in a world devoid of truth." On the contrary, conscience, substantively considered, "makes the subject transparent to the divine."[54] Conscience signifies "the perceptible and commanding presence of the voice of truth in the subject itself ... The abolition of mere subjectivity when man's intimate sphere is touched by the truth that comes from God."[55] Ratzinger, as does Newman, gives primacy in moral decision-making to individual conscience over external authority. Recall Odozor's affirmation of same in his analysis of Okonkwo's behavior. Ratzinger cites Newman's famous *Letter to the Duke of Norfolk* (1874), which reads thus, "Certainly, if I am obligated to bring religion into after-dinner toasts ... I shall drink – to the Pope, if you please, – still, to Conscience first, and to the Pope afterwards."[56] Newman's point here, Ratzinger explains, is to articulate the centrality and arbitrating role of "truth" which mediates between the objective or external authority and the subjective or internal authority of conscience. Based on truth, Ratzinger's and Newman's understanding of conscience is far from the sort of Cartesian subjectivism or Nietzschean moral agnosticism commonplace today. The primacy of the individual's conscience and thus consciousness and freedom, is not identical with one's own wishes and taste, nor with that which is more advantageous socially speaking or with respect to group consensus.[57]

There is a link here between conscience and Ratzinger's understanding of natural law, which he characterizes as "rational law," that which belongs to man as such, man as subject of rights. "Man's existence," he states, "bears in itself values and norms that must be discovered but not invented."[58] When this rational nature of man, or natural law, or conscience as the voice of truth, is lost or falsified, as is evident in today's world, we enter into a second Copernican revolution whereby, for lack of a true frame of reference, reality ceases to make meaning.[59] It then devolves into the self-creating autonomy of Nietzsche's *Übermensch* to establish new frameworks of (moral) reference as he wishes.

A way out of this predicament, Ratzinger proposes, is to return to "truth," to rediscover the true and authentic individual freedom and its burden of responsibility toward its Creator, discerned within conscience itself. In a little book he co-authored in 1986 with Schürmann and Balthasar, Ratzinger argues, "Conscience is shown to be what it is [voice of God] precisely because it says the same thing that God proclaimed to the Jews in the word of the Covenant."[60] Conscience, as such, "uncovers what is constant and thus necessarily leads to the 'mind of Christ.'"[61] Like we have said before, Christ is the perfection and measure of authentic humanity. Furthermore, Ratzinger discusses the two levels of conscience, in a manner that supports Odozor's utilization of Achebe's story in his moral discourse on conscience. The first level of conscience is *anamnesis* (*synderesis*), which is that primal remembrance of the good and the truth bestowed upon us, a remembrance of the Creator lodged in our interior being. This is what Augustine regarded as a basic understanding of good imprinted upon us, and which St. Basil called the love of God not imposed on us from without but infused into us a priori.[62] The second level is *conscientia*, understood by Aquinas as an act which entails three steps: recognition (*recognoscere*), bearing witness (*testificari*), and judgment (*iudicare*).[63] These distinctions are quite important for what follows. In a story from Greek mythology, quite like that of Okonkwo used by Odozor, Ratzinger further illustrates the point we are making here.

The story is about Orestes who killed his mother. Orestes committed this action (like Okonkwo) as an act of obedience to the god Apollo. Ratzinger calls this "obedience" an act of "conscience," that is, *conscientia*. But as the myth unfolds, Orestes is haunted by the Erinyes, the goddesses of vengeance in Greek mythology. Erinyes are an embodiment of the conscience that torments Orestes after his gruesome act. (We could liken Obierika and Ogbuefi in the story of Achebe to the Erinyes in this Greek myth.) Now in this second case, "conscience" is used to refer to that deeper level of being—*anamnesis*—that is, the deeper memory or remembrance of good and truth which convicts Orestes of guilt because of his misguided act of obedience to the repulsive divine oracle. In other words, his *conscientia* (recognition, judgement, and witness) had failed to heed the deeper memory of goodness and truth calling for restraint.[64] But once his conscience reflected upon itself post-action, it re-discovered or remembered (*anamnesis*) that deeper memory of truth and good that torments it for choosing wrong or evil over truth or good. This is the self-balancing objectivity of the law of conscience. Thus, Ratzinger would correctly argue that it is only in an initial phase that the erring conscience is comfortable.[65]

Odozor understands and adopts these Ratzingerian differentiations, albeit implicitly. He does so, among other ways, through his many references to John Paul II's *Veritatis Splendor,* wherein the Pontiff discusses human freedom among other things. Moral problems, the Pope notes (and Odozor concurs), arise when "freedom" or "conscience" is dissociated from "truth." When this happens, there arises an alleged conflict between freedom and law, which is engendered by, and in turn fuels, the claim that individuals or social groups have "the right to determine what is good or evil."[66] John Paul II and Odozor see in this tendency a crisis of truth, a false primacy of individual conscience considered independently of truth. This crisis, we could further note from a Ratzingerian perspective, arises when the two dimensions of conscience—*conscientia* and *anamnesis*—are not integrated. As a corrective to this erroneous tendency, Odozor offers Joseph Boyle's reading of Vatican II's teaching on conscience, namely, "that within the foundations of the conscience of all human beings there are nonconventional, non-arbitrary moral standards which make possible genuine moral self-criticism, and true moral knowledge even for those who have not received the moral instruction of divine revelation."[67]

We once again see quite clearly the connection between natural law and conscience as guarantors of moral objectivity. We also see how the other two guarantors, that is, God and the uniqueness of Christ, are related to these two. Natural law and conscience hinge on the eternal will of God for his creation, which has been revealed in and through Christ. That is, God has chosen to reveal himself such that even where the natural light of reason to perceive the natural law is darkened by sin, and the light of conscience to discern good is dimmed by concupiscence, we might understand God's will for us as moral agents, in Christ. In the end, therefore, I think that Bujo argues in vain when he states that "to reject natural law reasoning is not to call into question 'the possibility of universal validity' in ethics."[68] It actually is! Furthermore, his rejection of natural law based on the fact that it is non-African is scandalous, or at best counterintuitive even for his own purposes of promoting Africa. For the fact that a concept, in this case, natural law, was not coined by Africans, does not make it useless to the African, let alone the reality of what it stipulates, that is, the existence of such a law. More rhetorically, "Are Africans any less rational?"

III. Conclusion: Objective Morality—Truly African, Truly Christian?

Odozor does a great job in showing how morality can be at one and the same time objective and both Christian and African. In articulating this, he steers clear of the moral pluralism and relativism in vogue today. His approach offers what I might call a constructive plurality. He embraces the plurality of moral criteria hinged on the plurality of cultures. However, by his implicit adoption of the principle of the "finality" or "interior openness" of every culture, a principle which is explicated by Ratzinger as shown above, Odozor is able to argue that these plural cultures, African culture included, and their criteria for moral valuations are imperfect and limited as self-contained systems. Thus, every culture stands in need of an external and objective system against which to judge and measure its own validity. From his distinctive Christian background, and even from a philosophical, logical, and commonsensical perspective, he advocates for certain guarantors of moral objectivity, which we have identified as God, the uniqueness of Christ (and the Church), natural law, human nature, and conscience. These guarantors constitute the external and objective system against which to judge the ethical claims of every culture. All five guarantors form an integrative non-contradictory but corroborative unity.

With respect to our present discussion, the merit of Odozor's work, therefore, rests in how he integrates all five guarantors of moral objectivity, showing how they are both corrective and corroborative of the African ethical system. In the process, the latter is neither annihilated nor diminished but comes most fully to itself. His project is successful, we have tried to show, because of underlying crucial assumptions which he takes for granted, but which have been profoundly conceptualized by Ratzinger, namely, the universality of human nature in every culture, the interior openness of every culture, and the tending toward the universal in every culture. Precisely for this reason, bringing Odozor's project into dialogue with these aspects of Ratzinger's theology proves most beneficial. At this point, we are even better placed to appreciate the success of Odozor's work, as he satisfies the initial goal of his work, namely, to show that "a renewed and renewing sense of Christian identity [is] the basis for ethics and for reimagining the relationship between African cultures and Christianity, [and the relationship] between cultures everywhere and Christianity."[69]

In accomplishing this task, Odozor refuses to take the default position of some African theologians for whom Christianity ought simply to validate, uncritically, whatever culture has to say; and when this is not the case, they tend to brand Christianity as "hostile" to culture. A case in point which Odozor himself engages elaborately is Bujo's rejection of natural law as a "limited" Western creation. Generally speaking, for Odozor, granting the supremacy and uniqueness of Christ over every human culture, all culturally inspired ethics must eventually "test their soundness by exposing themselves to the gospel and the tradition of the Church."[70] Applying this principle to the African context, Odozor details three crucial assumptions which must be integrated in such a stance: (1) The uniqueness of the African as a subject and a moral agent, having his own unique history, culture, language, etc. (2) The recognition of the fact that something "happened" to Africans as a result of their encounter with faith in Jesus Christ and as a result of their membership in the Church. (3) Traditions and cultures provide the platform on which all stand to name and make sense of reality, by providing us with language and other tools for describing and evaluating reality.[71]

To this, I add a fourth, borrowing from Ratzinger, namely, (4) the principle of interior openness and the tending of every culture toward Christ. When all these principles are well integrated, a cultural norm can be truly African and truly Christian, and where conflict arises, Christ becomes the guiding principle, since it is only in him that every truly human (and hence, truly African) aspiration find its meaning and fulfilment. This is what we have tried to demonstrate throughout this essay. We could at this point reformulate Odozor's basic thesis as follows: "There is an objective morality that is truly African, and truly Christian, marked by five guarantors of moral objectivity."

It behooves me, at this point, to touch on the too often nagging question, "Why the adjective 'African'?" When speaking of Western ethical theories, we simply use the expression, "Ethics." So why "African" in this case? Odozor suggests a possible answer to this question. Borrowing from Edward W. Fasholé-Luke, he writes, "The emphasis here on African theology is deliberate, for even though African theology is theology in every other sense, it is a type of theology whose task is additionally 'to translate the one faith of Jesus Christ to suit the tongue, style, genius, and character of African peoples.'"[72] It is evident from this statement that rather than see it as a denigration, as some authors tend to do, this appellation speaks to the very contextual nature of theology. It is about a people owning the discipline of theology as well as the Christian message—owning it precisely as a people of *this* cultural, historical, linguistic, and religious heritage, called African. Today, there is noticeable an increasing awareness of the contextual nature of theology, which in no way denies its universality, but rather fosters it. We are hearing more and more divisions such as German theology, Orthodox theology, Latino theology, Asian theology, Black womanist theology, etc. It would be remiss of me not to note that there is a potential danger in these divisions, for they can very easily become idiosyncratic and competitive. This happens when the center shifts from Christ to vested interests and ideologies, which tend to make individual cultures into self-contained absolutes. Odozor and Ratzinger, we have demonstrated, show us how that must not be the case.

Chapter 13

African and Christian: Black Sanctity and the Future of African Catholicism

Emmanuel Ojeifo

I. Introduction

There is a growing interest in the academic study of black sanctity today, but available literature in this area looks too much to the past to unearth stories and narratives about black saints rather than to the present and future. A focus on black sanctity in the present is worth considering. For the enduring value of sanctity in the church in Africa is tied not solely to those of ages past who have gone before us but also to the ability of African Christians today to clearly perceive the signs of God working in members of their communities. For as Pope Francis tells us in his Apostolic Exhortation *Gaudete et Exsultate*, the Holy Spirit constantly bestows "holiness in abundance upon God's holy and faithful people."[1] A discussion on black sanctity in African Catholicism today therefore needs to contemplate the "holiness *present* in the patience of God's people."[2]

In discussing black sanctity in contemporary African Catholicism, three key issues come to the fore. The first issue is that contemporary African Catholicism is plagued by what may be called a "saintly inferiority complex."[3] While saints are part and parcel of the warp and woof of Catholic life, there are few officially recognized modern-day Catholics from sub-Saharan Africa in that vast spiritual company that the Letter to the Hebrews refers to as "a great cloud of witnesses" (12:1). With the exception of the Martyrs of Uganda who were canonized during the Second Vatican Council in 1964, there is only one African that has been canonized since after the Council—the Sudanese Saint Josephine

Bakhita, in the year 2000. Pope John Paul II, who opened the post-Vatican II register of holy men and women from Africa, showed great interest in raising new saints from Africa. However, in the 27 years of his papacy, during which he canonized 482 saints—more than the total number of saints canonized in the previous 600 years—only one African made it to sainthood. While he beatified six other Africans at different times—three on African soil and three in Rome—the African number is still so little compared to the total number of 1,341 persons that he beatified during his pontificate. Moreover, an overwhelming number of those beatified and canonized by John Paul II were bishops, priests, and members of monastic and religious communities. Laypeople were conspicuously absent. This explains why on All Saints Day, the internet and social media are awash with photographs of saints in which non-white faces are largely absent. As Sharon Prentis rightly observed, we may be surrounded by a cloud of witnesses, but the non-white faces in the crowd are hidden in "a fog of white, male, European hegemony."[4]

The second issue is connected to the first and has to do with saintly amnesia. Although there are not many modern African saints and blesseds, few African Catholics know the names and can recognize the faces of those saints and blesseds in their midst. Conversing with a number of young Nigerian Catholics during All Saints Day in November 2023, I inquired how many modern-day holy persons of African descent that they know. Most of those I asked could only come up with two names. While sampling a few persons cannot yield a general conclusion, there is sufficient reason to believe that Africa's heritage of sanctity is not well known even among African Catholics and in African local churches. What is at issue here is a crisis of memory, of remembering. By remembering, I do not mean the ability to merely recall names and faces of African saints, but a way of learning the stories of the saints well enough to form and initiate African Christians into concrete lived practices, disciplines, and performances that display the public-political character of the church as a community of memory in the world. It is this sort of memory "that allows the foundations of a people's life together to be remembered, retold, and creatively reinterpreted."[5]

I will return to this challenge later in this essay. In the present moment, it suffices to say that the inability of many African Catholics to "remember" their African brothers and sisters who are in the company of the saints does not augur well for the future of African Catholicism. Not only will this amnesia serve to de-historicize the church, it will also make African Catholicism unable to summon the moral and spiritual energies to disrupt "the spell of the ruling consciousness"[6] that prefers to maintain the status quo in the church and in society. For one of the prime gifts of the saints is their capacity to disrupt the status quo.

The two issues I have raised give rise to a third one, namely the dearth of a lively cult of saints in African local churches. Some scholars have argued that popular Catholicism flourishes in Africa. The appeal of this form of Catholicism finds expression in the growth of Marian piety, deep devotion to the Eucharist, and adherence to an enchanted worldview that is associated with charismatic prayers, exorcism, fasting, use of holy water, and wearing of religious articles.[7] However, popular Catholicism in Africa has not really touched the area of veneration of saints, as it is in Latin America where popular piety, shaped by devotion to local saints, forms part of the spiritual air that most Catholics breathe. Commenting on the Latin American context, Elizabeth A. Johnson notes that "popular saints are helpers of the people in their daily struggle for life. By providing them with understanding and power to deal effectively with harsh situations, these saints open up an avenue of relationship to God who can then be thought to be actively present in their midst."[8] What popular devotion to the saints does is that it works "to build personal and communal meaning where life is desperately hard. It is an expression of an existential faith."[9]

Most Africans today are living under conditions where life is desperately hard, shaped as it is by the realities of poverty, hunger, disease, violence, civil war, political instability, and environmental destruction. These conditions which are mainly produced by the acts of both state and non-state actors have conspired to make nation-state politics in Africa the "work of death."[10] At any rate, these death-dealing situations pose a serious ethical challenge to the church in Africa that is called to be "salt" and "light" for a continent in distress. How can such a church appropriate the resources of her saints and martyrs to disrupt the flow of oxygen into the machineries of death that continue to carefreely sacrifice African lives?

The example of diasporic African Catholics in early modern Catholic history can offer some insight here. In her work, *Black Saints in Early Modern Global Catholicism,* based on detailed archaeological and historical research, Erin K. Rowe shows how the existence of cults of black saints in 16th century Iberian Peninsula were influential in transforming social and ecclesial spaces in the context of the trans-Atlantic slave trade. Rowe's research focuses on the 16th century black African, Benedict the Moor (also known as Benedict of Palermo), born of slave parents, who later became a Franciscan friar in Sicily where he earned recognition for his holiness. Through the formation of confraternities, African converts to Catholicism mobilized Benedict's sanctity and that of other African holy persons to "create distinct spaces for black community members to gather and protect one another."[11] Although black confraternities were widely spread across the Iberian world and helped to foster group consciousness among diasporic African communities, the devotion to black saints also flourished among white Catholics as well. It was the flourishing of local devotion to Benedict that led to his canonization in 1743. Commenting on the general situation, Rowe notes:

> While the number of saints is few, their influence was vast—cults to one saint can spread to hundreds, even thousands, of sites across the globe. There were altars dedicated to black saints in southern Italy, Portugal, Brazil, Spain, Angola, Mexico, Guatemala, Venezuela, Peru, and the Rio de la Plata, for just a few examples. In every place affected by the African slave trade, we find veneration to black saints, whose presence altered the spiritual landscape of global Catholicism.[12]

While devotion to black saints during this period did not bring an end to the trans-Atlantic slave trade or mitigate the sufferings of millions of victims, it however helped to challenge ecclesiastical, racial, and social hierarchies and provided vital opportunities for claims-making about the brutal treatment of enslaved peoples and a push for universal humanity. Additionally, the existence of cults of black saints transformed spiritual practice in European societies and participated in the co-creation of new forms of Catholic ritual and devotional life. It is a testament to the significant contribution of African Catholics to the evolution of early modern global Catholicism. Retrieving this popular sanctity in the context of holy persons that are emerging in the crucible of violence across African societies today will not only display the unique and diverse incarnations of holiness present among contemporary African Catholics but will also be a source of strength and hope for Africans and a unique gift that Africa can offer to the world church and to today's humanity that is suffering from a crisis of faith and hope.

Amidst the grisly sacrifice of African lives in various machineries of both brutal and slow death in Africa today, African Catholicism is challenged to write a narrative of life, faith, and hope, not from the top but from below, from the ordinary experience of the believer—a narrative that takes seriously the concrete life histories and stories of poor, oppressed, exploited, and dispossessed Africans. As such, remembering, telling, and retelling the stories of African saints and martyrs—not only those officially recognized but especially the vast array of those less-known and yet-to-be canonized—can play a determinative role in shaping the outlook of African Catholicism. Indeed, only by taking this memory seriously can African Catholicism be faithful to its mission of being an authentic sacrament of reconciliation, justice, and peace in Africa today.

II. Situating the Problem: Between Memory and Hope

To talk about African saints is to talk about models of moral living in Africa. Over the last few decades, there has been a growing interest in the demographic explosion of Christianity in Africa. In both academic and ecclesial circles, the refrain is heard over and again that Africa is the hope of the church. By 2025, Africa will be the most Christian continent in the world with a share of 695 million of the world's 2.6 billion Christians, and by 2030 there likely will be more Catholics in Africa than Europe.[13] While the numerical growth of Christianity in Africa cannot be denied, one African theologian has argued that African scholars must move beyond assessments of African Catholicism that are based solely on sociological and demographic changes and engage deeper questions about the identity and mission of African Catholicism. He asks

African theologians to ponder this question: "What does God say about who we are, where we are, and what is moving forward in the life of faith in our continent?"[14] If Africa is the hope or is to be the hope of the church, what does this hope mean in concrete terms? What are the signs of this hope and where can we find them?

My aim in this essay is to muse on these questions by deploying black sanctity as a determinative key for assessing the shape and future of African Catholicism. Ironically, while black and African sanctity has been a subject of interest for western scholars and writers, it has not been the same for African scholars. This is evident from the fact that most works published in this field have come mainly from the North Atlantic. There is hardly an African voice in the conversation. The absence of African theological and ecclesial voices reveals how little interest there is in this important issue in the church in Africa.

In the ninth and final chapter of his book *Morality Truly Christian, Truly African,* Paulinus I. Odozor discusses what a fully inculturated African moral discourse looks like in the church. In grappling with issues about "how to make the faith real and lived on the continent,"[15] he makes an important point about the ethical task of memory in the church in Africa. A fully inculturated African moral discourse must embody an ethic, argues Odozor, and this "must be an ethic that begins with remembering Jesus, his teaching and his deeds. Further, this ethic must also take seriously the teaching of Jesus' disciples and of those other members of the community of Jesus who through the centuries in every part of the world have kept the memory of Jesus alive."[16]

I like to appropriate this ethic of memory as inclusive of the saints. For the saints are the best exemplars of the community of Jesus who show us what faithful Christian discipleship is about. Citing the work of Robert Bellah and his colleagues, Elizabeth Johnson notes that a genuine community is formed and flourish as a community of both memory and hope. It is a community of memory when it does not forget its past and in order to not forget its past, it must be involved in "telling its story, its constitutive narrative, and in so doing it offers examples of the men and women who have embodied and exemplified the meaning of the community. These stories of collective history and exemplary individuals are an important part of the tradition that is so central to a community of memory."[17] Because these stories carry a vital energy, they can inspire good actions and practices of commitment in members of the community. This is how communities of memory also become communities of hope. Drawing on this analogy, Johnson grounds the memory and hope of the Christian community of faith in the foundational narrative of the life, death, and resurrection of Jesus and weaves this story with the stories of countless men and women who have responded in different ways through the ages to the call to follow Jesus. "Losing a sense of connection with these lives," she insists, "weakens the ability of the church to pass on gospel values and to empower the growth of constituted selves."[18] This understanding of embodied memory that I find in both Odozor and Johnson offers me a key for reflecting on the institutional disconnection that has given rise to the dearth of modern African saints in the context of the local churches in Africa.

III. Saint-Making in Africa: An Institutional Disconnection

The fact that the church's register of saints has fewer modern-day African Catholics is a symptom of an institutional and structural problem. While it is taken for granted today that an unprecedented shift in the demography of world Christianity from North to South has occurred in our lifetime, this transformation has not yet resulted in making the voices of Christians in the global South to be heard. Notwithstanding the good intentions and efforts of Popes John Paul II, Benedict XVI, and Francis to make the church more inclusive of and attentive to the plight and concerns of Christians in the global South, the church's institutions, structures, and processes are still skewed in favour of the global North. Metz sees this as a class problem which the church must address. He challenges the church to commit to an ethic of global solidarity, a preferential option for those that are discriminated against. Otherwise, the church will not only risk mirroring the world's social divisions but also fall short of its mission "to be a place where hope is at home, that hope in the God of the living and the dead, who calls *all* men and women to be subjects in God's presence."[19]

The presence of this class problem means that for as long as African Catholics continue to rely solely on the formal process of canonization to name and memorialize their holy persons, they will continue to lag behind. In addition to length of time and rigor, the process of canonization is capital intensive. African local churches are still financially handicap and depend significantly on financial aid coming from the church's center of wealth in the global North. The huge expense of canonization processes already leaves African ecclesial communities at a distinct disadvantage. African local churches will need to decide whether it is worthwhile spending their meagre resources on the canonization of prospective saints rather than channelling the resources to attend to the barrage of life-and-death issues constantly staring at local churches in the face.

Another issue with the modern process of canonization is the penchant for a cult of celebrity among prospective candidates for sainthood. Michael Plekon notes that "it is not easy to find saints whose lives were ordinary."[20] Modern canonization process tends to favour people with a certain degree of privilege due to racial, gender, religious, ecclesiastical, or educational status. Many, if not most, are bishops and priests, monks and nuns, ascetics and martyrs. Although they are our brothers and sisters in the faith, modern saints come across very often as beyond human because of the way the narratives of their lives are enhanced. Stories and narratives of their lives, which is called hagiography (literally writing about that which is holy) often run "the risk of idealizing or romanticizing real human beings who had real human failings and who struggled with very difficult choices in the midst of conflictual and ambiguous historical circumstances."[21] The loss of connection with the joys and hopes, struggles and failings of many modern-day saints is partly what has made them so distant and out of touch with the ordinary daily experiences of many of us with jobs and debts and a range of socio-economic and spiritual deprivations.[22]

This was not always so. Many of the early Christians revered as holy people were ordinary members of the community of faith. Although the heroic example of the early Christian saints and martyrs shines forth in their hagiographies, many are still recognizable in their humanity. The biblical portraits of holiness are even more scandalous, full of life, and humanity in all their beauty and messiness. Whereas kings, princes, governors, and the high religious and social classes of society did not walk in the way of the Lord, prostitutes, tax collectors, mothers, widows, and aged couples are put forward as models of faith, love, and righteous living. Recovering the full humanity of the saints can help to displace the kind of celebrity status and extraordinariness that has clung to the perception of holiness today, and thus make it possible for us to recognize everyday African Catholics in the ordinariness of their lives as models of saintly living.

Noting that the word "hero" does not appear in the New Testament, but the word "saint" occurs sixty-four times, the Christian ethicist Samuel Wells has made five important distinctions between the hero and the saint, which foreground the conviction that Christians are called, not to be heroes, but to be saints. Firstly, the hero is always at the center of the story, whereas the saint is at the periphery of a story that is really about God. Secondly, while the hero's story is told to celebrate the virtues and qualities of the hero, the saint's story is told to celebrate faith and faithfulness. Thirdly, the soldier is the emblem of the hero, while the martyr is the emblem of the saint. Whereas the soldier faces death in battle and earns his reward by virtue of this heroism, the martyr faces death by not going to battle. The sanctity of the martyr makes no sense unless it is rewarded by God and finds its place in the story of Christ's redeeming sacrifice and the martyr's heavenly crown. Fourthly, the hero is not expected to fail, for failure would be fatal and not make the story come out right. Thus a hero fears failure and avoids making mistake. On the contrary, the saint expects to fail. If the saint's failures are honest, they highlight the wonder of God's greater glory. If they are less admirable, they open up the cycle of repentance, forgiveness, reconciliation, and restoration, which are all part of what Christians call new creation. Finally, the story of the hero shows how the hero stands apart from the community by the excellence of his or her virtues. The hero depends on himself. On the contrary, saints are never alone. They are part of a community within which their sanctity is formed and grows. They learn to depend on God and on the community of faith—a special kind of community, the communion of saints.[23]

For Plekon, what the church needs today is a more ordinary and less noticeable, hidden holiness, an everyday sanctity "one founded on the baptismal calling of all to be prophets and priests, witnesses to the

Gospel."[24] In his foreword to Plekon's book, Rowan Williams reinforces some of the ideas that Wells already noted above. "The saint is not primarily the high achiever of the moral life, the honours graduate in discipleship, but the person in whom the depths of the ordinary become visible."[25] The former Archbishop of Canterbury adds: "Holiness is nothing to do with measurable success, not even with an unbroken record of triumphantly negotiating temptation and avoiding error and hurt. Yet, in the light of the Gospel, what matters is their fidelity to the source of light and energy, their freedom to let their fractured humanity be upheld and saturated in that infinite gift that is God in Christ at work in the Spirit."[26] This appeal of ordinary, everyday sanctity that refuses to see sanctity as the cult of superheroes or larger-than-life personalities, is what has led Pope Francis to speak of the holiness that is found in "our next-door neighbours."[27] For Francis, when we talk about the saints, we need not think "only of those already beatified and canonized." The Holy Spirit bestows holiness in abundance among God's faithful people amidst the "complex fabric of interpersonal relationships present in a human community."[28] Thus Francis invites us to contemplate the holiness present in the patience of God's people which is often hidden and almost imperceptible "in those parents who raise their children with immense love, in those men and women who work hard to support their families, in the sick, in elderly religious who never lose a smile." Borrowing from the subtitle of a novel by Joseph Malègue, a modern French Catholic writer, Francis calls them "the middle class of holiness."[29]

I find Pope Francis' notion of holiness very innovative in terms of the immense possibilities that it holds for the local churches of Africa. In thinking about its saints and martyrs, the church in Africa is challenged to go beyond those already beatified and canonized and develop communal practices of memory that account for the many unknown and forgotten saints and martyrs from local ecclesial communities. For these practices to enjoy the status of popular piety, they need to evolve from the grassroots and respond to the deep spiritual yearnings of the typical contemporary Christian in Africa today, which includes a poor woman in the slum of Kibera in Nairobi, a school dropout in the suburb of Ajegunle in Lagos, or a farmer on the outskirts of Juba.

In the remaining part of this essay, I identify and discuss five key areas of concern, albeit sketchily, that the church in Africa needs to pay attention in order to effectively appropriate the precious gift of its saints and martyrs "so that their memory can stand out as a treasure safeguarded by the Christian community."[30]

IV. African Saints and Martyrs: Five Key Areas of Concern

The Challenge of Naming

I start with an anecdote that Matthew Hassan Kukah, a well-known Nigerian Catholic bishop, shared with me in July 2023. In March 1998, Pope John Paul II visited Nigeria for the beatification of Father Cyprian Michael Iwene Tansi. Tansi had been parish priest and schoolteacher to Cardinal Francis Arinze, and many believe that Cardinal Arinze, then serving in the Vatican, played a key role in Tansi's beatification, being the first holy person to be so officially recognized in West Africa. After the beatification Mass in Onitsha, then archbishop of Onitsha, Albert K. Obiefuna, was recalling to Bishop Kukah how much financial resources went out of his diocese for Father Tansi's beatification process. "If this is how expensive it is to get one saint, I don't think I want another," Obiefuna told Kukah. While Archbishop Obiefuna may have meant that remark as a joke, the point he makes is valid: saint-making is pretty much an expensive business. As I stated earlier in this essay, it is very unlikely that the local churches in Africa with their measly financial resources and many pressing needs will be able to muster the kind of resources needed to promote the causes of many saints and martyrs. Here is why the broader understanding of saints and martyrs that Pope Francis advances needs to be taken seriously by the local churches in Africa. Local churches in Africa do not have to wait until canonization processes are started and concluded before they can name their holy persons. They can draw a portrait of holiness from below, from the margins where the history of the church is being written by the witness of many unknown, unnamed, and forgotten members of the Christian community "whom no history book ever mentions"[31]

Matthew Hassan Kukah, bishop of Sokoto diocese in the predominantly Muslim region of northern Nigeria where Christians have been victims of violence and persecution for many decades, is quite aware of this need to name the martyrs of his own local church. On January 8, 2020, Islamist bandits attacked Good Shepherd Catholic major seminary in Kaduna and abducted four seminarians. One of the abducted seminarians, 18-year-old Michael Nnadi, who had just begun his philosophical studies, belonged to Kukah's Sokoto diocese. While the other seminarians eventually regained their freedom, Michael did not return to the seminary. He was killed by his abductors, mostly likely on January 28, 2020. In his confessional statement after he was apprehended, 26-year-old Mustapha Mohammed, leader of the gang of marauders that attacked the seminary, admitted killing Michael. He said the seminarian bravely "continued preaching the Gospel of Jesus Christ," telling him to his face to "change your evil ways or perish."[32]

In his homily at the funeral Mass for Michael at Good Shepherd seminary, Kukah extolled the heroic witness of his slain seminarian, calling him a representative of Sokoto diocese in the "national team of martyrs." "We are honoured that our son Michael has been summoned to receive the crown of martyrdom at the infancy of his journey to the priesthood," he continued. Placing Michael's sacrifice within a Eucharistic context, Kukah said: "He was a priest by desire but he is concelebrating the fullness of the priesthood beside His Master. He was lifted up even before his hands could lift up the sacred chalice." In his national Christmas day message in 2021, Kukah recalled the martyrdom of Michael saying, "When Michael Nnadi our teenage seminarian from Sokoto Diocese stared down the nozzle of the guns of terrorists and called them to repentance, he knew he was signing his signature with the blood of martyrdom." Not only has Kukah made effort to craft a moving martyrial narrative of his seminarian, he has gone ahead to erect a monument in one of his parishes in Katsina State (formerly part of Sokoto diocese but created as an independent diocese in 2023) where Michael's memory will be honored. The irony is that though ethnically Igbo from eastern Nigeria, Michael choose to become a seminarian for the northern diocese of Sokoto where he had been born. In a country marked by intense ethno-religious competition and rivalry, where many tend to assume that ethnic and religious identities are natural constructs, the story of Michael tears down the walls of tribalism and confirms that "there is neither Jew nor Greek" (Gal. 3:28) in the household of God.

The Challenge of Memorialization

By most accounts Christianity is the most persecuted religion in the world today, and Africa is indeed the epicenter of this global war on Christians.[33] In terms of the scale of violence, there are few modern parallels to the context in which African Christians live today. To say that Africa has become the new Golgotha of the modern world is no exaggeration. For many Christians in Africa today, when the accounts of the martyrs of our tradition are read, it is not a matter of remote historical interest or pious curiosity, but an expression of their own concrete situations within which they are living. However, as a result of the poor state of record keeping and data collection in many local churches in Africa, there is a high possibility that the names and stories of many of the new martyrs emerging from some of the crucibles of violence and terror across Africa will be forgotten. In a 1994 apostolic letter, Pope John Paul II noted that the end of the second millennium has brought the church back to the age of martyrs: "*In our own century the martyrs have returned,* many of them nameless, *'unknown soldiers'* as it were *of God's great cause.* As far as possible, their witness should not be lost to the Church.... *the local Churches should do everything possible to ensure that the memory of those who have suffered martyrdom should be safeguarded, gathering the necessary documentation.*"[34] Similarly, Pope Francis has said that there are more martyrs today than in the first centuries of Christianity, and that "we cannot forget them."[35] Memory is therefore central to the ongoing task of Catholicism in Africa today.

Metz has observed that ours is a time in which the Christian is "more and more radically exposed to the loss of memory."[36] Despite the huge amount of information at our disposal, modern societies are more and more devoid of history and memory. Yet without memory, Christians know that there can be no genuine community. At the heart of Christianity is a living and shared memory of the word and deed, life, death, and resurrection of Jesus Christ and of those followers of Jesus who through time and space have kept alive in the community the life of

Jesus. Without this memory, there can be no solidarity, and without solidarity there is no hope. A genuine community is thus one that is involved in "telling its story, its constitutive narrative, and in so doing it offers examples of the men and women who have embodied and exemplified the meaning of the community."[37] The stories of collective history and exemplary individuals that a community tells carry a vital elan and can inspire good actions and practices of commitment in members of that community. The ability of the church to pass on gospel values and to empower the growth of constituted selves will thus be weakened if it were to lose a sense of connection with its memory.[38]

Emmanuel Katongole has argued that one of the strange gifts of memorializing the martyrs is that it keeps the church from sleeping. By the constant pounding of their memory, the church breaks out of the prison of fear, is reenergized into a life of vigilance and relentless struggle for the realization of a better world, and is invited to really become what it professes: "a resurrected community on the other side of death."[39] Remembering the martyrs is onc way to remind Christians about the dangers, threats, and temptations on the Christian journey. Forms and practices of remembrance include vigils, feast days, storytelling, and renaming.[40] For Katongole, the call to develop forms and practices of remembering the martyrs is a reminder to us Christians that "the journey of reconciliation is a journey of tactics and gestures—a story here, a lesson there, and some insights along the way."[41] This offers a countercultural sign to a world that is so obsessed with big projects and grand strategies for enacting social change.

This is what makes the example of the Catholic diocese of Auchi in southern Nigeria so remarkable. On Sunday, June 26, 2022, as he stepped out of his parish rectory at St Michael Catholic church Ikabigbo to go for Mass, Father Christopher Odia, a priest of Auchi diocese and my classmate in the seminary, was abducted by some gunmen and taken into the forest. Getting wind of the incident, some brave youths and the local vigilante in the community trailed the kidnappers. Realizing that the bush where they were located had been encircled by the vigilante, the kidnappers opened gunfire and in the process killed Father Odia and injured several others. Ahead of the one-year memorial Mass for the slain priest, the diocese erected and unveiled a large cross made of concrete at the exact spot where Father Odia was gruesomely murdered in the thick forest. If the concrete cross reminds us of the historical cross of Jesus Christ, it also symbolizes the crosses of historical time borne by all those Christians who, like Father Odia, have fallen to the assassin's bullet or have "simply vanished into the maws of various killing machines."[42] The cross challenges African Catholics today to enter into the dynamic of Calvary and to appropriate the fruits of Christ's redemptive sacrifice in order to thwart the works of death that are emblazoned in the chaotic politics of Africa. The hope is that Catholics and other Christians in Auchi diocese will make the site of the erected cross a place for memorializing Father Odia and of the sacrifice he bore in following the example of his Lord and Master Jesus Christ.

When Christians forget their martyrs, they kill them a second time. Memory is what holds our feet to the fire, reminding us that we are not yet as free as we might like to think, but that remembering those who have fallen asleep in Christ, amidst the battles of this world, impels us to not rest until we arrive at the Promised Land of liberty, justice, and peace. Using the cross to offer a socio-theological critique on the devaluation of human life in Nigeria today, Gabriel G. Dunia, bishop of Auchi diocese, in his homily at the memorial Mass for his slain priest invited his diocesan flock, especially the priests, to a sense of heroic witness in the face of trials and persecution. "Priests must brace up for battle. There are spiritual battles, there are moral battles, there are physical battles, there are psychological battles. We must be prepared and defend ourselves, not with machine guns, but with weapons of spiritual power." Earlier in the homily, Bishop Dunia said, "The priest must brace up and know that he is doing the work of God, anytime, any day. You must be bold, be courageous. You are a soldier of Christ."

The gesture of Auchi diocese is a powerful glimpse of the point Katongole makes about the journey of reconciliation as a journey of tactics and gestures with simple stories, lessons, and insights. It also shows that the first point of call in the remembrance of the martyrs is the local ecclesial community where the saints and martyrs lived, died, and continue to live. The gestures and stories told about the martyrs "can empower communities of memory in their identity formation, in their resistance to injustice and evil, in their articulation and embodiment of an alternative moral imagination, and in their communal power to act with love in the face of violence and oppression."[43]

The Challenge of Formation

Growth in sensibility of the presence of many saints and martyrs in African Catholic ecclesial communities is not automatic. It is a discipline that needs to be formed. Without adequate formation, African Catholics are not likely to learn how to appreciate the great significance of the universal call to holiness that Vatican II popularized. What does this formation look like? When I visited Sokoto diocese in northern Nigeria during the 2022 Christmas break, I attended the Christmas vigil Mass at the diocesan cathedral where the bishop in his homily spoke about the heroic witness of his slain seminarian Michael Nnadi. Homilies are a powerful medium for educating, forming, and reminding today's Catholics about the call to holiness through the lived experiences of their own brothers and sisters. Apart from the homily, catechesis in the local ecclesial communities needs to include moral instruction on the virtue of sanctity by drawing on the concrete portraits of exemplary witnesses within the local ecclesial community. Through songs and poems composed to honor models of holy living in local ecclesial communities, African Catholics will come to learn about their brothers and sisters whose examples are worth emulating and why their memories are worth preserving.

Another important way of forming today's African Catholics in the sensibility of emerging African saints and martyrs is through books and articles. This should be targeted at the literate audience in African Catholic ecclesial communities, especially to candidates in formation for priestly and religious life. Across sub-Saharan Africa, there is currently no record of courses in the curriculum of seminaries, novitiates, and theological institutions that focus on black/African sanctity in contemporary global Catholicism. If future African priests and nuns are not educated and formed in this sensibility, how can they transmit this knowledge of embodied forms of holiness to the laity? Catholic educational institutions in Africa can learn from the example of Camille Lewis Brown.

While teaching a course on the history of black Catholics in the United States to seminarians at St Charles Borromeo Seminary in Pennsylvania,

Brown realized the importance of including content on holy men and women of Africa in the course syllabus. Sensing how little she knew about the saints from Africa, she undertook to travel across Africa for over a decade collecting data on African holy persons, both canonized and not-yet-canonized, which aided her to design and teach a course on African saints in the seminary, and to write a book titled *African Saints, African Stories*.[44] I reference Brown's effort not only to demonstrate the importance of courses in black African sanctity in the curriculum of studies in major seminaries and novitiates in Africa, but also to highlight the need for African priests, religious, and scholars to invest in collecting data and producing works which focus on how African Christians are living and dying for their faith in Jesus Christ. The effort of Dr Brown and of Frederick Quinn in his anthology of a diverse cast of holy persons from Africa[45] is worth commending.

Given the modern stress on historical and written accounts over oral tradition in saint-making, effort needs to be made to reach the non-literate African audience that might be marginalized if we were to limit ways of forming African Catholics in sanctity to written texts. As the anthropological theologian Todd Whitmore notes, "in sub-Saharan Africa alone there are 200 million people who do not read or write."[46] For this reason, attention needs to be given to how such socially located people figure in what and to whom we write. While written texts may not reach the needs of this audience, through homilies and catechesis in vernacular languages, the local ecclesial communities will be able to reach them and form them in the sensibilities of African saints—past and present, hidden and renowned—and thus challenge them to embrace the call to holiness using vernacular idioms.

The Challenge of Discernment

Emerging African saints and martyrs point us in the direction of critical areas of social and ecclesial life where witness to gospel values are most needed in our time. According to Pope Francis, "Each saint is a mission, planned by the Father to reflect and embody, at a specific moment in history, a certain aspect of the Gospel."[47] Discerning those aspects of the gospel embodied by African saints and martyrs is of great importance for the meaning and message of black sanctity in contemporary African

Catholicism. Looking at Africa's present social condition today, shaped by the realities of violence, civil wars, poverty, tribalism, corruption, political instability, mismanagement of national resources, repression of women, abuse of children, and environmental destruction, there is no doubt that Africa direly needs emancipation and salvation. What if the church in Africa deploys the witness of modern African saints and martyrs to shed a deeper light on these issues?

Here, I argue that the contemporary relevance of saintly figures in Africa depends significantly on how their narratives and stories are appropriated and reappropriated to beam a light on challenges facing the church and the social and political ills facing the continent. For instance, the Sudanese saint, Josephine Bakhita, has been deployed as an advocate of genuine emancipation in her country. During the second civil war in Sudan that began in 1983 and ended in 2005, the Sudanese bishops delivered strong messages that injected Bakhita's life and struggles into calls for the respect of human dignity. As a freed slave girl Bakhita's memory played a huge role in the rhetoric of human rights and freedom. The Catholic radio station, Radio Bakhita, was also instrumental in advocating for the referendum that gave birth to the independent nation of South Sudan in 2011, just as the Christian population of Sudan saw Bakhita as a symbol of emancipation from forced Islamic rule. Around the world, Bakhita is considered the patron saint of victims of trafficking, and there are several initiatives named after her that continue to raise awareness about the horrors of trafficking in women and girls. These varied appropriations of Bakhita confirm the ongoing relevance of saintly figures in beaming a searchlight on social and political ills.[18]

In light of the oppression, exploitation, and victimisation of women and girls in Africa today through patriarchal cultural practices, there seems to be a strong need for an African saint whose memory and legacy can be marshalled to attend to the situation of women. The Kongolese St Anthony, Dona Beatriz (1684–1706), who was accused of heresy and burned at the stake is a good fit. Beatriz, a young Kongolese woman, claimed to be possessed by St Anthony and founded a prophetic movement for the restoration of the divided kingdom of the Kongo. She fought against European colonization and worked hard to indigenize Christianity until her unjust execution. When Pope Paul VI visited

Uganda in 1969, there were calls for him to declare Beatriz a martyr. Though the advocacy did not succeed, the memory of Beatriz remains a powerful force for critiquing the alliance of religion and power in relation to gender. In a similar vein, the church in Africa needs to project the witness of the murdered Congolese archbishop Christophe Munzihirwa of Bukavu as an example of courageous leadership in an African context where pastoral leaders can sometimes lack the prophetic boldness to confront structures of sin and evil.[49]

The same argument could be made of Julius Nyerere, the first post-independent president of Tanzania, whose cause of beatification is underway. In many sub-Saharan African nations where the noble art of politics has for the most part lost its moral hygiene, there is a sign of hope in Nyerere's beatification cause. Already his legacy is being deployed to make a point about the fact that "Africa needs saints in high political office"[50] who will eschew personal benefit and work for the good of their people. His legacy offers the church in Africa the possibility of deploying a concept of political holiness that can speak to the challenge of politics and governance in Africa. This ongoing discernment needs to be extended to those emerging saints and martyrs from African local ecclesial communities so that the witness of their lives can serve to disrupt the death-dealing situations that shape the realities of life in contemporary Africa.

The Challenge of Translation

If emerging African saints are to be relevant to the daily life of Catholics in Africa, the choice of who to name or memorialize has to be negotiated within local churches. I do not use the word negotiated in terms of financial transaction but in terms of translation of meaning. A salient question that the American Jesuit church historian John W. O'Malley prods us to ask about prospective candidates for sainthood is, "For whom, to what degree, and with what qualification is this blessed or saint a model?"[51] O'Malley asks us to raise this question because saint-making deals with the lives of people in the past but are actions carried out in the present and for the present. It is therefore important to carefully identify what a prospective candidate stands for and which sector of the church or particular need might be better served by the promotion of a particular candidate. While this is possible in many cases, I take the risk of pointing out the possibility of some causes being lost in translation. When Pope John Paul II beatified Father Tansi in Onitsha, Nigeria, in 1998, he referred to Tansi in his beatification homily as "a model of reconciliation" in a country marked by ethnic and religious strife, and urged Nigerians and Africans to look up to him and emulate him. On three separate occasions the next day—his homily at the national Mass in Abuja, his audiences with Nigeria's head of state and the leadership of the Nigerian Muslim community—John Paul II reiterated the significance of Tansi as a model of reconciliation. However, no one, it seems, not even within the church in Nigeria, remembers Tansi in such light. When the topic of reconciliation comes up in ecclesial circles and discussions, no one ever mentions the name of Tansi.

Could this be the result of the fact that Tansi's religious and cultural context shaped by his conversion from Igbo traditional religion to Christianity is quite different from the religious, ethnic, and cultural context to which John Paul II was trying to insert him? While Tansi's legacy can stand for other things, in this particular context his name hardly evokes ideas about reconciliation in a way that can strike the spiritual and social imagination of Nigerian and African Catholics. Here therefore, it seems to me, is a cause that is being lost in translation. If O'Malley notes that "the model provided by every saint and blessed must be translated if it is to be meaningful in our lives,"[52] it becomes clear that local churches in Africa need to negotiate carefully not only who is named or memorialized as a saint or martyr but what they stand for and how that might be relevant to the everyday life of African Christians.

V. Conclusion

This essay began by raising three critical issues about black sanctity in contemporary African Catholicism: the fact that there are only few officially recognized modern African holy persons in the church, the lack of awareness among contemporary African Catholics of the holy persons in their midst, and the dearth of a lively cult of saints in the local churches in Africa. With respect to the first issue, I situated the problem within the broader structural and institutional dynamics of the Catholic

Church and the parameters of the modern saint-making process, which has led to the marginalization of the church in Africa. Regarding the second and third issues, I locate the cause of the problem in the structures of education and formation in African local churches. Consequently, in the remaining section of the essay, I discussed five areas of concern that the church in Africa needs to pay attention in order to effectively appropriate the precious gift of its saints and martyrs to positively shape the present and future of African Catholicism.

There is a lack of local stories (oral and written) about holy people in Africa. The social and religious reality of Africa, plagued as it were by an underdeveloped culture of record keeping, poses a challenge to the flourishing of a viable and authentic culture of holiness. That African holy persons are not being recognized, even in vernacular contexts, remains a cause for concern and calls for a reimagination of both the concept and performance of holiness in the African social context. My emphasis on the need to write and tell stories of modern-day African saints presupposes that the stories are bountiful and waiting to be written and told. What role can Christian preaching and catechesis play in the religious and cultural transmission of stories of holy people in Africa today, both known and yet-to-be-known? What paradigms of local, popular, vernacular sainthood need to be proposed for the church in Africa? These questions need to be explored further. What I have tried to do here is to show that the present and future of African Catholicism will be significantly shaped by how narratives of the lives of modern African saints can capture the spiritual imagination of Catholics in Africa and the world. By keeping alive the memory of Africa's holy heroes—both known and unknown—the church in Africa will be better able to continuously set out afresh on the journey of living the Gospel in Africa. If what a people remember is integral to their identity, to forget or ignore that "great cloud of witnesses" that have emerged and are emerging from the soil of Africa is tantamount to cutting off a vital support system for the church in Africa.

Chapter 14
Trinitarian Conception of God as Basis for an African Christian Ethics

Bede Ukwuije, C.S.Sp.

Introduction

What difference does the Christian understanding of God as Trinity make in the conception of Christian ethics in Africa? This question was provoked by the reading of Paulinus Odozor's *Morality Truly Christian and Truly African*[1] and a later article, "One and the Same? Invoking Joseph Ratzinger/Benedict XVI in the Debate on God and Question of God-Language in African Christianity."[2]

Odozor strongly contends that Morality truly Christian, in Africa or anywhere, will have to be anchored on a correct conception of the Christian God. He takes a distance from the position of pioneer African theologians who, in defence of African identity, argue in favour of a continuity between the Christian God and the African God, generally conceived as the *Supreme being*. Odozor believes that this conception of God is not strong enough to anchor a "Morality truly Christian and truly African." Not only does it not respect the flexibility of the conception of God in African traditions, but also it does not do justice to the Christian conception of God and the difference the confession of this God makes in the life of an African.

Odozor proposes to move beyond the classical question: how can God be conceived in African theology in such a way that safeguards African understanding of God? If one takes seriously the fact that being a Christian involves a person entering into a new community, what will govern that person's life is the Christian tradition, that is, the rules and lifestyle of the Christian community. Since the Christian community confesses God as Trinity, Odozor poses the question in such a way that makes the Christian responsible for Christian confession of faith in a particular context: How can Africans confess the God who revealed himself in Jesus Christ and in the activities of the Holy Spirit in a way that such confession can make them more authentically African? In other words, what is the ethical import of the doctrine of the Trinity?[3]

Odozor's approach resonates with the thoughts I developed in my works, *Trinité et Inculturation*[4] and *The Trinitarian God: Contemporary Relevance and Challenges*.[5] While journeying with his thought, I prefer, nevertheless, to move away from what may appear as the trap of the equation, "truly Christian and truly African." As we shall see here below, the quest for a "Morality Truly Christian and Truly African" is a response to the question whether one can be Christian and African at the same time. The question was initially asked by African intellectuals in search of cultural authenticity. Caught up between two traditions that make demands on them, they desire to harmonize Christianity and African religious thoughts in order to minimize the scandal of Christianity considered as alien religion.[6]

As Odozor rightly stated, this question implies an assumption that there is something about Africa and Christianity which makes them antithetical to each other to the point where being one would pose problems for, or be an obstacle to, being the other.[7] The approach also involves some sort of mental gymnastics to define what is truly Christian and what is truly African. Such gymnastics overlooks the fact that cultures are dynamic and that what could be considered as "truly African" or truly Christian could already be a product of previous encounters of both cultures with other cultures. No culture is chemically pure. Moreover, it is difficult for Christian theology to minimize the scandal which is determined by the irreconcilable tension between the dangerous memory of the passion, death and resurrection of Jesus Christ and the different conceptions of God and human beings in all cultures.

I, therefore, opt for a more flexible expression, "African Christian ethics" which will take responsibility for the Christian God (Trinitarian God) while dialoguing with the conceptions of God in African traditional religions. It is my conviction that this approach corresponds better to

Odozor's work and conclusions than the "truly Christian and truly African" equation.

This reflection does not intend to provide an outline of African morality and virtues, rather to see what the Christian trinitarian conception of God can offer to the search for African Christian ethics. First, I contextualise the problem by presenting the strengths and the limits of the proposals from African inculturation theology, which seeks to ground African Christian ethics on the apologetics of African monotheism, on one hand and, the Christology of *Christ-the-ancestor* on the other. Second, I elaborate on the Trinitarian conception of God with particular attention to the understanding of God as love. Third, I indicate some implications of the Trinitarian conception of God for an African Christian ethics. I argue that an African Christian Ethics informed by the Trinitarian conception of God will be theocentric, theofilial, pneumatological/ecological, and eschatological.

I
The Apologetics of African Monotheism and Ancestral Christology

The apologetics of African monotheism (*Supreme being*) and the Christology of *Christ-ancestor* had three goals. The first was to demonstrate against Western rationalists—particularly Hegel—and Western missionaries that Africans have a religion, hence they are human beings. Second, to pave a way for the evangelization of Africa, by demonstrating the continuity between the God of the African Traditional Religion and the God of Christian revelation. Third, to guarantee the bases for African Christian ethics in a context of cultural crisis created by the advent of modernity.

The Apologetics of African monotheism

The apologetics of the continuity between the God of African traditional religions and the Christian God is assured with the concept of God as the *Supreme being*. When John Mbiti sought to establish the continuity between the God of African religions and the God of the Christian faith, he wrote: "I assume in this book, that there is one Supreme God. I take it also that the majority of the concepts presented here, have sprung independently out of African reflection on God."[8] He followed in the footsteps of Bolaji Idowu, who concluded his demonstration on the Yoruba religion as monotheism, with particular reference to the unique position of the deity, Olodumare, by saying: "[W]e can predicate that the religion of the Yoruba was, or consisted in a 'Primitive Monotheism.'"[9] In his remarkable 1960 doctoral dissertation, Francis Arinze argued that "[t]he Iboman believes firmly in the existence of a Supreme being."[10] He noted that the Igbo think highly of this "Supreme Spirit" that they give him innumerable names, three of which are prominent: "*Chukwu* (*Chi-ukwu*, the great Spirit), *Chineke* (the Spirit that creates), and *Osebuluwa* (Lord who upholds the world)."[11]

Although the belief in God as the ultimate principle, the Creator and sustainer of the universe, pervades majority of African traditional religions, there is debate however as to whether this conception of God could be fairly represented by the Western monotheistic concept of the *Supreme being*.

First, the idea of the Supreme Being is a product of the 17th and 18th centuries' theism. It was developed by French philosophers, especially Voltaire, Jean-Jacques Rousseau and Denis Diderot, as a moral postulate to guarantee peace in the society. The idea was a negation of the God of revelation which supported the superiority claims of positive religions, Judaism, Islam and Christianity. It was the central idea in what the philosophers called *natural religion*. The cult of *l'Être Supreme,* developed by protagonists of the French Revolution, was meant to liberate the society from religion. The philosophers claimed that this idea of God was not accessible to the so-called primitives. The conception culminated in Hegel's *tabula rasa*, which denied humanity to the Africans on the ground that they had no idea of God, law and freedom.[12]

While trying to account for the cultures of the different peoples discovered in the new world, in the light of Darwinian evolutionism, 18th Ethno-anthropologists argued that the so-called "primitive cultures" were the pre-civilization stages of which the European cultures represent the apogee. However, another group led by the German Wilhelm Schmidt postulated the idea of *primitive monotheism* (*Urmonotheismus)* and *primitive revelation (Uroffenbarung*). They argued that the idea of monotheism which philosophers reserved for civilized societies was in fact a primitive idea before it degenerated to polytheism and magic. The reasoning followed Herbert Spencer's *Principles of Sociology* which, translating the Darwinian theory of evolution into sociological principles, stated that civilization can evolve from *heterogeneity to homogeneity*, but can as well degenerate from homogeneity to heterogeneity.

19th-century Christian missionaries exploited the postulate of primitive monotheism for the benefit of Christian apologetics. Their intention was to defend the Christian truth claim and the supernatural revelation against modern rationalism. The most famous protagonists were the French Spiritan Alexander Le Roy and the Belgian priest Placid Tempels, who defended the idea of the possibility of the belief in the Supreme Being in Africa.

In addition to the position of ethno-anthropologists, Christian apologetics mobilized the philosophy of religion of Friedrich Schleiermacher, Mircea Eliade, and Rudolf Otto. This suggests that the disposition to religion is created in man by an external reality called the Sacred, which for them is no other than *Being as such* or *Supreme Being*. It follows that the human being, *homo religiosus*, has the faculty or the natural emotion to perceive and tend towards the *Supreme Being*.

Following this argument, Christian ethno-anthropologists identified the *Supreme Being* with the God of Christian revelation. In other words, for them, the idea of the *Supreme Being* does not contradict the idea of God in Christianity. By consequence, Africans have the natural disposition to adhere to the Christian God without contradicting what is fundamental in their religion.

The conception of African God as the Supreme being has met with severe criticism. For example, some Igbo scholars have insisted that reducing the Igbo conception of God to the western/missionary concept of the *Supreme being*, does violence to Igbo traditional religion.[13] Donatus Ibe Nwoga argues that the Supreme being is a stranger in Igbo religious thought where the earth deity, *Ala* is the custodian of morality. It is more revered and feared than the other deities.[14] Others argue that the position of *Chukwu* as Supreme God, Creator, Omniscient and Providence, is difficult to confirm in the religious practice of Igbo traditional religion. It is not confirmed in ritual practice, since there are no places of worship, priests or festivals dedicated to *Chukwu*. Worship is addressed to the ancestors and the multiple deities as the case may be. This lack of worship of a Supreme God gave rise, in the 1950s and 1960s, to Mircea Eliade's theory that the African God was a deus *incertus*, *deus remotus*, or *deus otiosus.*[15]

In his response to the above criticism, Francis Arinze explains that "God (*Chukwu*) has an honored place in Ibo prayer [...]. Ibo morning prayer is addressed principally to God."[16] However, "Ibo ideas of Chukwu are too high and perhaps too vague for them to haul statues of wood and red clay for him."[17] Chukwu's awe and majesty perplex the Igbo. This explains why they prefer to deal with the various *spirits* or lower deities. Nevertheless, Arinze concedes that "Ibo morality is not clearly referred to God."[18] The control of morality is left to the *spirits,* mostly *Ala* (the Earth Spirit) and the ancestors.

Recent studies, obviously influenced by modern secular thought, attempt to explain the absence of direct worship of God in traditional religions differently. They claim that the distancing of God is both the condition for the birth of human freedom and the desire of ATR to respect God's freedom.[19] The absent God is seen as a possibility of meaning and the affirmation of truth. It is meant to prevent an individual or a group from monopolizing the truth and consequently, dominating others. It therefore guarantees fairness in the socio-cultural and political systems of the society. René Luneau and Louis-Vincent Thomas explain the "retreat of God" in the myth of the Giziga of Northern Cameroon and its parallels (in Mosi country, among the Bwa and the Bambara) in the sense the resolve of those traditions to maintain the radical otherness of God.[20] The absence of God is said to give room for human maturity and responsibility.

For his part, the Nigerian theologian Elochukwu Uzukwu believes that the distancing of God is a proof that the traditional Igbo religion does not want to involve God in the management of violence in society.[21] Violence is left in the hands of other deities[22] who are easily mobilized for war. God is not partisan. "H(e) who is Father/Mother of the whole world, instead of being God of a single chosen people or ethnic group, would not become a prisoner of an ethnic group or civilization."[23]

African humanists, particularly Chinua Achebe and Wole Soyinka, maintain that the idea of African monotheism is not enough to guarantee pluralism and living together.[24] They consider monotheism as absolutist and violent. Over and against this tendency, they propose a conception of life in the society as complex integration of singularity and plurality among persons who know that they are dependent on one another and that they share the same community of destiny.

Achebe argues that it is difficult to support the absolute power of a Supreme Being, *Chukwu*, in a traditional Igbo religion that hesitates to concentrate power in the hands of a single deity. He insists that the conception of *Chukwu* as the *Supreme Being* and creator is a product of Western-Christian influence. He demonstrates that in the Igbo worldview, it is a deity *chi,* who assigns a destiny to each person.[25] This also means that there is as many *chi* as there are individuals. Moreover, each phenomenon has its deity: for example, *Amadioha* (lightning) is considered to be the deity responsible for thunder. Other deities, such as *Ibinukpabia, Igwekala* and *Agbala*, play various roles as judges or oracles. People have the right to worship and confess the god of their choice. They can even confess many at a time. No power is absolute and no one should pretend to the monopoly of God.

Wole Soyinka on his part sees the idea of monotheism as religious absolutism. He pleads for the respect of the polytheistic imagination of Yoruba religion. He argues that the affirmation of the existence of a Supreme God belongs to Christianity and Islam and that Africans are not obliged to subject themselves to a Supreme Being in order to accomplish their humanity.[26] Like David Hume,[27] Soyinka maintains that the polytheistic imaginary would be more apt to encourage sharing and participation in society than the monotheistic imaginary.[28] In the polytheistic imaginary communities, everything is done to limit the natural temptation of human beings to assume absolute power, to take control of the lives of others, their personal relationships, their social behavior and their thoughts.

From the foregoing, we can infer that the apologetics of monotheism based on the concept of God as the *Supreme being* does not appear to be a solid basis to guarantee an authentic African Christian ethics. First, it falls short of accounting for the flexibility of the conception of God in African traditions. Second, it is not a sure ground for building a conception of Christian understanding of God who revealed himself to the world in Jesus Christ through the Holy Spirit.

The Christology of Christ-the-Ancestor

The Christology of *Christ-the-ancestor* proposed by Charles Nyamiti and Benezet Bujo was meant to supply for the limits of the apologetics of African monotheism, namely, provide a basis for African Christian ethics in such a way that respects African religious traditions and the specificity of the Christian God.

Ancestor-kind in African traditions is a model that expresses the deepest aspirations of the Africans, which is definitive happiness, solidarity between the living and the dead. It is also meant to motivate and sustain the desire for good life with others in the society.

Charles Nyamiti designates Christ as "brother Ancestor." He clarifies that brother Ancestor is "a relative of a person with whom he has a common parent, and of whom he is mediator to God, archetype of behaviour, and with whom—thanks to his supernatural status acquired through death—he is entitled to have regular sacred communication."[29] He argues that by his life, death and resurrection, Jesus qualifies as an ancestor in the African understanding.

However, Bénézet Bujo is the theologian who elaborated more deeply on the moral implications of considering Jesus Christ as an ancestor. He notes that African ethics is based on a rational framework which is at the same time anthropocentric, cosmic and theocentric. These dimensions are connected by the concept of community, which embraces the visible community, the invisible community, which in turn "embraces not only one's ancestors but also those not yet born and even God."[30]

Bujo specifies that the designation, *ancestors*, refers to only those who have lived in a good relationship with God (God-fearing ancestors) and who though dead, continue to exert a good influence on their descendants.[31] "The ancestors share in the life that comes from God and pass this life on to the community."[32] They represent the perpetuation of the solidarity beyond death.

Ethical behavior in an African community "involves reenacting the presence of one's ancestors… in order to actualize anew the protological foundational act which first called the clan to fellowship into life."[33] This plays out clearly in process and rituals surrounding marriage; the serious preparation for a responsible sexual life through initiations, which is a school of self-control oriented to the future of the community.

Bujo's presentation of ethical behavior in Africa is in line with the thoughts of Zahan who argues that the basis of behavior in the African society is the virtue of self-control, which depends on self-knowledge.[34] Self-knowledge "signifies being conscious of one's humanity, of the place once occupies in the universe as a human being. Self-knowledge underlines the unique character of the human being vis-à-vis the rest of creation."[35] Zahan argues that the respect Africans accord to someone depends on one's capacity to master one's passions, emotions, behavior and actions. The place where self-mastery is verified is in speech (*parole*) which goes together with the capacity to observe silence, to keep secrets. Silence is the virtue that defines the human being. Silence is wisdom. It englobes integrity, courage, strength of character, prudence, modesty, temperance.[36]

Bujo notes also that ancestral memory also plays a central role in the process of *palaver*, where everyone participates in the word (*parole*) received from the ancestors and reinterpreted in the community. In the palaver community (*assemblée palabrique*) "each person is obliged to safeguard interpersonal relationship that constitutes the human person, and where the good use of the word is one of the constitutive elements. Each person must be conscious of pronouncing only edifying and life-giving words."[37]

The functioning of the palaver process conceived by Bujo leads to the question of the connection individual freedom and the community. Does the community not suffocate the individual? While recognizing this possibility, Bujo clarifies that a shortcoming does not efface the ideal.

For Bujo, Christ is the *proto-ancestor*, the ancestor par excellence. "This signifies that Jesus did not only realize the authentic ideal of God-fearing African ancestors, but also infinitely transcended that ideal and brought it to new completion. No ancestor can be thought of who was capable of such a complete and effective realization of the ideal."[38] This makes the ancestrality of Jesus Christ the measure of all other conceptions of ancestor. He suggests therefore, that Christian anthropology "discover the significance for African anthropology of Jesus Christ as the proto-ancestor which draws from the Pauline analogy of Christ as the "firstborn of those who sleep, or the second Adam."[39]

Considering Jesus as proto-ancestor has implications for morality in Africa.[40] First, Jesus becomes for the African a model par excellence of good life here on earth and of hope of redemption for the world to come. Second, since African ethics is articulated in the framework of anamnesis which involves remembering one's ancestors, the memory of the incarnation, death and resurrection of Jesus Christ, will be at the heart of African anamnestic ethics. The memory of Christ the ancestor, will induce a certain praxis in the community. Ethical behavior will thus consist in reenacting the presence of Christ the ancestor in view of followship into new life. Third, Christ proto-ancestor can bring Africans to look beyond the desire for earthly fulfillment here and now in marriage and child bearing. He can also motivate them to care for the poor, the handicapped the marginalized with who he identifies in the Gospel. Finally, anamnestic remembering with Christ pro-ancestor at its center can also move the community beyond ethnic boundaries to embrace all humanity born from the word of God and the salvation procured by Jesus Christ. Africans can also walk in the footsteps of Christ proto-ancestor to overcome tyrannies, political oppressors and dictators.

Nevertheless, the Christology of *Christ the Ancestor* tends to minimize the complexity of the role of the ancestral model in African societies. It is known that in some societies social organization is based either on family alliances, clans or ethnic groups. In this context, reference to ancestors may serve to support the monolithic management of society and to justify inequalities: everyone has their place and only their place. Moreover, reference to the ancestors of particular clans may not be strong enough to anchor morality that would be universal and inclusive beyond the clan or ethnic group.

Secondly, presenting Christ as the ancestor risks reducing Christ to ancestral traits. For example, Nyamiti notes that the relationship of sacrifice of the descendants to the ancestor is an obligation whose oblivion would automatically trigger the anger and punishment of the ancestor.[41]

If this is the case in traditional religions, the handling of this argument in Christology may prove to be delicate. All the more so since the logic of Christ's excellence leads Nyamiti to argue that Christ's anger towards members of his body who refuse to honor him would be more serious than that of an ordinary African ancestor. Thirdly, this has also consequences for the understanding of the relationship between Jesus and God. Christian faith confesses Jesus as the incarnation of God who is love and through whom humanity is saved. Human worship of God should be based on freedom and not on reward or the fear of punishment.

Theology should, therefore, move beyond the Ancestor Christology and the apologetics of the *Supreme being* in order to establish the basis of an African Christian ethics. As Odozor rightly argued, authentic African Christian ethics cannot be built on minimalist assumptions about God found in African culture as in all cultures.[42] Courageous confession of the God who revealed himself in Jesus Christ through the Holy Spirit could contribute to enriching the being human of Africans. In other words, the Trinitarian conception of God could broaden the basis for authentic African Christian ethics.

II
Trinitarian Conception of God: God Is Love

Faith in God as Trinity, Father, Son and the Holy Spirit is the specificity of Christianity. It was the Swiss theologian Karl Barth who declared that *Trinity is the Christian name for God.* The mystery of the Trinity is the mystery of love, totally manifested in the freedom of self-donation of the Father, the Son and the Spirit.

What does it mean that God is love? First it is important to expose anthropologically the phenomenon of love. This phenomenological understanding of love will clear the ground for the theological understanding of the essence of love. Then we see how it applies to God's being. Special attention will be given to the Trinity as the story of God's being which is totally revealed in the event of the life, death and resurrection of Jesus Christ.

The Essence of Love

The German theologian Eberhard Jüngel, following Karl Barth, defines love as "the unity of life and death for the benefit of life." He uses different expressions to define the concept of love: *overflowing being* (*überströmenden*),[43] *self-forgetfulness* (*Selbstlosigkeit*), *self-surrender* (*sich Hingeben*).[44] The essence of love is the overflowing of a being which by the same token exposes itself to nothingness.

However, self-exposure to nothingness does not annihilate the lover. Jüngel observes that those who engage in love experience both a self-dispossession and a reunion with oneself. "The loving I has itself only as though it did not have itself. It wants to be had by that very Thou that it wants to have. In order to have this Thou, it must surrender to it, that is, cease to have itself."[45]

Formally, love is "the event of a still greater selflessness within a great, and justifiably very great self-relatedness. Judged materially, love (is)…the event of the unity of life and death for the sake of life."[46]

In the essence of love reigns the dialectic of being and non-being: to lose oneself in order to win oneself. This dialectic is determined by an unassailable inner movement. Concretely, to become attached to the other, one must detach oneself from oneself, thus abandoning oneself at the risk of losing oneself, but a free abandonment of oneself without expecting anything in return.

But at the same time, Jüngel emphasizes that, in the event of abandonment, the beloved Thou gives to the loving I, without the other claiming it, a new being. The fact that they love each other makes each one receive from the other. This means, says Jüngel, that those who live in love exist *ex nihilo*, from nothing.[47] Love makes new.

This is what gives love that singular closeness to death. Jüngel points out that this closeness of love to death is revealed when love is confronted with that which is not love.[48] For love brings not only joy but also sorrow. As long as the loving self and the loved self agree to walk a common path, love is strong. But as soon as love is confronted with what is not love, it discovers itself to be vulnerable. But love does not give up. It wants to radiate beyond this confrontation until death.

The vulnerability of love is its strength and weakness. Jüngel says that one who accepts to die will triumph. Vulnerable on the outside, love is indestructible on the inside. It does not destroy what is opposed to it but transforms it. Thus, love "unites life and death in favor of life."[49]

God's Being as Love

Theologically, it is not the human understanding of love that gave birth to the expression, "God is love." It is rather God's being as revealed in Scripture that led to the confession that "God is love. The Doctrine of the Trinity is the conceptualization of the being of God as revealed in the history of the man-Jesus of Nazareth, announced and believed as the Son of God.[50] In the New Testament, 1 John 4:9 states that God expressed his love by sending his Son, by separating himself from his Son.

The New Testament's interpretation of God's being as love was anticipated in the Old Testament. The God who defined himself from himself in Jesus Christ is the God who speaks from himself in the Old Testament. This clearly affirms the eschatological focus of the promises of the Old Testament Scripture.[51] Certain features of the Israelite depiction of God become clearer or come into focus only in the light of the revelation of Christ and his Spirit in the New Testament. The central feature is the fact that the One God who revealed himself at Sinai is the Creator of all things visible and invisible, the sovereign Lord of all things.[52]

God's-Being-as-Love Expressed in the Conception of God as Creator

The biblical narrative affirms that God is not a solitary being. God is God for others. The word that first describes this God is Creator. God created the world and all that is in it.[53] Creation is a product of God's graciousness. Creation is an expression of God's beauty and love.

That God freely and graciously created the world is expressed in the idea of *creatio ex nihilo*. Some scholars question the idea of *creatio ex nihilo* as imposed on the biblical tradition. Although this idea became very clear in the 2nd and 3rd centuries, it is not alien to the biblical tradition.[54] The stories of creation emerged from the understanding of God as liberator. They "reflect the grammar of exodus and covenant."[55] As Brian Robinette stated, "By declaring that God freely originates created reality, with no preexistent constraints against which God must contend, whether passive matter, cosmological laws, or choral indeterminacies, *creatio ex nihilo* affirms God's relationship to creation as utterly gratuitous."[56]

The priestly account of creation (Genesis 1:27) notes that God created humanity male and female in his image and likeness. It does not mean that God is male and female. In the Hebrew tradition, God is transcendent. "Gen 1:27 suggests that it is human community, both male and female, that most adequately images God as personal and relational, even if what it means to speak of God as person remains an incomprehensible mystery to us."[57] Image of God as male and female speaks in an analogous way of the inviolable mystery, dignity and transcendence of the human creatures who image such a God. To be human means to be in-relation, to-be-with, in the light of God's being.

This understanding of God's being as love will be prolonged in the Trinitarian conception of God in the New Testament. God's being as love is revealed in the kenosis of the Father, the Son and the Holy Spirit. A kenosis that led to the confession of God as love.

God's-Being-as-Love Expressed in the Kenosis of Jesus Christ

The New Testament presents Jesus' kenosis, his self-emptying on the cross, as the event that definitively reveals his divine identity, as Son of God. Pauline writings (Cf. Philippians 2:5–11; Colossians 1:15–20; 1 Timothy 3:16; Hebrews 1:1–14) show that Christ partakes of the attributes of the One God of Israel: the unique creator of all things visible and invisible, sovereign Lord of all things, who revealed himself at Sinai; the only God who is to be worshiped and adored; the eschatological savior of humanity.[58] They go further to affirm that "It is when the Lord God of Israel is crucified and raised from the dead in his human nature that God is truly recognized among the nations as Lord, the only true God, who has revealed himself to Israel alone and through Israel to all the world."[59]

For John as well, the trinitarian life of God is the mystery underlying incarnation. The Trinity is revealed in the life, mission, crucifixion and glorification of Jesus Christ. The Gospel of John (John 8: 23–24; 8:28; 8:58) presents Jesus' crucifixion as "an exaltation that establishes Jesus' status as the Suffering Servant, reveals God's glory and serves as the standard for the salvific ingathering together of the human race.[60]

The Synoptic Gospels go further to demonstrate that Jesus' kenosis was determined by God's prior opening to him. Jesus is presented as a man totally turned towards God and others; in other words, a being totally turned towards others because entirely determined by God.

Eberhard Jüngel indicates that Jesus' identity shines out clearly from the point of view of the proclamation of the Kingdom and how he announced the Kingdom. Jesus announced the kingdom in parables. The parables confront God with the individual who is *addressed* (who is listening). This calls each person to a personal existential decision. This is clear in the parables of Jesus, like the Good Samaritan (Lk 10:3), the woman who was double bent for eighteen years (Lk 13:10–17), the Lost Sheep (Lk 15:1–6), the prodigal son (Lk 15:11–32), and so on.

Secondly, the proclamation of God's reign through parables has a communal structure (*eine sozietare Structure*). First, on Jesus' side, he experienced communion with God (*Gemeinschaft*) which individualizes him. In the same way, the hearers are drawn nearer into fellowship with God such that they gain a new understanding of themselves which is not only communion with God but also openness to the neighbor.

The joy produced by the Kingdom produces fear on those who defend the status quo, the law. This is what Martin Luther, the reformer, calls "the terror of the law."[61] The new communion accomplished in the person of Jesus brings together the present and the future of the world.

This is possible because of the deeper identity of Jesus. Jüngel explains that Jesus's being is made possible because God primarily identified himself with Jesus. Jesus understood himself as entirely determined by God. In other words, he understood his unique relationship to God as the expression of God's unique relationship to him.[62] Hence, Jesus' humanity radiates the characteristics of God's being as love, overflowing being, selflessness, self-abandonment, royal freedom, not wanting to be anything for oneself, absence of concern for self-preservation.

The death that was imposed on Jesus is a confirmation of his earlier experience. The freedom to be nothing for himself. His death on the cross is a consequence of his total surrender to God. That is why the cross of Jesus is interpreted as the cross of Christ, the cross of the Son of God.

The Gospels confirm that it is on the cross of Jesus that God revealed himself as Father; a Father who does not withhold his son but allows him to assume his fight against evil and violence for the benefit of the human being. John says that God revealed himself as love by dispossessing himself of all he had (cf. 1 John 4:8).

The history of God in Jesus Christ would have remained a history of suffering without the resurrection. The Paschal faith proclaims that God demonstrated his fidelity as Father by raising Jesus from the dead; hence, with the life he lived. Through this self-identification with the dead man, God turned death into life. The resurrection of Jesus shows that the last word does not belong to death because God is the father of life. In fact, God did not contradict himself in his self-dispossession, rather by giving himself totally, he revealed himself as the living and true God.

The resurrection is the victory of love. The Holy Spirit is the *vinculum caritatis*, the bond of love, the unity of the Father and the Son. He assumed the unity of both in their distinction on the cross.[63] The Holy Spirit is also characterized as kenosis per excellence. The mode of presence of the Spirit and his manner of accompanying creation involves self-emptying, self-humiliation on the part of the Spirit. He is a gift of the Father and the Son. He works tirelessly on our behalf, bringing human beings to participate in the Trinitarian communion. In fact, the Spirit of God continues the solidarity of God with the entire creation.

God's-Being-as-Love as Basis for the Unity and Distinction of the Divine Persons

The discovery of God's being as love led Christian tradition to deepen the understanding of God's nature as ecstatic. In fact, Bonaventure in his *Breviloquium* notes that love is the basis of showing plurality in the Godhead. Borrowing from the Neoplatonic tradition, reinterpreted by Pseudo Dionysius and Richard of Saint Victor, Bonaventure understands God as the Good. The Good itself is self-diffusive (*bonum diffusivum sui*). Divine nature is love and by its nature seeks to share itself.[64] Since the Good is self-diffusive, it follows that God is necessarily self-communicative. The perfection of love requires a lover a beloved and the fruit of love. The love shared between the Father and the Son is expressed in a third person (Holy Spirit).

If God is essentially love, the ultimate basis of God as love is the primacy of the Father.[65] The Father is the dynamic, fecund source of the trinitarian procession. He is the unbegotten (innascible) fountain of fulness, self-communication. With this Neoplatonic principle, Bonaventure unites as opposites two properties of the father, innascibility and paternity. "The unbegottenness of the father is the paternity or generative power of the Father.[66] The Father here is not the transcendent unknowable one of the philosophers. We can know the Father only from the Son. The mystery of the self-diffusive Good, the total self-giving of the Father is revealed in the mystery of the Son Jesus Christ. As Jordan Wood stated, the profoundest insight is this: "the unity and identity and distinction in God is revealed in the Son's kenosis as the Father's own intra-trinitarian kenosis—that the father himself in constituted only in his act of originating the Son and with the Son, the Spirit. The Father is who he is solely in giving all of what he is for the Son to be who he is."[67]

It is this mystery that the Fathers of the Church tried to express through the designation of the Trinitarian relations as *persons*. It was Tertullian who first designated the three divine relations with the term, *persona*. *Persona* signified "the being in and for themselves of the Father, Son and the Spirit respectively."[68] The Cappadocians, uncomfortable with the Greek equivalent, *prosopon* (mask), preferred the word *hypostases* which identifies being not with *ousia* but with personhood.[69] This means, according to Catherine Mowry Lacugna "that the ontological question of 'what something is' is not answered by pointing to the 'self-existent', to a being as it is determined by its own boundaries but to a being which in its *exstasis* breaks through these boundaries in a movement of communion."[70] Thus a person is not an individual but an open and ecstatic reality, turned towards others. "The actualization of the person takes place in self-transcendence, the movement of freedom toward communion with other persons."[71]

This means that God cannot be located in 'substance' alone (what God is in himself) but also in his personhood (what God is toward another). In fact, what God is in himself is manifested in what God is towards another. God exists as a mystery of persons. "Only in communion can God be what God is, and only as communion can God be at all."[72]

The Trinitarian conception of God exposed herein could have radical implications for African Christian ethics. Christian life is a life that corresponds to the triune God. That will be the concern of the last section of our reflection.

III
Implications of the Trinitarian Conception of God for African Christian Ethics

Theocentric Ethics

Theological anthropology insists on the primacy of God's action for the understanding of the human being and human action in society. It is derived from the conception of God as love, on the basis of God's self-identification with the man Jesus Christ.

As Jüngel stated, "All judgments about God and humanity can only be made on the basis of one and the same event. For Christian faith, this event is God's identity with the life and death of the one-man Jesus, revealed in the resurrection of Jesus from the dead."[73] By defining himself as God in a human person, God defined humanity. This is the meaning of the doctrine of the image of God in humanity. Humanity is a gift of God's love.

Being human, therefore, consists in corresponding to God's love. That is, living a life of self-donation. To be human is to correspond to the Trinitarian communion in which no one tries to preserve the self, rather, each person lives for others. Being for others is not a product of voluntarism. It presupposes faith, the act through which the human person abandons oneself to God. In the words of Jüngel, "the humanity of a human 'I' consists in allowing another to be there for me."[74] The human person exists by accepting to receive the self from God who loved us first. Jesus Christ is the ultimate realization of humanity and of the freedom to which we are called: freedom-for; freedom to love.

The understanding of the human being in the light of God has a greater advantage over the modern understanding of self-actualization.

Biblically, the category of *self-realization* is understood as sin. Authentic life is not self-realization. On the contrary, it is God who by becoming human justifies, that is, makes human those to whom he comes.

The above reflection can be brought to resonate with the African conception of the human person. As Bujo stated, the person is not an individual in terms of self-realization but "as a process of coming into existence in the reciprocal relatedness of individual and community, where the latter includes not only the deceased by also God."[75] This means that the being of the individual as a person is expressed through active participation in the life of the community. Freedom is therefore understood as "the capacity and responsibility for human community and divine communion."[76]

Theofilial Ethics

The event of humanity's correspondence to God through Jesus Christ can be designated with Archbishop Anthony Obinna's neologisms, theofiliance/theofiliation. It is "creation's new and integral sense of kinship with God derived from its relationship with the Son of God who has become the Son of Man."[77] It is the event of the redemption of humanity and the entire creation through Jesus' kenosis on the cross.

Theofiliation is closely related to confiliation, that is, our adoption as children of God in Jesus Christ. This is different from co-filiation or co-filiality which refers to the natural relationship of people by birth. Theofiliation includes and transcends confiliation. "It is humanity's new kinship with God, through His Son Jesus Christ born of the Virgin Daughter Mary, which makes of humans new sons and daughters of God endowed with the Spirit of Christ."[78]

A theofilial ethics will therefore aim at *reconfiliation*, that is, the restoration of the dignity of every human person as son and daughter of God and the unity of humanity wounded by sin and divisions. Archbishop Obinna designates reconfiliation as a "corrective-redemptive dynamic," the rectifying or corrective force which assures that the dignity of every son or daughter in the human family is held and defended beyond all biological, cultural or religious divides. Re-confiliation, he writes, affirms "the primacy of sonship and daughtership of every human ahead of the still important category of brother and sister."[79] In that sense, "the sociological or religious extension of brotherhood and sisterhood, fraternity and sorority are secondary to the primacy of filiality, confiliality or cofiliality."[80] This work, requires a confrontation "with persons, groups, ideas, practices, customs, institutions and systems that distort and assault the dignity of humans in so many places on earth."[81]

This resonates with Bujo's suggestion that Christian anthropology "discover the significance for African anthropology of Jesus Christ as the proto-ancestor"[82] which draws from the Pauline analogy of Christ as "the first born of those who sleep, or the second Adam."[83] Christian ethics helps to correct perversions in the culture. "Where Africans have introduced many practices under an erroneous appeal to the life that comes to them from the ancestors, the proto-ancestor opens their eyes to the true life and corrects abuses and misunderstandings."[84]

In contexts where systemic discriminations, like the Igbo caste system—osu/diala/umeh/ohu divides—have distorted relationships and institutionalized inhumanity, theofiliation can lead to the *recti-valuing* of one another, that is, bringing people to think of one another correctly; *new-joining*, *con-joining* or *new-kining* of humans into fellow sons and daughters in equal dignity.

Pneumatological/Ecological Ethics

Theofiliation is a cosmic event which transcends the community of those who believe in Jesus Christ. While it is a fact that humans participate in Jesus' filiation to creation and humanity through baptismal-conversional experience, the filiation and radiation of Christ in creation is a historic-cosmic given which continues to attract and reach persons and cultures not yet visibly reached.

Hence, theofiliation is also made possible through the activity of the Holy Spirit, since it is the Spirit that brings us into the intimate union of the Father and the Son. It is also the Holy Spirit that assures the presence of God through the entire creation. The Spirit (ruach) was present at the beginning of creation, creating space for life to emerge (Genesis 1:2). The Spirit is the breath God breathed into the human being to give them life. Everything that lives does so through the breath of the God in the Spirit (Psalm 104:29–30). The Spirit works towards the glorification of God through creation, uniting the past, the present and the future.

Pneumatological ethics, therefore, invites all humans to understand themselves as members of the community of creation. The Trinitarian conception of God which declares God as Creator and creation as the expression of God's glory, determines a renewed way of conceiving the relationship between human beings and the environment. The image of God as Creator and creation as fruit of the gratuitousness can helps to appreciate the kinship between human beings and the environment. A discovery of humanity's kinship with and responsibility for the creatures of the earth will dispose human beings to experience the world as the glory of God.

Pope Francis' radiant theologico-ecological project, expressed in *Laudato Si'* and *Laudate Deum*, calls on the entire humanity to take care of "our common home," by rediscovering respect for nature and the environment, not only as a gift of God, but also as an expression of the Creator. In his Apostolic Exhortation *Querida Amazonia*, the Pope speaks almost like an African. He insists that our life depends on the environment: "the forest is not a resource to be exploited; it is a being, or various beings, with which we have to relate."[85] Therefore, "to abuse nature is to abuse our ancestors, brothers and sisters, creation and the Creator, by mortgaging the future."[86]

African Christian ethics will insist with Pope Francis that the best way to avoid humans dominating and exploiting the earth violently is to keep in mind the image of God as Creator. "Creation can only be understood as a gift from the outstretched hand of the Father of all, and as a reality illuminated by the love which calls us together into universal communion."[87] Every creature is the object of the Father's tenderness and love who gives it a place in the world.

Eschatological Ethics

African Christian ethics will be eschatological. The Trinitarian conception of God as love, relation and communion is itself an eschatological principle. It performs the function of *interruption* of the *status quo*, of what people consider as evident or normal. In a world where cultures, traditions, religious movements seek to master reality, to give meaning to the existence of a people, the trinitarian conception of God relativizes ideologies. It shows that ideologies and their conditionings are transitory.

As we saw earlier, Jesus' proclamation of the nearness of God through the parables poses a judgment on the world. As an eschatological principle, the message of Jesus stands in contrast to the present. The qualitative change it brings goes beyond borders, overturns hierarchies, transgresses limits, puts an end to the duplication between life and death, between the promise and its fulfilment, reverses signs, brings opposites closer together.[88]

The Congolese pastor Kä Mana expresses this eschatological principle with the utopic principle of *the coming-Christ* (*le Christ-à-venir*).[89] Kä Mana asks Africans to abandon the search for a safeguard of African past and identity and to trust in *the coming-Christ*. Kä Mana drew this principle from two sources. The first is an understanding of the human being as a beginning, a principle of freedom, following Hannah Arendt and St Augustine. The second is an understanding of Christ as *utopia*. Utopia here is positively understood as a force of action and creativity. Hence the idea that Christ is the measure of humanity, the model of love. The limit of Kä Mana's utopia is that it does not confront its Christology with the doctrine of the Church, with the New Testament understanding of the paschal mystery. The coming-Christ cannot be dissociated with the crucified Jesus. The *memoria passionis et resurrectionis Christi*, constitutes the heart of the Christian faith, without which, Christian theology risks becoming quite simply a political "utopia."

African Christians have to factor in the subversive nature of Christian confession of faith. The story of the universal love of God in Jesus Christ plays the role of critique of societies, cultures and traditions. At the same time, African Christian ethics will teach Christians and others to yield to God's freedom and mystery. God cannot be subjected to history. This conviction can free the believers from the quest for immediate judgment or the temptation to equate God's kingdom to the realizations of the present moment.

This can resonate with Igbo sense of duality, which is based on the understanding of life as a mystery beyond the human person and even the community. Several Igbo proverbs expressed this duality. For example, *Ife kwulu, ife ozo akwudebe ya* (Wherever something stands, something else will stand beside it)[90] No one masters knowledge. Another Igbo proverb says, "The hand does not throw as far as the eye sees." It means that the deepest aspirations of the human person cannot be reduced to and judged by the successes and failures of the present moment. When Igbo wisdom wants to teach about the limits of human knowledge, it says *K'ịma nkea, ịma nke ọzọ*? (If you know one thing, do you know the other?).

Human institutions and laws are not perfect. Even institutions with the best intentions can produce ambiguous and adverse effects. Joyce Schuld, interpreting Augustine's "ethic of humility," puts it this way: "Our political expectations and desires must not be confused or equated with social harmony of creation or redemption."[91] Our future is in God and this future has already been inaugurated in the death and resurrection of Christ. Augustine's "ethic of humility." is "based on the paradoxical power of the cross" which should lead to "chastened knowledge…which recognizes the limitations of any finite perspectives, standards and projects."[92]

Genuine hope brings us to welcome our limits and those of the world. This is not despair. Eschatological African Christian Ethics will help Africans to embrace human existence without surrendering. It urges us to place our own limitations and successes within the horizon of God's kingdom.

Conclusion

I have argued that the Trinitarian conception of God provides a broader basis for an authentic African Christian ethics, or what Paulinus Odozor calls, "morality truly Christian and truly African."

The reflection intended to go beyond the apologetics of early African inculturation theology. This apologetics has two ramifications. On one hand, the apologetics of African monotheism sought to ground African Christian ethics on a supposed continuity between the Christian God and the African God-named the *Supreme being*. The Christology of Christ the ancestor, on the other hand, identified Christ with the African conception of Ancestors as custodians and models of morality.

I have shown that the two apologetic attempts do not provide adequate basis for African Christian ethics. First, the theistic concept of the *Supreme being* and the analogy of Christ as ancestor do not account adequately for the complexity and plasticity of the conception of God and ancestors in African traditional religions. They remain within the conception of the idea of God as a moral postulate. Second, they do not give adequate account of the Christian confession of God as Trinity revealed in the event of life, death and resurrection of Jesus Christ and in the activities of the Holy Spirit and its implication for Christian life in society.

Consequently, I opted, in consonance with Odozor's thought, for a change of approach. Instead of arguing whether Africans knew God before the coming of Christianity and how Christianity can preserve what is considered as the ancestrally supported basic African moral values, our research went on to register the fact that an authentic African Christian ethics should be grounded in the confession of God being as love, revealed in God's self-identification with Jesus Christ through the powers of the Holy Spirit. This we described as the kenosis of the Father, the Son and the Holy Spirit.

The confession of God's being as love opens the way for an African Christian ethics that does not destroy African world vision and moral values but takes them up and transforms them in the light of the revelation. African Christian ethics will understand human life as correspondence to God's being through Jesus Christ (theocentric ethics). Corresponding to Jesus Christ, human beings can discover an integral sense of kinship with one another, as sons and daughters of God, beyond social, cultural, ethnic divides (theofilial ethics). Following the inspiration of the Holy Spirit, they will also understand themselves as members of the same community of creation with other people beyond the Christian folk and with the entire creation as expression of God's glory (pneumatological/ecological ethics). Finally, they will also understand that God's kingdom cannot be equated with our dream of social harmony here and now. They will believe and hope in God who comes to transform their earthly existence (eschatological ethics).

Chapter 15

Continuing the Quest for a Morality Truly Christian and African[1]

Paulinus Odozor, C.S.Sp.

Introduction

I wrote *Morality Truly Christian, Truly African* after several years of leading a doctoral seminar on African Christian theologies at the University of Notre Dame. In this course we read some of Africa's finest minds, especially of the generation before and after Independence, that is, the 1950s to the early years of the present millennium. These African pioneers did their work against the immediate backdrop of colonialism, the Independence of various African nations, the African Church as basically a missionary Church, and the optimism unleashed on the Church by Vatican II, to name just a few. They lamented the woes visited on Africa from the outside ; they struggled with the devaluation of the African reality in all its aspects by outsiders; they did whatever they could to prove to anyone who cared to listen that Africa was not a continent of hopelessness, darkness, sans history, or culture; and they made concrete suggestions on how to move Africa forward theologically, economically and socially.[2]

These African pioneers formalized the subject of African theology and made it respectable as a particular branch and approach to the craft of theology. I teach these African pioneers with great devotion and awe and my research work owes a lot to their genius. However, while *Morality Truly Christian, Truly African* acknowledges and builds on their work, it seeks to take the work of theologizing in and from Africa towards a slightly different trajectory. While acknowledging the harm done by outsiders, the book under discussion in these chapters is intended as a blueprint for the future and therefore believes that certain things or issues need to be attended to, especially from the theological point of view in Africa to affect the much desired renewal of African life.

Dreams Not Yet Realized

The dawn of the present Millennium coincided with a desire for rebirth in Africa, for something the onetime president of South Africa, Thabo Mbeki, and other African leaders often referred to as "an African renaissance." This was to be a new contemporary African self-assertion to build an African civilization which would be "responsive to the dictates of our times, namely, economic prosperity, political freedom and self and social solidarity."[3] Since the start of the present millennium African governments and organizations have taken some extraordinary measures to address the issues which continue to plague the continent.

> [These leaders] put several administrative mechanisms in place on the continent to help Africa face the challenge of alienation and achieve continental integration. To accelerate political integration on the continent, the Organization of African Unity (OAU) metamorphosed into the African Union (AU); while on the economic front a new mechanism, the New Economic Partnership for African Development (NEPAD), was established as a strategic framework for development, while an African Peer Review Mechanism (APRM) was also set up to monitor and measure the compliance of the AU members to the development goals which the continent's leaders had set for themselves and their nations. The continent still had its troubles, but there was the feeling that, given a little push, Africa would join the rest of the world to avail of the opportunities which the dawning new millennium seemed to hold for the entire world.[4]

Despite all these plans Africa's prospects do not seem to improve much, however one looks at it. The much hoped-for African renaissance is yet to materialize. As Pope Benedict XVI puts it in various parts of *Africae Munus*,[5] there are situations of grave concern which make the rebirth we seek in Africa difficult. Africa's memory is still scared painfully as a result of "fratricidal conflicts between ethnic groups, the slave trade and colonialization" (AM 9). There are new forms of enslavement and colonialization all over the continent. Africa is "facing a culture—shock which strikes at the age-old foundations of social life and makes it hard for her to come to terms with modernity. Wars, conflicts, and racist xenophobic attitudes which plague many human societies are also held by a minority to the detriment of entire peoples" (AM 21). Africa is also suffering the ravages of alcohol and drug abuse and "the plundering of the goods of the earth" is destroying "the continent's human potential" (AM 72). Africa is also grappling with many pandemics and endemic situations such as malaria, HIV/AIDS, and tuberculosis, which, according to the Pope, call for serious medical intervention and behavioral changes such as sexual abstinence and fidelity within marriage. The list goes on.

There are a number of ways to evaluate Africa's prospects. One is to throw up one's hands in despair in the belief that Africa is beyond redemption. This is pessimistic attitude fails to honor the much Africans are actually achieving or can achieve, thanks to the triumph of God's grace on the continent. *Morality Truly Christian, Truly African,* the book under discussion in the present volume, makes some noteworthy assumptions: that Africa is not beyond redemption; that the church is uniquely placed to help Africa's redemption; that the Church's contribution to the African renaissance we all hope for is theological and not merely social or even economic. Even though it might sometimes appear that despite all the efforts the churches have made so far in the social life of Africa the timbre and tone of African societies do not appear to change much or that in fact African societies seem to be sinking more and more into chaos and barbarity, this is no reason to give up on Africa. As Pope John Paul said a long time ago, Africa is not destined for death but for life. It is my view, as already indicated above, however, that

> the one area in which the church must effect transformation in Africa is theological. Although the church's mission is not merely the transmission of doctrine its efforts at social transformation in Africa as elsewhere must come from a well-articulated and openly stated doctrinal core; unless it focuses

> with razor like intensity on its theological task it cannot any longer be an effective agent of transformation in Africa; it will ultimately become irrelevant in Africa. If the church carries itself merely as another NGO it will die in Africa.[6]

The book under discussion is a result of these convictions.

To put it another way, I believe that African Christian theology must be at the forefront in the search for ways to bring about a new Africa. The theology I speak about is one that helps the Church and Christians refocus their attention on Jesus Christ, his mission and his message in addition to whatever else that is useful and helpful in African societies. This book was meant to start and stimulate discussions on a number of issues which are of utmost importance to Africa, to the African Church, and to our world. Judging by the various essays in this collection and by other reviews and reactions which it has elicited since its publication, the book has succeeded beyond my wildest dreams.

An Old Question

Morality truly Christian, Truly African is also intended to supply some answers to questions about the distinctiveness of Christian ethics which agitated the field of Christian moral discourse especially in the years after Vatican II and to show how acknowledgment of that distinctiveness can help Christians contribute more meaningfully to the renewal of African life. That the question of the distinctness of Christian ethics is no longer being raised very vociferously today does not mean that it has been answered adequately or that it is no longer cogent. There were two important aspects to the debate on the distinctiveness of Christian ethics, namely whether there was anything else apart from the normal human morality which as the Catholic tradition itself in espousing the natural law insists is both knowable to and doable by everyone, and secondly, whether Jesus taught any things that were unique to him and subsequently to his community, morally. There were those like Joseph Ratzinger who insisted that Jesus taught unique moral truths and that there was a specificity to Christian morality. There were also those who, like Josef Fuchs, held that there was nothing specific to morality from a uniquely Christian perspective.

Basically, for Fuchs, morality is about the way human beings organize life in this world. Thus it has no bearing on the salvation of the individual before God. The question about the specificity of Christian morality has to do with whether there are distinctively 'categorical' ways of life which are unique to Christians, "that is whether there are ways of being just, pure, and faithful, which are specifically Christian or whether 'genuinely human attitudes and lifestyles in various areas of life are not also those of non-Christians."[7] In the end, Fuchs denies that there is any morality distinct and unique to Christianity, other than normal human morality. One implication of this is therefore that the Church, as Church, cannot teach authoritatively on moral matters. Its domain is in the area of salvation which is utterly gratuitously given by God and has no connection with the categorical choices we make in this world. To put it more technically, there is a sphere of moral goodness and a sphere of moral rightness. The former is the sphere where the church has competence and in which it urges people to live religiously, and the former is the area of human morality where even good people can make wrong choices without any consequence to their eternal destiny.

An African Slant to the Old Question

Morality Truly Christian, Truly African is basically a book about moral theory and foundations—a kind of Catholic theological metaethics, written by an African with African realities both secular and religious in mind and as background. It raises questions about what being an African Christian has to do with the way one thinks about matters of right and wrong. What difference does faith make to the way I think about moral matters? How, if at all, does my being an African influence my moral judgments, decisions, or perceptions? Can an African Christian be different from his/her compatriots as a moral actor, and in what ways? To be even more specific, what difference does, can, or should faith in Jesus Christ make in the way African Christians think or act morally? What proof can one adduce for whatever assertions, positive or negative, one makes on this issue?

Christian morality is the morality of those who have found faith in Jesus Christ. It is the morality of those who, moved by the events of the stunning deed of God in Jesus look at the world from the reality of Jesus.

And African Christian morality follows from this: *It is the morality of Africans who have found faith in Jesus Christ as Africans*. Faith in Jesus has an originating and grounding effect in that it provides an angle of vision on reality, tutors our imagination, directs our motivations, and influences our choices in a most profound way. "As Joseph Sittler puts, "to be a Christian is to accept what God gives. What God gives is Jesus Christ as God's self-giving love. The faith response is itself empowered by God who himself is the author of our redemption."[8] Christian ethics in whatever place and time is therefore a response ethic and thus a call to discipleship. And as the William Spohn once put it, to be a disciple of Jesus is to take seriously what Jesus took seriously. And what did Jesus take seriously? Among many other things, Jesus took God, the human person, forgiveness, reconciliation, seriously. Jesus provides us an angle of vision, by drawing our attention to certain facets and realities of life, such as the need to pay attention to the poor and the abandoned. In some other cases Jesus teaches us either by his words and deeds the truths about human life, truths which come from God such as when he teaches us about the indissolubility of marriage. At other times, Jesus reinforces what are universally shared values with a particular intentionality and attitude. In this regard, as Joseph Ratzinger argued, the originality of Christian morality does not lie in the fact that Christian morality consists of principles which are not found anywhere else. What makes Christian morality unique is the place these principles do or do not occupy in the spiritual structure of Christianity. This is to say that in some ways the uniqueness of Christian morality comes from its narrative embedding.

Even in the ancient world, there was no ready morality to be taken over. In ancient Israel the dividing line, as Joseph Ratzinger points out, was faith in Yahweh which served as the rallying point, and which gave meaning to the moral code. In other words, even moral knowledge which had been arrived at by reason in other circumstances were admitted or rejected on the grounds that they corresponded to the teaching and figure of Yahweh or not.[9] The teaching of Christ and the memory of the person of Jesus figured decisively in the evolution of Christian morality and still constitute the architectonic framework on which this approach to ethics rests. The Christian Church was not born in a sanitized world where there was no sin, and everything was alright. The world of the early church was as much a morally complex world as our own. In this world, for example, divorce and remarriage was the norm. Child neglect in parts of the Roman empire was rampart and, homosexuality was wildly practiced, etc.[10] Christianity made its choices on these matters despite the prevailing ethos of the period.

It is noteworthy, however, that the first order of interest for Christianity was not morality. Christianity was first of all about the kerygma, the good news of salvation from God in Jesus. The disciples of Jesus who had witnessed this stunning deed fanned out into the world to proclaim that in the man from Nazareth God had done something new, gratuitous and utterly unique and unrepeatable. They wanted the whole world to hear of this engendering deed and to join up in this move to recreate the world.[11] But, even though morality was not the first order of business for the Christian community the community also insisted that faith in Jesus had consequences for the way we organize our world. What we do here on earth and what we refuse to do here have consequences for our eternal destiny. The rightness of what we do or the wrongness of it was measured by what Christians heard Jesus say and on the basis of what they imagined he would say on the basis of who he was and what he taught. It is this reality that gave the Christian moral tradition a flavor all its own and a distinction from everyone else around them. Christians were thus able to take a stance on certain ways of being in the world in the area of politics, sex and sexuality, marriage and relationships etc. Christianity has continued to draw from its *Memoria Jesu* and from the explicit teachings of Jesus to address many issues and challenges which humanity faces right to our day, including those which could not have been foreseen or imagined by the Lord Jesus in his second century Palestinian context.

Christian Morality in the African Context

As in the ancient world, African Christianity was not born in a religiously neutral world. Christianity came to Africa in a world where there were primal religions in place already. I deliberately stress this point of similarity between African Christianity and the first Christian communities to remind us that the African experience was not as unique as we sometimes think it is, and also to point us to the early Christian communities for help with our own search for solutions regarding what we often refer to as inculturation. Kwame Bediako has attended to these parallel situations in his magisterial work on theology and identity and in his other writings as well.[12] In its contact with the ancient world, Christianity had to make choices about the moral rightness or otherwise of certain human institutions and situations, based on the two criteria I talked about already, namely, the explicit teaching of Jesus and the example of his life and the inferences drawn, or which could possibly be drawn from any or both of these.

African traditions, closely tied to African traditional religion as they are, have had a lot to say to Africans about life and about how it is to be organized. Many Africans have been tutored in them and by them as regards what is morally right or wrong. This system has produced men and women who have lived or who continue to live morally upright lives. So, African Christianity in its current phase, like the early church has the good fortune of being in a context which is suffused with ethical concerns, especially with ethical concerns that are theistically informed. But here also lies the challenge. As in its previous history, Christianity in Africa has also had to do two things, first, it has had to preach the good news of Jesus Christ. This in itself is a labor of love which signals the belief in the universality of God's concern and salvation. If the gospel is good news for the European or for the first century Palestinian, it must also be good news for the African. Secondly, aside from proclaiming the kerygma, African Christianity insists as in the first centuries and all through history that faith has implications for the ways we organize life in this world. What is ethically upright human behavior and practice has now to be seen through the lenses provide by the life, example, and teaching of Jesus. By taking such a stance in Africa Christianity was bound to come in conflict with the existing worldview, namely African traditions and religion, in a number of areas. This arises basically because of the sometimes incompatible understandings of reality between the Christian faith and aspects of African traditional worldviews.

II
Conversations

Two Important Questions Answered

In the introduction to *Morality Truly Christian, Truly African* I raised the following two questions: "(1) given the largely Eurocentric nature of Catholic moral theology thus far in the history of the church, what will it take to invest the rest of the church, especially the theological community, through sustained intellectual attention and solidarity, in the history and moral challenges of the church in other parts of the world, in this case Africa? (2) What is to be gained, for the whole church were this to happen in a deep and lasting way?" I also stated in that introduction that "my hope is that theologizing in such an open way, as I tried to do here in this book, will help to bring the church and the entire theological community into conversation about Christian ethics (moral theology) in the African context so that what goes on in that part of the Christian community will be of interest to all as a 'Christian theological thing' and not just as an 'African thing.'"[13] This collection adequately addresses these concerns. The scholars whose essays appear in this volume have shown that the "African thing" is indeed "a Christian theological thing" and that conversations started within the African context can indeed be of interest to the whole Church and indeed the whole human community.

The essays in this volume clearly capture the major issues in the book and in some cases take many of these issues to much greater lengths than I had imagined. The contributors collectively accomplish two of the important aims of the books stated above; they show that despite geographical differences African Christian ethics shares many of the same interests and concerns as Christian ethics done in other places in the world, and they show that merely discussing any issues of right and wrong from an African perspective does not necessarily mark that discussion off as merely an "African thing" which is too unimportant to occupy the lofty minds of western theological thinkers. Inculturation—the process whereby theology engages culture—is not merely an African thing; anamnesis—the way Christians remember Jesus—is not only important in the liturgy or relevant only for African remembrances of ancestral deeds and past, it is also key for moral life everywhere. What we remember and what we forget are important for the way we all construe morality and for the ways we treat each other. In short, Africa's theological musings can no longer be relegated to footnotes or to dusty shelve spaces in libraries. Secondly, the scholars represented in this volume show in their various essays that African theological discourse has valuable lessons and insights to teach the rest of the world. Africa is no longer just a consumer of foreign theological products, Africa is brewing theology in its "pots" and kitchens, to paraphrase Orobator.[14] The food might sometimes be spicy, but it is always tasty and intended for the nourishment of the consumer. As David Clairmont puts it in his contribution to this volume,

> What Odozor (and many other Catholic theologians) are doing is not simply unfolding the logical implications of the Catholic profession of faith rooted in the churches credal formulae. They are doing ethics: they are critically reflecting on how people live—both Catholics and non-Catholics—in conversation with Catholic moral teaching but their sources, their approaches and the forms of reflection are critical. They want the lives of Catholic Christians to become better, more deeply reflective of their humanity and the message of the gospel, and that standard for measuring what is better and what is worse is not to be found only in the church's history or in its present teaching. Another way to put this point is to say that Catholic theological ethics is a kind of comparative activity in the sense that the process of critiquing involves a comparative spirit.[15]

The African Christian comes to this comparison not a tabula rasa but fortified with some important assumptions, as Christian ethics in Africa is today faced with three formidable opponents/ interlocutors: a resurgent African traditional religion; an uncompromising Islamic religion which is intent on total takeover and conquest of Africa; and a secularist worldview which is also seeking total dominance through some of the proverbial forces of globalization—namely the media and African intelligentsia, especially domiciled in the West, who, though still in the minority; are strong purveyors of wokeism and some secular tendencies which are dominant in Western Europe and in the United States of America. Africa is in flux. But despite the fluidity of the situation African Christian ethics is marked by several tendencies or constants. Here is a partial listing of these: (a) Jesus Christ; (b) the primacy of charity; (c) the notion of natural law; (d) a new and expanded anthropology; (e) an optimistic view of reality and of the human person in the created order; and (f) a healthy but critical attitude to culture as a human creation—hence the attention given to the question of inculturation. The contributors to this volume have, as already indicated, noted many of these issues. I am not going to repeat what they have said, nor will I talk about any of these issues at any length since I have written extensively about them in the book under discussion. What I will do in the next section is to emphasize again some of those issues which mark African Christian ethics as unique as well as some of the factors which African Christian theology and African Christian theological ethics must stress as essential contributions to the African renaissance we all seek.

III
What Christian Ethics Must Emphasize; What It Must Bring to the Table in Africa

1. A New Face of God

African Christian Ethics as ethics done in a theological way assumes the existence and relevance of God; it assumes that God has a new face in Africa as mediated by the Lord Jesus Christ. Since it is commonly accepted that ethical commitment in Africa, as elsewhere, is anchored in the people's concept of the God they worship,"[16] African Christian ethics as theology assumes responsibility not just for mediating the face of the one Jesus called his father but also for drawing Africa's attention to the implications of this belief with regard to the way Africans construe life on the continent. As Bede Ukwuije indicates in his essay in this volume, following Karl Barth, "Trinity is the Christian name for God. The mystery of the Trinity is the mystery of love, totally manifested in the freedom of self-donation of the father, the Son and the Spirit."[17] For Ukwuije, "humanity is a gift of God's love." Human life is to be lived in a way to correspond to God's love—in self-donation, that is in correspondence to the Trinitarian communion. It must be "a life in which no one tries to preserve the self, rather each person tries to live for others."[18] It is therefore clear that at the center of Christian morality, as has been recognized down the ages is love. It is not simply about our love for God. It is about God's love for us which in turn generates our love for God which is manifested in our love for each other. The ultimate expression of God's love for us is in the Incarnation, the death and Resurrection of Christ.

2. Jesus, the Human Face of God's Love

An essential of Christian ethical discourse in Africa and elsewhere is God's stunning revelation of himself in Jesus Christ. I have stressed this point everywhere in this essay and in the book as well. Christian ethics in Africa has to provide a very clear image of the Lord. Professor Melanie Barrett, using the work of Hans Urs von Balthasar, has tried to show how African theology can recover the face of Jesus and what it brings to the table by doing so. The retrieval of the face of Jesus according to Barrett,

> involves enabling a fresh engagement with the New Testament: neither by providing intellectual summaries of the ideas therein, nor by rehearsing abstract theological arguments derived from the Bible by well-regarded theologians in the western tradition, but rather by facilitating an *aesthetic* encounter with the person of Christ as portrayed in the gospels (and to a lesser extent, in the lives of the apostles and saints). Not only would such an approach avoid the dreaded European attire that can render theology unattractive; it would holistically engage the whole person (both mind and heart) while also communicating the needed concepts regarding both God and the human person due to its Christ-centered focus.[19]

The ultimate intention would be to invite people into communion with Christ who is himself the way and the ultimate expression of divine love. The New Testament needs to be read by Africans in their cultural contexts with fresh eyes,

> so as to deepen their own discipleship. By contemplating Jesus aesthetically, with open hearts and minds, they can perceive the harmony between his existence and his mission, his effortlessness, his utter humility, his unwavering obedience to the father, and the radicality of his love: the contours of which are not sentimental but sacrificial, not self-aggrandizing but self-emptying, and poured out for all human beings, not just some of them.[20]

From Jesus we learn that neighborly love grows from love of God, and aims at helping anyone in need, simply because he is a fellow human being.

3. Moral Epistemology

The question of moral epistemology is important in African Christian ethics. The issue is whether we can know moral truths; how we can know moral truths; and what we are capable of doing or not doing morally. This is not solely an African question, but it begs to be raised in this context principally because of the claim by some that natural law is a western imposition. What GS 16 says of the human ability to know moral truths and to act morally in upright ways applies equally to Africans. Africans do not make up the moral standards as they go along. In moments of moral conflict, Africans enter into deliberations to decide the morally upright way to go. However as Matthew Levering puts it, "since human reason knows the core precepts of natural law there are universally knowable moral absolutes… These absolutes ground community deliberation about what is to be done rather than arising out of community deliberation."[21] But that is not all. Catholic tradition acknowledges that natural law is not by itself sufficient in mapping out all the details for the moral life of individuals. As Stephen Brock points out, it is the case that "under the conditions of sin, even many of the precepts that belong to natural law absolutely, and indeed the most important of them, seem to need divine help, not only for actual compliance with them—that certainly requires grace—but also for a more than tenuous, merely notional or theoretical hold on them."[22]

4. An Expanded Anthropology

Ethics is about human conduct; it is about the human being as a free, rational creature. It matters therefore what we understand about the human being as a moral agent. But what is the human person? The African context answers this question in several ways. One key element, among many others, in the definition of the human person is relatedness, which is often described with the Bantu word *ubuntu.* As the South African philosopher Thaddeus Metz puts it, *Ubuntu* roughly translated, means "humanness." It is a word which connotes the idea that a person is a person through other persons or as is often generally stated, "I am because we are." This is the essence of the so-called relationality principle. For Metz, living an ideal human life among black Africans is not so much about acting in conformity to principles of right actions; it is rather about acting in ways that exhibit some excellent character. In African ethics, according to some other African scholars, there is less emphasis on moral rules. Rather, the focus is on what kind of person one should become.[23] Africans as characteristically community-oriented people determine the rightness or wrongness of a moral act based largely on the relationality principle. According to Thaddeus Metz, the relationality principle in African ethics is a means to granting moral status to beings. "The more a being is capable of being part of a communal relationship, the greater its moral status."[24]

This means that there are different levels of "personhood." One can be more or less a person, self, or human being, where the more one is, the better. One's ultimate goal should be to become a full person, a real self, or a genuine human being; and African traditional societies much like the early Christian community value the importance of community solidarity. Anything which undermines community cohesion is frowned upon.

Although relationality is a major sustaining idea and ethos in the African worldview, I have a number of concerns with the emphasis which some authors place on it as the hinge norm for African ethics, forcing it to provide all the answers to African moral needs. Africans adhere to more than one moral principle to make their moral choices. First, one has to ask the question which Africans we are talking about. This question is not the usual one about Africa's regional, geographical, and cultural variations and complexities. The question arises here because authors like Metz, Christopher Simon Wareham, and others seem to speak of an Africa still untouched by any other influences, secular or religious, an Africa where villages are intact and moral decisions are conducted much like in secluded human pockets. In that world, *ubuntu* or relatedness would be an easy approach to many of life's moral challenges. The African world is a different world from the world of *ubuntu* as originally conceived and lived. Even South Africa, pre- or post-apartheid, could not bring back the era of unsoiled *ubuntu*. The basis of the relatedness motif in African life is crumbling before us. Consider for instance the inter-ethnic and intra-ethnic conflicts which continue to bedevil the continent.

A second related issue about *Ubuntu* ethics is that in *Ubuntu* ethics, humanness is a gift bestowed by the community. And it is a category which is possessed in varying degrees. This means, then, that the community can refuse to bestow humanness or personhood to a particular individual or to groups of individuals for whatever reason it considers important. According to this understanding, *ubuntu* could indicate a kind of "cancel culture" in which people are refused membership in a human community for whatever reason. Here we find a clue to many of Africa's human-rights problems. In this understanding, some people are more human than others and society can refuse to confer humanness to some others or decide to treat them differently according to the perceived degree of humanity they possess. The strength of *Ubuntu* as a viable moral theory has to be measured against the plight of the lowliest members of Africa's societies, the poor, the marginalized, and Africa's various caste systems which are found all over Africa. Doing so involves a number of things including determining the moral rules which guide or promote humane living and the kind of persons which are expected to create or grow these rules.

In Christian anthropology, humanness is an endowment from God. One's personhood is non-negotiable and beyond human calculation because it is not a gift from any institution or person and not dependent on human achievement or even moral standing. Human beings have their origin in God who created them in his own image and likeness; they are also redeemed by and destined for God. "Creation in the image of God confers dignity and makes everyone equally valuable. As the foundation of human dignity, it dictates who is to be considered worthy: every individual regardless of condition, and highlights human equality, regardless of functional importance."[25] The principle of relationality and its attendant virtue of solidarity is an important anthropological marker for doing ethics anywhere, but it cannot stand on its own. It needs the transcendent mooring which is only made possible by the Christian understanding of the human being as created in God's image. Africa needs this expanded anthropological understanding to address the many challenges the human person is facing on the continent. As already stated in this book, the discussion of inculturation in African theology comes from a deeply optimistic place which acknowledges that God has been good to Africa and that Africa has used its talents and opportunities to create cultures that speak of God. At the center of this undertaking is the human person, made in the image and likeness of God, the only creature God willed for himself, the one who has worth from natural conception to natural death, the one whose value is inviolable and beyond any utilitarian calculation.

5. Inculturation

Inculturation remains a staple of African theological discourse. It arises basically as an exercise of gratitude to God for his blessings on Africa. African theologians through inculturation debate have sought to consider God's blessings on their continent as they reflect on the gospel. God has not left Africa without gifts. And Africa is not a passive recipient of those gifts especially the gifts of faith from other people. Even Pope Benedict XVI acknowledged this fact both in his opening homily at the second Africa Synod in 2009 and in *Africae Munus* which he published after the Synod. African traditional religions have celebrated the gifts of God through rituals, and moral commitments. Inculturation discourse started initially as a way to enter into the great gifts of God in African cultures and religions. As the Second Vatican Council put it, when the gospel enters into any space, it throws the light of truth upon those circumstances, affirming what is true and noble and critiquing what is unacceptable and wrong. As indicated in *Morality Truly Christian, Truly African*, the requirements for the interaction of Christianity with the various aspects of the Christian faith and aspects of African traditional religion varies considerably from one theological subspecialty to another. But faith must engage culture. The question is which culture? And how to do it.

Although inculturation discourse began as an exercise of dialogue between Christianity and African primal religions, it must not no longer be limited to this one dialogue partner. African cultures have expanded beyond the mainly religious culture which characterized the initial internal interaction between Christianity and Africa in modern times. Today there are many aspects of African cultures which are posing serious challenges to the Christian faith and indeed to all faiths and to belief in general. Therefore we now need a new and expanded view of inculturation. This discussion would have to include the challenges from not just African traditional religion but Islam and the secular world. Christian ethics in Africa is today facing three formidable opponents/ interlocutors: a resurgent African traditional religion; an uncompromising Islamic religion which is intent on total takeover and conquest of Africa; and a secularist worldview which is also seeking total dominance through the proverbial forces of globalization. The media and African intelligentsia, especially those domiciled in the West, though still in the minority, are strong purveyors of wokism and all secular tendencies which are dominant in Western Europe and in the United States of America. Africa is in a flux. And the dominant concerns for African theology are no longer those which come from or reflect the era of *Things Fall Apart* (figuratively speaking). It is now time to move beyond this phase. We are in an era when the continent is not at ease. Christian ethics must continue to participate in the effort to articulate clearly why the unease and what can be done about it. One of the things Christian theology must do in the contemporary era is to articulate carefully the cultural trends in Africa today with a view to supporting those which are life-giving/affirming, dialoguing with those which need purification and critiquing those which drag Africa or African persons down.

6. *Sex/Sexuality/Marriage/Gender as Issues for African Christian Ethics*

Another area which is also in need of critical engagement between Christianity and cultures in general is the area of human sexuality/ marriage, and gender. Even within Christianity itself, sex and matters related to it continue to pose serious challenges to Christian morality.[26] As Peter Nichols noted long ago, "The question of women, the question of divorce, even the question of the priesthood, contains a powerful element of sex, and if there is one issue which it is fair to say that Christianity as a whole… has failed to handle successfully, it is sex."[27] Even though a lot has been written on these matters by theologians and authorities of the various churches, there is still plenty of discussion and disagreements even among Christians on them. Although the Christian faith was not understood in the early church as a code of morality, since the announcement of the good news was paramount for the apostles and early disciples of Jesus, the good news was not without ethical implications. As interpreted by Luke in the various discourses of Acts, for example, first evangelization "constituted a general invitation to conversion and life's reorientation. This bond between the gospel's proclamation and a Christian ethical stance can also be discerned in Paul's writing when he exhorts his readers to model their behavior on the attitude attributed to Christ in the Philippian's hymn (Phil.2:3–5) or when argues for faith attitudes or behaviors consistent with the Christian creedal and liturgical formulas (1 Cor. 15:12–58; 11:26–34)." Therefore, from the very beginning, Christians were aware that "the fundamental gospel proclamation had ethical implications" in all aspects of human life, including human sexuality. The problem has often been what conclusions to draw from it for the way they organize their lives, since not everything was specified.[28]

It did not take too long for the Christian position on matters of sex and sexuality to become clear. As Lisa Cahill has pointed out, the Christian position on sex and sexuality in the New Testament hinges on four important assumptions: the importance of Christian identity; the need for preservation of Christian community; eschatological expectation of the church; and finally, of course, the teachings of Jesus himself.[29] The

Christian church was born into a world with a lot of sexual challenges: there were widespread homosexual practices especially among upper class stoics;[30] divorce and remarriage were rife; child abandonment and prostitution were endemic in many societies. Yet, in both the New Testament and the early fathers, the Christian community developed a solid and united moral stance on these matters.

Consider, for example, the issue of divorce and remarriage. Even though the Jewish and Roman laws allowed for divorce and remarriage, the teaching of Jesus in Mark 10:2–12 with parallels in other New Testament sources solidly put the early Christian Church on the side of indissolubility of validly entered marriages. Marriage was understood as a union between a man and a woman. And there was a consensus that sexual difference between man and woman ought to be treated as morally significant. "From Augustine to the reformation, there was a consensus that God created human beings in sexual differentiation, that Christian social life will affirm this difference through marriage and the regulation of life, and that sexual difference will be redeemed in the eschaton."[31] For much of Christian history up until the Protestant Reformation the prohibition of Jesus against divorce and remarriage was considered absolute to the point where not even adultery of one of the spouses was considered grounds enough for dissolution of an otherwise validly arranged marriage or grounds enough for remarriage when separation had in fact occurred. With the Reformation, Christians became split in their understandings of the marital union and various aspects of its meaning and on the moral force of the teaching of Jesus especially in the so-called exception clause of Matthew's Gospel. There was also debate on the theological legitimacy of celibacy, and the role of the Christian conscience in determining the morality of these issues vis-a-vis what some considered the imposition on these matters by ecclesiastical authority.[32]

There has also been considerable discussion on the question of the regulation of birth, beginning from the fathers down to our day. For much of that history up until the 20th century there was consensus on this matter across the spectrum of Christian communities all of which taught that contraception was morally wrong. All that changed in 1930 when at the Lambert conference of that year, the Anglican communion voted to allow artificial contraception, at least under certain circumstances. The Christian consensus on this matter broke down completely at the WCC convention of 1959 when entire Protestant communities voted to permit the use of contraception, thus leaving the Roman Catholic Church and the Eastern Orthodox Church as the only Christian communities still holding to the ancient Christian position. The reasons for this split were many, based on theological, medical, and other considerations. These forces were also to influence discussions around birth control in the Catholic Church which ultimately led to the papal stance in *Humanae Vitae* which was issued by Pope Paul VI in 1968.

The debate over contraception exposed a growing rift within Christian communities and within the Catholic Church itself over some fundamentally important theological assumptions which had carried the Church through much of its history and which have since the Second Vatican Council and the publication of *Humanae Vitae* become the subject of serious discussions in various ways within the Christian churches themselves—the question of authority, the meaning and extent of moral norms and the sources of moral insights, such as scriptures and human experience, etc. These debates have had a lot of impact in the discussion on the distinctiveness of Christian ethics as was discussed above in this essay. Africa has been on the receiving end of the question of contraception and reproduction. Many organizations such as Planned parenthood and the Gates foundation have currently set up shop all over Africa, often under the guise of the empowerment of women and the protection of women's reproductive rights. The Protocol to the Charter on Human and Peoples' Rights on the Rights of Women in Africa, otherwise known as the Maputo Protocol, contains a section, Article 14, which provides for "the right to health of women, including sexual and reproductive health, including (a) the right to control their fertility; (b) the right to decide whether to have children, the number of children, and the spacing of children; and (c) the right to choose any method of contraception." This protocol also requires African governments and societies to "protect the reproductive rights of women by authorizing medical abortion in cases of sexual assault, rape, incest and where the continued pregnancy endangers the mental health of the mother or the life of the mother or the fetus."[33] Many African Churches and Muslim communities have consistently strongly opposed certain sections of this protocol on the grounds especially that it sanctions abortion and does not respect the right to life of human beings from conception to natural death.[34]

Another issue of moral concern for Christians in the post-Vatican II era is homosexuality and homosexual marriages, and in more recent years, transgenderism. In the past twenty years or so, the world has witnessed an increasing movement towards acceptance of same-sex marriages as normative. Some of the Christian churches themselves have come under serious attacks for refusing to accept the entirety of mostly Western societies position on this issue or for questioning societies positions on the matter. From formerly predominantly Catholic Ireland to Canada, the United States, and Australia, western societies have increasingly shown support for homosexual unions as normatively marital unions. On the other hand, some persons within these societies and even governments within these places consider anyone who holds a contrary view on this matter as closed minded and homophobic. Even within the Christian community, the acceptance of homosexual unions as equally marital unions has become increasingly high. Theologians, priests, bishops, and other church workers and even episcopal conferences appear increasingly reluctant to question the basic assumption behind the movement for same-sex marriage: namely that no one should ever be prohibited from marrying whomever he or she 'loves' for whatever reason. This assumption in some ways runs headlong against the previous and long held position of the churches that sexual difference is morally significant, that sex in marriage has a purpose, that man and women are complementary in their anatomical, psychological, and spiritual makeup, and that as Christians we understand that God made them from the beginning male and female, and for this reason "a man leaves his father and mother and joins his wife" (Gen 2:24).

The same-sex marriage phenomenon is one of the most serious challenges the Christian faith has faced in all its existence, both theologically and socially. A lot of theological capital has been invested in the theology and theological anthropology of sexual difference and for good reasons based on human experience and on the scriptures. All of this work faces an assault which is in many ways unprecedented in the history of the Church. The resolution of this challenge could give us either a Christian community in which all that matters is love, in that loose sense used by Joseph Fletcher, or a situation where love and normativity meet as partners in the search for human common good.

The Challenges for African Christian Ethics

The received Christian tradition on human sexuality and marriage is being increasingly challenged in Africa as well. The challenges in Africa come from various points all at once: African traditional societies, Islam; African Initiated Churches; various Christian communities who were formerly in agreement on a number of issues but can now hardly see any unity between them and the Catholic community. At the root of these disagreements is the so-called Sexual Revolution which "at the least reflects changes in understandings and assessments of the nature and purposes of human sexual relations and in turn understandings of gender roles and of the family or household in relation to society at large."[35] The so-called Sexual Revolution has now struck at all this with the argument that the two do not necessarily have to go together. As Professor Maurice Agbaw-Ebai points out in his essay in this volume, at the root of the sexual revolution which we speak of is what he refers to as "immanentist visions of the human person" which manifest themselves in various forms. According to Agbaw-Ebai these views of the human person are

> reflected in the controversies surrounding gender and sexual expression, in which once-widely-held beliefs about maleness and femaleness as anthropological givens, and that about the complementarity of the sexes regarding the question of sexual expression are largely being rejected especially by contemporary western culture. Added to the question of gender and sexual expression is the fundamental question regarding the inviolable dignity of human life, hitherto considered as a gift, but increasingly being degraded to such a degree that the right of the mother is considered to trump the right of the child to life. And besides this, is the very reality of scientific/genetic manipulation in which that which is possible by science is immediately translated to that which is doable. And alongside these cultural and scientific challenges and

> rejection of classical anthropology is likewise present, in very real forms, the rejection of the humanity and personhood of the other, seen in conflicts that never seem to diminish across Africa, the Middle East, and other parts of the world.[36]

Africa is at the receiving end of this immanentist view of the human person. At the second African synod, Cardinal Sarah decried seriously what he referred to as gender ideology which was being forced down the throat of Africa often as condition for foreign aid.[37] Pope Benedict also in the opening homily at that synod spoke of cultures and world-views which were infesting Africa with viruses which would damage and kill the continent. This attitude to the human person is combining forces with a neo-pagan fringe in Africa acting in pretense as "revivers" of African sexual worldviews (which had ostensibly been suppressed by Christianity) to create a climate in Africa where everything is okay, and nothing should be questioned by society in any form.[38] What can African Christianity bring to the discussion on these matters? The answer is simple. Christianity has fought these wars before, and the battles have raged in various guises. Christian unified attitude to sex and sexuality had been built on the understanding that sex was good, that it had its purposes in the union of man and woman called marriage; that sexual relations were normatively consummated in marriage between man and woman who had committed themselves to forming a stable union under oath "until death do us part." It is an exclusive union into which people enter freely and from which they could not dissociate themselves freely since their free consent creates an indissoluble bond. This union is also marked by exclusivity and has both unitive and procreative aspects which must be upheld.

However one looks at it, there is a lot of sexual license today. It is not the work of the Christian ethicist to show how much more license we can create on this matter. People will eventually make their choices. It is not the work of the Church or the theologian to be a morality police either. That does not mean therefore that the Christian Church will cease to speak about what is right or wrong about our current expressions of our sexuality. African Christian ethics must continue to be a prophetic voice on this matter.

7. *Memory*

A lot has been written about memory and remembrance in African life. The intention in this section is not to repeat what has already been said but to stress further how important this area is for Christian theological ethical engagement with the continent. Remembering is a very complicated thing as many of the authors in this collection have indicated. Africans remember. We remember our great ancestors; we celebrate them privately and publicly through ritual processes and narratives, passed on orally or communally and in folklores and through festivals dedicated to them. As I noted in *Morality Truly Christian, Truly African*, recalling or celebrating the past can be very complicated because the past is not always what we think it was.

In the celebrated play which he published on the eve of Nigeria's Independence in 1960, Wole Soyinka, the Nigerian Nobel prize playwright, demonstrates this reality very clearly. As Aroni, one of the characters in the play announces in this play, the human community is celebrating the Gathering of the Tribes. "Their councilors met and said, our forefathers must be present at this feast. They asked us for ancestors, for illustrious ancestors."[39] In response, the living community passed a resolution: "We must bring home the descendants of our proud ancestors. The builders of empires. The descendants of our great nobility. Find them. Bring them here. If they are half-way across the world, trace them. If they are in hell, ransom them. Let them symbolize all that is noble in our nation. Let them be our historical link for the season of rejoicing. Warriors. Sages. Conquerors. Builders. Philosophers. Mystics. Let us assemble around the totem of the nation and we will drink from their resurrected glory."[40] As these illustrious ancestors begin to show up the organizers discover that the past was not what they had imagined it to be. It was full of unjust wars fought over trifles; the past is full of intrigues and murders. As one of the characters in this play puts it, "we asked for statesman instead we got executioners: dead man and dead woman.... The guests we were sent are slaves and lackeys. They are often disgruntled creatures who have come to accuse the present as if in a court of law."[41]

The point here is not to caricature Africa's past or to join in the untrue discussion about that past which has for so long dominated western historical discourse on Africa. That said, we must look at that past with maturity and honesty. As many African historians have shown, Africa's past has much to commend it and much that is not so commendable about it. Africans do not always remember the past with happiness. Many of these negative remembrances continue to plague African life today ensuing in much of the continent's many strifes, rivalries, and violent outbursts. The Christian ethicist in Africa must always remember this reality. And this is where Christian sense of remembrance, at its best, that is, as anchored around the events of the cross, is needed in African life. Christian memory is built on faith and hope. It is anchored on the thoughts and experiences of a God who so loves the world that he gave his only son that we might all have life and have it to the full. It is anchored around a God who even when we disobeyed him and lost his friendship did not abandon us to the power of death. It is anchored around the God whose mercy is boundless. There are three important tools that are thus necessary for Christian evangelization of African memory. First, the Christian faith must continue to find ways of keeping this narrative of God alive and well. Africans love celebrations. The more we find ways in Africa to celebrate God's mercy the better for the continent. Secondly, the Christian faith must find ways to establish agencies of reconciliation in local communities, within the church itself, and in the broader regional or national communities in various African states. What I mean here is that there ought to be avenues or departments for conflict resolutions at all levels of African life, ecclesial, familial, community, national. Finally, the African church must take seriously the effort to raise African Saints. As Emmanuel Ojeifo points out in his essay, "the saints are the best exemplars of the community of Jesus who show us what faithful Christian discipleship is about.[42] They are embodied testimonies of the triumph of God's grace.

IV
Conclusion:
African Christian Theology, an Exercise in Faith and Hope

Christianity is a religion of hope. All Christian theology must be an exercise in hope. This is true in Africa as in other parts of the world. This hope is founded on faith in God who so loves the world that he gave us his Son for our salvation. In his encyclical *Lumen Fidei*, on the *light of faith*,[43] Pope Francis reminds us that "Christian faith is centered on Christ, it is the confession that Christ is Lord, and that God has raised him from the dead (Rom 10:19). "The history of Jesus," says Pope Francis, "is the story of God's reliability… the life of Jesus, now appears as the locus of God's definitive offer of his supreme love for us. Faith as a gift from God opens us up to the vast horizons, beyond ourselves and empowers us to trust God with courage and to entrust ourselves to him with complete confidence" (LF 14).

There is another thing faith does to us; it provides us with a unique angle of vision on reality by transforming our senses and clothing us as Christian with the mind of Christ. Given the gift of faith we become transformed to become disciples of Christ who see with the eyes of Christ and who thus are able to take seriously what Jesus takes seriously—God, human beings, the redemptive power of suffering for the will of God, the relativization of certain aspects of life, in light of the higher good of loving and being loved by God, and so on. Faith comes from the assurance that God is reliable and believable. Faith comes from the understanding that I am loved, and that the ground of all existence is not only reliable but knows me and cares for and about me. Jesus himself notes that we are so loved by God and that God so cares for us that a strand of hair would not drop off our head without him knowing. In God there is no caprice, for the Lord of Hosts is with us, the God of Jacob is our stronghold. We cannot speak of Christian faith without talking of Christian hope. Faith precedes hope, hope precedes charity. As Pope Francis puts it, "Faith is bound up with hope" (LF 9).

Pope Benedict XVI before him had stated that hope is the other side of faith, and that it is so central to biblical faith that both of them are seen to be interchangeable (*Spe Salvi*, no. 1).[44] Faith transforms us and provides us with fresh vision, new eyes to see. We realize that contains a great promise of fulfillment and a vision of the future opens before us (LF, 4). Hope is one of the theological virtues. As Aquinas puts it, through this virtue the Christian believes that he or she will be granted the gift of eternal happiness which lies in the vision of God (*Summa theologiae* II-II, q. 17, a. 2). "Hope gives the believer a confident movement toward the future that enables him or her to overcome everything that restricts this movement towards God."[45] "As James M. Gustafson puts it, "Hope is a disposition that correlates with trust in the goodness of God and the power of goodness in life. Hope is carried by the confidence that life is more reliable than unreliable, that the future is open, that new possibilities of life exist, that the present patterns of life are not fated by the blind god Necessity, but are susceptible to change, to a recombination of aspects and elements of the world."[46] Christian hope is grounded in the goodness and power of God, "a goodness and power that has a vaster time- and-space span than the particular experiences of one man in one time, or a generation of men in one place." It is a disposition which is grounded in the goodness of God "who makes all renewal, reconciliation, and fulfilment possible, who secures the future as one in which people can respond creatively to new possibilities of human achievement and well-being."[47]

The opposite of hope, the disposition or emotion that is opposed to hope, is despair. Despair emerges where confidence is gone, where "there are no signs of the possibility of a human and moral good coming into being in personal and communal experience, where there is no confidence in the goodness of one's own life to break into meaningful and rewarding experience and relations."[48] If hope is a result of belief in the goodness and trustworthiness of what Paul Tillich would refer to as the ground of our existence, and from the fact that the ground of our existence is not in competition with us and does not seek to sabotage us, despair arises from an emotion of fear and from a sense that reality is untrustworthy or outright capricious. It is therefore an absence of faith in God as savior or capable of saving people from the immediate problems and challenges of now and perhaps of the future, if there is a future to talk about.

Despair is an emotional challenge which can arise from a number of issues: suffering, failure to see primal reason or logic in life, lack of confidence in life and in any possibilities that life seems to offer or promise. It stems from a sense of fatedness or lack of meaning. As James Gustafson points out, despair is evoked more by the "the degeneration of humanness through loss of vision of new possibilities, through lack of confidence that the future is open and worthy of trust. Despair is hopelessness."[49] This is an emotional disturbance which can strike even the most ardent believer. Consider the case of the prophet Elijah. The first book of the Kings has many stories about the running battles between Elijah the prophet and King Ahab and his wife, Jezebel. In Chapter 18 and 19 we read of the contest between the prophets of Baal and Elijah. As the story goes, Elijah succeeds in bringing down rain after many years of severe drought in Israel through his invocation of Yahweh while the prophets of Baal were not able to do so. This feat was considered proof enough of the reality and efficacy of Yahweh as the one and only true God. Because of their failure to prove the worth and reality of Baal as god, Elijah commanded the people to seize the prophets of Baal and let not one of them escape. "Then they seized them; and Elijah brought them down to Wadi Kishon and killed them there" (I Kgs 18:40).

After this incident, Ahab and Jezebel decide to avenge the death of the prophets of Baal resolve to kill Elijah who now, in fear, flees to Mount Horeb to hide. While there, the Lord visits him in the gentle breeze and asks why he was there. Elijah' responds thus: "I have been very zealous for the Lord, the God of Hosts; for the Israelites have forsaken your covenant, thrown down your altars and killed your prophets with the sword. I alone am left, and they are seeking my life, to take it away" (1 Kgs19:14). This was an utmost cry of despair to which God responded by making Elijah aware of the thousands of people who had not confessed faith in Baal but had remained committed to Yahweh. For his giving in to despair, God asked Elijah to prepare to anoint his servant Elisha to succeed him and to go into retirement. Elijah had committed the ultimate sin of giving in to hopelessness, the one sin no believer in God should ever commit. He could no longer be a veritable spokesperson for God.

The Christian theologian must never forget that the primary mission of the theologian is not to find some "clever" formulae or to merely get people to circumvent the harsh realities of life. His task is not to impose heavy and unbearable burdens on people either. The Christian theologian must be a prophet of hope, one who believes in and lives the truth that the ground on which we stand, God himself, is good, firm, and reliable. This is the way, theology ought to be done in Africa and elsewhere. The theologian, especially in Africa, must be a faith leader of hope, real hope, not cheap faith, a faith that comes from the understanding that the God of hosts is with us. The theologian in Africa, as elsewhere, must be someone who like Moses has gone up the mountain and seen afar, beyond the horizons, and returned with a message of hope which is founded a theologically grounded faith in God. Since the future is utterly eschatological one, the task of the theologian is to lead the people to learn to wait in goods works, in hope for their master's return.

Endnotes

Introduction Endnotes

1 See James Nkemngong, *Odozor: The Man, the Priest and the Scholar: Interview with Rev. Fr. Paulinus Odozor* (self-published, 2024).

2 See Thomas J. Bouquillon, "Moral Theology at the End of the Nineteenth Century," in *Readings in Moral Theology*, no. 11, *The Historical Development of Fundamental Theology in the United States*, ed. Charles E. Curran and Richard E. McCormick, S.J. (New York: Paulist, 1999), cited in Paulinus Ikechukwu Odozor, *Moral Theology in an Age of Renewal: A Study of the Catholic Tradition since Vatican II* (Notre Dame: University of Notre Dame Press, 2003), 1.

3 Nkemngong, *Odozor: The Man, the Priest and the Scholar*, 58.

4 Odozor, *Morality Truly Christian, Truly African*, 185.

5 Odozor, *Moral Theology in an Age of Renewal*, 9.

6 Odozor, *Moral Theology in an Age of Renewal*, 280–81.

7 Nkemngong, *Odozor: The Man, the Priest and the Scholar*, 61.

8 Nkemngong, *Odozor: The Man, the Priest and the Scholar*, 62.

9 Nkemngong, *Odozor: The Man, the Priest and the Scholar*, 63.

10 Nkemngong, *Odozor: The Man, the Priest and the Scholar*, 63.

11 Odozor, *Morality Truly Christian, Truly African*, 154. On this point, see Wilson Muoha Maina, *The Making of an African Christian Ethics: Bénézet Bujo and the Roman Catholic Tradition* (Eugene, OR: Pickwick, 2016), although Maina agrees with Bujo's perspective more than Odozor does.

12 Odozor, *Morality Truly Christian, Truly African*, 256.

13 See Agbonkhianmeghe E. Orobator, S.J.'s evaluation of "the uses and abuses of Christianity" through "the dual category of *prophetic practice* and *pathological performance*" (Orobator, *Religion and Faith in Africa: Confessions of an Animist* [Maryknoll, NY: Orbis, 2018], 81). On numerous points of theological assessment, Orobator and Odozor agree; but in important respects their respective perspectives represent quite different paths for the future of African Catholicism.

14 Odozor, *Morality Truly Christian, Truly African*, 298.

15 Odozor, *Morality Truly Christian, Truly African*, 298.

16 Robert Cardinal Sarah with Nicolas Diat, *The Power of Silence: Against the Dictatorship of Noise*, trans. Michael J. Miller (San Francisco: Ignatius, 2017), 41.

17 Nkemngong, *Odozor*, 69. Odozor continues, "That doesn't mean I'm always living up to it but that's something I strive for—how do you treat other people? How do you take human beings? What is the quality of your interaction with those above you, those below, those beside you? What do you do? That is the most important question for me. I mean, that doesn't make it the fact that I should not work very hard to write the next book like I'm struggling now to write my next book. I'm struggling now, there are so many articles in my computer that are begging to be finished. I will do them, as long as I have life; lots of them over this summer but in the end, those things have very limited value. They're important but have very limited value. So, wherever I find myself, in what circumstance I find myself, whatever office I hold, whatever place I occupy, I must do so in love" (69).

18 See Cyril Orji, *Unmasking the African Ghost: Theology, Politics, and the Nightmare of Failed States* (Minneapolis, MN: Fortress, 2022); Emmanuel Katangole, *The Sacrifice of Africa: A Political Theology for Africa* (Grand Rapids, MI: Eerdmans, 2011); and Katangole, *Born from Lament: The Theology and Politics of Hope in Africa* (Grand Rapids, MI: Eerdmans, 2017). These problems are also addressed—sometimes, admittedly, with more theological idealism than erudition about economic and political structures that actually serve to remove people from poverty, corruption, and despotic statism—in the essays in *African Public Theology*, ed. Sunday Bobai Agang (Bukuru, Nigeria: Hippo Books, 2020). See also Katongole's less-known but important work *A Future for Africa: Critical Essays in Christian Social Imagination* (Scranton, PA: University of Scranton Press, 2005).

19 Orji, *Unmasking the African Ghost*, 77. Orji directs attention to a number of helpful works, including Jason K. Stearns, *Dancing in the Glory of Monsters: The Collapse of the Congo and the Great War of Africa* (New York: Public Affairs, 2012) and the essays in *Failed and Failing States: The Challenges to African Reconstruction*, ed. Muna Ndulo and Margaret Grieco (Newcastle: Cambridge Scholars, 2010). Orji comments, "As the apparatus of states crumbled due to the inability to enshrine workable democratic practices, and the ineptitude of the African leaders became more and more pronounced, new groups of African leaders gradually began to emerge. They fashioned and crafted ghost states, styling themselves as the new messiahs and claiming to have the magic wand to fix Africa's problems and lead Africans to a land flowing with milk and honey. Using the creative energy latent in the traditional African worldview, its religiosity, and the

dynamism of ethnic configuration, some of the new leaders claimed to be visionaries who could return their countries to the pristine old glory days. They claimed that the progress of the continent would not have been blunted had the colonial rulers not disintegrated the traditional African political system. To make themselves appealing the West, they began to throw around the word *democracy*, even conducting sham elections [...]. Rhetoric aside, it does not take political astuteness to see that the new crops of African leaders are nothing but reincarnations of their predecessors. The ghost lives on" (*Unmasking the African Ghost*, 205–206).

20 Orji, *Unmasking the African Ghost*, 227.

21 Paulinus I. Odozor, C.S.Sp., "The Church as Family of God in Africa," in *Handbook of African Catholicism*, ed. Stan Chu Ilo (Maryknoll, NY: Orbis, 2022), 573–85, at 575.

22 Odozor, "The Church as Family of God in Africa," 580. He goes on to say, "Since the church is more fundamentally a theological and religious community, it can help further in the transformation of Africa by addressing some of those specifically theological themes that stand in the way of the transformation of African societies, such as the question of God-language in Africa and the issue of anthropology" (583). See also the fruitful emphasis on the God of Jesus Christ by one of Odozor's mentors: Elochukwu Eugene Uzukwu, C.S.Sp., *God, Spirit, and Human Wholeness: Appropriating Faith and Culture in West African Style* (Eugene, OR: Pickwick, 2012), in dialogue with African Traditional Religion (in West Africa). Uzukwu notes, "The West African context poses serious problems because it is rooted in a worldview that is suffused with, and related to, a multiplicity of divine beings that are still active in the world where Christians live [...]. The deities are ambivalent—they have both positive and negative attributes" (*God, Spirit, and Human Wholeness*, 169).

23 Odozor, "The Church as Family of God in Africa," 581. As he emphasizes, "Christian morality is therefore an ethic of response, a response to the stupendous love of a friend; it is an invitation to give back in love to a friend who has shared so much with us. It is never an imposition" (582).

24 For further discussion of the issues, see Idara Otu, M.S.P., *Communion Ecclesiology and Social Transformation in African Catholicism: Between Vatican Council II and African Synod II* (Eugene, OR: Pickwick, 2020), although Otu's book would be improved by a deeper engagement with Odozor's work. See also *The Church We Want: African Catholics Look to Vatican II*, ed. Agbonkhianmeghe E. Orobator (Maryknoll, NY: Orbis, 2016), which shockingly neglects Odozor's contributions (he is not mentioned in the index), and which as a result is seriously impoverished.

25 Nkemngong, *Odozor*, 71.

Chapter 1 Endnotes

1 Henri de Lubac, S.J., *The Motherhood of the Church* (San Francisco: Ignatius Press, 1983).
2 Augustine of Hippo, *Sermones* 43, 9.
3 Augustine of Hippo, *Contra Academicos* III, 20, 43.
4 Paulinus Ikechukwu Odozor, C.S.Sp., *Morality Truly Christian, Truly African: Foundational, Methodological, and Theological Considerations* (Notre Dame, IN: University of Notre Dame Press, 2014), 236.
5 Second Vatican Constitution, Pastoral Constitution on the Church in the Modern World, *Gaudium et Spes*.
6 Odozor, *Morality*, 229.
7 Joseph Ratzinger, *"In the Beginning ... ": A Catholic Understanding of the Story of Creation and the Fall*, trans. Boniface Ramsey, O.P. (Grand Rapids, MI: Eerdmans, 1995), 48–49.
8 Odozor, *Morality*, 214–33.
9 Odozor, *Morality*, 216.
10 Agbaw-Ebai, *Light of Reason, Light of Faith, Joseph Ratzinger and the German Enlightenment* (South Bend, IN: St. Augustine's Press, 2021), 243.
11 Odozor, *Morality*, 217–22.
12 Odozor, *Morality*, 225.
13 Odozor, *Morality*, 214.
14 Odozor, *Morality*, 207.
15 Odozor, *Morality*, 233–236.
16 Joseph Ratzinger, *Feast of Faith*, 30.
17 Andrew T. J. Kaethler, *The Eschatological Person, Alexander Schmemann and Joseph Ratzinger in Dialogue* (Eugene, OR: Cascade Books, 2022), 155.

Chapter 2 Endnotes

1 Paulinus Odozor, *Morality Truly Christian, Truly African: Foundational, Methodological, and Theological Considerations* (Notre Dame, IN: Notre Dame University Press, 2014).
2 Bénézet Bujo, *Foundations of an African Ethic: Beyond the Universal Claims of Western Morality*, trans. Brian McNeil (Nairobi: Paulines Publications Africa, 2003).
3 Paulinus Odozor, "An African Moral Theology of Inculturation: Methodological Considerations," *Theological Studies* 69, no. 3 (September 2008): 583–609. This article eventually became the sixth chapter of *Morality Truly Christian, Truly African*.
4 Bénézet Bujo, *Plea for Change of Models for Marriage*, trans. Gregor

Hucke, Andreas Hugentobler and Katrin Stucky (Nairobi: Paulines Publications Africa, 2009).

5 Paulinus Odozor, "Thoughts on African Christian Theology of Marriage and Sexuality," *Bulletin of Ecumenical Theology* 6, no. 2 (1994): 56–74.

6 Odozor, "Thoughts," 59.

7 Odozor, "Thoughts," 62.

8 Odozor, "Thoughts," 64.

9 Odozor, "Thoughts," 64–69.

10 Odozor, *Morality Truly*, 226–27.

11 Odozor, *Morality Truly*, 227.

12 Odozor, *Morality Truly*, 227.

13 Odozor, *Morality Truly*, 227.

14 Odozor, *Morality Truly*, 228.

15 Odozor, *Morality Truly*, 228.

16 Odozor, "Thoughts," 60–62.

17 Rita M. Gross, *Gender and Religion: On the Complexity of Symbols* (Boston: Beacon Press, 1996).

18 Cheryl J. Sanders, "Christian Ethics and Theology in Womanist Perspective," *Journal of Feminist Studies in Religion* 5, no. 2 (Fall 1989): 83–112; Kwok Pui-lan, "Feminist Theology in a Postcolonial Context," in *Feminist Theology: A Reader*, ed. Rita M. Gross (Boston: Beacon Press, 1996), 257–74; Elizabeth Schussler Fiorenza, *In Memory of Her: A Feminist Theological Reconstruction of Christian Origins* (New York: Crossroad, 1983).

19 Kate Millett, *Sexual Politics* (New York: Doubleday, 1970); Michel Foucault, *The History of Sexuality, Volume 1: An Introduction* (New York: Vintage Books, 1990); bell hooks, *Feminist Theory: From Margin to Center* (Boston: South End Press, 2000).

20 This list is not exhaustive; it is meant to be illustrative only: Mercy Amba Oduyoye, *Becoming Whole: African Women's Journey to Healing and Wholeness* (Maryknoll, NY: Orbis Books, 2004); Musimbi R. Kanyoro, *The Power We Have: African Women in Church and Society* (Maryknoll, NY: Orbis Books, 2002).

21 See "Rev. Paulinus I. Odozor, C.S.Sp., Th.D., STD 2020," https://theology.nd.edu/assets/387598/fullsize/odozor_curriculum_vitae_2020..pdf (accessed August 22, 2023). While some online sources cite works purportedly authored by Odozor, such as "African Christian Moral Theology: A Proposed Framework" in *African Christian Ethics: A Reader* (edited by Emmanuel Katongole and Jacob K. Olupona [Maryknoll, NY: Orbis Books, 2010], 249–70) and "The Inclusion of Women in African Christian Moral Theology," published in *African Journal of Gender and Religion* (4, no. 2 [2016]: 1–15), these works are not authentic and have been invented by persons other than Odozor without his knowledge.

22 Odozor, *Morality Truly*, 26–27.
23 Odozor, *Morality Truly*, 78–79, 80, 311n51.
24 Odozor, *Morality Truly*, 80.
25 Odozor, *Morality Truly*, 80–84.
26 Odozor, *Morality Truly*, 84–85, 311n51.
27 Odozor, *Morality Truly*, 199–201.
28 Odozor, *Morality Truly*, 234.
29 Odozor, *Morality Truly*, 288–91.
30 Odozor, *Morality Truly*, 289.
31 A commentary on *Amoris Laetitia*, edited by Professor Stan Ilo from an African perspective, is a welcome addition to the ongoing discussions on the document in Africa. However, I believe that the contributors to the commentary largely avoided or circumvented many of the most controversial issues, thereby missing opportunities to highlight the nuances that *Amoris Laetitia* offers the Church in Africa in its application of the balance between love, law, and mercy. See Stan Chu Ilo, ed., *Love, Joy, and Sex: African Conversations on Amoris Laetitia and Gospel of Family in a Divided World* (Nairobi: Paulines Publications Africa, 2022; originally published 2019).
32 Raymond Olusesan Aina, "*Amoris Laetitia* on Marriage and Family Life: Theological and Pastoral Reception in Nigeria," *Nigerian Journal of Religion and Society—JORAS* 8 (2018): 9.
33 Raymond Olusesan Aina, "*Amoris Laetitia* and the Church in Sub-Saharan Africa: On Dashed Hopes, Discerned Promises, and Sundry Challenges," *Asian Horizons* 11, no. 1 (March 2017): 163.
34 Samuel Kleda, "Pastoral Care to Wounded Families," in *Christ's New Homeland—Africa: Contribution to the Synod on the Family by African Pastors* (San Francisco: Ignatius Press, 2015), 158.
35 Aina, "*Amoris Laetitia*," 164.
36 Aina, "*Amoris Laetitia*," 165.
37 Paulinus Ikechukwu Odozor, "Humanae Vitae Fifty Years Later," *Spiritan Horizons* 13, no. 13 (2018): 74–75, https://dsc.duq.edu/spiritanhorizons/vol13/iss13/11.
38 A hermeneutics of multiplicity and inclusion is an exegetical approach that acknowledges and embraces the diversity of voices and perspectives within the Catholic Church. It is an attitude of receptivity to the Holy Spirit and to the ongoing revelation of the meaning of the faith. This approach is grounded in the belief that there is no single correct way to interpret the Catholic faith, and that all voices have value. It is an essential approach in a world where the Catholic Church is composed of people from many different cultures and backgrounds. Overall, a hermeneutics of multiplicity and inclusion is an approach that seeks to create a more inclusive and diverse Catholic Church, one that is better equipped to respond to the needs and challenges of the modern world. Stan Chu Ilo, "Contested Moral Issues

in Contemporary African Catholicism: Theological Proposals for a Hermeneutics of Multiplicity and Inclusion," *Journal of Global Catholicism* 1, no. 2 (2017): 60–61, DOI: 10.32436/2475-6423.1015.

39 Ilo, "Contested Moral Issues," 69.

40 Paulinus Ikechukwu Odozor, "Casuistry and AIDS: A Reflection on the Catholic Tradition," in *Catholic Ethicists on HIV/AIDS Prevention*, ed. James F. Keenan (London: Continuum, 2002), 298–99.

41 Odozor, "Casuistry and AIDS," 298–99.

42 John Segun Odeyemi, "'Justice and Mercy': The Question of Discordancy, the Development of Doctrine and African Catholicism," *Journal of the Black Catholic Theological Symposium* 10 (2017): 117–37.

43 Odozor, "Casuistry and AIDS," 297–302.

44 John L. Allen Jr. and Inés San Martín, "Theologian says 'Amoris' Communion debate is settled in Africa," *Crux*, March 21, 2017, https://cruxnow.com/africaund/2017/03/theologian-says-amoris-communion-debate-settled-africa.

45 Bujo, *Plea for Change of Models for Marriage* (2009).

Chapter 3 Endnotes

1 Plato's Socrates, in Books I–IX of dialogue on the *Republic*, painted the ideal city with his words. But, by way of an irony, in Book X, the conclusion of the dialogue, he banished poets from his republic because, for him, poets are artists, and art is mimetic. Artists imitate reality, and, by so doing, disseminate false information and corrupt the minds of the youth.

2 The description of philosophy as "ancilla theologiae" is often rendered as "handmaid of theology." In this essay, I describe philosophy not as handmaid but as ally of theology. "Ancilla" is translated in this sense as that which offers necessary support for theology as opposed to servant of theology.

3 Thomas Aquinas, *Summa theologiae*, I, q. 1, a. 7.

4 Thomas Aquinas, *Summa Contra Gentiles*, Bk 1, ch. 1.

5 "You must therefore be perfect, just as you heavenly Father is perfect" (Mt 5:48), reiterates Lev 11:45: "you must therefore be holy because I am holy."

6 Cf. Augustine, *City of God*; Aquinas, *Summa theologiae*, I-II, q. 90.

7 See Jean-Jacques Rousseau, *Discourse on Inequality* and *Social Contract* in *The Basic Political Writings of Jean-Jacques Rousseau*, trans. Donald A. Cress (Indianapolis: Hackett, 1987).

8 See Thomas Hobbes, *Leviathan*.

9 Second Vatican Council, *Gaudium et Spes*, 26. See also the *Catechism of the Catholic Church*, 1906–1909.

10 Pope John Paul II, *Sollicitudo Rei Socialis*, 38.
11 Pope John Paul II, *Sollicitudo Rei Socialis*, 39.
12 John Paul II, *Centesimus Annus*, 48; Pius XI, *Quadragesimo Anno*, 184–86.
13 If, for example, university education is on the concurrent legislative list in the Constitution of the Federal Republic of Nigeria, should one commission oversee the establishment of every university in Nigeria and regulate all the faculties, departments, and programs in all universities in a country as vast and as diverse as Nigeria?
14 Second Vatican Council, *Lumen Gentium*, 35.
15 Second Vatican Council, *Lumen Gentium*, 36.
16 Aristotle, *Politics*, Bk 1, ch 2, 1252a2–1253a3.
17 Second Vatican Council, *Dei Verbum*, 10.

Chapter 4 Endnotes

1 Thomas Aquinas, *Summa theologiae* (henceforth, *ST*) I-II q. 85, a 1.
2 Aquinas, *ST* I-II q. 109, a. 2.
3 Aquinas, *ST* I-II q. 109, aa. 3–4.
4 Paulinus Odozor, *Morality Truly Christian, Truly African: Foundational, Methodological, and Theological Considerations* (Notre Dame: University of Notre Dame Press, 2014), 297.
5 Odozor, *Morality Truly Christian, Truly African,* 296.
6 Odozor, 296.
7 Odozor, 10. Here Odozor cites his agreement with theologian Edward Schillebeeckx.
8 Odozor, 152.
9 Odozor, 156–58.
10 Odozor, 159–60.
11 Odozor, 161–63.
12 Odozor, 164–65.
13 Odozor, 166–69.
14 Odozor, 169.
15 Odozor, 169–73.
16 Odozor, 158.
17 Odozor, 173–74.
18 Odozor, 174–75.
19 Odozor, 186.
20 Odozor, 186 and 201–202.
21 Odozor, 202–203.
22 Odozor, 204.

23 Odozor, 204.
24 Odozor, 204–205.
25 Odozor, 189.
26 Odozor, 193–98.
27 Odozor, 200.
28 Odozor, 208, 228, 234–35.
29 Odozor, 212–13.
30 Odozor, 213.
31 Odozor, 215.
32 Odozor, 229.
33 Odozor, 229.
34 Odozor, 229.
35 Odozor, 204.
36 Odozor, 216 and 226–28.
37 Odozor, 226.
38 Odozor, 209 and 228.
39 See for example Odozor, 108.
40 Hans Urs von Balthasar, "Conversion in the New Testament," *Communio* (1974), 47.
41 Balthasar, "Conversion in the New Testament," 48.
42 Balthasar, "Conversion in the New Testament," 48.
43 Balthasar, "Conversion in the New Testament," 53 and 56–57.
44 Balthasar, "Conversion in the New Testament," 56.
45 A fuller version of this argument can be found in chapters two and three of my book on Balthasar. See Melanie Susan Barrett, *Love's Beauty at the Heart of the Christian Moral Life: The Ethics of Catholic Theologian Hans Urs von Balthasar* (Lewison, NY: The Edwin Mellen Press, 2009).
46 See for example, Hans Urs von Balthasar, *Dramatis Personae: Persons in Christ,* vol. 3 in *Theo-Drama: Theological Dramatic Theory* (San Francisco: Ignatius Press, 1992), 461. There he conjectures, "It can happen that the example of a single person who is really serious about his faith" and who actively is witnessing to Christ though the power of the Holy Spirit "can suffice to override other factors that are unconvincing or downright repellent," leading the perceiver to grasp the qualitative difference between "God's epiphany in Jesus Christ…[and all] other religious epiphanies."
47 Hans Urs von Balthasar, *Theology: The Old Covenant,* vol. 6 in *The Glory of the Lord: A Theological Aesthetics* (San Francisco: Ignatius Press, 1991), 37, 10, 415.
48 Hans Urs von Balthasar, *Seeing the Form*, vol. 1 in *The Glory of the Lord: A Theological Aesthetics* (San Francisco: Ignatius Press, 1982), 182.
49 Balthasar, *Seeing the Form*, 182.
50 See, for example, Balthasar, *Seeing the Form*, 186–88 and 464–65.

51 Balthasar, *Seeing the Form*, 182.
52 Balthasar, *Seeing the Form*, 188.
53 Balthasar, *Seeing the Form*, 188–89.
54 Balthasar, *Seeing the Form*, 468–70.
55 Balthasar, *Seeing the Form*, 470–72.
56 Balthasar, *Seeing the Form*, 488–90.
57 Balthasar, *Seeing the Form*, 482.
58 Hans Urs von Balthasar, *Love Alone: The Way of Revelation*, trans. Alexander Dru (London: Burns & Oates, 1968), 69.
59 Balthasar, *Love Alone: The Way of Revelation*, 71.
60 Hans Urs von Balthasar, *Theology: The New Covenant,* vol. 7 in *The Glory of the Lord: A Theological Aesthetics* (San Francisco: Ignatius Press, 1989), 291 and 29.
61 Balthasar, *Theology: The New Covenant,* 202, 129–42, and 146–47.
62 Hans Urs von Balthasar, *Moment of Christian Witness,* trans. Richard Beckley (San Francisco: Ignatius Press, 1994), 50; and *Word and Revelation*, trans. A.V. Littledale with Alexander Dru (New York: Herder and Herder, 1964), 146 and 135.
63 Balthasar, *Seeing the Form*, 502–507 and 463.
64 Balthasar, *Persons in Christ,* 460.
65 Balthasar, *Persons in Christ*, 460.
66 Balthasar, *Persons in Christ*, 460–61.
67 Balthasar, *Persons in Christ*, 461.
68 Hans Urs von Balthasar, *The Action,* vol. 4 in *Theo-Drama: Theological Dramatic Theory* (San Francisco: Ignatius Press, 1994), 77.
69 Balthasar, *The Action,* 73–76.
70 Balthasar, *The Action,* 12.
71 Balthasar, *The Action,* 11.
72 Balthasar, *Seeing the Form*, 247.
73 Balthasar, *Seeing the Form*, 320–21.
74 Balthasar, *Seeing the Form*, 220.
75 Hans Urs von Balthasar, *Heart of the World*, trans. Erasmo S. Leiva (San Francisco: Ignatius Press, 1979), 27.
76 Hans Urs von Balthasar, "Movement Toward God," in *Creator Spirit*, vol. 3 of *Explorations in Theology*, trans. Brian McNeil, CRV (San Francisco: Ignatius Press, 1993), 15. See also chapter five of *Love Alone: The Way of Revelation.*
77 Balthasar, "Movement Toward God," 16.
78 See Balthasar, *Love Alone: The Way of Revelation*, 37–39, and 41.
79 Balthasar, *Love Alone: The Way of Revelation*, 83.
80 Balthasar, *Love Alone: The Way of Revelation*, 68.
81 Balthasar, *Seeing the Form*, 297.

82 See Christopher Steck, *The Ethical Thought of Hans Urs von Balthasar* (New York: Crossroad, 2001).
83 Balthasar, *Theology: The New Covenant*, 303.
84 Balthasar, *Love Alone: The Way of Revelation*, 92
85 Balthasar, *Love Alone: The Way of Revelation*, 82.
86 Balthasar, *Love Alone: The Way of Revelation*, 83.
87 Balthasar, *Theology: The New Covenant*, 293. Italics added for emphasis.
88 Balthasar, *Theology: The New Covenant*, 294; and *Seeing the Form,* 246.
89 Hans Urs von Balthasar, *Studies in Theological Style: Clerical Styles*, vol. 2 in *The Glory of the Lord: A Theological Aesthetics* (San Francisco: Ignatius Press, 1984), 270–71.
90 Balthasar, *Theological Style: Clerical Styles*, 290.
91 Balthasar, *Theological Style: Clerical Styles*, 272. Italics added for emphasis.
92 Balthasar, *Theological Style: Clerical Styles*, 272–73.
93 Balthasar, *Theological Style: Clerical Styles*, 272–73. Here Balthasar quotes Bonaventure, *Perf. vit. ad sor.* 6 (VIII 123b).
94 Balthasar, *Theological Style: Clerical Styles*, 273. Here Balthasar quotes Bonaventure, *De regim. animae* 7 (VIII 130a).
95 Balthasar, *Seeing the Form*, 242.
96 Balthasar, *Seeing the Form*, 243–44.
97 Balthasar, *Seeing the Form*, 244–46.
98 Balthasar, *Seeing the Form*, 247.
99 Balthasar, *Seeing the Form*, 221.
100 Balthasar, *Seeing the Form*, 220.
101 Balthasar, *Seeing the Form*, 224.
102 Balthasar, *Seeing the Form*, 220.
103 Balthasar, *Seeing the Form*, 224.
104 Balthasar, *Seeing the Form*, 224.
105 Balthasar, *Theological Style: Clerical Styles*, 272–73.
106 Balthasar, *Seeing the Form*, 225.
107 Balthasar, *Seeing the Form*, 225.
108 Hans Urs von Balthasar, *The Christian State of Life*, trans. Mary Frances McCarthy (San Francisco: Ignatius Press, 1983), 59.
109 Balthasar, *The Christian State of Life*, 63.
110 Balthasar, *Love Alone: The Way of Revelation*, 96–97.

Chapter 5 Endnotes

1 Stanley Hauerwas and Samuel Wells, "Why Christian Ethics Was Invented," *Blackwell Companion to Christian Ethics* (Malden, MA: Blackwell, 2004), 30.

2 Hauerwas and Wells, "Why Christian Ethics Was Invented," 14.
3 Tony Alonso, "Damaged Goods," *Worship* 97 (April 2023): 108–126.
4 Lauren Winner, *The Dangers of Christian Practice: On Wayward Gifts, Characteristic Damage, and Sin* (New Haven: Yale University Press, 2018), 16.
5 Odozor, 164.
6 Walter Benjamin, cited in Marsha Hewitt, "The Redemptive Power of Memory: Walter Benjamin and Elizabeth Schussler Fiorenza," *Journal of Feminist Studies in Religion* 10.1 (Spring 1994): 76–7.
7 Hewitt, 77.
8 Walter Benjamin, *Illuminations*: *Essays and Reflections*, trans Harry Zohn, edited and with an introduction by Hannah Arendt (New York: Schocken Books, 1969), 265.
9 Hewitt, 78, citing Walter Benjamin, *Illuminations*: *Essays and Reflections*, trans Harry Zohn, edited and with an introduction by Hannah Arendt (New York: Schocken Books, 1969), 263.
10 Hewitt, 79, citing Walter Benjamin, *One Way Street and Other Writings*, trans Edmund Jephcott and Kingsley Shorter (London: New Left Books, 1979), 359.
11 Johann Baptist Metz, F*aith in History and Society: Toward a Practical Fundamental Theology* (New York: Crossroads, 2007), 68.
12 Bénézet Bujo and Juvenal Illunga Muya, eds., *African Theology: The Contributions of the Pioneers* (Nairobi: Kolbe Press, 2002), 115 n. 30.
13 Bujo and Muya, *African Theology*, 124. See further 119.
14 Bujo and Muya, *African Theology*, 123.
15 Bujo and Muya, *African Theology*, 123.
16 Bujo and Muya, *African Theology*, 137, citing Bénézet Bujo, *African Theology in Its Social Context* (Maryknoll: Orbis Books, 1992), 120.
17 Bujo and Muya, *African Theology*, 141, citing Bénézet Bujo, *African Christian Morality at the Age of Inculturation* (Paulines Publications Africa, 1998), 373.
18 Ghislain Ndondji-Tshiwisa-Adidem, "An African Reconsideration of Christian Anamnesis," *Exchange* 27:1 (1998): 38.
19 Ghislain Ndondji-Tshiwisa-Adidem, "An African Reconsideration," 40–41.
20 Bujo, *Foundations of an African Christian Ethic: Beyond the Universal Claims of Western Morality* (New York: Crossroad, 2001), 12; cited in Odozor, 162.
21 Odozor, 165.
22 Odozor, 165.
23 Odozor, 205.

24 Odozor, 233.
25 Odozor, 216.
26 Odozor, 228.
27 Odozor, 212.
28 Odozor, 239.
29 Odozor, 239.
30 Odozor, 251.
31 Odozor, 167.
32 Odozor, 165.
33 Odozor, 173.
34 Odozor, 165.
35 Odozor, 165.
36 Odozor, 219
37 Odozor, 219.
38 Odozor, 219.
39 Odozor, 234.
40 Odozor, 165.
41 Odozor, 165.
42 Bruce T. Morrill, *Anamnesis as Dangerous Memory: Political and Liturgical Theology in Dialogue* (Collegeville: Liturgical Press, 2000), xv.
43 *Psalmos*, Cited in L. Edward Phillips, "Liturgy and Ethics," 88.
44 See proceedings online here: https://ctsa-online.org/resources/Convention%202023/CTSA2023PrintProgram.pdf.
45 Tony Alonso, "Damaged Goods." *Worship* 97 (April 2023): 108–26; citing Katie Grimes, *Christ Divided: Anti-Blackness as Corporate Vice* (Minneapolis: Fortress Press, 2017), 110.
46 Grimes, *Christ Divided*, 201, cited in Alonso, 120.
47 Alonso, "Damaged Goods," 122.
48 L. Edward Phillips, "Liturgy and Ethics," *Liturgy in Dialogue* (1995): 88 101, at 98.
49 Odozor, 169–70.
50 Cavanaugh, *Torture and Eucharist: Theology, Politics, and the Body of Christ* (Oxford: Blackwell, 1998), 193.
51 William Cavanaugh, "Torture and Eucharist: Theology, Politics, and the Body of Christ," *Landas* 26.2 (2012): 1–15, at 15.
52 Cavanaugh, "Torture and Eucharist," 7.
53 Morrill, *Anamnesis as Dangerous Memory*, 140.
54 Morrill, *Anamnesis as Dangerous Memory*, 161.
55 Winner, *The Dangers of Christian Practice*, loc 635.
56 Winner, *The Dangers of Christian Practce*, loc 653.

Chapter 6 Endnotes

1 I am grateful to Professor Anthony Reddie for his astute comments and criticisms on an earlier draft of this essay.

2 Chinua Achebe, *Things Fall Apart* (1958), reprinted in Chinua Achebe, *The African Trilogy: Things Fall Apart, No Longer at Ease, and Arrow of God* (New York: Doubleday, 2010).

3 Odozor variously uses 'exceptionless moral norms', 'absolute norms' and 'intrinsically evil', in referring to such prohibited classes of action (e.g. MTCTA, 163, 239).

4 The notion of 'abomination' is of course not limited to African traditional religion, but can also be found, not only in Scripture, but among e.g. the African diaspora in the Caribbean and elsewhere.

5 Anscombe takes up the question of absolute prohibitions her essays 'Modern Moral Philosophy' (1958) and 'War and Murder' (1961), both of which are reprinted in G.E.M. Anscombe, *Collected Philosophical Papers, Vol. 3: Ethics, Religion, and Politics* (Oxford: Blackwell, 1981).

6 MTCTA, 163.

7 Anscombe, 'War and Murder,' 58.

8 "It has been characteristic of [the Judaeo-Christian] ethic to teach that there are certain things forbidden whatever consequences threaten, such choosing to the kill the innocent for any purpose, however good .... The prohibition of certain things simply in virtue of their description as such-and-such identifiable kinds of action, regardless of any further consequences, is certainly not the whole of the Hebrew-Christian ethic; but it is a noteworthy feature of it." Anscombe, MMP, 34. "These absolute prohibitions of Christianity by no means exhaust its ethic; there is a large area where what is just is determined partly by a prudent weighing up of consequences. But the prohibitions are bedrock, and without them the Christian ethic goes to pieces." See Anscombe, 'War and Murder,' in *Nuclear Weapons and Christian Conscience*, ed. Walter Stein (London: Merlin Press, 1961). Reprinted in Anscombe, *Collected Philosophical Papers, Vol. 3: Ethics, Religion, and Politics* (Oxford: Blackwell, 1981), 58.

9 Anscombe glosses the command "Thou Shalt not Kill" as meaning "Thou Shalt not Murder," where murder is defined as the intentional killing of the innocent.

10 Anscombe and Daniel, *The Justice of the Present War Examined: A Criticism Based on Traditional Catholic Principles and on Natural Reason* (Glasgow: John Burns and Co., 1940).

11 G. E. M. Anscombe, *Mr. Truman's Degree* (Oxford: Oxonian Press, 1956). This pamphlet was privately printed by Anscombe, and was available for sale beginning on June 1, 1956 at numerous bookshops in Oxford. Part of

the pamphlet was reprinted in Anscombe, *Collected Philosophical Papers, Vol. 3*, 62–71.

12 "Now, it is one of the most vehement and repeated teachings of the Judaeo-Christian tradition that the shedding of innocent blood is forbidden by the divine law. …For a long time the main outlines of this teaching have seemed to be merely obvious morality … And indeed, that it is terrible to kill the innocent is very obvious; the morality that so stringently forbids it must make a great appeal to mankind, especially to the poor threatened victims." Anscombe, "War and Murder," 57.

13 MMP, 38.

14 Anscombe, *Mr. Truman's Degree*, 71.

15 I will add more on the relationship between wrongful acts and divine judgments in Anscombe.

16 MTCTA, 262 (bottom of page).

17 MTCTA, 262.

18 As Odozor puts it, "some sins so injure relationships and are so disruptive of communion that they require public penance and a public process of reconciliation" (MTCTA, 261). What Odozor does not clearly indicate is whether the penance is required of those who have committed an *aru*, or whether penance is required from the whole community. On the one hand, he says, "The fact is that because some of our members have sinned in such a big way, we are all implicated […] because we are […] members of the same body" (262). But this raises the question: Should one do penance for sins that one has not committed? While I think it is possible to justify this claim, it seems to me that an alternative paradigm for articulating what is going on is that it is analogous to a community making reparations for historical wrongs done either to some in their community, or to those of another community, as in reparations for slavery.

19 MTCTA, 263.

20 In MTATC, Odozor emphasizes that

21 Adichie, Introduction to Chinua Achebe, *The African Trilogy*, vii–viii.

22 NB: In TFA the initial evangelization is followed almost immediately by the colonisation of that part of Nigeria by the British government.

23 NB: some abominations seem to be more or less universally accepted—twins, osu, etc. Other abominations clearly not agreed upon.

24 For example, Okonkwo's father was afflicted with a kind of swelling that the gods identify as an abomination, and his father is exiled to die alone in the Evil Forest. (TFA, 15) The same is true any twins that are born, who must also be abandoned in the Evil Forest. A third example of a cultic abomination are the *osu*: inter-generational families dedicated to the gods and therefore excluded from most ordinary privileges of members of the clan.

25 For example, Okonkwo considers his oldest son Nwoye an abomination because he is insufficiently manly. In Okonkwo's world, a man is one who revels in exploits in warfare and is disposed to resolve conflict more generally by means of violence, especially, but not only, within his household of women and children.

26 For a definition of an *osu*, see the previous footnote.

27 Which was the original meaning of 'paganism', albeit a negative characterization from the beginning.

28 For example, Odozor discusses the work of Magesa and Mbita, who emphasize that African Traditional Religion is ultimately monotheistic (Odozor, *MTATC*, 77–78). Be that as it may be for some African Traditional religions, in Achebe's novel, the understanding of deity as it is presented is universally or almost universally presented as polytheistic. Thus, in what follows, I am following the understanding of the deities in the Igbo Traditional Religion as presented by Achebe in *Things Fall Apart*, and make no claim to be characterizing the understanding of the divine in any other African Traditional religions.

29 Contraventions of fundamental religious rituals—e.g. around Eating unclean foods is a secondary way in which one becomes an abomination.

30 Anscombe, "Paganism, Superstition and Philosophy," in *Thoreau Quarterly,* no. 17 (1985). Reprinted in G.E.M. Anscombe, *Faith in a Hard Ground: Essays on Religion, Philosophy and Ethics* (Edinburgh: Imprint Academic, 2005), 59–73. Henceforth PSP.

31 "What then is the complaint against the Jews? Clearly, that they do not worship the gods. ... their singularity is so great that it has to be put into their history that Moses persuade them to abandon hope of any help from the gods." Anscombe, PSP, 63.

32 "Moses invented novel rites, contrary to what everyone else does." Anscombe, PSP, 61.

33 "circumcision ... which they do to be *recognisably* different." Anscombe, PSP, 62.

34 Tacitus, *Histories*, quoted in Anscombe, PSP, 59–60.

35 Another difficulty is that it is never quite clear in the novel who is to be included on a clan or town or village, and who is not. Early on in the novel we are told that Okonkwo has previously gone to war and killed five men. Although the novel says Okonkwo had been involved in two inter-tribal wars, it seems that the wars were intra-tribal wars, wars with other Igbo towns or clans. But considering that there is considerable intermarriage between clans, it is at best hazy as to who is considered one's clansmen and who is not.

Second, there is no clear mechanism for justice between clans. When a daughter of Umuofia is murdered by a neighbouring clan, there is no clear mechanism for defusing the situation. Because Umuofia is a feared clan compared to the one of the murderers, Umuofia makes a demand on the other clan that is not commensurate with the evil done. Rather than demanding that the perpetrators be brought to justice (if that is possible), the Umuofians instead demand that the other clan sacrifice to them two young teenagers.

36 TFA, 15.

37 "Every clan and village had its "evil forest." In it were buried all those who died of the really evil diseases, like leprosy and smallpox. It was also the dumping ground for the potent fetishes of great medicine men when they died. An "evil forest" was, therefore, alive with sinister forces and powers of darkness" (TFA, 105).

38 "It was [the evil] forest that the rulers of Mbanta gave to the missionaries. They did not really want them in their clan, and so they made them an offer which nobody in his right senses would accept [...]. The next morning the crazy men actually began to [...] build their house. The inhabitants of Mbanta expected them all to be dead in four days [...]. [N]one of them died. Everyone was puzzled" (105–106).

39 "[the white man] came quietly and peaceably with his religion. We were amused at his foolishness and allowed him to stay." (TFA, 124)

40 Odozor gives an extensive quotation from the exchange between Okonkwo and friend Obierika (TFA, 49). Okonkwo challenges his friend for not being part of the execution party. Obierika says he does not question the decision of the Oracle, but that does not mean he had to participate in carrying it out. Obierika then goes on to say that that the Oracle commanded went against the Earth goddess Ani, who oversees the morality of the Igbo. He says that Okonkwo's action is the kind for which Ani destroys whole families. Here we seem to have a disagreement about the relative authority of the Oracle and that of the Earth goddess Ani. Odozor says that it may be OK for the gods to command evil, but not for humans to obey such commands. Odozor says that this story shows that according to traditional African religion people are bound to do as their conscience tells them.

41 In the novel, there is a hint that the father of Ikemefuna may have been involved in the murder.

Chapter 7 Endnotes

1 Paulinus Ikechukwu Odozor, C.S.Sp., *Morality Truly Christian, Truly African* (Notre Dame, IN: University of Notre Dame Press, 2014), 148.

2 *Ibid.*

3 *Ibid.*, 88.

4 *Ibid.*, 21.
5 *Ibid.*, 64
6 *Ibid.*, 88.
7 *First Apology* 21–22; 54.
8 *Ibid.*, chapters 9, 13, 24, 64
9 *Ibid.*, chapter 62.
10 *Ibid.*, chapter 66.
11 For example, *Contra Celsum* 7.5; 64–70.
12 These issues are treated at John C. Cavadini, "Epilogue: The Architectonic Plan of the *City of God*," in David Vincent Meconi, S.J., ed., *The Cambridge Companion to Augustine's City of God* (Cambridge: Cambridge University Press, 2021), 297–320.
13 Odozor, *Morality Truly Christian, Truly African*, 86.
14 *Ibid.*, 98, summarizing the view of John Mbiti.
15 *Ibid.*
16 *Ibid.*, 99.
17 *Ibid.*
18 See the entry *doctrina* in *The Oxford Latin Dictionary* [*OLD*] (Oxford: The Clarendon Press, 1982), 568.
19 The fundamental meaning of the word *doceo*, from which *doctrina* is built, is simply "to tell, inform (a person of a fact, etc.)," for which see the *OLD*, 568.
20 The meaning of the word *doctrina* and its relation to what we today might call "culture," see the discussion of Madeleine Moreau in *Oeuvres de saint Augustin: La Doctrine Chrétienne, Bibliothèque Augustinienne* vol. 11 / 2 (Paris: Institut d'Etudes Augustiniennes, 1997), 22–26. See also G.A. Press, "'Doctrina' in Augustine's *De doctrina christiana*," in *Philosophy and Rhetoric* 17 (1984): 98–120. I think it is also fair to say that in his essay, "Sign and Language," Luigi Alici has in mind an understanding of "doctrina" that evokes a broader meaning than simply "teaching,' but a system of sign and signification that constitutes the spiritual and intellectual medium of communication characterizing a particular culture. See Saint Augustine, *Teaching Christianity: De Doctrina Christiana: A New Presentation by Edmund Hill, O.P.* (Hyde Park, NY: New City Press, 1996), 28–53.
21 Prologue.1. All translations are taken from Hill's translation, sometimes (as here) adjusted. All citations of the Latin text are taken from *BA* 11 / 2, as above, which offers an updating of the critical edition by J. Martin in *Corpus Christianorum, Series Latina,* vol. 32 (Turnhout: Brepols, 1962).
22 *De doctrina christiana* 1.1.1.
23 *Ibid.* 3.2.2, cf. 2.6.8; 2.9.14; also see 3.28.39 on the plainer passages of Scripture.

24 *Ibid.*, 3.2.2 mentions the connection between the Rule of Faith and Book 1.
25 *Ibid.*, Prologue.2
26 *Ibid.*, 4–5.
27 *Ibid.*, 6.
28 *Ibid.*, 7.
29 *Ibid.*, 8.
30 *Ibid.*, 1.11.11.
31 *Ibid.*, 1.12.13.
32 *Ibid.*, 1.2.2. There is a very large literature on Augustine's theory of signs. One of the best places to start would be R.A. Markus, "Signs, Communication, and Communities in Augustine's *De doctrina christiana,*" in *De doctrina christiana: A Classic of Western Culture,* ed. Duane W.H. Arnold and Pamela Bright (Notre Dame: University of Notre Dame Press, 1995), 97–108. Also in the same volume: David Dawson, "Sign Theory, Allegorical Reading, and the Motions of the Soul in *De doctrina christiana*," 123–42; and John C. Cavadini, "The Sweetness of the Word: Salvation and Rhetoric in Augustine's *De doctrina christiana*," 164–81. This latter essay is also available, slightly updated, in John C. Cavadini, *Visioning Augustine* (Oxford: Wiley Blackwell, 2019), 23–44.
33 *De doctrina christiana* 2.7.10.
34 *Ibid.*, 2.7.9.
35 See *ibid.*, 2.7.6.
36 *Ibid.*, 1.17.16, though the Latin is slightly more reserved, Hill's translation captures the effect well: "qui se ipsum nobis, qua rediremus, substernere voluit" (*BA* 11 /2 p. 96, translated there as "lui qui a voulu se mettre lui-même sous nos pas, comme un chemin qui permette le retour," *BA* 11 /2 p. 97, cf. Jn. 14.6).
37 *De doctrina christiana* 2.18.28.
38 *Ibid.*, 2.39.58.
39 *Ibid.*, 2.20.30. On this topic, see the article by Markus, referenced above, n. 32.
40 *Ibid.*, 2.34.27.
41 *Ibid.*, 2.40.60.
42 *Ibid.*
43 *Ibid.*, 2.41.62.
44 *Ibid.*
45 See above, at the outset of this essay.
46 Odozor, *Morality Truly Christian, Truly African,* 189.
47 *Ibid.*
48 *Ibid.*, 189–90.
49 *Ibid.*, 190.

50 See *De doctrina christiana* 4.12.27, etc.
51 See *ibid.*, 4.24.53.
52 *Ibid.*, 4.21.45–50.
53 Odozor, *Morality Truly Christian, Truly African,* 261.
54 *Ibid.*
55 *De doctrina christiana* 4.5.8.
56 Cited at *De doctrina christiana* 2.41.62.

Chapter 8 Endnotes

1 Thanks to the Maurice Agbaw-Ebai and Matthew Levering for their work organizing the conference to honor of the scholarship of my friend and colleague, Paulinus Odozor, at which an original draft of this essay was presented. I am grateful for the feedback received at the conference and for subsequent conversations about these topics with the conference participants.

2 In this analogy of comparison to farming and gardening, I draw on two inspirations: the contemplative religious orders which share a certain commitment to place that also characterize the diocesan clergy's commitment to parish life, and the apostolic religious orders which share with the wider Church the mission to preach the Gospel to all the nations and to bring Christ's healing to all people. Although the ecclesial affiliations do not track precisely, my inspiration for the former is the Benedictine tradition, which in the following is going to frame my discussion of the inculturation theology of the Spiritan theologian Paulinus Odozor. For the Benedictine reflection on rootedness in place, see Kyle T. Kramer, *A Time to Plant: Life Lessons in Work, Prayer, and Dirt* (Notre Dame: Sorin Books, 2010). My inspiration for the latter is the Armenian Orthodox theologian Vigen Guroian whose writings on the theological image of the garden provide a useful way of thinking about the rootedness in the Church of the comparative theology of the Jesuit theologian Francis Clooney. See Vigen Guroian, *Inheriting Paradise: Meditations on Gardening* (Grand Rapids: William B. Eerdmans Publishing, 1999) and *The Fragrance of God* (Grand Rapids: William B. Eerdmans Publishing, 2006).

3 The introductory paragraphs of the third part of the *Catechism of the Catholic Church* quotes the ancient Christian treatise *Didache*: "The way of Christ 'leads to life'; a contrary way 'leads to destruction.' The Gospel parable of the two ways remains ever present in the catechesis of the Church; it shows the importance of moral decisions for our salvation: 'There are two ways, the one of life, the other of death; but between the two, there is a great difference.'" (par. 1696) https://www.vatican.va

/archive/ENG0015/__P5D.HTM The Second Vatican Council's 1965 "Decree on Priestly Training" (*Optatam Totius*) describes moral theology as a science, with its own ends and proper methods: "Special care must be given to the perfecting of moral theology. Its scientific exposition, nourished more on the teaching of the Bible, should shed light on the loftiness of the calling of the faithful in Christ and the obligation that is theirs of bearing fruit in charity for the life of the world." (par. 16) https://www.vatican.va/archive/hist_councils/ii_vatican_council/documents/vat-ii_decree_19651028_optatam-totius_en.html

4 Here I follow the formulation offered by the Christian theologian Robin Lovin: ""The study of ethics begins with critical reflection on a way of life." See Robin W. Lovin, *An Introduction to Christian Ethics* (Nashville: Abingdon Press, 2011), 3. Lovin argues that the spirit of critical reflection that animates a distinctively Christian ethics springs from two sources: the Hebrew prophetic tradition which critically reflected on the failure of Israel to live according to the demands of the Covenant, and the Greek philosophical tradition, which in its Socratic formulation critically reflected on whether the Athenians were living a truly good life or simply one that confirmed to base desires and accepted patterns of behavior. I have used a similar formulation in my coauthored (with William Schweiker) *Religious Ethics: Meaning and Method* (Malden: Wiley—Blackwell, 2020).

5 Critique itself has a number of meanings. Here, I am following Lovin and others who think about critique as an expression of the Hebrew prophetic spirit and also the Greek philosophical spirit. In the modern period, critique took on a different meaning, as an inquiry into the conditions necessary for a certain kind of knowledge or for the emergency of a certain kind of action. There are important connections between these two meanings of critique but cannot be examined here in any detail.

6 As I develop this comparison, I acknowledge that I am reading each of the two main authors I explore here "against the grain" so to speak. For exam ple, I am arguing that although Odozor describes his own work as Cathoic moral theology, I read is work as closer to a Catholic theological ethics. So too am I aware that Francis Clooney, whose work I examine further along, does not view his work as ethics—as a critical reflection on how to live. In each case, I hope that the arguments I present give each scholar, and those who read their work, a different way of interpreting what they are doing.

7 Paulinus Ikechukwu Odozor, "An African Moral Theology of Inculturation: Methodological Considerations," *Theological Studies* 69 (2008): 583–609.

8 Ibid., 594.

9 Paulinus Ikechukwu Odozor, C.S.Sp., *Morality Truly Christian, Truly African: Foundational, Methodological, and Theological Considerations*

(Notre Dame: University of Notre Dame Press, 2014).

10 Ibid., 584–6.

11 Aylward Shorter, *Toward a Theology of Inculturation* (Eugene: Wipf and Stock, 1999), 5–9.

12 Ibid., 4–5.

13 Odozor, "An African Moral Theology of Inculturation," 586.

14 Ibid., 594.

15 Ibid.

16 Odozor, *Morality Truly Christian, Truly African*, 58–9.

17 Odozor, *Morality Truly Christian, Truly African*, 59.

18 Ibid., 59.

19 Ibid., 14–15.

20 Ibid., 15.

21 Ibid., 21.

22 Ibid., 21–22.

23 Francis X. Clooney, S.J., *Comparative Theology: Deep Learning Across Religious Borders* (Malden, MA: Wiley Blackwell, 2010), 10.

24 Ibid., 9.

25 Ibid., 10.

26 Ibid., 10.

27 Francis X. Clooney, S.J., "Reading Religiously across Religious Borders: A Method for Comparative Study," in *Religions* 9.42 (2018): 2.

28 Ibid., 2.

29 Ibid.

30 Ibid., 3.

31 Francis X. Clooney, S.J., *Reading the Hindu and Christian Classics: Why and How Deep Learning Still Matters* (Charlottesville, VA: University of Virginia Press, 2019), 1.

32 Ibid., 118–9.

33 While Clooney is arguably one of the leading Catholic comparative theologians in the world (and is probably without equal among comparative theologians working in the United States today), his projects have still been criticized, not so much for their analyses of ancient texts but for what their almost exclusive focus on texts misses as viable sites for comparative theology and in the audiences and purposes for comparison that he pursues. For example, Catherine Cornille has been interested in the phenomenon of multiple religious belonging and views investigating these instances as a promising site for comparative theology which involves a wider field of comparative data than Clooney's focus on texts and on his assumptions that comparison should proceed from two clearly defined traditions. See Catherine Cornille, "Double Religious Belonging: Aspects and Questions," *Buddhist-Christian Studies* 23.1 (2003): 43–49; also her *Many Mansions?:*

Multiple Religious Belonging and Christian Identity (Maryknoll: Orbis, 2002). Similarly, Tracy Sayuki Tiemeier has challenged Clooney to consider how his comparisons benefit the wider Church, particularly those involved in local inter-religious dialogue at the parish or other local community level, especially when those engaged in such dialogues have not acquired the linguistic or other scholarly apparatus to undertake the kinds of comparisons Clooney performs. See Tiemeier's "Comparative Theology as a Theology of Liberation" in *The New Comparative Theology: Thinking Interreligiously in the 21st Century*, ed. Francis X. Clooney, S.J. (London: T&T Clark, 2010), 129–50.

Chapter 9 Endnotes

1 Paulinus Ikechukwu Odozor, *Morality Truly Christian, Truly African: Foundational, Methodological, and Theological Considerations* (Notre Dame, IN: University of Notre Dame Press, 2014), 22. See also 26.

2 "General Audience of 6 June 2007: Saint Cyprian | BENEDICT XVI," accessed June 10, 2024, https://www.vatican.va/content/benedict-xvi/en/audiences/2007/documents/hf_ben-xvi_aud_20070606.html.

3 "General Audience of 30 May 2007: Tertullian | BENEDICT XVI," accessed June 10, 2024, https://www.vatican.va/content/benedict-xvi/en/audiences/2007/documents/hf_ben-xvi_aud_20070530.html.

4 For a discussion of the early African Church, see Peter Brown, *Augustine of Hippo: A Biography*, rev. ed. (Berkeley: University of California Press, 2000), 7–15, 207–11, 408, and elsewhere.

5 Odozor, *Morality Truly Christian, Truly African*, 46.

6 "31 July 1969: Eucharistic Celebration in Kampala (Uganda) at the Conclusion of the Symposium of Bishops of Africa | Paul VI," accessed June 10, 2024, https://www.vatican.va/content/paul-vi/en/homilies/1969/documents/hf_p-vi_hom_19690731.html. Cited by Odozor at *Morality Truly Christian, Truly African*, 306.

7 For example, of the "four sources for the development of African theology," Odozor has written that "The first is the Bible, which as the Second Vatican Council puts it, is "the soul" of all theology" (*Morality Truly Christian, Truly African*, 21). Describing what was distinctive in the ancient African Church, Pamela Bright writes that it likewise "Above all [...] immersed in the Word. It was the common delight in the Scriptures that provided the dynamic link between the different factions," in *Augustine Through the Ages: An Encyclopedia*, ed. Allan Fitzgerald and John C. Cavadini (Grand Rapids, MI: Eerdmans, 1999), 190. Further, both the ancient and contemporary African Churches show lively awareness of the

angelic and demonic realms in contrast to the overall more muted approach of the contemporary Western Church (see the discussion in Matthew Michael, *Christian Theology and African Traditions* [Cambridge, UK: The Lutterworth Press, 2013], 92–100). Odozor has also discussed various effects of colonialism upon Africa (see *Morality Truly Christian, Truly African*, 14–19, 32, 167, 204.) In this connection we may note Peter Brown's poignant discussion of Africa in St. Augustine's time as a "'colony,' administered by strangers across the sea" (*Augustine of Hippo*, 13).

8 See "31 July 1969: Eucharistic Celebration in Kampala (Uganda) at the Conclusion of the Symposium of Bishops of Africa | Paul VI."

9 Second Vatican Council, *Optatam Totius*, no. 16.

10 Paulinus Odozor, "Christology and Moral Theology," *Journal of Moral Theology* 2.1 (2013): 31–32.

11 Katharine Breen, *Imagining an English Reading Public, 1150–1400* (Cambridge: Cambridge University Press, 2010), 43.

12 See *De Virt.,* q. 1, a. 9; *ST* I-II, q. 51, aa. 2–3; *De Malo,* q. 2, a. 11, ad 4, 6.

13 *ST* III, q. 69, a. 4. The base metaphor is liquid: *infundere* means "to pour into."

14 See *ST* I-II, q. 114; *De Virt.* q. 2, a. 10, rep.; *ST* II-II, q. 184, a. 2; and Joseph P. Wawrykow, *God's Grace and Human Action: 'Merit' in the Theology of Thomas Aquinas* (Notre Dame, IN: University of Notre Dame Press, 1996), 221–38.

15 *ST* II-II, q. 24, a. 9.

16 For a helpful treatment of accustomization, see William Mattison, "Aquinas, Custom, and the Coexistence of Infused and Acquired Cardinal Virtues," *Journal of Moral Theology* 8.2 (2019): 1–24.

17 See for example *De Car.* a. 10 resp.; *ST* I-II, q. 52, a. 3; *ST* I-II, q. 114, a. 8, ad 3; *ST* II-II, q. 24, a. 6; *ST* II-II q. 184, a. 3, co.; I *Sent*, dist. 17, q. 2, a. 3. For a full discussion of the distinction, see Gulielmo Lynn, S.J., *Christ's Redemptive Merit. The Nature of Its Causality According to St. Thomas Aquinas* (Rome: Gregorian, 1962), 45–73.

18 *ST* II-II, q. 24, a. 6.

19 *ST* I-II, q. 65 a. 3, ad 2; *DQVG* 10, ad 16.

20 *ST* III, q. 86, a. 5, co.

21 For a helpful treatment of this problem, see Michael Sherwin, "Infused Virtue and the Effects of Acquired Vice," 29–52; and Knobel, *Aquinas and the Infused Virtues*, 170–79.

22 *De Malo,* q. 3, a. 13, ad 3.

23 Second Vatican Council, *Lumen Gentium*, no. 40.

24 For a full treatment, see my "'Spiritual Training' and Growth in Infused Virtue: Aquinas' Model in Historical Context," *Studies in Christian Ethics*

36.2 (May 2023): 287–310. For texts in St. Thomas, see, for example, *ST* I-II, q. 186, a. 1, s.c. and ad 4; q. 188, a. 1, co.; q. 188, a. 5, co.; q. 188, a. 6, co. and ad 3, q. 188, a. 7, co.; q. 189, a. 1; q. 189, a. 5; and also q. 184, a. 3, co.; q. 186, a. 1, s.c.; q. 186, a. 7, co. and ad 2; q. 187, a. 3, co.; q. 188, a. 7, co.; *ST* III, q. 69, a. 3; *De Perf.* IX; *Contra retrahentes*, cap. 6; *Quodlibet* IV, q. 12 a. 1 ad 18, q. 12, a. 2 ad 2; *Contra impugnantes* 5.4; and *Collationes in decem praeceptis*, a. 1–2. See also *ST* II-II, q. 185, a. 6, ad 1; II-II, q. 186, a. 4, ad 2; II-II, q. 186, a. 1; and II-II, q. 184, a. 3.

25 See Jean Leclercq, *La spiritualité de Pierre de Celle, 1115–1183* (Paris: J. Vrin, 1946), 232; Giles Constable, *The Reformation of the Twelfth Century* (Cambridge: Cambridge University Press, 1998), 1–43, 272–77.

26 His precise term varies and tracks a semantic field set by customary practice, but standard terms include *exercitium/exercitia* (joined to *spirituale/spiritualia* or not), *exercitia perfectionis*, *exercitium tendendi in perfectionem*, *observantia*, and *disciplina*.

27 St. Thomas, *De perfectione spiritualis vitae*, c. 9.

38 For example, Dominicans in Thomas' time fasted more days of the year than not (fasting was widely practiced in his time: even lay persons might fast for fifty-two days a year or so with a Ramadan-like intensity), they were wakened around midnight for a long vigil office that could stretch to three hours, and they were directed by the Master General Humbert of Romans to meditate just about anytime and anywhere: 'on the road, walking through the cloister, garden, or house [...] in the cell, or when in bed.' These were not token efforts, but were undertaken with the consistency to shape moral agency. They were real "training," as Thomas calls it, and were far from limited to his religious order or era. See for example Donald Prudlo, *Thomas Aquinas: A Historical, Theological, and Environmental Portrait* (New York: Paulist Press, 2020), 162; William Hinnebusch, *The History of the Dominican Order: Origins and Growth to 1500* (Staten Island, NY: Alba House, 1966), 350; Humbert of Romans, *Instructiones* in *Opera De Vita Regulari*, vol. II (Marietti 1956), 231.

29 Katharine Breen, *Imagining an English Reading Public, 1150–1400* (Cambridge: Cambridge University Press, 2010), 68.

30 The topic is discussed in W. H. Shewing, *The Passion of Ss. Perpetua and Felicity: A New Edition and Translation* (London: Sheed and Ward, 1931), who wrote, "Of [the author's] identity there is no absolute proof, but such evidence as we have is strongly in favor of Tertullian," p. xx.

31 Tertullian, *Ad Martyres* 3, translation from *Tertullian: Disciplinary, Moral, and Ascetical Works*, trans. Rudolph Arbesmann et al. (New York: Fathers of the Church, Inc., 1950), 22–23. Related points are made throughout St. Cyprian of Carthage's *De Mortalitate* (see especially chapters 12–16).

32 St. Cyprian of Carthage, *De Zelo et Livore* ("On Jealousy and Envy").

33 See the brief but scholarly treatments by Jean Leclerq, "Exercices Spirituels" and "Disciplina," in *Dictionnaire de spiritualité ascétique et mystique, doctrine et histoire* (Paris: G. Beauchesne, 1937), vol. 4, col. 1902 and vol 3, col. 1291, respectively; and the entries for "Exercitatio/Exercitium" as well as "Disciplina" in *Thesaurus linguae Latinae* (Munich: K.G. Saur, 2002), 1383–89 and 1316–25. I address the well-known work of Pierre Hadot and others on this topic in my "Spiritual Training."

34 For fine exceptions, see Gilles Emery, "Trinitarian Theology as Spiritual Exercise," in *Aquinas the Augustinian*, ed. Michael Dauphinais, Barry David, and Matthew Levering (Washington, DC: Catholic University of America Press, 2007), 1–40, and M. Kruger, "Aquinas, Hadot, and Spiritual Exercises," in *New Blackfriars* 98.1076 (July 2017): 414–26.

35 For example, already in the twelfth century Peter Comestor wrote: 'There are those who do more praying than reading: they are the cloister dwellers; there are others who spend all their time reading and rarely pray: they are the schoolmen.' See his Sermo IX, *Patrologia Latina* (PL) 198.1747.

36 See *ST* I-II, q. 65, a. 3, ad 2; *De Virt.*, q. 1, a. 10, ad 16; *ST* III, q. 86, a. 5, co.

37 See *ST* II-II, q. 189, a. 1 and *De Perf.* IX; see also *ST* II-II, q. 186, a. 1, ad 4 and q. 189, a. 5, ad 2.

38 'Contraria contrariis curantur', *De Malo*, q. 3, a. 15, arg. 4. See also Aristotle, *Nic. Eth.* 1104b17, and Hippocrates, *De Flatibus* 1.

39 *ST* II-II, q. 24, a. 6

40 *De Virt.* q. 5, a. 3, ad 1.

41 *ST* II-II, q. 82, a. 2, ad 2, a. 3. See also *ST* II-II, q. 180 aa. 1–4, and *Sent.* IV. dist. 15, q. 4.

42 *Collationes in decem praeceptis* a. 1–2, translated by Joseph B. Collins and available at https://isidore.co/aquinas/TenCommandments.htm.

43 A full treatment of this important subject is beyond my present scope. Yet here I will note that while Thomas insists on the superiority of religious life and holds that the counsels function as an overarching or comprehensive form of spiritual training, he adds that lay persons may practice the counsels themselves in a qualified form (*secundum quid*) appropriate to their state of life, that in this sense spiritual exercises constitute acts of the counsels for those who practice them, and that lay persons may be spiritually perfect in the counsels and *exercitia* generally. In this they are aided through moral preparation (*reparation animi*) to forgo created goods as necessary as well as through cultivation of inner detachment. See *ST* I-II, q. 108, a. 4, co; *ST* II-II, q. 184, a. 3; q. 184, a. 7, ad 1; q. 186, a. 4; a. 7, ad 1; and q. 189, a. 1, ad 4, and my "Spiritual Training."

44 *ST* II-II, q. 185, a. 6, ad 1; q. 186, a. 4, ad 2.

45 *Super Psalmo* 48, n. 1.

46 *ST* II-II, q. 184, a. 3.

47 See for instance *Summa contra Gentiles* [hereafter, *SCG*] III, c. 132, no. 14; *ST* II-II, q. 186, a. 1, s.c. and ad 4; q. 188, a. 1, co.; q. 188, a. 5, co.; q. 188, a. 6, co. and ad 3; q. 188, a. 7, co.; q. 189, a. 1; q. 189, a. 5; and also q. 184, a. 3, co.; q. 186, a. 1 s.c.; q. 186, a. 7, co. and ad 2; q. 187, a. 3, co.; q. 188, a. 7, co.; III, q. 69, a. 3; *De Perf.* IX; *Contra retrahentes*, cap. 6; *Quodlibet* IV, q. 12 a. 1 ad 18, q. 12, a. 2 ad 2; *Contra impugnantes* 5.4, and *Collationes in decem praeceptis* a. 1–2.

48 *ST* II-II, q. 186, a. 1, s.c.

49 J. Patout Burns and Robin M. Jensen, *Christianity in Roman Africa: The Development of Its Practices and Beliefs* (Grand Rapids, MI: Eerdmans, 2014), xlvi.

50 See Thomas' comments in IV *Sent.*, d. 4., q. I, a. 2, qla. 1.2, and IV *Sent.*, d. 4, q. II, a. 3, qla. 3.2; and the parallel discussion in my review of *Virtue and Grace in the Theology of Thomas Aquinas* in *The Thomist* 86.2 (2022): 299–303.

51 Joseph Wawrykow, "'Perseverance' in 13th-Century Theology: The Augustinian Contribution," in *Augustinian Studies* 22 (1991): 125–40, citation at 126.

52 Odozor, *Morality Truly Christian, Truly African*, 231.

53 While Thomas sometimes uses *auxilium* to refer to even to habitual grace, he reserves a proper or specialized sense of it to this specific divine motion. As Joseph Wawrykow says: "For auxilium in this [narrow] sense, see such texts as I–11 109, 1c, where he calls it divinum auxilium, I-II 109, 2c (divinum auxilium), I-II 109, 3c (auxilium Dei moventis, auxilium Dei), I-II 109, 4c (auxilium Dei moventis), I-II 109, 5 ad 3 (auxilium gratiae), and 109, 6c (auxilium gratuitum Dei interius animam moventis)" (Wawrykow, *God's Grace and Human Action*, 171).

54 See the thorough and fine treatment by Shawn M. Colberg, "Aquinas and the Grace of Auxilium," *Modern Theology* 32, no. 2 (2016): 187–210; and my "Cultivating Infused Virtue: How Aquinas' Late Turn to Auxilium Grace Reframes the Virtuous Life," in *Vetera novis augere. Le risorse della tradizione tomista nel contesto attuale*, III. *Temi teologicim*, ed. Serge-Thomas Bonino and Luca F. Tuninetti (Città del Vaticano: Pontificia Universitas Urbaniana, forthcoming).

55 *ST* I-II q. 109, a. 10.

56 See footnotes 53 and 54 above.

57 St. Augustine, Sermo LVI, de oratione Dominica, *Patrologia Latina* 38, Col. 0381, quoted in *Catechism of the Catholic Church*, no. 2559.

58 See *Quaestiones disputatae de veritate* q. 24, a. 13, ad 2; *ST* II-II, q. 109, a. 9, co.; and Joseph Wawrykow "Grace," in *The Theology of Thomas Aquinas*, ed. Rik Van Nieuwenhove and Joseph P. Wawrykow (Notre

Dame: University of Notre Dame Press, 2005), 192–221.

59 Pioneering twentieth centuries studies include Henri Bouillard, S.J., *Conversion et grace chez S. Thomas d'Aquin. Etude historique* (Paris: Aubier, 1944), and Bernard J. F. Lonergan, S.J., *Grace and Freedom: Operative Grace in the Thought of St. Thomas Aquinas* (London: Darton, Longman & Todd, 1971), among others. A helpful overview of these developments is found in Wawrykow "Grace."

60 Augustine, *On the Gift of Perseverance*, 2. The passage is cited by St. Thomas at I-II, q. 109, a. 10, s.c.

61 See footnote 59 above for references.

62 Alister McGrath, *Iustitia Dei: A History of the Christian Doctrine of Justification* (Cambridge: Cambridge University Press, 2005), 107.

63 McGrath, *Iustitia Dei*, 107. See also Lonergan, *Grace and Freedom*, 41–61.

64 See my "Cultivating Infused Virtue," in *Vetera novis augere*, forthcoming.

65 I note in passing that Aquinas quotes Cyprian at least 73 times, including his major works, whereas Bonaventure quotes Cyprian a total of 12 times, and mostly his letters not his treatises.

66 See Odozor, *Morality Truly Christian, Truly African*, 36.

67 I am indebted to my colleague Thomas Clemmons for this observation.

68 Brown, *Augustine*, 408–409.

69 In ancient Africa, Brown writes, "Church was thought of as a preserve of safety and cleanliness in a world ruled by demonic powers. It existed to protect the believer. The African came to church, less because he was 'thirsty and heavy laden,' but that he wished to survive in a battlefield" (*Augustine*, 207). As Augustine had said: the "gift of perseverance" was the "greatest of God's gifts" (407).

70 Brown, *Augustine*, 22.

71 See Jonathan Conant, *Staying Roman: Conquest and Identity in Africa and the Mediterranean, 439–700* (Cambridge: Cambridge University Press, 2012), 188.

72 St. Augustine, *Contra Julianum*, Bk 3, c. 17, cited from *Against Julian (The Fathers of the Church, Volume 35),* trans. Matthew A. Schumacher (Washington, D.C.: Catholic University of America Press, 1957), 135.

73 Ibid., p. 136.

74 Brown, *Augustine*, 408.

75 See footnote 1 above.

76 Significant portions of this essay have included and reworked material from my earlier publication, "'Spiritual Training' and Growth in Infused Virtue: Aquinas' Model in Historical Context," as well as a few paragraphs from my forthcoming publication, "Cultivating Infused Virtue." I am grateful to the publishers for permission to reuse this material.

Chapter 10 Endnotes

1 Bernard Lonergan, *Method in Theology* (New York: Herder and Herder, 1972), 237.

2 Lonergan, *Method in Theology*, 237.

3 "Empowerment" in this sense is enabling the individual to respond to the action of the Holy Spirit, the operation of grace in his or her life to bear fruit.

4 Bonaventure, *Breviloquium, Prologus,* 5.2. Cf. Bonaventure, *Breviloquium*, trans. Dominic Monti (St. Bonaventure, NY: Franciscan Institute Publications, 2005), 15.

5 Paul VI, "Homily at the Canonization of the Martyrs of Uganda," *AAS 56* (1964): 905–906.

6 The distinctiveness of the local Church in Africa in antiquity has been exposed by Peter Brown, "Christianity and Local Culture in Late Roman Africa," *Journal of Roman Studies* 58 (1968): 85–95.

7 Cf. Karl Delahaye, *Ecclesia Mater chez les Pères des trois premiers siècles* (Paris: Cerf, 1964), 98, 108.

8 Alan Kreider, "Baptism, Catechism, and the Eclipse of Jesus' Teaching in Early Christianity," *Tyndale Bulletin* 47.2 (1996): 315.

9 *Didache,* 7.1. (Citations of patristic sources can be found at *New Advent*. See Web Archive: https://www.loc.gov/item/lcwaN0008071/).

10 *Didache*, 1.1.

11 Justin Martyr, *1 Apology*, 61. Cf. Everett Ferguson, *Baptism in the Early Church: History, Theology, and Liturgy in the First Five Centuries* (Grand Rapids, MI: Eerdmans, 2009), 202.

12 The stress on the moral content of Baptism can also be seen not only in the *Didache* and Justin Martyrs *Apology* but also in 2 Clement (3.1–4.1), Ignatius (*To Polycarp* 6.2); Hermes (*Mandates* 4.3.1–4), and Barnabas (6.16; 11.6; 16.7).

13 *Barnabas,* 18–21.

14 For instance, in the works of Cyprian, Origen, and eventually Augustine. Cf. Ferguson, *Baptism in the Early Church*, 351.

15 Cf. Pontius, *Vita Cypriani*, 4–6; Augustine, *Confessions*, 8.1–12. Regarding Origen, although the Neoplatonist philosopher Porphyry claims that Origen was born of pagan parents, Eusebius of Caesarea states the opposite. According to Eusebius's account of Origen's life, Origen's father, Leonides, died a Christian martyred in the persecution of 202. Cf. Eusebius, *Historia Ecclesiastica*, 6. 2–3.

16 Cf. Cyprian, *Ad Quirinus*, Praef.

17 William Harmless, *Augustine and the Catechumenate*, rev. ed. (Collegeville, MN: Liturgical Press, 2014), 50.

18 Thomas M. Finn, *Early Christian Baptism and the Catechumenate: West and East Syria* (Collegeville, MN: Liturgical Press, 1992), 4–5.
19 Harmless, *Augustine and the Catechumenate*, 39.
20 Tertullian, *Prescription Against Heretics*, 41.
21 Tertullian, *On Baptism*, 18.
22 Tertullian, *Apologeticum*, 22.
23 Kreider, "Baptism, Catechism, and the Eclipse of Jesus' Teaching in Early Christianity," 332.
24 Kreider, "Baptism, Catechism, and the Eclipse of Jesus' Teaching in Early Christianity," 332.
25 Augustine, *On Faith and Works*, 18.33.
26 Kreider, "Baptism, Catechism, and the Eclipse of Jesus' Teaching in Early Christianity," 336–37.
27 Kreider, "Baptism, Catechism, and the Eclipse of Jesus' Teaching in Early Christianity," 338.
28 Founded by Cardinal Charles Lavigerie in 1868. Originally, they were known as the "White Fathers," because of their white habit (gandoura) and a white hooded cloak (burnous). Both pieces of attire were based on traditional North African garb. Later, they insisted on being called "Missionaries of Africa."
29 Waliggo, "Bible and Catechism in Uganda," in *The Bible in African Christianity: Essays in Biblical Theology*, ed. Hannah W. Kinoti and John M. Waliggo (Nairobi, Kenya: Acton Publishers, 1997), 179.
30 Waliggo, "Bible and Catechism in Uganda," 181.
31 Waliggo, "Bible and Catechism in Uganda," 183.
32 Fr. Waliggo noted that the Trinity was presented as a mathematic puzzle, which created the greatest difficulty in understanding the doctrine. Waliggo, 182.
33 Bishop Hirth, "Introduction" to *Edhiini ya Katonda*, cited by Waliggo, 185.
34 Bishop Hirth, "Introduction" to *Edhiini ya Katonda*, cited by Waliggo, 185.
35 Waliggo, "Bible and Catechism in Uganda," 185.
36 Waliggo, "Bible and Catechism in Uganda," 183.
37 Lavigerie quoted in Renault, *Cardinal Lavigerie*, 138. Cited by Jay Carney, "Making Disciples of all Nations: Adaptation and Christian Civilization in the Missiological Thought of Charles Lavigerie," *Engaging Particularities Conference,* Boston College, 2007, 7.
38 Jay Carney, "Making Disciples of all Nations: Adaptation and Christian Civilization in the Missiological Thought of Charles Lavigerie," 7.
39 Jay Carney, "Making Disciples of all Nations: Adaptation and Christian Civilization in the Missiological Thought of Charles Lavigerie," 4–5. An example was Lavigerie's plan of "doctor catechists" or "medical catechists" who would be trained in both medicine and the truths of the Catholic faith.

They would bring healing to the people, which was so needed at that time due to the prevalence of diseases in Buganda, and at the same time evangelize.

40 Jay Carney, "Making Disciples of all Nations: Adaptation and Christian Civilization in the Missiological Thought of Charles Lavigerie," 6.

41 Waliggo, "Bible and Catechism in Uganda," 182.

42 Waliggo, "Bible and Catechism in Uganda," 184.

43 "There had been a handful of African Catholic priests in the Christian Kingdom of Kongo in the 16th century, but this priesthood soon died out. In the 19th century, a few African priests were ordained but this small collection of priests belonged to missionary groups." Cf. "Lumu, Bazilio," *Dictionary of African Christian Biography*, https://dacb.org/stories/uganda/lumu-bazilio/ accessed on October 26, 2023. For an archival study, cf. John Mary Waliggo, *A History of African Priests, Katigondo Major Seminary 1911–1986*, Uganda: Katigondo National Seminary, 1988.

44 Paulinus Odozor, *Morality Truly Christian, Truly African: Foundational, Methodological, and Theological Considerations* (Notre Dame, IN: University of Notre Dame Press, 2014), 165.

45 Odozor, *Morality Truly Christian, Truly African*, 165–74.

46 Cardinal Sarah and Edward Pentin, "Cardinal Sarah's Cri de Coeur: The Catholic Church Has Lost Its Sense of the Sacred" *National Catholic Register*, September 23, 2019, https://www.ncregister.com/interview/cardinal-sarah-s-cri-de-coeur-the-catholic-church-has-lost-its-sense-of-the-sacred.

47 Cardinal Sarah and Edward Pentin, "Cardinal Sarah's Cri de Coeur."

48 Odozor, *Morality Truly Christian, Truly African*, 166.

49 Odozor, *Morality Truly Christian, Truly African*, 168.

50 Odozor, *Morality Truly Christian, Truly African*, 169.

51 Waliggo, "Bible and Catechism in Uganda," 182.

52 Odozor, *Morality Truly Christian, Truly African*, 169.

53 Carney, "Making Disciples of all Nations," 4.

54 Odozor, *Morality Truly Christian, Truly African*, 171.

55 Odozor, *Morality Truly Christian, Truly African*, 172.

56 Odozor, *Morality Truly Christian, Truly African*, 172.

57 Odozor, *Morality Truly Christian, Truly African*, 173–74.

58 Cf. *Catechism of the Catholic Church*, 2nd ed., nos. 2659–60.

59 *Catechism of the Catholic Church*, no. 2659.

60 Odozor, *Morality Truly Christian, Truly African*, 174.

61 Cf. Pope Francis, *Evangelii gaudium* (24 November 2013), AAS 105 (2013): 1019–1137, no. 43.

62 Pope John Paul II, *Catechesi trandendae* (16 October 1979), AAS 71 (1979): 1277–1340, no. 18.

63 Pope Francis, *Evangelii gaudium*, no. 43.

Chapter 11 Endnotes

1 Vincent W. Lloyd, *Black Natural Law* (Oxford: Oxford University Press, 2016), ix.

2 Paulinus Ikechukwu Odozor, C.S.Sp., *Moral Theology in an Age of Renewal: A Study of the Catholic Tradition since Vatican II* (Notre Dame: University of Notre Dame Press, 2003), 164. See also the chapter on "Natural Law in the Catholic Moral Tradition" in *Moral Theology in an Age of Renewal*, 165–88. Odozor notes "the reluctance of many theologians to grant moral significance to natural human faculties," and in response he approvingly observes: "*Veritatis splendor* reacts strongly to those who deny that human nature has moral significance. The encyclical's reaction is given against the backdrop of what it considers a misunderstanding of the idea of human freedom. This misunderstood freedom claims to be absolute and tends to treat the human body as 'a raw datum, devoid of any meaning and moral values until freedom has shaped it according to its design'" (184–85).

3 Both Odozor and Bujo have written on Aquinas's natural law doctrine: see Odozor, *Moral Theology in an Age of Renewal*, 168–76; Bujo, *Moralautonomie und Normenfindung bei Thomas von Aquin: Unter Einbeziehung der neutestamentlichen Kommentare* (Paderborn: Ferdinand Schöningh, 1979), 232–83. Bujo delves deeply into Aquinas's New Testament commentaries, and for this I commend him. See also Bujo's Habilitation, published as *Die Begründlung des Sittlichen: Zur frage des Eudämonismus bei Thomas von Aquin* (Paderborn: Ferdinand Schöningh, 1984). For valuable background to, and analysis of, Bujo's theological corpus, see Juvénal Ilunga Muya, "Bénézet Bujo: The Awakening of a Systematic and Authentically African Thought," in *African Theology: The Contribution of the Pioneers*, ed. Bénézet Bujo and Juvénal Ilunga Muya (Nairobi: Paulines Publications Africa, 2003), 107–45. Muya notes that Bujo, in the year after the publication of the encyclical *Humanae Vitae*, completed an S.T.L. with a thesis on "Loi ancienne, loi nouvelle et loi naturelle. Analyse de la pensée de S. Thomas d'Aquin dans ses commentaires néotestamentaires de 1259–1265." Muya comments, "Already at the time, one can spot the fundamental question concerning him: 'Can the moral law be founded on something other than the natural law?'" (108). He credits Bujo's Dominican seminary teachers, who had been students of Edward Schillebeeckx, for interesting Bujo in Aquinas and in "the problem of the specificity of Christian morals" (109). In Bujo's S.T.L. thesis, says Muya, "The dialogue with St Thomas's theology was the occasion for showing the transformations and the reciprocal changes occurring when the Gospel meets various cultures"; whereas in his doctoral dissertation and Habilitation, he sought to identify "the

fundamental principles for a fruitful dialogue between the autonomy of morals, the biblical message and the Magisterium of the Church" (109). Muya adds that Bujo drew from Aquinas a method that "does not place at its origin a dualism matter-spirit, profane-sacred, natural-supernatural, transcendence-immanence, interior-exterior, but an integration, an original unity maintaining differences, while always presupposing correlations […]. Through the commentaries of biblical texts, Thomas developed a whole method of doing theology rooted in symbols, analogy and metaphors, closer to the Fathers and to African thought" (110–11).

4 Bénézet Bujo, *African Theology in Its Social Context*, trans. John O'-Donoghue, M.Afr. (Maryknoll, NY: Orbis, 1992), 76. Notably, Odozor reverses the terms, placing "truly Christian" first. For Bujo's sharpest critique of natural law as he understands it, see his *La vision africaine du monde. Pour un enseignement social de l'Église sans loi naturelle* (Basel: Schwabe, 2021).

5 Bénézet Bujo, *Foundations of an African Ethic: Beyond the Universal Claims of Western Morality*, trans. Brian McNeil (New York: Crossroad, 2001), xi. For the original German edition, see Bujo, *Wider den Universalanspuch westlicher Moral: Grundlagen afrikanischer Ethik* (Berlin: Herder, 2000).

6 Bujo, *Foundations of an African Ethic*, xii.

7 Ibid. In Bujo's view, "it is inappropriate to talk in the plural about ethics or religion in sub-Saharan Africa. Except for a few non-African researchers and scientists, most tend to agree on the unity of religion—and ethics—in Black Africa […]. The differences we can observe among African religions do not concern the substance of the African conception itself, but the way that conception is translated and put into practice (costumes, rites, etc). It is inappropriate to look for the kind of divergence in African religion we find, for instance, within the various Christian denominations (Catholicism, Protestantism, Orthodoxy) or the various Buddhist, Muslim, and other traditions. The African conception centers on life. Life articulates itself thanks to and through the community of the living, the dead, and the not-yet born, and it never forgets to refer to God, the actual foundation of this three-dimensional community" (Bujo, "Differentiations in African Ethics," trans. Philippe Eberhard, in *The Blackwell Companion to Religious Ethics*, ed. William Schweiker [Oxford: Blackwell, 2005], 423–37, at 423). For discussion, see Wilson Muoha Maina, *The Making of an African Christian Ethics: Bénézet Bujo and the Roman Catholic Tradition* (Eugene, OR: Pickwick, 2016), 8–13. Maina emphasizes diversity: "It is my view that there are as many African traditional religions as there are ethnic groups in the continent" (13).

8 Bujo, *Foundations of an African Ethic*, 51.

9 Ibid., 53.

10 For the significance of the whole cosmic order in African understanding, see also Bujo, "Differentiations in African Ethics," 425–26.

11 Bujo, *Foundations of an African Ethic*, 100. Bujo's comments in this context on Aquinas's theology of nature and grace, and on Aquinas's theology of law, exhibit misunderstandings that lead him to draw unnecessarily sharp contrasts between Thomistic ethics and African ethics. Like many Catholic moral theologians in the 1970s and 1980s, Bujo argues that Christ does not add anything to human morality in terms of ethical content, but Christ does make a large "qualitative" difference. Bujo explains with regard to the latter, "Jesus Christ, the proto-ancestor, develops the primary concern of the African tradition in a radical way; where Africans have introduced many practices under an erroneous appeal to the life that comes to them from the ancestors, the proto-ancestor opens their eyes to the true life and corrects abuses and misunderstandings" (103). Bujo names three examples of such misunderstandings and abuses: the view that a childless marriage justifies divorce or polygamy; the view that handicapped children can licitly be killed; and the problem of ethnocentrism. In each case, Bujo holds that the basic thrust of African ethics is oriented to what Christ brings, even though Christ also changes the African practice. For example, "Where sterility leads to contempt for the married couple, the proto-ancestor [Christ] points to the true dimension of life, since it is precisely the weak to whom he wishes to give the fullness of life. Childless couples are the weak ones in society, and these must be protected and supported, so that they too may have the life of the proto-ancestor in its fullness" (103). See also Bujo's "Die christologischen Grundlagen einer afrikanischen Ethik," *Freiburger Zeitschrift für Philosophie und Theologie* 29 (1982): 223–38, an essay that was published in multiple languages.

12 Bujo, *Foundations of an African Ethic*, 161. See Bujo, "Differentiations in African Ethics," 428: "African ethics is not based on the concept of Western natural or moral law, but in the framework of the community. The community is actually the place where norms take shape. In all of this, life in its widest sense is what functions as the hinge for the elaboration of ethical norms. Everything that contributes to maintaining, strengthening, and perfecting individual as well as communal life is good and right. Whether it is an ethical judgment on property, marriage, or sexuality, etc., palaver will determine if it is appropriate for life in abundance for all." This seems a fairly straightforward proportionalist approach to ethics. indebted to Fuchs, since the community makes its contextually normative decisions on the basis of whether the particular action serves to foster "life in abundance for all." Bujo, however, maintains that the communal emphasis provides a crucial "difference from Western styles of argument" (428). I note that Bujo

wants to retain some shared (universal) norms, a point emphasized by Maina, *The Making of an African Christian Ethics*, 108, citing Bujo, *The Ethical Dimension of Community: The African Model and the Dialogue between North and South*, trans. Cecilia Namulondo (Nairobi: Paulines Publications Africa, 1998), 143—and see also Bujo, *Foundations of an African Ethic*, 82–83, arguing (mistakenly in my view) that Aquinas considers that the natural law arrives at certain general principles, from which however one cannot derive practical norms applicable in all contexts. Insofar as Bujo does this, natural law remains a necessary category. As Maina observes, Bujo relies here on "autonomous ethics" as understood by Alfons Auer and Josef Fuchs, among others: Bujo "uses autonomous ethics to show that through reason, ethical principles are related, and they are transcultural," while also insisting that "Christianity is always lived in a particular historical and cultural context that shapes moral reasoning" (Maina, *The Making of an African Christian Ethics*, 110, 137). There is a tension in Bujo's thought, but insofar as "autonomous ethics" can be considered to follow what Maina calls "the natural law approach" (139; cf. 161), Bujo can be said to have some place for "natural law," since autonomous ethics justifies denying that there are moral norms that necessarily apply in every "concrete historical and cultural setting" (163).

13 Bujo, *Foundations of an African Ethic*, 161.

14 Ibid., 159.

15 Ibid., 148; see Josef Fuchs, S.J., "Magisterium und Moraltheologie," in Fuchs, *Für eine menschliche Moral: Grundfragen der theologischen Ethik*, vol. III: *Die Spannng zwischen objektiver und subjektiver Moral* (Freiburg i. Br.: 1991), 127–38, at 128. This position of Fuchs contradicts his own amply argued earlier position, as I note below. See also Bujo's remark in his *Le Diaire d'un théologien africain* (Kinshasa: 1987), 24: "The Bible has not invented moral norms—not even Jesus has—but [...] everything goes back to man created in the image and likeness of God and questioned by his word in order to deepen and radicalise the existing, or better pre-existing ethos. The Christian must, starting from the Word of God, criticise, stimulate and integrate the human ethos" (translated and quoted in Muya, "Bénézet Bujo," 110n10). For a critique of Fuchs's postconciliar position, see Russell Hittinger, "Natural Law as 'Law,'" in his *The First Grace: Rediscovering the Natural Law in a Post-Christian World* (Wilmington, DE: ISI Books, 2003), 39–62.

16 See also, however, Bujo's attempt to explain (and in certain ways defend) such practices as polygamy and female circumcision in his *The Ethical Dimension of Community*, 96, 127. In her book review of *The Ethical Dimension of Community*, published in *Philosophia Africana* 4 (2001): 79–82, Chielozona Eze raises concerns about these passages and others. She

remarks critically that "by the end of the book, one even wonders whether any dialogue really did take place between 'northern' and 'southern' worldviews. 'Northern' [i.e. Western, European] ideas are put forth by the author only to be dismissed summarily as 'imperialistic,' with African ideas then proposed as worthy alternatives [...]. Many issues raised in the book end up as mere assertions. Only a more systematic study could have given enough substance to the issues to satisfy the philosopher or, for that matter, the contemporary African. Our world, North or South, needs to rediscover a sense of community. What still needs answering, though, especially with regard to Bujo's African community, is the question of how to create it, especially if one is not a descendant of a revered ancestor. Bujo's book does not offer any clue. Neither does it grant a young African mind the right to challenge the relevance of the ancestors' experiences to the demands of the present. Bujo does not seem to be disturbed that the strongest prerequisite for entering into the pantheon of the ancestors is to beget a child" (Eze, 81). Eze warns that the idealization of solidarity and the palaver feeds, in actual practice, into political systems of persisting dictatorship.

17 Bujo, *Foundations of an African Ethic*, 140–41.

18 Bujo's perspective on inculturation is similar to that of Laurenti Magesa, for whom, as Odozor says, "the interaction between Christianity and African traditions has to be between equal partners and not between a superior and an inferior tradition" (Odozor, Review of Laurenti Magesa's *What Is Not Sacred? African Spirituality* [Maryknoll, NY: Orbis, 2013], *Theological Studies* 76 [2015]: 378–79, at 378). In his *African Theology in Its Social Context*, Bujo argues: "The incarnation of Christianity in Africa can only come about when it has been shown to the people of that Continent that the message of Jesus, far from destroying the liberation which traditional religion sought, provides it with a new, purifying and total stimulus. To achieve this, we must get beyond general questions, like the justification of African theology, or its aims and benefits; our task must be to bring together the fundamentals of both Christian faith and the African tradition, so that the Africans may find their own way in the resulting Christianity and feel at home therein" (75). See also Bujo's reflections on Christian morality as the purification of African morality—rather than as something sharply different from African morality—in Bujo, *Morale africaine et foi chrétienne* (Kinshasa: 1976); and his *African Christian Morality at the Age of Inculturation* (Nairobi: Paulines Publications Africa, 1990).

19 Bujo, *Foundations of an African Ethic*, 129; and for the same point see Bujo, "Differentiations in African Ethics," 433, including his remark that "my freedom as an individual can only be real and total if I free the community at the same time. In the same way, the community as a whole can

enjoy true freedom only if it frees me as an individual. Strong and abundant life for all is possible only in this continual interaction." Bujo's distinction between "freedom from" and "freedom for" likely comes from the work of Bujo's Fribourg colleague Servais Pinckaers, O.P., *The Sources of Christian Ethics*, trans. Mary Thomas Noble, O.P. (Washington, D.C.: Catholic University of America Press, 1995).

20 Bujo, *Foundations of an African Ethic*, 119.

21 Ibid.

22 Ibid.

23 Ibid., 126. Earlier Bujo clarifies, "The impression is often given that community solidarity in Black Africa leads to the dissolution of individual identity. Certainly, one must not overlook the danger that the community may put the individual under pressure and force him to conform to the group; this is in fact often the case. But one must distinguish (as in Christianity) between the ideal and human shortcomings [...]. The community gets entangled in contradictions and destroys itself if it disregards or disparages the identity of the individual. The individual can enrich the community only when he is made a person by its individual members, so that he in his turn can share in the process by which others become persons. No one is dispensable in this process; the individuals are not exchangeable" (ibid., 93).

24 For a range of perspectives on *Veritatis Splendor*, see the essays in the following three volumes: *Veritatis Splendor and the Renewal of Moral Theology*, ed. J. A. Di Noia, O.P. and Romanus Cessario, O.P. (Chicago: Midwest Theological Forum, 1999); *The Splendor of Accuracy: An Examination of the Assertions Made by* Veritatis Splendor, ed. Joseph A. Selling and Jan Jans (Grand Rapids, MI: Eerdmans, 1995); and *Considering* Veritatis Splendor, ed. John Wilkins (Cleveland, OH: Pilgrim Press, 1994), including Fuchs's "Good Acts and Good Persons," 21–26. More recently, see Michael Dauphinais, "The Splendor and Gift of the Christian Moral Life: *Veritatis Splendor* at Twenty-Five," *Nova et Vetera* 16 (2018): 1261–1312. For Odozor's defense of aspects of the encyclical's critique of proportionalism, see Odozor, *Moral Theology in an Age of Renewal*, 222–24—although Odozor emphasizes that "all parties to the discussion on norms [including the proportionalists] insist that they uphold the existence of moral absolutes, even when they disagree on how these are to be determined or what particular norms are to be so regarded" (246).

25 As noted above, insofar as Bujo accepts some kind of natural law reasoning, he is indebted to the "autonomous ethics" of Auer and Fuchs, who in my view misread Aquinas. For accurate Thomistic presentations of "intrinsically evil actions," see Romanus Cessario, O.P., *Introduction to Moral Theology* (Washington, D.C.: Catholic University of America Press, 2000),

167–70; and Servais Pinckaers, O.P., "A Historical Perspective on Intrinsically Evil Acts," trans. Mary Thomas Noble, O.P. with Craig Steven Titus, in *The Pinckaers Reader*, ed. John Berkman and Craig Steven Titus (Washington, D.C.: Catholic University of America Press, 2005), 185–235. As Pinckaers notes, "the conviction that there are actions evil in themselves, things one may never do even for a good intention, was a constant conviction in the tradition, firmly established in the consciences of theologians and faithful alike even before the theological formulation and its systematization came into being" (232). It is no surprise that Fuchs's student James F. Keenan, S.J. privileges Bujo—and entirely ignores Odozor's *Morality Truly Christian, Truly African*—in his misleading portrait of African moral theology in *A History of Catholic Theological Ethics* (Mahwah, NJ: Paulist Press, 2022), 320–27.

26 Bujo, *Foundations of an African Ethic*, 83.

27 Ibid., 83. For discussion of Bujo's critique of *Veritatis Splendor*, see Maina, *The Making of an African Christian Ethics*, chapter 6. Maina is indebted in this chapter to Joseph Selling, a strong critic of *Veritatis Splendor* who taught Raymond Aina, and whose views are reflected in Aina's chapter in the present volume. For Bujo, as Maina says, "In an attempt to emphasize the universality of the magisterium of the church, the encyclical forgets that universality has to be understood in particular cultural and historical settings" (Maina, *The Making of an African Christian Ethics*, 164).

28 Bujo, *Foundations of an African Ethic*, 83.

29 Ibid., 37.

30 Ibid., 39. Mark Graham sums up Fuchs's post-conciliar perspective: "On the issue of artificial contraception [...] the preconversion [i.e. pre-conciliar] Fuchs located moral normativity in the 'natural' end of intercourse, procreation. By directly impeding the natural finality of the marital act, artificial contraceptives contravened the natural order and were deemed contrary to natural law by Fuchs. Within this framework does experiential data, understood very broadly, contribute to the determination of artificial contraception's liceity? Does it matter morally that artificial methods of contraception might be more effective than the rhythm method in regulating births? Does it matter that married couples using artificial contraception might be more satisfied with their sex lives, or that their marriages might be more stable and healthy? Does it matter that serious medical problems might arise for some women if they become pregnant? Does it matter if more babies afflicted by Down's Syndrome are born to couples using the rhythm method than those using artificial contraception? For the preconversion Fuchs, the answer is 'no' because the process of uncovering natural law on this particular issue depends on knowing the natural finality of conjugal intercourse, not on the cumulative knowledge gained through the

insights or empirical data of medical doctors, married couples, or anyone else. The postconversion Fuchs, in contrast, claims not only that natural law analysis must consider the insights of married couples, population experts, medical doctors, social scientists, philosophers, and theologians to determine the liceity of artificial contraception, but maintains that recent advances in various disciplines have culminated in an entirely new understanding of conjugal intercourse" (Graham, *Josef Fuchs on Natural Law* [Washington, D.C.: Georgetown University Press, 2002], 156). Fuchs's reconceived "natural law" holds that "new insights, new evidence, and advances in the physical and social sciences [...] have altered our conception of the human person" (157). I think Fuchs is mistaken. For further discussion, see my *Engaging the Doctrine of Marriage: Human Marriage as the Sign and Sacrament of the Marriage of God and Creation* (Eugene, OR: Cascade, 2020) and my *Aquinas's Eschatological Ethics and the Virtue of Temperance* (Notre Dame: University of Notre Dame Press, 2019).

31 Bujo, *Foundations of an African Ethic*, 39. Bujo comments, "Marriage is one of the fundamental elements which strengthen and reestablish the community; it signifies the anamnetic solidarity with one's ancestors. Moreover, it is a *communio* with one's ancestors which ultimately achieves a communicative fellowship that transcends death" (ibid., 35).

32 Bujo states, "Understanding or reason alone cannot suffice to make a person capable of living and of giving life—for this, each one needs to be integrated *actively* into the community, seeking contact with its other members, and in particular taking into consideration the experience of past generations. It is only thus that the young person can become wise and prudent" (ibid., 26).

33 Ibid., 45. Bujo carefully distinguishes his position from the "communitarianism" popular in the 1980s and 1990s in the West. He states, "the communitarianism that is put forward by important representatives of modern philosophy deserves this name from the African viewpoint only in a *limited* sense, especially since it does not understand the dead as agents and pays no attention at all to the significance of the unborn. Despite all its criticism of liberalism, communitarianism ultimately cannot detach itself from its Western origin" (ibid., 29). See also Bujo, "Differentiations in African Ethics," 430: "Western anthropology leaves a fundamental mark on communitarian thinking. It is true that communitarians strongly oppose the atomization of the individual and that they stress the bond between individual and community. Nevertheless, if one compares their conception of community with the African conception, it appears that, as far as moral action is concerned, the individual, though bound to environment and group, is not bound in his or her personal decisions to the extent of referring to his or her community. In other words, the community can shape the individual,

but it does not accompany them in their personal dealings: ultimately, decisions belong to the private sphere, in which the community must not meddle. By contrast, in African ethics community is so important that one goes so far as to involve its deceased members in a decision to be made: this is not a passive attitude but, rather, an *active* participation of the whole community which must help the individual before, during, and after a decision in order to put it into practice—always as a community." In order to differentiate this from the Church's understanding of its Spirit-filled (and saint-filled and angel-filled) communal and Magisterial ethics, Bujo adds in a proportionalist key: "the communal character of African ethics does not necessarily turn it into a kind of fiction and dogmatism but provides leeway for innovations and creativity: traditions that no longer encourage abundant life must be abolished" (430). I should note here, however, that Bujo strongly rejects the liceity of abortion and euthanasia, and he does so in a beautiful and persuasive way ("Differentiations in African Ethics," 435–36). For Bujo's further remarks along these lines, see Bujo, *The Ethical Dimension of Community*.

34 Bujo, *Foundations of an African Ethic*, 16.

35 Ibid., 19.

36 Ibid., 21.

37 Ibid., 11.

38 Ibid.

39 Ibid., 18.

40 For further discussion, see Bujo, *Plea for Change of Models for Marriage* (Nairobi: Paulines Publications Africa, 2020).

41 Bujo, *Foundations of an African Ethic*, 22.

42 Bujo notes that "among Ghana's Ashanti the rule is to exclude no one from palaver"; and he adds that "the rule of the Ashanti (a rule similar to those of several other African ethnic groups) really embraces everybody, including the handicapped, even if they cannot express themselves at the level of language. They can […] communicate and make themselves understood through symbolic actions and gestures, for instance. Such actions and gestures […] can be decisive for palaver" ("Differentiations in African Ethics," 429).

43 Bujo, *Foundations of an African Ethic*, 22.

44 Ibid., 23.

45 Ibid., 21–22.

46 Paulinus Ikechukwu Odozor, C.S.Sp., *Morality Truly Christian, Truly African: Foundational, Methodological, and Theological Considerations* (Notre Dame: University of Notre Dame Press, 2014), 153.

47 Ibid., 154.

48 Ibid. For discussion of how Bujo in his early work attempted to ground

this position in Aquinas's theology, see Muya, "Bénézet Bujo," 118–19. Muya states, "Asserting the autonomy of morals does not contradict God's law. If human reason is the foundation of ethics, it itself rests on another foundation: the *lex aeterna* and the divine promise of fulfilment. Thomas can then insist on the responsibility on the part of every human being towards the self and the others. His mission is not to repeat nature, but to transform and perfect it" (119). Odozor's trenchant description and critique of Auer's and Fuchs's ethics is found in *Moral Theology in an Age of Renewal*, 108–16.

49 Odozor, *Morality Truly Christian, Truly African*, 156.

50 For Bujo's perspective, see (in addition to Bujo's *Foundations of an African Ethic*) his "Differentiations in African Ethics," 424–25, 427–28. Bujo notes that "it must be strongly emphasized that, in general, African tradition does not forget the common origin of all humans, which precisely grounds a common membership. Consequently, there is the obligation to see every person as a member of a universal human community in which every individual moves and attempts to be moral. This is what the Baluba of Kasayi in Congo-Kinshasa bring to light through their expression 'Muntu-wa-Bende-wa-Mulopo,' which means 'Human from Bende from God.' In other words, every human being comes from Bende, who comes from God. *Bende* here becomes synonymous with the common origin of humans and of the cosmos, an origin that makes sense only with reference to God" (425).

51 Odozor, *Morality Truly Christian, Truly African*, 157.

52 Ibid.

53 Ibid., 158.

54 Ibid., 159.

55 Ibid., 160.

56 Ibid., 162.

57 *Gaudium et Spes*, §16, in *Vatican Council II: The Basic Sixteen Documents: Constitutions, Decrees, Declarations*, ed. Austin Flannery, O.P. (Northport, NY: Costello, 1996), 178, quoted in Odozor, *Morality Truly Christian, Truly African*, 163.

58 Odozor, *Morality Truly Christian, Truly African*, 164.

59 Ibid.

60 Ibid.

61 Ibid., 168. See also Odozor, Review of Laurenti Magesa's *What Is Not Sacred?*, 379: "Speaking as an African theologian myself, I would give pride of place to the gospel's power to enculturate and transform, not to the African traditions, no matter how lofty their insights." Odozor developed the position on inculturation found in his book in his "An African Moral Theology of Inculturation: Methodological Considerations," *Theological*

Studies 69 (2008): 583–609. For further background, see Odozor, "Classical Catholic Moral Theology and the World Church," *Louvain Studies* 30 (2005): 276–96.

62 Odozor, *Morality Truly Christian, Truly African*, 168.

63 Ibid., 169. See also Odozor's "Christology and Moral Theology," *Journal of Moral Theology* 2 (2013): 24–45.

64 Odozor, *Morality Truly Christian, Truly African*, 175.

65 Ibid., 238.

66 Ibid., 239.

67 Ibid.

68 Ibid. Odozor discusses at some length a scene from Chinua Achebe's novel *Things Fall Apart* in which a palaver arrives at a radically unjust conclusion.

69 Ibid., 240.

70 See ibid., 245. Here, the role of the Church's condemnation of certain "objectively or 'intrinsically' morally wrong" actions is important, since it provides standards (grounded in natural law and in divine revelation) for determining what true community-building entails, beyond a consequentialist evaluation of benefits.

71 Ibid., 250.

72 Ibid., 251.

73 Ibid. See also Odozor, *Moral Theology in an Age of Renewal*, 147: "One must be careful […] not to infer […] that there is a total inconsistency or fragmentation in the Bible. The truth the Bible teaches must be deciphered from a total reading of the biblical text. The idea that the Bible cannot be treated as a source of 'timeless moral rules' must not be exaggerated. No serious Catholic theologian would doubt the need to go beyond the cultural and authorial limitations of the biblical text in order to get to the truth of what the Bible says or what the biblical text can mean for us today. However, I think it is too much to say that the historical and cultural factors in the Bible show that we cannot treat the Bible as a direct source of timeless moral rules. The Bible is indeed not just a rule book. But it does contain rules which are perennially valid for ordering human life and human society for all times and places. The Bible does indeed carry some heavy cultural and historical baggage which obscures the truth it contains. However, it does still function for the Christian faithful and others as a source of guidance and moral regulation, among other things. Christian and other readers of the Bible can and do draw the conclusion based on the Bible and as part of the teaching of the Bible that certain things are right and some are wrong, always and everywhere" (147–48).

74 Ibid.

75 Ibid.

76 Odozor comments further, "For the Christian involved in this process in whatever time or culture the teaching of Jesus takes precedence over any other insights or cultural and historical considerations. Part of the task of Christian ethics today should be to emphasize its awkward and difficult aspects and to resist the temptation to adapt itself to and to conform to the thoughts and practices of the world which are clearly against its founding inspiration in Jesus Christ. This is as true elsewhere as it is in Africa. The New Testament is certainly concerned that Christians should be 'the salt of the earth' and the 'light of the world' (Matt. 5:13–14; cf. Phil. 2:15) and maintain their distinctiveness even in their 'good works'" (ibid., 254).

77 Ibid., 261.

78 Ibid., 262.

79 Odozor sums up his perspective on the relationship between African Catholic ethics and African traditional religion: "African Traditional Religion as the main interlocutor with African Christian ethics in Africa is both a blessing for and in some instances a restriction on African theological ethics. Some of the blessings include the following: an ever-present sense of the divine which ensures that theological ethics in Africa remains theological and grounded on firm metaphysical and transcendental foundations; fundamental dispositions about life and therefore about ethics as a search for what constitutes the good life or what enhances life; the sacredness of the human person and of all reality in general. All these make it possible for the African theologian to do his or her work as a Christian ethicist without having to reinvent the wheel, so to speak, or being distracted by extreme secularist concerns. On the other hand, the restricting marks of African religions on African Christian ethics are also obvious. These include a limited notion of God, which, although it may have been adequate for another time or for other purposes, can no longer adequately express the Christian view of reality; the operative understanding of the notion of the human person in African Traditional Religion, which [...] also can no longer fully carry the weight of Christian ethical reasoning, because it is based on a limited anthropology" (ibid., 295). He adds that the cultures built by African traditional religions cannot be the basis for dialogue because they are changing rapidly in the new Africa, both for good and for ill.

80 Ibid., 269.

81 For background, see my *The Abuse of Conscience: A Century of Catholic Moral Theology* (Grand Rapids, MI: Eerdmans, 2021).

82 Stephen L. Brock, *The Light That Binds: A Study in Thomas Aquinas's Metaphysics of Natural Law* (Eugene, OR: Pickwick, 2020), 224.

83 See ibid., 122.

84 Ibid., 198.

85 Ibid., 206.
86 See ibid., 113.
87 Ibid., 114.
88 See ibid., 126.
89 Ibid., 128.
90 Ibid.
91 Ibid., 139. Brock goes on to elucidate this point: "If we observe a desire for something—say, a desire for food, perhaps our own desire for it—but we do not see how the object desired perfects the desirer, we wonder why the desire exists. But when we see that the object enhances or favors or perfects the desirer's own being, we no longer wonder. We do not ask: why does it desire to enhance its being—what good is that? Rather, now its desire makes sense. We have traced the observed desire to something desirable *per se*. We might as well ask, why does the mind find acceptable the propositions that state the case as it is, and unacceptable the ones that do not? It is just the nature of the mind" (ibid., 150). Similarly, he adds, "Desire does not explain goodness. It is goodness that explains desire [...]. The good, then, is first of all an explanatory notion, none that governs an entire mode of explanation. It is primarily a speculative notion. In 94.2 Thomas says that the good is the first thing to fall into the apprehension of practical reason. He does not say, however, that what the good first falls into is the apprehension of practical reason [...]. Once the notion of the good has been achieved in the course of the mind's natural process of sizing things up and understanding them, the practical way of apprehending the good comes as a natural result" (ibid., 154; cf. 167–68). Brock also explains that the first practical principle (the first precept of natural law) that calls us to seek the good and avoid evil has in view not any good whatsoever, but the "unqualifiedly good," the good in itself or the total good (beatitude) (ibid., 156).
92 Ibid., 122.
93 Ibid., 124.
94 Ibid., 223–24.
95 Ibid., 226.
96 Ibid.
97 Ibid., 200.
98 Ibid., 254.
99 Ibid., 234.
100 Bujo, *African Theology in Its Social Context*, 91.
101 Nor would Odozor agree with Bujo's view that "to attack the African religious system is to condemn all those human beings who live by it, and to deprive them, not only of their natural dynamism, but of their very identity" (Bujo, *African Theology in Its Social Context*, 49–50). Odozor states simply, "What would be unacceptable as African Christian theology would be

to water down the universal and absolute significance of Jesus as Lord and Savior or to put African Traditional Religion on a par with Christianity as means of salvation" (Odozor, *Morality Truly Christian, Truly African*, 148).

102 Emmanuel Katongole, Review of Paulinus Ikechukwu Odozor, C.S.Sp., *Morality Truly Christian, Truly African: Foundational, Methodological, and Theological Considerations*, in *Modern Theology* 32 (2016): 449–51, at 449.

103 Ibid., 450.

104 Ibid. The interior quotation is from Odozor, *Morality Truly Christian, Truly African*, 251. Katongole adds a further quotation from Odozor: "not the 'abstract,' idealized church but 'the concrete visible communion of hierarchical and charismatic gifts'" (Katongole, Review of Odozor, *Morality Truly Christian, Truly African*, 450, quoting Odozor, *Morality Truly Christian, Truly African*, 271–72). I note that Katongole, in his review, mounts a sharp critique of Odozor's book, arguing that Odozor treats a narrow range of African theologians (mainly from Nigeria, and only one woman), and moreover that "it is not clear what is 'African' in Odozor's *Morality Truly Christian, Truly African* […]. There is something of a feigned 'interreligious dialogue' in Odozor's search for a morality that is at once truly Christian and truly African, for the 'dialogue' at times feels like nothing more than a search for usable 'insights' from the African heritage for the African moral life. In the end, it is not even clear whether there are any such insights that are uniquely or distinctively African since what might be positive contributions from Africa are depicted as insights available *everywhere* through the natural light of reason […]. The only exception to this universal flattening of moral insights seem to be in the area of sexuality, where the African traditional understanding seems to provide a bulwark against the 'toxic' lifestyles, values, and attitudes that threaten the family, and in relation to the clergy sex abuse scandal in the West when Odozor suggests that 'we should borrow from African Traditional Religion and deal with it through a carefully worked out communal process of atonement and reconciliation' (262)" (Katongole, Review of Odozor, *Morality Truly Christian, Truly African*, 450). To my mind, this critique is far too sharp. Odozor's book is a work of a Catholic moral theologian suffused with, and profoundly giving voice to, the concerns and debates and traditions of Africa. Odozor well knows the failures of Catholics in Africa and elsewhere, but he does not think the revision of divinely revealed Church structures and moral teachings is the answer.

105 For discussion of the Church Fathers on Romans 2, see my "Christians and Natural Law," in Anver M. Emon, Matthew Levering, and David Novak, *Natural Law: A Jewish, Christian, and Islamic Trialogue* (Oxford: Oxford University Press, 2014), 66–110. See also my "Knowing What Is 'Natural':

Thomas Aquinas and Luke Timothy Johnson on Romans 1–2," *Logos* 12 (2009): 117–42.

106 See David VanDrunen, *Divine Covenants and Moral Order: A Biblical Theology of Natural Law* (Grand Rapids, MI: Eerdmans, 2014); and David Novak, *Natural Law in Judaism* (Cambridge: Cambridge University Press, 1998). See also Donald R. Davis, Jr., in *The Spirit of Hindu Law* (Cambridge: Cambridge University Press, 2010), 10: "all religious legal systems recognize a diversity of the sources of law, including sources that are natural (reason, deity), positive (ruler's edict, legislation), and traditional (custom, precedent)." For further discussion, see C. S. Lewis, *The Abolition of Man* (New York: HarperOne, 2015).

Chapter 12 Endnotes

1 Kant, "On a Supposed Right to Tell Lies from Benevolent Motives." http://philosophical.space/f325/KantLies.pdf. Accessed November 01, 2023. First published in a Berlin periodical in 1797. See Immanuel Kant, *The Critique of Practical Reason*, in *The Philosophy of Kant*, ed. Carl J. Friedrich (New York: Modern Library, 1949), 211.

2 Paulinus Ikechukwu Odozor, *Morality Truly Christian, Truly African: Foundational, Methodological, and Theological Considerations* (Notre Dame: University of Notre Dame Press, 2014), 266.

3 For the full story, see John 8:3–11.

4 Jack Gist, "Individualism, Relativism, and the Most Extreme Form of Idolatry," in *The Catholic World Report* (blog), accessed October 7, 2023, https://www.catholicworldreport.com/2021/08/30/individualism-relativism-and-the-most-extreme-form-of-idolatry/.

5 Friedrich Nietzsche, *The Gay Science,* BK IV, 335. See Nietzsche, *Thus Spoke Zarathustra* (1883–85). Tegha A. Nji, "Etsi Veluti Deus Non Daretur (As If God Does Not Exist)," *BIA: Benedict Institute for Africa* (blog), October 7, 2023, https://www.b16ia.org/essays/etsi-veluti-deus-non-daretur-as-if-god-does-not-exist/.

6 Odozor, *Morality Truly Christian, Truly African,* 213.

7 Besides the many references here and there throughout the text under consideration, Odozor structures Chapter Nine, "Moral Theology Christian and African: The Ecclesial Dimension," around a dialogue with Benedict XVI via his Post-Synodal Apostolic Exhortation, *Africae Munus*.

8 Joseph Ratzinger, "Homily of His Excellency Card. Joseph Ratzinger, Dean of the College of Cardinals during the Mass 'Pro Eligendo Romano Pontifice'" (Vatican Basilica, April 18, 2005), https://www.vatican.va/gpII/documents/homily-pro-eligendo-pontifice_20050418_en.html. Emphasis is

mine. Henceforth referenced as "Homily Before the 2005 Conclave."

9 According to Odozor, "Traditions generally provide the world of meaning on which people, including Africans, stand to make sense of all reality" (*Morality Truly Christian, Truly African,* 57). See Robert Schreiter, *Constructing Local Theologies* (Maryknoll, NY: Orbis Books, 1985).

10 Writing as a Catholic African Theologian, Odozor makes a particularly im portant point regarding this last source of African Morality: He extends the sense of Christian tradition to include not just the first centuries of Christianity but every aspect of the Church's self-understanding and teaching on divine revelation, through the centuries till date; and this includes the Magisterium: the teaching authority of the pope and the bishops, as well as the teachings of the church's various ecumenical councils. See Odozor, *Morality Truly Christian, Truly African,* 21, 22.

11 Ratzinger, "Homily Before the 2005 Conclave."

12 Edward W. Fasholé-Luke, "The Quest for an African Christian Theology," *Ecumenical Review* 27:3 (July 1975): 263. Emphasis is mine. See Odozor, *Morality Truly Christian, Truly African,* 9.

13 Joseph Ratzinger, "Christ, Faith and the Challenge of Cultures" (Meeting with the Doctrinal Commissions in Asia, Hong Kong, March 3, 1993), https://www.vatican.va/roman_curia/congregations/cfaith/incontri/rc_con_cfaith_19930303_hong-kong-ratzinger_en.html.

14 Ratzinger, "Christ, Faith and the Challenge of Cultures."

15 Ratzinger, "Christ, Faith and the Challenge of Cultures."

16 Ratzinger, "Christ, Faith and the Challenge of Cultures."

17 Bénézet Bujo, *African Theology in its Social Context,* trans. John O'Donohue (Nairobi: St. Paul Publications Africa, 1992), 80–81. See Agbonkhianmeghe E. Orobator, "The Quest for an African Christ: An Essay on Contemporary African Christology," *Theology Faculty Research and Publications* 476 (1994): 84–85, https://epublications.marquette.edu/theo_fac/476.

18 See Yong-Bock Kim, "Jesus Christ Among Asian Minjung: A Christological Reflection," *Religion Online* (blog), August 1989. https://www.religion-online.org/article/jesus-christ-among-asian-minjung-a-christological-reflection/. Retrieved November 10, 2023.

19 New International Version (NIV).

20 See Luke 10:29–37.

21 See Luke 23:34—"Father, forgive them, for they do not know what they are doing"; John 12:32, "And I, when I am lifted up from the earth, will draw all people to myself" (NIV).

22 Odozor, *Morality Truly Christian, Truly African,* 212.

23 Tegha A. Nji and Valery Akoh, "The African Understanding of Solidarity and the Ratzingerian Concept of Pro-Existence: A Mutually Beneficial

Dialogue," in *Joseph Ratzinger and the Future of African Theology*, ed. Maurice Ashley Agbaw-Ebai and Matthew Levering (Eugene, OR: Pickwick Publications, 2021), 94. See pages 64, 81–82, 87.

24 Odozor, *Morality Truly Christian, Truly African,* 269.

25 Odozor, *Morality Truly Christian, Truly African,* 269.

26 Ratzinger, "Christ, Faith and the Challenge of Cultures."

27 Ratzinger, "Christ, Faith and the Challenge of Cultures."

28 Odozor, *Morality Truly Christian, Truly African,* 64. Emphasis is mine.

29 Odozor, *Morality Truly Christian, Truly African,* 85.

30 Romeo Igwebuike Okeke, *The Osu Concept in Igboland: A Study of the Types of Slavery in Igbo Speaking Areas of Nigeria* (Enugu, Nigeria: SNAAP Press, 1986), 9.

31 Odozor, *Morality Truly Christian, Truly African,* 84–85. See Chinua Achebe, *No Longer at Ease* (New York: Anchor Books, 1994), especially chapters 17–19.

32 Later, in chapter six, through an extensive treatment of the parables of Jesus, Odozor further shows some ways in which Christ stipulates and fulfills this perfection of culture. See Odozor, *Morality Truly Christian, Truly African,* 193–205.

33 Immanuel Kant offers three formulations of the categorical imperative in Kant. See *Foundations of the Metaphysics of Morals* (Akademie pagination): 1. "Act only according to that maxim by which you can at the same time will that it should become a universal law." (p. 422). 2. "Act as though the maxim of your action were by your will to become a universal law of nature." (p. 422). 3. Act so that you treat humanity, whether in your own person or in that of another, always as an end and never as a means only." (p. 429).

34 James Lee, "Pope Benedict XVI and Modernity: A Patristic Theologian's Perspective," in *Nova et Vetera* 15, no. 1 (2017): 89–110, at 89.

35 George Washington Northrup, "The Fatherhood of God," *The American Journal of Theology* 5, no. 3 (July 1901): 473–95, at 473, 474.

36 Northrup, "The Fatherhood of God," 474–76ff.

37 James M. Gustafson, *Ethics from a Theocentric Perspective*, vol. 2, *Ethics and Theology* (Chicago: University of Chicago Press, 1984), 98.

38 Odozor, *Morality Truly Christian, Truly African,* 71.

39 Odozor, *Morality Truly Christian, Truly African,* 77. See Laurenti Magesa, *African Religion: The Moral Traditions of Abundant Life* (Maryknoll, NY: Orbis Books, 1997), 35.

40 Odozor, *Morality Truly Christian, Truly African,* 77, 78.

41 Joseph Ratzinger, *Values in a Time of Upheaval*, trans. Brian McNeil (San Francisco: Ignatius Press, 2006), 64.

42 Joseph Ratzinger, *Introduction to Christianity*, trans. J. R. Foster (San

Francisco: Ignatius Press, 1990), 21. See Odozor, *Morality Truly Christian, Truly African,* 185—86.

43 "Faith in the one God of Abraham, Isaac, and Jacob—extended now in Jesus' new family and *all nations* over the bonds of descent according to the flesh – is the fruit of Jesus' work. It is what proves him to be the Messiah. It signals a new integration of messianic promise that is based on Moses and the prophets, but also opens them up in a completely new way" (Benedict XVI, *Jesus of Nazareth*, vol. 1, trans. Adrian J. Walker (New York: Doubleday, 2007), 116–17). See Odozor, *Morality Truly Christian, Truly African,* 92–193. Emphasis is mine.

44 Benedict XVI, *Jesus of Nazareth*, vol. 1, trans. Adrian J. Walker (New York: Doubleday, 2007), 44. In another passage in *Introduction to Christianity,* Ratzinger speaks of the "invocability" of God in and through Christ. "Christ himself, so to speak, appears as the burning bush from which the name of God issues to mankind" (*Introduction to Christianity,* 133). See pages 116, 132. Here, Ratzinger engages John 17:6, 11–12, 16).

45 Nietzsche, *The Gay Science,* Bk III, par. 125.

46 Aristotle, *Nicomachean Ethics*, trans. W. D. Ross and Lesley Brown (Oxford: Oxford University Press, 2009). See especially Bk I.

47 See Augustine, *Confessions,* 1, 1.

48 Aquinas treats the differing kinds of law in *Summa Theologiae* I-II, q. 91. A detailed treatment of each kind of law is found in the following: Eternal law (question 93); Divine law (q. 91, aa. 4 and 5); Natural law (question 94); Human law (95). Divine law considered as revelation is further divided into "Old Law" (questions 98–105) and "New Law" (question 106–108).

49 Bénézet Bujo, *Foundations of an African Ethic: Beyond the Universal Claims of Western Morality* (New York: Crossroad, 2001), 12. See Odozor, *Morality Truly Christian, Truly African,* 155.

50 Odozor, *Morality Truly Christian, Truly African,* 161. Cf. Bujo, *Foundations of an African Christian Ethic,* 12.

51 Odozor, *Morality Truly Christian, Truly African,* 163.

52 John Paul II, *Familiaris Consortio* (November 22, 1981), no. 34: "What is known as 'the law of gradualness' or step-by-step advance cannot be identified with 'gradualness of the law,' as if there were different degrees or forms of precept in God's law for different individuals and situations." Also see John Paul II, *Homily at the Close of the Sixth Synod of Bishops* (Oct. 25, 1980), 8, published in *AAS* 72 (1980), 1083.

53 Odozor, *Morality Truly Christian, Truly African,* 241–43. See Chinua Achebe, *Things Fall Apart* (New York: Anchor Books, 1994), 57 ff.

54 Ratzinger, *Values in a Time of Upheaval,* 83.

55 Ratzinger, *Values in a Time of Upheaval,* 86, 83.

56 Ratzinger, *Values in a Time of Upheaval,* 85.

57 Ratzinger, *Values in a Time of Upheaval,* 87. See Benedict XVI, *On Conscience: Two Essays* (San Francisco: Ignatius Press, 2007), 26.
58 Benedict XVI, *On Conscience*, 34, 39.
59 Ratzinger, *Values in a Time of Upheaval,* 88.
60 Heinz Schürmann, Joseph Ratzinger, and Hans Urs von Balthasar, *Principles of Christian Morality*, trans. Graham Harrison (San Francisco: Ignatius Press, 1986), 64.
61 Heinz Schürmann, Joseph Ratzinger, and Hans Urs von Balthasar, *Principles of Christian Morality*, 64.
62 Ratzinger, *Values in a Time of Upheaval*, 92, 93. There exists a striking relationship between Newman's understanding of conscience (see his 1875 *Letter to the Duke of Norfolk*) and his notions of *sensus fidei* or *sensus fidelium* (see his 1859 essay, *On Consulting the Faithful in Matters of Doctrine*).
63 Ratzinger, *Values in a Time of Upheaval*, 96.
64 Ratzinger, *Values in a Time of Upheaval*, 98. See Benedict XVI, *On Conscience*, 30–38.
65 Ratzinger, *Values in a Time of Upheaval*, 83.
66 Odozor, *Morality Truly Christian, Truly African,* 224. See John Paul II, *Veritatis Splendor* (August 6, 1993), nos. 32, 35, 36.
67 Joseph Boyle, "Natural Law," in *The New Dictionary of Theology*, ed. Joseph A. Komonchak, Mary Collins, and Dermot A. Lane (Collegeville, MN: Liturgical Press, 1987), 704. See Odozor, *Morality Truly Christian, Truly African,* 163.
68 Odozor, *Morality Truly Christian, Truly African,* 55.
69 Odozor, *Morality Truly Christian, Truly African,* 271.
70 Odozor, *Morality Truly Christian, Truly African,* 298.
71 Odozor, *Morality Truly Christian, Truly African,* 48, 49.
72 Fasholé-Luke, "The Quest for an African Christian Theology," 263; Odozor, *Morality Truly Christian, Truly African,* 9.

Chapter 13 Endnotes

1 Pope Francis, *Apostolic Exhortation Gaudete et Exsultate—On the Call to Holiness in Today's World* (Rome: Libreria Editrice Vaticana, 2018), no. 6.
2 Pope Francis, *Gaudete et Exsultate*, no. 7. Italics mine.
3 Kathleen S. Cummings, *A Saint of Our Own* (Chapel Hill, NC: University of North Carolina Press, 2019), 10.
4 Sharon Prentis, *Every Tribe: Stories of Diverse Saints Serving a Diverse World* (London: SPCK, 2019), 22.
5 Emmanuel Katongole, *Beyond Universal Reason: The Relation between Religion and Ethics in the Work of Stanley Hauerwas* (Notre Dame: University of Notre Dame Press, 2000), 120.

6 Johann Baptist Metz, *Faith in History and Society*, trans. by J. Matthew Ashley (New York: Crossroad, 2007), 182.
7 Emmanuel Katongole, "Africa," in *Handbook of African Catholicism,* ed. Stan Ilo (Maryknoll, NY: Orbis, 2022), 20.
8 Elizabeth A. Johnson, *Friends of God and Prophets* (New York: Continuum, 1998), 13.
9 Johnson, *Friends of God and Prophets*, 13.
10 Achille Mbembe, *Necropolitics* (Durham: Duke University Press, 2019), 66.
11 Erin Kathleen Rowe, *Black Saints in Early Modern Global Catholicism* (Cambridge: CUP, 2019) 3.
12 Rowe, *Black Saints*, 4.
13 Philip Jenkins, *The Next Christendom: The Coming of Global Christianity*, 3rd ed. (New York: Oxford University Press, 2011), 1–3.
14 Stan Chu Ilo, "The Church of Pope Francis," in *The Church We Want: African Catholics Look to Vatican III*, ed. Agbonkhianmeghe E. Orobator (Maryknoll, NY: Orbis, 2016), 13.
15 Odozor, *Morality Truly Christian, Truly African*, 271.
16 Odozor, *Morality Truly Christian, Truly African*, 269.
17 Cited in Johnson, *Friends of God and Prophets*, 22.
18 Johnson, *Friends of God and Prophets*, 23.
19 Metz, *Faith in History and Society*, 214.
20 Michael Plekon, *Hidden Holiness* (Notre Dame: University of Notre Dame Press, 2009), 4.
21 Elizabeth O'Donnell Gandolfo, *Ecomartyrs in the Americas* (Maryknoll, NY: Orbis, 2023), 70–71.
22 Plekon, *Hidden Holiness*, 4.
23 Samuel Wells, *Improvisation: The Drama of Christian Ethics* (Grand Rapids, MI: Baker Academic, 2018), 23–24.
24 Plekon, *Hidden Holiness*, 4.
25 See Plekon, *Hidden Holiness*, vii.
26 See Plekon, *Hidden Holiness*, viii.
27 Pope Francis, *Gaudete et Exsultate*, no. 7.
28 Pope Francis, *Gaudete et Exsultate*, no. 6.
29 Pope Francis, *Gaudete et Exsultate*, no. 7.
30 Pope Francis, *Letter of Pope Francis Constituting the Commission of New Martyrs* (July 3, 2023). www.vatican.va.
31 Pope Francis, *Gaudete et Exsultate*, no. 8.
32 "Murdered Nigerian seminarian was killed for announcing gospel, killer says." *Catholic New Agency* (May 2, 2020). https://www.catholicnewsagency.com/news/44401/murdered-nigerian-seminarian-was-killed-for-announcing-gospel-killer-says.

33 John L. Allen Jr., *The Global War on Christians* (New York: Image Books, 2013), 49.
34 Pope John Paul II, *Apostolic Letter Tertio Millennio Adveniente—On Preparation for the Jubilee of the Year 2000* (November 10, 1994), no. 37. www.vatican.va.
35 Pope Francis, *Commission on New Martyrs*.
36 Metz, *Faith in History and Society*, 183.
37 Johnson, *Friends of God and Prophets*, 22
38 Johnson, *Friends of God and Prophets,* 23.
39 Emmanuel Katongole, "'Threatened with Resurrection': Martyrdom and Reconciliation in the World Church," in *Witness of the Body: The Past, Present, and Future of Christian Martyrdom,* ed. Michael L. Budde and Karen Scott (Grand Rapids, MI: Eerdmans, 2011), 193–94.
40 Katongole, "Threatened with Resurrection," 203.
41 Katongole, "Threatened with Resurrection," 199.
42 Robert Royal, *The Catholic Martyrs of the Twentieth Century: A Comprehensive World History* (New York: Crossroad, 2000), 10.
43 Gandolfo, *Ecomartyrs in the Americas*, 71.
44 Camille Lewis Brown, *African Saints, African Stories* (Cincinnati, OH: Franciscan Media, 2008).
45 Frederick Quinn, *African Saints: Saints, Martyrs, and Holy People from the Continent of Africa* (New York: Crossroad, 2002).
46 Todd Whitmore, *Imitating Christ in Magwi: An Anthropological Theology* (London: T&T Clark, 2019), 4.
47 Pope Francis, *Gaudete et Exsultate*, no. 19.
48 Christopher Tounsel, "Two Sudans, Human Rights, and the Afterlives of St. Josephine Bakhita," in *Christianity and Human Rights Reconsidered,* ed. Sarah Shortall and Daniel Steinmetz-Jenkins (Cambridge: Cambridge University Press, 2020), 261–75.
49 See Emmanuel Katongole, *Born from Lament: The Theology and Politics of Hope in Africa* (Grand Rapids, MI: Eerdmans, 2017), chapter 8.
50 John Paul II, *Post-Synodal Exhortation Ecclesia in Africa* (September 14, 1995), no. 111, at www.vatican.va.
51 John W. O'Malley, *Catholic History for Today's Church* (Maryland: Rowman & Littlefield, 2015) 54.
52 O'Malley, *Catholic History for Today's Church*, 58.

Chapter 14 Endnotes

1 Paulinus Odozor, *Morality Truly Christian, Truly African. Foundational, Methodological, and Theological Foundations* (Notre Dame: University of Notre Dame Press, 2014).

2 See Paulinus Odozor, "One and the Same? Invoking Joseph Ratzinger/Benedict XVI in the Debate on God and Question of God-Language in African Christianity," in *Joseph Ratzinger and the Future of African Theology*, ed. Maurice Ashley Agbaw-Ebai and Mathew Levering (Eugene, OR: Pickwick, 2021), 17–39.

3 See Odozor, "One and the Same?," 35.

4 Bede Ukwuije, *Trinité et inculturation* (Paris: Desclée de Brouwer, 2008).

5 Bede Ukwuije, *The Trinitarian God: Contemporary Relevance and Challenges* (Mumbai: Paulines, 2013).

6 Pioneer African theologians claimed that Christianity rimed with colonialism, exploitation and alienation. Christianity was accused of stripping Africans of the God of their ancestors. Bolaji Idowu spoke of "the difficult and urgent problem […] of the seemingly alien character of Christianity" (Bolaji Idowu, "Préface," in *Pour une théologie africaine, Rencontre des théologiens Africains*, ed. Kwesi A. Dickson et Paul Ellingworth [Ibadan, Yaoundé: Edition CLE, 1969], 13). For his part, John Mbiti insisted that Christianity contributed to the African's "sense of frustration and uprootedness" (Mbiti, *African Religions and Philosophy* [London: Heinemann, 1969]; Mbiti, *Concepts of God in Africa* [London: SPCK, 1970], 2–3). The Congolese theologian, Kä Mana called missionary Christianity, "Christianity of catastrophe: a principle of death at the heart of African history" (Mana, *La nouvelle évangélisation en Afrique* [Paris: Clé, 2000], 83). This Christianity, he said, "emerged in Africa as a system of power and violence imposed on the weak" (85). The Cameroonian theologian Fabien Eboussi-Boulaga was even more virulent. He argued that the Christian God, preached by missionaries in Africa, appeared as a principle of exclusion and domination in the hand of a privileged group which claims to have entered into covenant with God. See Eboussi-Boulaga, *Christianisme sans fétiche. Révélation et domination* (Paris: Présence Africaine, 1981), 8.

7 Odozor, "One and the Same?," 23.

8 Mbiti, *Concepts of God in Africa*, xii. See also Mbiti, *African Religions and Philosophy*, 30.

9 Idowu, *Olodumare, God in Yoruba Belief*, 219.

10 Francis Arinze, *Sacrifice in Igbo Religion* (Ibadan: Ibadan University Press, 1970), 9.

11 Arinze, *Sacrifice in Igbo Religion,* 9.

12 Cf. G. W. F. Hegel, *Lectures on the Philosophy of History*, trans J. Sibree (London: Henri G. Bohn, 1857), 95–104.

13 See Donatus Ibe Nwoga, *The Supreme Being as a Stranger in Igbo Religious Thought,* (Ahiazu Mbaise: Hawk Press, 1984); Chinua Achebe, "Chi in Igbo Cosmology," in *Morning Yet on Creation Day* (New York: Anchor Books, 1976), 131–45; Raymond Arazu, "Chukwu and Yahweh: The

Problem of Naming God in Igbo Language," in *God, Bible and African Traditional Religion*, ed. Bede Ukwuije (Enugu: SNAAP Press, 2010), 6–30.

14 See Nwoga, *The Supreme God as Stranger in Igbo Religious Thought*, 71.

15 Mircea Eliade, *Fragments d'un Journal* (Paris: Gallimard, 1973), 305.

16 Arinze, *Sacrifice in Igbo Religion*, 11.

17 Arinze, *Sacrifice in Igbo Religion*, 10.

18 Arinze, *Sacrifice in Igbo Religion*, 30.

19 See Éloi Messis-Metogo, *Dieu peut-il mourir en Afrique? Essais sur l'indifférence religieuse et l'incroyance en Afrique Noire* (Paris: Karthala, 1997), chapter 1, 33–45; René Jaouen, *L'Eucharistie du mil, Langage d'un peuple, expressions de la foi* (Paris: Karthala, 1995), chapter 1, 17–45. These authors, in their turn, take up the ethnological research of Louis-Vincent Thomas and René Luneau, *Les sages dépossédés. Univers magiques d'Afrique noire* (Paris: Laffont, 1977). See also the collection of myths in Louis-Vincent Thomas and René Luneau, *Les religions d'Afrique noire. Textes et traditions sacrés*, 2nd ed., 2 vols. (Paris, Stock, 1981).

20 Louis-Vincent Thomas and René Luneau, *La terre africaine et ses religions* (Paris: L'Harmattan, 1980), 136.

21 See Elochukwu Uzukwu, "Quand Dieu s'éloigne de nos guerres," published online, no longer available (Paris: 2004).

22 For example, in Nigeria the Yoruba tradition, war belongs to Ogun, the god of war and irion, while the Igbo would convoke Ikenga, the god of strength and war. Ijaw people would trust their wars to Egbesu. The Akan and Asante people of Ghana would rely on Tano, the god of War and Strife, while the Ga tribe would rely on Sakumo, the deity of war and duels.

23 Elochukwu Uzukwu, "Quand Dieu s'éloigne de nos guerres," 3.

24 See a detailed exposition of this critique in Ukwuije, *Trinité et inculturation*, 98–103.

25 See Achebe, "Chi in Igbo Cosmology," 138.

26 See Soyinka, *This Past Must Address Its Present*, 10; Soyinka, *Que ce passé parle à son présent*, 37–38.

27 See Hume, *The Natural History of Religion*, 24.

28 See Wole Soyinka, "La saveur du partage," *Le monde,* Thursday 18 December 2003, p. 17.

29 Charles Nyamiti, *Christ Our Ancestor. Christology from an African Perspective (*Gweru, Zimbabwe: Mambo Press, 1984), 35.

30 Bénézet Bujo, *Foundations of an African Ethic. Beyond the Universal Claims of Western Morality* (New York: Crossroad, 2001), 1–2.

31 See Bujo, *African Theology in Its Social Context*, 73.

32 Bujo, *Foundations of an African Ethic*, 102.

33 Bujo, *Foundations of an African Ethic*, 35.

34 See Dominique Zahan, *Religion, spiritualité et pensée africaines* (Paris: Payot, 1970), 172.
35 Zahan, *Religion, spiritualité et pensée africaines*, 172.
36 Zahan, *Religion, spiritualité et pensée africaines*, 175.
37 Bénézet Bujo, *La vision africaine du monde. Pour un enseignement social de l'Eglise sans loi naturelle* (Fribourg: St Augustin, 2018), 37.
38 Bujo, *African Theology in its Social Context*, 74.
39 Bujo, *Foundations of an African Ethic*, 102.
40 See Bujo, *Foundations of an African Ethic*, 103–106.
41 See Nyamiti, *Christ Our Ancestor*, 19–21.
42 See Odozor, *Morality Truly Christian, Truly African*, 169.
43 Eberhard Jüngel, *God as the Mystery of the World. On the Foundation of the Theology of the Crucified One in the Dispute between Theism and Atheism*, trans. Darell L. Guder (Grands Rapids, MI: Eerdmans, 1983), 300.
44 Jüngel, *God as the Mystery of the World*, 317.
45 Jüngel, *God as the Mystery of the World*, 320.
46 Jüngel, *God as the Mystery of the World*, 317.
47 Jüngel, *God as the Mystery of the World*, 323.
48 See Jüngel, *God as the Mystery of the World*, 324.
49 Jüngel, *God as the Mystery of the World*, 326.
50 See Jüngel, *God as the Mystery of the World*, 344.
51 See Jüngel, *God as the Mystery of the World*, 350.
52 See Thomas Joseph White, O.P., *The Trinity: On the Nature and Mystery of the One God* (Washington, D.C.: Catholic University of America Press, 2022), 85–95.
53 Note that the Genesis 2 account does not use the verb "to create" (*bara*, Gen 1:1, 21, 27; 2:3) but uses the word "to make" (*asah*, Gen 2:4, 18) and "to form" (*yasar*, Gen 2:7, 8, 19).
54 See Brian D. Robinette, "The Difference Nothing Makes: *Creatio Ex Nihilo*, Resurrection, and Divine Gratuity," *Theological Studies* 72 (2011): 525–57, at 528.
55 Robinette, "The Difference Nothing Makes," 547.
56 Robinette, "The Difference Nothing Makes," 535.
57 John Sachs, S.J., *The Christian Vision of Humanity: Basic Christian Anthropology* (Collegeville: Liturgical Press, 1991), 18.
58 See White, *The Trinity*, 85–95.
59 White, *The Trinity*, 89.
60 See White, *The Trinity*, 101. Christ identifies himself with the God of Israel. Christ is revealed on the Cross not only as the Suffering Servant, but also as the Lord, the God made flesh. "Jesus […] ascribes to himself the preexistence of the Godhead, the Lord of Israel who created all things and who called Abraham into the covenant" (103).

61 Jüngel, *God as Mystery of the World*, 355.
62 See Jüngel, *God as Mystery of the World*, 357.
63 See Jüngel, *God as the Mystery of the World*, 374.
64 See Ilia Delio, "Bonaventure's Metaphysics of the Good," *Theological Studies* 60 (1999): 228–46.
65 Cf. Bonaventure, *Breviloquim* 1,3; Delio, "Bonaventure's Metaphysics of the Good," 223.
66 Cf. Delio, "Bonaventure's Metaphysics of the Good," 234.
67 Jordan Daniel Wood, "The Father's Kenosis: A Defense of Bonaventure on Intra-Trinitarian Acts," *Pro Ecclesia* 30 (2021): 3–31, at 5.
68 Barth, *Church Dogmatics*, 1.1, chapter 2, part 1.8. See also Eberhard Jüngel, *The Doctrine of the Trinity: God's Being is in Becoming* (Grand Rapids, MI: Eerdmans, 1976), 17.
69 Cf. Catherine Mowry Lacugna, *God for Us: The Trinity and Christian Life* (San Francisco: HarperSanFrancisco, 1991); John Zizioulas, *Being as Communion* (Crestwood, NY: St Vladimir's Seminary Press, 1985), 15.
70 Catherine Mowry Lacugna, *God for Us* p. 260.
71 Catherine Mowry Lacugna, *God for Us,* p. 260.
72 Catherine Mowry Lacugna, *God for Us,* p. 260.
73 Eberhard Jüngel, "Humanity in Correspondence to God: Remarks on the Image of God as a Basic Concept in Theological Anthropology," in *Theological Essays 1*, trans. and ed. John B. Webster (Edinburgh: T&T Clark, 1989), 124–153, at 132.
74 Jüngel, "Humanity in Correspondence to God," 134.
75 Bujo, *Foundations of an African Ethic*, 87.
76 Sachs, *The Christian Vision of Humanity*, 34.
77 Anthony Obinna, "African Cultures and Development: The Rectifying Challenge," *Cultures and Faith* 18 (2010): 321–33.
78 Obinna, "African Cultures and Development," 328.
79 Anthony Obinna, "Confiliating Americans: Recti-valuing One Another. A Theology and Practice of Reconfiliation (Unpublished manuscript, 2004), 5.
80 Obinna, "Confiliating Americans," 5.
81 Obinna, "Confiliating Americans," 5.
82 Bujo, *Foundations of an African Ethic*, 102.
83 Bujo, *Foundations of an African Ethic*, 102.
84 Bujo, *Foundations of an African Ethic*, 102–103.
85 Pope Francis, Apostolic Exhortation *Querida Amazonia* (Rome: Libreria Editrice Vaticana, 2020), no. 42.
86 Pope Francis, *Querida Amazonia,* no. 42.
87 Pope Francis, *Laudato Si'*, no. 76.
88 Cf. Eboussi-Boulaga, *Christianisme sans fétiche*, 105–106.

89 Cf. Kä Mana, *L'Afrique va-t-elle mourir?* (Cerf : Paris, 1991); *Foi chrétienne, crise africaine et reconstruction de l'Afrique* (Nairobi: CETA, 1992); *Christ d'Afrique. Enjeux éthiques de la foi chrétienne en Afrique* (Karthala: Paris, 1994).
90 Cf. Achebe, "Chi in Igbo Cosmology," 133.
91 Joyce J. Schuld, *Foucault and Augustine. Reconsidering Power and Love* (Notre Dame: University of Notre Dame Press, 2003), 216.
92 Schuld, *Foucault and Augustine*, 218.

Chapter 15 Endnotes

1 I consider it a very high honor that the book *Morality Truly Christian, Truly African* was chosen for attention in this way and that so many serious scholars from different backgrounds have been participated in discussing some of the issues which this book raises. It is a rare honor when colleagues like these can think your work important enough to merit this kind of attention. I sincerely thank every one of these colleagues for their various contributions. Special thanks to Professors Matthew Levering and Maurice Agbaw-Ebai for organizing the conference in Mundelein Seminary at which these papers were delivered and for working to have the essays appear in published form.
2 Some of these pioneers include Vincent Mulago, Engelbert Mveng, Msgr. Tharceisse Tshibangu, Alphonse Mushete, Sidbe Sempore, Oscar Bimwenyi, Barnabas Okolo, Benezet Bujo, Eugene Uzukwu, Barthelemy Adoukonou; Laurenti Magesa, Francois-Marie Lufuluabo Mizeka, Alexus Kagame, Meinrad Pierre Hebga, Laurent Mpongo, Ikenga E. Metuh, Bolaji Idowu, John Mary Waligo, Justin Ukpong, Charles Nyamiti, Jean-Marc Ela, Patrick Kalilombe, Mercy Amba Oduyoye, Theresa Okure, Kwame Bediako, Kwesi A. Dickson, and so on.
3 Paulinus I. Odozor, "*Africae Munus* as Christian Policy Statement for an African Renaissance" in *Africae Munus: Ten years Later*, ed. Maurice Agbaw-Ebai and Matthew Levering (South Bend, IN: St Augustine's Press, 2022), 4. See also Nana Akuffro-Addo, Foreign Minister of the Republic of Ghana (2001–2008), quoted in "The Church in Africa in Service of Reconciliation, Justice, and Peace. 'You are the Salt of the earth [...]. You are the light of the world' (Matthew 5:13, 14)," *Relatio Ante Disceptationem* for the 2nd African Synod by Peter Cardinal Turkson (Vatican, 2009), 10.
4 Odozor, "*Africae Munus* as Christian Policy Statement for an African Renaissance," 5.
5 Pope Benedict XVI, *Africae Munus: Post-Synodal Exhortation of His Holiness Pope Benedict XVI on the Church in Africa in Service to Rec-*

onciliation, Justice and Peace (Vatican City: Editrice Libreria Vaticana, 2011).

6 Paulinus I. Odozor, "The Church as Family of God in Africa," in *Handbook of African Catholicism*, ed. Stan Chu Ilo (Maryknoll, NY: Orbis, 2022), 583–84.

7 Josef Fuchs, "Is there a Specifically Christian Morality?," in *Readings in Moral Theology*, no.3: *The Magisterium and Morality,* ed. Charles Curran and Richard A. McCormick, S.J. (New York: Paulist Press, 1982), 6.

8 Joseph Sittler, *The Structure of Christian Ethics* (Baton Rouge: Louisiana State University Press, 1958).

9 Joseph Ratzinger, "Magisterium of the Church, Faith, Morality," in *Readings in Moral Theology*, no.2: *The Distinctiveness of Christian Ethic*s, ed. Charles E. Curran and Richard A. McCormick, S.J. (New York: Paulist Press, 1980), 177.

10 See Peter Brown, *Body and Society: Men, Women, and Sexual Renunciation in Early Christianity* (New York: Columbia University Press, 1988), 28, 261, 438.

11 Cf. Eugene A. LaVerdiere, "The Witness of the New Testament," in *Sexualit6y, Marriage, and Family: Readings in the Catholic Tradition*, ed. Paulinus I. Odozor (Notre Dame: University of Notre Dame Press, 2001),

12 See Kwame Bediako, *Theology and Identity: The Impact of Culture Upon Christian Thought in the Second Century and in Modern Africa* (Cumbria, UK: Regnum Books, 1999).

13 Paulinus I. Odozor, *Morality Truly Christian, Truly African: Foundational, Methodological, and Theological Considerations* (Notre Dame: University of Notre Dame Press, 2014), 3.

14 See Agbonkhiameghe Orobator, *Theology Brewed in an African Pot* (Maryknoll, NY: Orbis Books, 2008).

15 David Clairmont, "Catholic Comparative Theological Ethics: Elements of an Approach to Tradition, Ethics and Dialogue (with Odozor and Clooney, in the Church)."

16 Laurenti Magesa, *African Religion: The Moral Traditions of Abundant Life* (Maryknoll, NY: Orbis Books, 1997), 35.

17 Bede Ukwuije, C.S.Sp., "Trinitarian Conception of God as Basis for an African Christian Ethics."

18 Ukwuije, "The Trinitarian Conception of God as Basis for an African Christian Ethics."

19 Melanie Susan Barrett, "Aquinas, Balthasar, and African Tradition: Christian Conversion of Individuals and Cultures."

20 Barrett, "Aquinas, Balthasar, and African Tradition," 30.

21 Matthew Levering, "Natural Law in Bénézet Bujo, Paulinus Odozor, and Stephen L. Brock."

22 See Stephen L. Brock, *The Light That Binds: A Study in Thomas Aquinas's Metaphysics of Natural Law* (Eugene, OR: Pickwick, 2020), 254. Cited in Matthew Levering, "Natural Law in Bénézet Bujo, Paulinus Odozor, and Stephen L. Brock."

23 Olusegun Steven Samuel and Ademola Kazeem Fayemi, "Afro-Communal Virtue Ethic as Foundation for Environmental Sustainability in Africa and Beyond," *South African Journal of Philosophy*, 18 May 2019, https://doi.org/10.1080/02580136.2019.1581393.

24 Thaddeus Metz, "An African Theory of Moral Status: A Relational Alternative to Individualism and Holism," *Ethical Theory and Moral Practice* 15, no. 3 (2012): 388.

25 Paulinus I. Odozor, *Richard A. McCormick and the Renewal of Moral Theology* (Notre Dame: University of Notre Dame Press, 1995), 75.

26 Thomas F. Sedgwick, "Exploring the Great Divide: Sex, Ethics, and Ecumenism," *Journal of Ecumenical Studies* 45, no. 3 (2010): 422.

27 Peter Nichols, *The Pope's Divisions: The Roman Catholic Church Today* (London: Faber and Faber, 1981), 239.

28 LaVerdiere, "The Witness of the New Testament," 5.

29 See Lisa Sowle Cahill, *Between the Sexes: Foundations for a Christian Ethics of Sexuality* (Philadelphia: Fortress Press, 1985).

30 Brown, *Body and Society*, 20, 128–30.

31 Christopher C. Roberts, *Creation and Covenant: The Significance of Sexual Difference in the Moral Theology of Marriage* (London: T&T Clark, 2007), 8.

32 See Eric Fuchs, Christianity and Sexuality: An Ambiguous History," in Odozor, *Sexuality, Marriage and Family*, 22–75.

33 Protocol to the African Charter on Human and Peoples' Rights on the Rights of Women in Africa: The Maputo Protocol, https://icj-kenya.org/wp-content/uploads/2017/05/Maputo-Protocol-A5.pdf. See also Paulinus I. Odozor, "Christianity and Law in Africa Today," in *The Oxford Handbook on Christianity and Law*, ed. John Witte, Jr. and Rafael Domingo (Oxford: Oxford University Press, 2024), 273–74.

34 Odozor, "Christianity and Law in Africa Today," 274.

35 Sedgwick, "Exploring the Great Divide."

36 Maurice Agbaw-Ebai, "Ratzinger's Theological Anthropology in Conversation with Aspects of Paulinus Odozor's Understanding of the Human Person in Christ."

37 "La theorie du genre est une ideologie sociologisante occidentale des relations hommes-femmes, qui s'attaque à l'identitė sponsale de la personne humanine, à la complémentaritė anthropologique entre l'"homme et l femme, au mariage, à la maternité et la paternité, à la famille et à la procreation. Elle est contraire à la culture africaine et aux veriės humaınes

éclaireés par la Révelation divine en Jésus Christ." (This quotation is taken from the synodal intervention of Archbishop Sarah entitled "L'eglise et la theorie du genre en Afrique.")

38 See for example, Sylvia Tamale, ed., African *Sexualities: A Reader* (Pambuzuka Press, 2011).

39 Wole Soyinka, "A Dance of the Forests," in *Wole Soyinka: Collected Plays 1* (Oxford: Oxford University Press, 1973), 5.

40 Ibid., 31.

41 Ibid.

42 Emmanuel Ojeifo, "African and Christian: Black sanctity and the future of African Catholicism."

43 Pope Francis, *Lumen Fidei*, https://www.vatican.va/content/francesco/en/encyclicals/documents/papa-francesco_20130629_enciclica-lumen-fidei.html.

44 Pope Benedict XVI, *Spe Salvi*, https://www.vatican.va/content/benedict-xvi/en/encyclicals/documents/hf_ben-xvi_enc_20071130_spe-salvi.html.

45 See Stephen Pope, "Virtue Ethics in Aquinas," in *Readings in Moral Theology*, no.16: *Virtue*, ed. Charles E. Curran and Lisa A. Fullam (New York: Paulist Press, 2011), 5–6.

46 James M. Gustafson, *Christ and the Moral Life* (New York: Harper and Row, 1968), 250.

47 Gustafson, *Christ and the Moral Life*, 251.

48 Gustafson, *Christ and the Moral* Life, 250.

49 Gustafson, *Christ and the Moral Life*, 250.

Maurice Agbaw-Ebai is a priest of the Roman Catholic Diocese of Mamfe, Cameroon. He is Professor of Philosophical Anthropology and Professor of Dogmatic Theology at the Catholic Institute of Technology, Castel Gandolfo, Rome, and Professor of Dogmatic Theology at the Pontifical University of St. Thomas Aquinas (Angelicum), Rome. His publications include: *Light of Reason, Light of Faith: Joseph Ratzinger and the German Enlightenment*; *Joseph Ratzinger and the Future of African Theology* (editor with Mathew Levering); *The Essential Supernatural: A Dialogical Study in Kierkegaard and Blondel*; *An African Perspective on the Thought of Benedict XVI* (editor with Kizito Forbi, S.J); *Benedict XVI Rethinking Africa: Tasks for Today* (editor with Kizito Forbi, S.J.); *Africae Munus: Ten Years Late*r (editor with Mathew Levering); and *Journeying Together With God As A Missionary Church in Africa* (editor with Ikenna U. Okafor). He is the editor of the journal, *Religions – issue: Kierkegaard's Philosophy of Religion.*

Matthew Levering holds the James N. Jr. and Mary D. Perry Chair of Theology at Mundelein Seminary, where he also serves as the director of the Center for Scriptural Exegesis, Philosophy, and Doctrine. He is the author or editor of numerous books, including most recently *The Abuse of Conscience: A Century of Catholic Moral Theology*; *Aquinas's Eschatological Ethics and the Virtue of Temperance*; and *The Oxford Handbook of Deification*. He is the co-editor of two quarterly journals and the Senior Editor of *The New Ressourcement.*